After the Fall

After the Fall

The Failure of Communism
and the Future of Socialism

———————◆———————

Edited by

ROBIN BLACKBURN

VERSO

London · New York

First published by Verso 1991
© Verso 1991
Chapters 2, 5, 6, 7, 8 & 16 © *New Left Review*;
all others © individual contributors

Verso
UK: 6 Meard Street, London W1V 3HR
USA: 29 West 35th Street, New York, NY 10001-2291

Verso is the imprint of New Left Books

British Library Cataloguing in Publication Data
After the fall : the failure of communism and the
    future of socialism.
    I. Blackburn, Robin, *1940–*
321.8

    ISBN 0-86091-320-1
    ISBN 0-86091-540-9 pbk

Library of Congress Cataloging-in-Publication Data
After the fall : the failure of communism and the future of socialism
    / edited by Robin Blackburn.
        p.   cm.
    ISBN 0-86091-320-1. — ISBN 0-86091-540-9 (pbk.)
        1. Communism—1945–   2. Socialism.   3. Communism—Europe,
Eastern.
        4. Europe, Eastern—Politics and government—1989–   I. Blackburn,
Robin.
    HX44.A367   1991
    335.43′09′043—dc20

Typeset by Leaper & Gard Ltd, Bristol
Printed in Finland by Werner Söderström Oy

Contents

Acknowledgements

'The Upturned Utopia' was first published in *La Stampa*, 9 June 1989; this translation first appeared in *New Left Review* 177, September–October 1989. 'Reflections on the Crisis of Communist Regimes' first appeared in *New Left Review* 177, September–October 1989. 'Ways of Walking' was first published in *New Statesman & Society*, September 1990. 'What Does Socialism Mean Today?' was originally published as 'Nachholende Revolution und linker Revisionsbedarf: Was heisst Sozialismus heute?' in *Die Nachholende Revolution: Kleine Politische Schriften VII*, Frankfurt am Main 1990; this translation first appeared in *New Left Review* 183, September–October 1990. 'The "Woman Question" in the Age of Perestroika' was first published in *New Left Review* 183, September–October 1990. 'The Ends of Cold War' was given as a lecture at the University of Sheffield on 5 March 1990; it subsequently appeared in *New Left Review* 180, March–April 1990. 'The Ends of Cold War: A Rejoinder' and 'A Reply to Edward Thompson' were first published in *New Left Review* 182, July–August 1990. 'Goodbye to All That' was first published in *Marxism Today*, October 1990. 'Marxist Century, American Century' was prepublished in *New Left Review* 179, January–February 1990, and is reprinted from S. Amin, G. Arrighi, A.G. Frank and I. Wallerstein, eds, *Transforming the Revolution: Social Movements in the World-System*, New York 1990, courtesy of Monthly Review Press. 'Radical as Reality' was first published in *The Nation*, 16 September 1991. An earlier version of 'Fin de Siècle: Socialism after the Crash' was published in *New Left Review* 185, January–February 1991. 'A Child Lost in the Storm' was first published in *The Guardian* weekly, May 1990. 'The Intellectuals in Power?' was first published in *Against the Current*, September–October

1990. 'Whose Left? Socialism, Feminism and the Future' was first published in *New Left Review* 185, January–February 1991. 'The New Agenda' was first published in *New Left Review* 184, November– December 1990. 'Vorsprung durch Rethink' was first published in *Marxism Today*, and reprinted in *New Times*, ed. Stuart Hall and Martin Jacques, Lawrence & Wishart 1989. 'Out of the Ashes' was first published in *Marxism Today*, April 1991. All permissions to reprint are gratefully acknowledged.

Preface

The essays in this book explore the historical meaning of Communism's meteoric trajectory across the twentieth century. They also assess the consequences for socialism and socialists of the debacle and disaster of Communism since 1989. The concern here is with understanding the reasons for Communist failure and exploring its wider significance, not with telling the story of the various dramatic, heartening or tragic events of that and subsequent years. However the reader should bear in mind the time at which each of the essays was written, since they are published here with little or no revision. They were all written while the shock of the events they concern was still palpable, though they have been selected because they succeeded in putting those events in a wider theoretical and historical perspective. Indeed, even the briefest of these reflections are the fruit of a lengthy prior critical engagement with the fate of Communism and the other topics they concern.

The brutal suppression of the Democracy movement in Beijing in June 1989 was the occasion for the essays by Norberto Bobbio and Ralph Miliband which open this collection. The killings in Beijing and a dozen other major centres, numbering several thousand in only a few days, were especially shocking because the Chinese government was here shooting young people who were urging Communism to reform itself, to deal with corruption and democratize the structures of power. Bobbio, in his brief but pithy reflections, saw these events as revealing the way in which the Communist exercise of power has inexorably turned into a cruel caricature of the noble ideals it proclaimed. In scholarly works and political polemics which range over more than fifty years Bobbio has maintained that the norms and institutions of liberal democracy are essential to socialism.[1] While he sees the tragic slaughter

ix

in China as bearing out the need for democracy there he also observes that the epochal discrediting of 'historical Communism' leaves intact the very conditions of global want and misery which produced the desperate Communist alternative.

Miliband concedes that few of the Communist revolutions were born in conditions favourable to a democratic polity. But he nonetheless argues that the characteristic emphases of Leninism—its excessive faith in itself, its rejection of representative procedures in favour of 'council democracy' and its ferocity towards opponents—created an arrogant vanguard which was to transform itself into the bureaucratic oligarchy of Stalinism. And, once in place, such oligarchies have been peculiarly resistant to reform in a socialist direction.

Recoil from the events in Beijing may have helped to restrain the reaction of Soviet and local Communist authorities when they faced a spreading popular revolt in Eastern Europe in the latter part of 1989. Yet this more humane response confirmed in a different way the difficulty, perhaps impossibility, of reforming Communism in a socialist rather than capitalist direction. Long years of Stalinist misrule and oppression meant that the popular movements in Eastern Europe in 1989 no longer aspired to the 'socialism with a human face' of 1968 in Czechoslovakia, instead rejecting all socialist models and aiming at a Western conception of 'normal society'. And in the Soviet Union as well as in China, Communist rule, together with the corruption and cynicism it has bred, has gravely compromised the very idea of socialism. In this, of course, lies a challenge to which many essays in the book are responding.

Hans Magnus Enzensberger offers a radical criticism of the state socialist project, arguing that it placed false hopes in the conscious control of economic life, underestimating its necessary complexity and spontaneity. With characteristic iconoclasm he argues that even libertarian leftists have been disconcerted by the capacity of the capitalist 'bad fairy' to grant the Left's wishes, albeit in travestied ways. The scathing verdict on utopianism offered here is not shared by several later contributors—notably Jameson and Therborn—but in a book mainly about Communism it is important to be reminded that capitalism at least remains an unpredictable and even subversive force.

Jürgen Habermas surveys both the East European revolutions of 1989 and the theories which have sought to explain them. In his view these revolutions represented the attempt to catch up of societies whose development had been arbitrarily retarded where it threatened the rule of the Communist bureaucracy. He suggests that Marx's own account of how capitalism undermined and destroyed pre-capitalist civilizations paradoxically helps us to grasp this process of 'recuperation' of the East

by the West. Habermas sees the economic worsting of Communism as
driving home the lesson that it is dangerous and unrealistic to suppose
that a modern economy can dispense with the complexity and autonomy
of market relations. But at the same time he insists that a purely economic logic will not respect or sustain the lifeworld upon which we all
depend. Realization of the values of liberty, equality and solidarity
requires the construction of a new discursive public space which could
revise the workings of the economy, and in which all citizens could
find themselves.

Maxine Molyneux examines the Communist record in promoting the
emancipation of women and equality between the sexes. She does not
deny the real if limited attempts made by Communist regimes to further
these goals as they understood them. Women have broken through
traditional barriers, and gained entry to higher education and professional employment. Official childcare programmes have been comparatively extensive but have still left women bearing a heavy load of
domestic responsibilities and forced to cope with the failure of the
command economies to meet consumer needs. Women have remained
shut out of decisive structures of power and imprisoned by restrictive
gender stereotypes. Molyneux argues that the ending of Communism
will give women more opportunity to discover their interests but she also
warns that the newly powerful religious and nationalist ideologies are
often tied up with patriarchal conceptions of the woman's role.

Fred Halliday sees the Cold War as expressing a clash of systems, in
which an economically superior West was able to prevail over the East
by imposing on it an unsustainable burden of military competition. The
Soviet Union was brought to the point where it saw an advantage in
leaving Eastern Europe to its own devices, thus reducing the Soviet
military budget and allowing it to find hard-currency markets for Soviet
oil and raw materials. Halliday also stresses the ways in which the
Western culture and information industries revealed Communist backwardness to Eastern rulers and citizens alike. Edward Thompson objects
to the thesis that the Cold War was mainly about political differences; in
his view Soviet militarism partook of a logic which was shared with its
Western antagonist. He argues that the peace movements should be
given some of the credit for the unfreezing of Cold War mentalities, and
that a 'third way' does exist beyond Stalinism and capitalism. Halliday
and Thompson both express concern at the West's ungenerous response
to collapse in the East, and at the exploitation of popular disillusionment
there by illiberal nationalism and doctrinaire laissez faire.[2]

Eric Hobsbawm puts the rise and fall of Communism into the context
of the history of the twentieth century. The Communist challenge did
much to transform the Western capitalism and imperialism that was so

discredited by the slaughter of the First World War and the misery of the Great Depression. The decisive Soviet contribution to the defeat of Nazism helped to promote reformism and decolonization in the Western empires. Communist claims to have banished unemployment and instituted comprehensive educational and health programmes put Western governments on their mettle. While Communism's vaunted utopia might have failed miserably in the East, it set targets in the West.

Giovanni Arrighi sketches a bold periodization of the history of the world labour movement, suggesting that Marx's prediction that social misery and social power would be united and concentrated in the Western proletariat did not hold true in the twentieth century—the Communist cause became rooted in those countries where capitalism had produced social misery; while labour movements in the advanced countries, having accumulated real social power, were pacified by the fruits of reform. Arrighi concludes that capitalism today is again concentrating social power and social misery in the proletariat of a range of Third World countries which have experienced capitalist development over recent decades. He sees new working-class movements in Brazil, South Africa, South Korea and a range of intermediate countries as now possessing both the power and the motive for challenging the grotesque inequalities embodied in the world capitalist system. Arrighi's essay was completed in the early months of 1989, when the tenacious survival of *Solidarność* in Poland had convinced him that 'historical Marxism', in the shape of the Communist governments, did not, and could not, meet the demands of the new working class it had brought into existence. The subsequent role of Soviet miners in challenging the monopoly of the CPSU would be a further example of this phenomenon.

Eduardo Galeano writes on the awesome spectacle of Communist collapse from the standpoint of the Third World. Writing shortly after the Nicaraguan elections of 1990 he contrasts the political and moral qualities of the Sandinista revolution with the cynicism and accommodation of Communist bureaucracy in Eastern Europe. He also points out that while Communism may have failed to reverse global inequalities, capitalism has actually maintained and enlarged them. Moreover the unjust international order over which the West presides has been defended and policed with great ruthlessness and violence, with blockades, sabotage, murder squads, contra wars and the like. In pointing to the harsh polarization of wealth and life opportunity that structures the world Galeano develops a theme taken up in different ways by a number of contributors, notably Bobbio, Habermas, and Hobsbawn.[3]

While these essays are concerned to chart the impact of Communism on the history of the twentieth century they also seek to assess the extent to which that history demands a new development of socialist theory and of historical or cultural materialism. Underlying several of the essays is the view that the Communist states have undergone an incomplete, lopsided and perverse modernization; their newly urbanized and educated citizens, aware of life in the West, were drawn to complete the process in a new species of bourgeois democratic revolution.

Iván Szelényi, writing in early 1990, argues that the transformations in Eastern Europe are bringing intellectuals a new privileged position in society, thus bearing out the predictions made in the book he co-wrote with George Konrad in 1974, *The Intellectuals on the Road to Class Power*.[4] The first fruits of the attempts to restore capitalism in the post-Communist states have often been sour. Cultural and productive resources have been laid to waste. New forms of intolerance, and new threats to democracy, have emerged.[5] As Iván Szelényi observes, the post-Communist attempt to join the First World is likely in most cases to fall short of its objective. In some countries the former nomenklatura are the main beneficiaries of privatization; in others, members of the mafia. Yet other outcomes remain possible, if less likely. In the Soviet Union and China, labour collectives themselves are breaking loose from ministerial control and demanding forms of self-management. To the extent that democratic conditions are being, or will be, established and respected, trade-union action and other forms of independent civic life may allow the new forms of corruption and exploitation to be contested.[6]

While socialists will quite properly insist that the instability and injustice of capitalism be scrutinized, the failings of capitalism in no way reduce the onus on socialists to show that a viable alternative can be built. The articles by André Gorz, Diane Elson, Göran Therborn, Lynne Segal and myself propose central themes of such an alternative. One key motif here is the exploration of ways in which economic processes can draw on the skills and initiative of millions or hundreds of millions of independent agents (households, enterprises, communities) and yet remain responsive to democratically agreed social priorities. The aim of socializing the market—detaching the market from blind and obsessive accumulation—can be both a goal of current struggles and a stepping-stone to a non-capitalist, but complex and self-governing, society.

Gorz argues for a trade unionism which would rediscover its commitment to general interests, as in the demand for a drastic shortening of the working week. Lynne Segal sees no reason today to abandon her long-held libertarian socialist convictions. While she welcomes the new diversity which characterizes the formations of the Left, she urges that a new awareness of 'difference', and of the distinct experience of those disadvantaged by their sex or ethnicity, should not displace the commitment to substantive social and civic equality for all.

Several essays reflect the sensibility and programme of the 'new social movements', constituted by Green politics, feminism and a concern with global inequality and militarization.[7] There is, in fact, a natural kinship between movements aiming at social equality and those which hope to ensure a sustainable relationship with the natural world. Any attempt to ensure equal outcomes for women or for ethnic minorities on the market, or to impose respect for ecological limits, is likely to be scarcely less difficult and complex than that of securing a full socialization of market processes. Diane Elson sketches how a 'socialized market' might work, while Göran Therborn transports us into an imagined future beyond capitalism (and socialism?). My own essay considers the key programmatic ideas of the Left, tracing a subterranean dialogue which links Bakunin and Kautsky, Trotsky and Hayek, Che Guevara and Gorbachev. The conclusion, as with Habermas, Elson and Gorz, is that the Left must respect the complex structures of self-determination which the market embodies, while vigorously resisting its propensity to promote social division and stimulate an oblivious and greedy consumerism.

Communism failed as a project for a different type of society, but as a movement it was by no means always contemptible. Alexander Cockburn urges us not to forget the human qualities of those Communists who did so much to resist racism, Fascism, and colonialism. It could be that Communism shared with Social Democracy the quality of being far more important as a corrective within and against capitalism than as a politics aiming beyond it. But both Communism and Social Democracy have over-invested in the state and centralizing bureaucracy as the key levers for social advance. The project of socialism, or even reformism, in one country was always flawed—but in an age of accelerated globalization its narrowness and weakness is even more striking. The socialism of the future will be obliged to strike deeper local roots and to keep in view wider international horizons.

The world we live in is now more than ever dominated by capitalism and the West, leading Fredric Jameson to suggest that it is scarcely the time to forget what we have learnt from Marx. While the G7 powers respond with great speed and violence to any challenge to their control of the world's resources and refuse to abandon a protectionism which blocks the development of the Second and Third Worlds, they do nothing to tackle world poverty or a variety of manifest threats to global ecology. Communism claimed, falsely, to embody a more responsible and just social order. It would be quite illogical and wrong to see its failure as vindicating capitalist injustice and irresponsibility. As Eric Hobsbawm points out, a rational Left, aware of its own fallibility and having learnt from the past, has a vital role to play in ensuring a livable future for all and subordinating the remarkable productive capacities unleashed by capitalism to truly human purposes.

The outcome of Russia's August revolution only reinforces the points made by the contributors to this book. Yet there is, perhaps, one aspect of this remarkable event to which attention should be drawn – namely, the virtually bloodless character of the popular victory over a power apparatus of legendary ruthlessness. The explanation suggested by these essays would seem to be as follows. Latter-day Soviet Communism formed an increasingly sophisticated and skilled elite but failed to furnish the appropriate context for complex economic development. The command economy and party-state regime were widely experienced as a fetter on broad social development and as an obstacle even to many in the privileged elite itself. Many of the latter not only knew better than anybody else how badly the system was failing but possessed skills that would be marketable even if there was a change of system. While the great mass of the Russian people played little active part, they voted for change and certainly longed to see the deadweight of bureaucratic tutelage lifted from their lives. Socialists will hope that Russia's bourgeois democratic revolution does indeed remain democratic – to the extent that it does, it will be possible to contest the impetus of new forms of inequality and callousness associated with laissez faire capitalism.

Democratization and respect for minority rights should also be encouraged in the other formerly Soviet republics where, often, it is Communists who have formed the national elite. If the West really wished to improve the chances of a democratic consolidation in the East it should forgive old debts, offer generous new aid and dismantle its own trading restrictions. As it is, the gloomy economic prospects of the formerly Communist lands will not favour democratic development. Paradoxically, China has continued to make a far more successful transition to the market economy than those states which have been following Western economic advice. This is not because of the repressive policies of the Beijing government but because the command economy was scrapped in China more than a decade ago. The dynamic sectors of the Chinese economy are agriculture and rural industry, the latter often owned by municipal authorities or labour collectives. This allows us to hope that the eventual settling of accounts with China's gerontocracy will not only reverse the verdict of Tien An Men Square, but do so without further bloodshed and without the economic devastation and social regression which threatens many parts of Eastern Europe and the former Soviet Union.

Robin Blackburn
August 1991

Notes

1. This is, of course, not to say that Bobbio has not also attended to the tension between liberalism and democracy. See Norberto Bobbio, *Liberalism and Democracy*, London 1988; and the helpful discussion in Perry Anderson, 'The Affinities of Norberto Bobbio', *New Left Review*, 170, July–August 1988.

2. The new nationalism in Eastern Europe is analysed by Slavoj Žižek,' The Republics of Gilead', *New Left Review*, 183, September–October 1990.

3. In 1990 the World Bank reported that during the 1980s, when the economies of the advanced countries were booming, real GDP per capita fell by 2.2 per cent per annum in Africa and by 0.6 per cent per annum in Latin America. Towards the close of the eighties the per capita GNP of the inhabitants of the Indian subcontinent was only 2 per cent of that of the inhabitants of the Group of Seven countries. In 1988, the World Bank reports, 'low and middle income countries' paid $53 billion to their creditors in the rich countries—a sum that comprised 20.5 per cent of their export earnings and 4.4 per cent of their GNP. The Bank estimated that there were 1,116 million poor people and 633 million 'extremely poor' people in the developing countries. World Bank, *World Bank Development Report: Poverty*, Oxford 1990, pp. 11, 29, 224–5.

4. Iván and Sonya Szelényi analyse the results of the 1990 elections in Hungary in 'The Vacuum in Hungarian Politics', *New Left Review*, 187, May–June 1991.

5. For an informative survey of the post-Communist experience see 'The Communist Aftermath', *The Socialist Register* 1991, edited by Ralph Miliband and Leo Panitch.

6. In this connection it is worth citing the views of a Soviet miners' leader whose analysis, albeit couched in a different idiom, chimes in with that of a number of contributors to this book: 'To put it briefly—perhaps abstractly and a bit crudely—a struggle is occurring today between the Communist *boyars* (aristocrats) and the new bourgeoisie that used to serve the *boyars* but has grown tired of that. They now have the desire to rise to the top themselves. The bourgeoisie are enterprising people, whose capital at present is their knowledge.... *You are talking about the intelligentsia?* Yes, the intelligentisia, economists and the like.... For us, workers and the workers' movement, it makes more sense now to support the bourgeoisie.... But we should never forget that ... when the new bourgeoisie tries to turn its knowledge into capital they will want to exploit us, that is part of their system. So while supporting at present the movement of democrats—though we know that they are really a bourgeoisie with a social-democratic orientation if judged from the point of view of world experience—we must never forget that sooner or later we will clash with them and are already clashing over a number of issues.' Aleksander Sergeev, interviewed by David Mandel, *International Viewpoint*, no. 207, 27 May 1991, pp. 26–7. Many Soviet workers favour wresting control from the ministries, though this trend would appear to be stronger in China where local collectives now dominate the dynamic sector of rural industry. Whether such labour collectives are able to promote socialist or capitalist objectives is another question which is likely to be decided not only on the local level.

7. There remains, of course, much more to be said on these, as on other questions raised in this book, and it is hoped to that a sequel will be able to pursue them. I hope it will be clear from the brief remarks in Therborn's article and in my own that Green politics should be both critically and enthusiastically embraced by the Left. For further discussion see *Defending the Earth: A Dialogue between Murray Bookchin and Dave Foreman*, ed. Steve Chase, Boston 1991; Rainer Grundmann, 'The Ecological Challenge to Marxism', *New Left Review*, 187, May–June 1991; and Rainer Grundmann, *Marxism and Ecology*, Oxford 1991.

PART I

The Forms of
Communist Collapse

1

The Upturned Utopia

Norberto Bobbio

The catastrophe of historical communism stands literally before
everyone's eyes—the catastrophe of Communism as a world movement,
born of the Russian Revolution, promising emancipation of the poor
and oppressed, the 'wretched of the earth'. The process of decomposition is continually speeding up, beyond anything predicted. This does
not yet spell the end of the Communist regimes, which might still last a
long time by finding new forces for survival. The first great crisis of a
Communist state occurred in Hungary more than thirty years ago, and
yet the regime did not collapse. In this respect, too, it is wiser not to
make any predictions.

What cannot be denied, however, is the failure not just of the
Communist regimes but of the revolution inspired by communist
ideology—the ideology which posed the radical transformation of a
society considered unjust and oppressive into a quite different society,
both free and just. The unprecedented sense of drama in the events of
the last few days lies in the fact that they have not involved the crisis of a
regime or the defeat of a great, invincible power. Rather, in a seemingly
irreversible way, the greatest political utopia in history (I am not
speaking of religious utopias) has been completely upturned into its
exact opposite. It is a utopia which, for at least a century, has fascinated
philosophers, writers and poets (think of Gabriel Pery's 'singing tomor-
rows'); which has shaken whole masses of the dispossessed and impelled
them to violent action; which has led men with a high moral sense to
sacrifice their own lives, to face prison, exile and extermination camps;
and whose unquelled force, both material and spiritual, has at times
seemed irresistible, from the Red Army in Russia to Mao's Long March,
from the conquest of power by a group of resolute men in Cuba to the

3

desperate struggle of the Vietnamese people against the mightiest power in the world. In one of his early writings—why should we not recall it?—Marx defined communism as 'the solution to the enigma of history'.

None of the ideal cities described by the philosophers was ever proposed as a model to be actually realized. Plato knew that the ideal republic of which he spoke with his friends was not destined to exist in any place on earth; it was true, as Glaucon put it to Socrates, only in our words. But the first utopia that tried to enter into history, to pass from the realm of 'words' to that of things, not only came true but is being upturned, has already almost been upturned in the countries where it was put to the test, into something ever more like those negative utopias which have so far also existed only in words (one thinks of Orwell's novel).

The best proof of failure is that all those who have rebelled from time to time in these years, and with particular energy in the last few days, have called precisely for recognition of the rights to liberty that are the first prerequisite of democracy—not, please note, of 'progressive' or popular democracy, or however else it might be called to distinguish and exalt it over our democracies, but precisely of the democracy that we can only call 'liberal' and which emerged and consolidated itself through the slow and arduous conquest of certain basic freedoms. I am referring, in particular, to the four great freedoms of modern man: individual liberty, or the right not to be arrested arbitrarily and to be judged in accordance with clearly defined penal and judicial rules; freedom of the press and of opinion; freedom of assembly, which we saw captured peacefully, but contested, on Tiananmen Square; and finally—the most difficult to achieve—the freedom of association out of which free trade unions and free parties were born, and with them the pluralist society in whose absence democracy does not exist. The completion of this centuries-long process was political liberty, or the right of all citizens to participate in collective decisions that concern them.

The explosive, and seemingly irrepressible, force of the popular movements shaking the world of Communist regimes stems from the fact that these great freedoms are now being demanded all at once. In Europe the state of freedoms came after the law-based state, the democratic state after the state of freedoms. But on those squares today people are simultaneously demanding the law-based state, the state of freedoms and the democratic state. The Chinese students, in one of their documents, have declared that they are fighting for democracy, freedom and law. Such a situation is objectively revolutionary. But when such a situation cannot have a revolutionary outcome—as seems to be the case in each of these countries—the resolution can only be either gradual (Poland apparently being the most advanced) or counter-revolutionary, as in China, unless it develops into civil war, that well-known historical form of failed or impossible revolutions.

The conquest of the freedom of the modern world—if and insofar as it is possible—cannot but be the starting point for the countries of the upturned utopia. But to go where? I ask this question because the founding of the law-based liberal-democratic state is not enough to solve the problems which gave birth to the proletarian movement of the countries that embarked upon a savage form of industrialization, and later among the poor peasants of the Third World, the 'hope of the revolution'. The poor and forsaken are still condemned to live in a world of terrible unjustices, crushed by unreachable and apparently unchangeable economic magnates on which the political authorities, even when formally democratic, nearly always depend. In such a world, the idea that the hope of revolution is spent, that it is finished just because the communist utopia has failed, is to close one's eyes so as not to see.

Are the democracies that govern the world's richest countries capable of solving the problems that communism has failed to solve? That is the question. Historical communism has failed, I don't deny it. But the problems remain—those same problems which the communist utopia pointed out and held to be solvable, and which now exist, or very soon will, on a world scale. That is why one would be foolish to rejoice at the defeat and to rub one's hands saying: 'We always said so!' Do people really think that the end of historical communism (I stress the word 'historical') has put an end to poverty and the thirst for justice? In our world the two-thirds society rules and prospers without having anything to fear from the third of poor devils. But it would be good to bear in mind that in the rest of the world, the two-thirds (or four-fifths or nine-tenths) society is on the other side.

Democracy, let us admit it, has overcome the challenge of historical communism. But what means and what ideals does it have to confront those very problems out of which the communist challenge was born?

'Now that there are no more barbarians,' said the poet, 'what will become of us without barbarians?'

June 1989
Translated by Patrick Camiller

2

Reflections on the Crisis of Communist Regimes

Ralph Miliband

The massacre at Tiananmen Square in June 1989 is unlikely to be the last violent expression of the deep and multiple crises—economic, social, political, ethnic, ideological, moral—which grip many Communist regimes, and which will in due course most probably grip them all. A vast 'mutation' is going on throughout the Communist world, and undoubtedly constitutes one of the great turning points in the history of the twentieth century. The outcome of this crisis is still an open question, though the alternatives, broadly speaking, are not difficult to list: at best, a form of regime approximating to socialist democracy, which the reform movement initiated by Mikhail Gorbachev in the Soviet Union may manage to produce; some form of capitalist democracy, with a substantial public sector; or a reinforced authoritarianism with a spreading market economy—what Boris Kagarlitsky has aptly called 'market Stalinism'—of which China is the most conspicuous example to date. At any rate, it seems clear that the form of regime which dominated the Soviet Union from the late twenties until a very few years ago, and all other Communist regimes from the post-war years onwards, is now unravelling in many of them, and is very likely sooner or later to unravel in them all.

We know what this immense historic process is taken to mean by the enemies of socialism everywhere: not only the approaching demise of Communist regimes and their replacement by capitalist ones, but the elimination of any kind of socialist alternative to capitalism. With this intoxicating prospect of the scarcely hoped-for dissipation of an ancient nightmare, there naturally goes the celebration of the market, the virtues of free enterprise, and greed unlimited. Nor is it only on the Right that the belief has grown in recent times that socialism, understood as a

6

radical transformation of the social order, has had its day: apostles of 'new times' on the Left have come to harbour much the same belief. All that is now possible, in the eyes of the 'new realism', is the more humane management of a capitalism which is in any case being thoroughly transformed.

What, on the other hand, does the crisis of the Communist world signify for people who remain committed to the creation of a cooperative, democratic, egalitarian, and ultimately classless society, and who believe that this aspiration can only be given effective meaning in an economy predominantly based on various forms of social ownership? An answer to this question requires first of all a clear perception of what kind of regimes it is that are in crisis so that lessons may be properly read from their experience.

The Primal Mould

Even though Communist regimes have differed from each other in various ways, they have all had two overriding characteristics in common: an economy in which the means of economic activity were overwhelmingly under state ownership and control; and a political system in which the Communist Party (under different names in different countries), or rather its leaders, enjoyed a virtual monopoly of power, which was vigilantly defended against any form of dissent by systematic—often savage—repression. The system entailed an extreme inflation of state power and, correspondingly, a stifling of all social forces not controlled by, and subservient to, the leadership of the Party/state. The 'pluralism' which formed part of the system, and which involved the existence of a large variety of institutions in every sphere of life, from culture to sport, was not at all intended to dilute the power of the Party/state, but on the contrary to reinforce it, by turning these institutions into organs of Party/state control.

Why these regimes were all set in this mould also requires close attention. To begin with, all of them, by definition, went through a massive revolutionary transformation of their economic, social, political and cultural life. In some cases—Russia, China, North Korea, Vietnam, Yugoslavia, Cuba—the revolution was internally generated. In Eastern and Central Europe, on the other hand, with the exception of Yugoslavia, it was imposed by Soviet command, from above. But whether internally generated or externally imposed, these *were* revolutions, of a very thorough kind, with fundamental changes in property relations, the elimination of traditional ruling classes, the access to power of previously excluded, marginalized and persecuted people, the complete transformation of state structures, massive changes in the occupational structure, and vast changes (or attempted changes) in the whole national culture.

However they are made, such revolutionary upheavals produce immense and long-lasting national traumas. The point hardly needs emphasis at the time of writing, the year of the bi-centenary of the French Revolution, an upheaval which remains to this day a subject of bitter, passionate debate and political division in France. The traumas are bound to be greatly accentuated if the revolutionary transformation is imposed as a result of external intervention and dictation; and all the more is this certain to be the case where the intervention is that of a foreign power which has traditionally been seen as an enemy. Poland is an obvious case in point. Regimes born in these conditions seldom have much legitimacy; and few Communist regimes were in fact viewed as legitimate in the eyes of a majority of their citizens.

Moreover, the problems which faced the new regimes were, in all Communist countries, aggravated by three crucially important factors. First, the revolutions were engineered or imposed in countries which, with the exception of Czechoslovakia and to a lesser degree East Germany (which became the German Democratic Republic in 1949), were at a low level of economic development, in some cases at an abysmally low level. This meant, among other things, that the revolution did not inherit the fruits of economic maturation: on the contrary, it was turned into a means of economic development, and was therefore associated with a painful and arduous process, slow to yield beneficial results. This would have been bad enough; but, secondly, Communist regimes faced conditions of war and civil war, foreign intervention, huge losses of life and appalling material destruction. Korea and Vietnam were involved in a major war with the United States, and subjected to murderously destructive saturation bombing; and Cuba, for its part, has endured a debilitating boycott and other forms of hostile intervention on the part of the United States.

Again, there is the scarcely negligible fact that, save for Czechoslovakia, hardly any Communist regime had had any previous experience of effective democratic forms. The European states which became Communist regimes had all previously had strong near-authoritarian or actually authoritarian regimes, with very weak civil societies, in which the state, allied to semi-feudal ruling classes, had enjoyed great power and used it to exploit and oppress largely peasant populations. As for Communist regimes in Asia, and the revolutionary regime in Cuba, they had all previously been either colonial, or semi-colonial, or dependent countries, subject to impressive external or indigenous rule, or both.

These are not the conditions in which anything resembling socialist democracy could be expected to flourish. Yet, all these factors do not adequately explain why Communist regimes, with the notable exception of Yugoslavia after 1948, never made any serious attempt, or indeed any attempt at all, to break the authoritarian mould in which they had been cast at their birth. Neither Nikita Khrushchev's reforms nor Mao Tse-tung's Cultural Revolution constituted any such break: top-down and monopolistic rule remained unimpaired in the Soviet Union, in China and everywhere else in the Communist world. Their rulers might well argue that the circumstances of their birth had determined the character of their rule in the early years of the regime; and that they had continued thereafter to face very difficult conditions, capitalist hostility and the constrictions of the Cold War. But all this can hardly serve to explain the fact that at no time throughout the life of these regimes had their rulers felt impelled to seek a genuine relaxation of their rule in democratic directions.

State and Society

Conservative ideologists have a simple explanation for this immobility: its roots are to be found in Marxism. In fact, Marxism has nothing to do with it. At the very core of Marx's thought there is the insistence that socialism, not to speak of communism, entails the subordination of the state to society; and even the dictatorship of the proletariat, in Marx's perspective, must be taken to mean all but unmediated popular rule. In the unlikely event of their wishing to find textual ideological inspiration for their form of rule, Communist leaders would have sought in vain in the many volumes of Marx's and Engels's *Collected Works*. Least of all would they have found any notion of single-party monopolistic rule. They might have fared rather better with Lenin's *Collected Works*, but even this would have required a very selective reading and a refusal to take seriously Lenin's strictures against the 'bureacratic deformation' of Communist rule. The real architect of the model of the rule which came to prevail in all Communist regimes was in fact Stalin, who first established it in the Soviet Union, and then had it copied by other Communist leaders nurtured in his school, or imposed it on the countries which came under his control after World War Two.

However, Stalin died in 1953, and it is not reasonable to attribute to his malign power the reason why Communist leaders chose to cling to authoritarian patterns of rule. The reason for it lies in the simple fact that it suited extremely well the people who ran the system and who came to constitute a large state bourgeoisie and petty bourgeoisie nurtured in the *nomenklatura*, and enjoying considerable power and privilege. No doubt, the motives of the people concerned were very mixed—certainly personal advantage, but also a kind of authoritarian paternalism, a fear of what loosening up might do not only to their position but to the nature of the regime, even a genuine belief that this *was* socialism, and that they were defending it against its many internal and external enemies.

But whatever the motives of those who led these regimes, their rule constituted an awful perversion of socialism. This is not to deny them various advances and achievements in economic and social terms; but it needs to be said, most of all by socialists, that they did nevertheless contradict in a multitude of fundamental ways the democratic and egalitarian promise of socialism. Communist regimes were, and most of them remain, what, some considerable time ago, I called the Soviet Union— oligarchical collectivist regimes.[1]

It is in their authoritarian nature, I believe, that must above all be sought the reason for the crisis which has engulfed them. For their lack of democracy and of civic freedoms has affected every aspect of their life, from economic performance to ethnic strife. It has been Mikhail Gorbachev's immense merit to have seen and proclaimed that the essential and imperative remedy for the parlous state to which the Soviet Union had been brought was democracy, and to have sought to act upon that perception. Perestroika came from above. But it did not come all by itself, out of the unprompted wishes and impulses of an inspired leader. It was in fact engendered by the need to enlist the cooperation and support of a population whose cynicism about its leaders had brought about a profound economic, social and political crisis. The same cynicism and alienation are at work in other Communist regimes. This may not result in perestroika, Soviet style, or take the forms which it has already produced in Hungary and Poland. But it is very unlikely to leave any Communist regime unaffected.

Lessons of the Communist Experience

What lessons, then, does the Communist experience hold for Western socialists? It would of course be easy to say that it is entirely irrelevant, given the very different conditions which Western socialists confront in advanced capitalist countries with capitalist-democratic regimes. But to say this would be much too easy. How could an experience extending over some seventy years, lived under the name of socialism, however unwarranted the label, be dismissed as irrelevant and of no account? At the very least, it might point to what is *not* to be done—for instance, in regard to planning and the organization of economic life.

However, the really important lessons to be learnt by socialists from Communist experience lie elsewhere than in the realm of techniques: by far the most important of these lessons has to do with the subject of democracy. For a start, it is clear that the character of Communist rule has greatly helped to give plausibility to a claim which has been one of the most effective items in the conservative repertoire, namely that socialism was inherently authoritarian and oppressive, and that capitalism alone was capable of providing freedom and democratic rule. One of the great triumphs of dominant classes in the West has been their appropriation of democracy, at least in rhetoric and propaganda; and it can hardly be doubted that Communist practices, from elections with 99.9 per cent majorities to the brutal suppression of dissent, have been of the greatest help in the achievement of that appropriation. The simple fact of the matter is that capitalist democracy, for all its crippling limitations, has been immeasurably less oppressive and a great deal more democratic than any Communist regime, whatever the latter's achievements in economic, social and other fields. Communist regimes might legitimately claim that they encouraged a far greater degree of participation in organs of power than did bourgeois democracy; but the claim was rendered spurious by the subordination of these organs to strict party and state control, with little (or no) real autonomy.

The experience of Communist regimes therefore forces upon Western socialists the need for further and deeper reflection on the exercise of power. There are, in this connection, two different issues which tend to become confused and which need to be disentangled. Marxists and other revolutionary socialists have always insisted that bourgeois democracy is fundamentally vitiated by the class context in which it functions, and by the degree to which the whole democratic process is undermined by the visible and the invisible power which capitalist interests and conservative forces are able to deploy vis-à-vis society and the state. Bourgeois democracy, in a context of class domination, is more often than not turned into an instrument of that domination, and also provides dominant classes with a precious element of legitimation. Also, bourgeois democracy is corrupted by the authoritarian practices to which governments in capitalist societies frequently resort; and it is vulnerable to abrogation when democratic forms threaten to turn into a serious challenge to class domination.

All this is one critique of bourgeois democracy which Marxists and others have rightly made. There is, however, a different critique, which complements the first one, and which is, in some ways, even more fundamental. That is that the kind of representative and parliamentary system which is an essential part of bourgeois democracy is *in any case*, and whatever its context, undemocratic, and that socialism requires more direct forms of expression of popular sovereignty and democratic power. Representation, in this mode of thinking, is inevitably misrepresentation, and perpetuates the alienation of the mass of people from political power which it is the purpose of socialism to overcome. Some degree of representation may be unavoidable; but it should be kept to the barest minimum, with representatives constantly and vigilantly supervised by their constituents, and subject to frequent election and recall.

This radical alternative to representative democracy is outlined in Marx's *The Civil War in France*, written as a defence and celebration of the Paris Commune, and even more specifically in Lenin's *The State and Revolution*, written on the eve of the Bolshevik Revolution. Such a system, Lenin said in a bitter polemic with Karl Kautsky, was 'a million times more democratic' than bourgeois democracy could ever be. Yet, it is of great significance that, by the time the claim was made, in 1919, the soviet or council system, which had emerged in the February Revolution, had all but withered, with the soviets under the ever more strict tutelage of the Communist Party.[2] Nor has it ever been resurrected; and 'council communism' has flourished nowhere else in the Communist world, not surprisingly since it so greatly contradicts the party dictatorship which has been the essence of Communist rule. Equally significantly, 'council communism' has had no substantial resonance in any capitalist-democratic regime. As a project, it remains what it has been since the Bolshevik Revolution—a marginal movement whose proponents constitute a small and barely audible voice in labour and socialist ranks.

This is not likely to change. Social democrats have always, and ever more emphatically, tended to accept bourgeois democracy as being synonymous with democracy *tout court*, and have shown very little concern with its limitations; and social-democratic leaders have in recent times been particularly emphatic in their celebration of it. Western Communist leaders for their part have been more critical, but they have nevertheless long been wholly committed to its essential mechanisms.

Socialism and Democracy

So too is it notable that the constitutional reforms which have occurred in the Soviet Union, Poland and Hungary have involved the rejuvenation of representative legislatures, issued from newly competitive electoral systems. The trend is likely to continue, and to spread. All reform movements everywhere, not only in Communist regimes, but in previously authoritarian regimes of the Right as well, as in Latin

America, tend in the direction of what might be called traditional representative government. For the relevant future, which is likely to extend over a considerable period of time, socialists will have to wage their battles within the confines of this system. What, concretely, does this mean?

First, it means full participation in electoral, representative struggles at local, regional and national levels. It will immediately be said that this is a sure recipe for 'parliamentary cretinism', unprincipled compromise, the opportunistic dilution of programme and purpose. These are real dangers; but even if the dangers cannot be fully overcome, they may at least be greatly attenuated by a democratic, open, responsive party life, with leaders and representatives truly accountable to the members of the organizations which had made their election possible. Nor of course does participation in representative institutions exclude extra-parliamentary and extra-institutional struggles wherever such struggles are to be waged. It is idle to pretend that, even in the best of circumstances, and even with saintly good will all round, a real tension can be avoided between the demands of politics within the framework of representative democracy, and the demands of socialist principle. The alternative, amply demonstrated by long experience, is for parties intent upon radical change to remain confined in a very narrow political space.

The second point is that, together with their involvement in the system, socialists have to conduct a permanent critique of the limitations and shortcomings of bourgeois democracy, of its narrowness and formalism, of its authoritarian tendencies and practices. Such a critique must bear on existing constitutional, electoral and political arrangements; but it also has to be directed at the hierarchical and oppressive aspects of daily life in a social order based on exploitation and domination. In other words, it is not only political arrangements which need sustained and convincing criticism, but also the exercise of arbitrary power in all walks of life—in factories, offices, schools and wherever else power affects people's existence. The notion that the battle for democracy has already been won in capitalist-democratic systems, save for some electoral and constitutional reforms at the edges, simply by virtue of the achievement of universal suffrage, open political competition and regular elections is a profoundly limiting and debilitating notion which has served conservative forces extremely well, and which has to be exposed and countered.

The question, however, is from what standpoint it should be exposed and countered. For many Marxists, past and present, the answer has seemed very simple. Of course, they would say, one has to function within the context of bourgeois democracy, but by having as little to do as possible with formal, electoral, cretinism-inducing procedures. The important thing was to concentrate on class struggle at the point of production, and beyond; and at some point, the class struggle would reach a moment of extreme crisis, out of the deepening and irresoluble contradictions of capitalism, and this would present the revolutionary, vanguard party with the opportunities for which it had been preparing itself over the years and decades. The moment of revolution would have arrived, the bourgeois state would be smashed, and the dictatorship of the proletariat would be proclaimed, on the basis of workers' councils and genuine as opposed to fake popular power.

The weakness of this perspective is not only that it has so far proved to be quite unrealistic, or that, as I have suggested, it has tended to ghettoize its proponents, but rather that it holds no promise whatever of avoiding the degeneration into authoritarianism which has befallen all Communist regimes. For it should be obvious that, however much an old state may be 'smashed', a new state, which really *is* a state, will have to replace it; and neither proclamations of its democratic credentials, nor even the good intentions of its controllers, will resolve the huge problems posed by the democratic exercise of power, particularly when vast changes in the social order are being implemented.

Checks on Power

To tackle these problems requires that attention be paid to some quite ancient propositions. Of these, none is more important than the proposition that only power can check power. Such checking power has to occur both within the state and from the outside. Within the state, it involves mechanisms which Communist regimes, to their immense detriment, have spurned: the checking of the executive and the administration by an effective legislature; the independence of the judiciary; the strict and independent control of police powers; the curbing and control of official discretion. Such devices could not properly operate in Communist systems, given the superior and supreme allegiance owed by all state organs to the Party and its leaders. In the light of this imperative requirement, it would have been idle to expect a legislative assembly to take seriously its formal constitutional powers. So too would it have been unreasonable to expect judges to make decisions that appeared to contradict what was wanted higher up.

This is not to imply that checks and balances are particularly effective in capitalist-democratic regimes, or even that they necessarily serve desirable purposes. It is only to argue that the checking of executive, administrative and police power—indeed all forms of power— is an intrinsic part of the politics of social democracy. Such politics cannot entail the wholesale rejection of traditional liberal principles in the conduct of government, but rather their radical extension, far beyond anything that was ever dreamt of by liberal thinkers. This means a fostering of many centres of power outside the state, in a system of autonomous and independent associations, groupings, parties and lobbies of every kind and description, expressing a multitude of concerns and aspirations woven in the tissue of society. Such pluralism can only flower in a regime where 'bourgeois freedoms' are fully guaranteed and extended, and vigilantly defended by a free press and other media, and from many other sources as well. Socialist democracy, on this view, is a system of 'dual power', in which state power and popular power complement each other, but also check each other.

Here too, it is as well to acknowledge that all this constitutes a difficult and fraught enterprise. But the whole experience of Communist regimes suggests that, in socialist terms, there is no other way. There is always bound to be a tension between what are perceived to be the needs of government by those who are in charge of it, and the claims of democracy. The crucial lesson which Communist regimes teach is that the attempt to resolve that tension by sacrificing the claims of democracy to what are taken to be the needs of government is self-defeating. What one ends up with is a bad government and no democracy. What is required is the maintenance of a balance between these conflicting claims—a difficult and precarious enterprise, but an essential one.

There is also a very different dimension to socialist democracy, related to the previous one, but which is never given the requisite attention and concern: this is that socialism stands, or should by definition stand, for *humane rule*. A good many years ago, in 1965, in the course of a series of interviews with Bertrand Russell for television, I asked him what he thought of Lenin. 'Lenin was a cruel man', he said, with great emphasis on the word 'cruel'. I then thought that this was an odd comment, not only because Lenin, from all accounts, was not a cruel man, but because the focus on *this* trait, true or false, seemed rather strange, irrelevant. But the concern with cruelty *is* of crucial importance. Political leaders may or may not be personally cruel. But the governments which they lead or of which they are members do many evil and cruel things, and tolerate, encourage and cover up many cruel actions, great and small, always of course in the name of democracy, freedom, national security, socialism, or whatever.

In the presidential campaign the Republican Party waged in the autumn of 1988—a campaign notable for the demagogic and unscrupulous depths which it plumbed—George Bush also spoke of his desire to see 'a gentler and kinder America'. Whoever wrote these particular lines for him had the right idea. Capitalist societies are inherently incapable of bringing the idea to fruition; but it should figure very high on the socialist agenda, and be seen to do so. One of the worst aspects of Communist regimes has been their seeming indifference, in practice, to humane values, their bureaucratic insensitivity, their resort to arbitrary action. It would not do to overlook the appalling cruelties which their bourgeois counterparts have often perpetrated. But bourgeois politicians in capitalist-democratic regimes have been constrained in their actions by the political framework in which they have had to act, at least—and the qualification is very large—in relation to their own citizens. Communist regimes, on the other hand, have been far less constrained, or all too often hardly constrained at all, and have had ample scope for acting in arbitrary, oppressive and cruel ways. Governments, of whatever kind, can never be trusted, by their own volition, to act decently. Socialist democracy would make it one of its main tasks to build strong barriers against their acting otherwise.

There are a good many socialists who will treat this whole line of argument with the deepest suspicion. They will sternly remind us that revolution is no picnic, and that there are extremely nasty people out there who are implacably determined to prevent at all costs, not excluding *any* means, however foul, the kind of changes in the social order which socialism implies. This is very true. Nowhere is there likely to occur a smooth transition to socialism—on the contrary, the process is bound to be fraught with great dangers and difficulties. But the dangers and difficulties are the more likely to be diminished, the greater the popular support for and involvement in the process. That support, and its resilience and depth, are in large part dependent on the degree to which a socialist movement is able to convince a majority of people that it stands, not only for material improvement and a more rational use of resources than lies within the capacity of capitalism, but also for humane government.

For many years to come, socialists will be something like a pressure group to the left of orthodox social democracy. It is social democracy which will for a long time constitute the alternative—such as it is—to conservative governments. In this perspective, one of the main tasks for socialists is surely to turn themselves into the most resolute and persuasive defenders of the democratic gains which have been achieved in capitalist regimes, the most intransigent critics of the shortcomings of capitalist democracy, and the best advocates of a social order in which democracy is at long last liberated from the constrictions which capitalist domination imposes upon it.

August 1989

Notes

1. 'Stalin and After', in *The Socialist Register 1973*, London 1973.
2. Soviets had of course emerged much earlier as well—in the 1905 Revolution. Originally, they were viewed with suspicion by Lenin and the Bolsheviks.

3

Ways of Walking:
A Postscript to Utopia

Hans Magnus Enzensberger

Walking upright, with one's head held high—which, as everyone knows, was invented by the German philosopher Ernst Bloch—remains a popular moral postulate. The principle is usually expressed with a certain degree of pathos; a reproachful undertone is unmistakable. It would be easy to gain the impression that the exhortation is addressed to a society of quadrupeds: one more proof that philosophy has considerable difficulty coming to terms with our more trivial achievements.

The attitude of Dr Renner, our blond physics teacher, who presented the results of his research to an astonished school class in the middle of the muted anarchy of the late forties, was quite different. As a student of the famous theorist Arnold Sommerfeld, he had written a thesis on the physics of walking. He maintained that until then science had been confronted by a puzzle; and he himself would not claim to have found a convincing explanation as to how such a disorderly form of locomotion was possible at all. Quite apart from the demands that walking upright made on a sense of balance and a capacity for co-ordination—demands which artificial intelligence failed to meet, since no automaton was equal to them—the simple kinetics of walking was so complex that it could only be very approximately calculated, proceeding from the theory of the spinning top. In fact, it was really a kind of staggering; the upright walk was an extremely precarious, unsteady, almost slithering motion, constantly on the verge of catastrophe. We left school in a thoughtful mood, carefully, indeed clumsily, placing one foot in front of the other— an example, to quote Kleist, of 'what disturbances to man's natural grace, consciousness can wreak'.

But if even such a simple system as a skeleton powered by muscles and nerves largely eludes analysis, what must things be like with that far more complexly structured subject to which Bloch's appeal is addressed—that is, the human race? Unless events leave it no other choice, it thinks just as little about the forward motion of the whole as an individual does about his own locomotion. If the spinning top of history begins to list and topples over, then astonishment is no less great than in Dr Renner's physics class, when he paused and began to give shape to an idea ...

No idea is dearer to the political class than stability. Kissinger and Brezhnev, Deng and Pinochet, Schmidt and Honecker could have easily agreed to that. But their successors too are united by the deep desire to remain in charge of the situation. A secret horror shakes the professional politicians of all countries at the thought that the sentence 'We are the people' could be taken seriously. Where would it all end if the people took the often-proclaimed right to self-determination literally?

The only answer to rule by the street is the water cannon: in an emergency other equipment can be made available too. All the apparatuses, whether in Beijing or Bonn, Leipzig or Paris, Sofia or Washington, are in fraternal accord with this unspoken conviction. And that is what is at stake when the planning staffs feverishly put together new 'peace settlements', always searching for 'inner security' and an eternal 'balance' that is supposed to put an end to the lurching forward motion. How nice it would be if everything that was on its feet would let itself be 'tied up', 'fastened down', 'integrated'!

However, it seems very likely that the longed-for stability was always an illusion. Even if these cleanly regulated, clearly organized, immobile structures of domination did exist, at some time and somewhere, then today at any rate they have disappeared. The traditional conception of the state is facing a paradigm collapse, such as classical physics underwent long ago. The control, which the chancelleries worship, is proving to be a phantom.

The awkward impression which governments are making in the face of the recent changes in Europe is therefore not an accidental embarrassment which could be redressed by changing individuals around. It follows from the impossibility of forecasting the social process and controlling it from above. This is not only true of the extreme case. It also makes visible to all that the swaying, unsteady course of things is at once very normal and quite unpredictable.

The spiteful glee of the intellectuals at the humiliation of politics by the tumble of events has stayed within bounds. It is not only the administrators of power who feel uneasy but the administrators of ideas too. No wonder; both imagined they could determine the direction society was to take; hence their traditional rivalry. They were quarrelling about the same privilege: that of defining and solving problems in the name of all the others.

As soon as a society comes in sight which no longer allows any regulatory ideas to be imposed on it from outside or from above, then both these classes of persons see themselves deprived of their hereditary role. An evolutionary process which cannot be predicted, and can even less be planned, does not, it is true, make them superfluous, but it necessarily involves a considerable loss of authority and influence.

The intellectuals are, then, suffering from withdrawal symptoms just as much as the politicians. Moreover, whether they want to preserve what already exists or to overthrow it is irrelevant. It is not only the solid facts that are tottering. The flying carpet of utopia, too, has been pulled out from under the feet of those who have made themselves at home on it. Anyone who believes he has taken out a lease on the future is in an even worse position than someone who imagines he is called upon to act as guardian of what already exists. Both had fallen for the illusion of the governability of the social sphere. Yet the losses to the left intelligentsia weigh more heavily, for the final goal, which they had in mind and which turns out to be mere make-believe, stood not under the dictate of reality but under the sign of hope.

The widespread complaint about the disappearance of utopia is understandable. Nevertheless, the lament easily clouds the vision of the lamenter. The often-heard assertion that one cannot live without a utopia is at best a quarter-truth. Because if one understands it to mean more than a straightforward dream of happiness, of paradise, then utopian thinking is by no means an anthropological constant. It is universal only in its claims. In fact it is a specific product of a very particular culture. As the name indicates, it was a Greek idea, which later on experienced a relatively brief flowering on our continent, from Bacon and Campanella to Fourier and Marx.

At its height, this mode of thought produced a series of schemes for society which were worked out in fantastic detail. In these thoroughly planned models there was an optimum of regulation of life from conception to death, as if the happiness of mankind could be got going with the precision of clockwork—an idea that should really put all worshippers of stability in a state of rapture.

That this way of thinking has not been ineffective should need no emphasis. Its export to the most remote parts of the world is one of the most devastating results of European culture. It would be an event of great significance if the Europeans too now discarded their obsession. It is not true that with such a self-correction they would surrender their desires. What would fall victim to it would above all be the most fatal elements of utopian thinking: the projective megalomania, the claim to totality, finality and originality. (The 'revolutions' which are now shaking the Eastern half of Europe have not brought forth any new demands. The only demands are those of 1848, which have remained unfulfilled until now.)

Instead of hoping for salvation from a single forceful idea, people would rather put their trust in an infinitely complicated, self-correcting process, which not only knows progress, but also retreat, not only grabbing what one can get, but also restraint. It may be that such a way of walking lacks grace. Nature plays tricks, the human being stumbles; without a degree of chaos there can be no self-organization.

But the farewell to utopia also has an ironic aspect. Its loss has also, in quite an odd way, brought about its fulfilment. The simple common-sense insight that things always turn out differently from what one had expected thereby comes to a head in a manner that no philosophy of history can cope with. To fully appreciate the position it is necessary to turn to the tellers of fairy tales.

A hero, whose circumstances are not enviable, meets a fairy who has nothing better to do than to promise him the fulfilment of his wishes. For some kind of magical reason these wishes are always three in number. There is probably no country in which this story is unknown; the twist is that the fairy sticks exactly to her promise to the point of pedantry. One cannot even accuse her of cheating. The hero is granted what he wished for, but always in such a way that either he does not recognize it or does not know what to do with it, which usually puts the dupe into a helpless rage. Three central promises of the European utopias have been fulfilled in a similarly disagreeable way.

The Withering Away of the State

One would have to look with a magnifying glass for anarchists who resolutely believe in a future world from which every form of domination has disappeared. But at the same time the forms of political domination have become strangely diffuse. To that extent we are dealing with, to borrow a term from anthropology, acephalic societies. The state is first to be affected. Its sovereignty, which was once its pride and joy, no longer counts for much, and the more intelligent of its representatives with good reason avoid using the words 'sovereign power'. Bound by a thousand threads like Gulliver, their room for manoeuvre grows ever smaller. That can be seen most clearly in countries whose political traditions were destroyed by their own efforts and outside help, a catastrophe which, as has since become evident, can have certain advantages.

The West Germans drew a noteworthy conclusion from their problematic situation by raising the most inconspicuous of places to be their capital city, and one can only hope that they leave the state in the village, where it belongs.

At all events there is no longer any state in Europe which expects of its citizens that they 'believe' in it, and even the boldest government spokesman would begin to stutter if he had to repeat Hegel's dictum that the state is 'God becoming visible'. Servitude has disappeared along with the halo. Yet, as in the fairy tale, the official denial follows close on the heels of the fulfilment of the wish: the disenchanted state is very far from withering away. It is true that the contention that some individual could 'lay down the guidelines of politics' has become pure fiction; but at the same time the 'administration of things' expands further and further.

Internationalism

The great European utopians were not local patriots. The social orders which they devised were supposed to make not one or other country happy, but the whole human race. This principle was most consistently formulated by proletarian internationalism. This promise too has found an ironic fulfilment. Not the workers, but the capitalists and technologists of all countries have put it into practice. More than a hundred years ago, without fanfares and brass bands, the World Postal Union, probably the first global organization, was founded in Berne and it has functioned smoothly up to the present day, regardless of political conflicts and ideological differences. Equally effective miracles were worked by the anonymous officials to whom we owe worldwide air traffic and telecommunications networks. Neither the First nor the Second nor the Third International established the idea of a world society; but the anonymous world market, symbolized by a handful of iconic brand names and dominated by the multinational companies, the big banks and the parastatal finance organizations.

Equality

It is superfluous to provide evidence yet again of increasing social polarization, even in many rich countries, or describe the desperate situation of many underdeveloped nations. But while real quality cannot be said to exist anywhere, a parodic version of the ideal has been realized in the industrial societies. That can easily be demonstrated using the example of road traffic.

Decades ago, traffic lights and traffic jams assumed power over just and unjust, rich and poor alike. This despotism is decentralized and guided by no overall interest, it knows no exceptions and pays no regard to class-position or origin. The £100,000 luxury model is no less subject to this despotism than the Trabant ready for the scrap heap. Social difference shrinks to an imaginary gain in distinction. The marginal utility of money and power sinks; neither offers protection against the risks of the future.

Even the differences which consumerism has to offer are becoming more and more illusory, at least in the richer countries. The writer Henryk Broder could recently assert, without anyone contradicting him, that the junk-food chain McDonald's has realized the principles of socialism in their purest form. It offers everyone, without respect of person, regardless of status, race, gender, nationality, the same product, the same service, the same quality, at the same price. It could therefore claim for itself the famous revolutionary slogan: To serve the people!

Disappointments can be overcome; but when old wishes are fulfilled in as malicious a manner as in the fairy tale, then frustration turns to hysteria and anger. That is evident, since the fall of the Wall, in the shrill and sterile debate on the unity of their country which German intellectuals are conducting. What is remarkable about this discussion is precisely its lack of productive substance, its regressive character, its resentful tone, its inability to deal with a new situation. It has no useful suggestions to offer. It is to be taken seriously only as a symptom.

'Never again Germany!' proclaims a group calling itself the Radical Left on 21 January 1990. The declaration begins with a comparison: 'In the Federal Parliament, a pan-German coalition of all the parties sang the *Deutschlandlied*—just as on 4 August 1914, at the start of the First World War, and just as on 17 May 1933, to endorse Hitler's foreign policy declaration.'

The intellectuals, against whose 'nationalist intoxication' the Radical Left is warning, behave like mirror images of their spiritual brothers. Common to both is a negative or positive fixation on the unified German state. Both fight over the altar of the Fatherland, as if this piece of furniture had not long ago become an anachronistic sham. (A further common feature of these feuding brothers is their cultural contempt for the base materialism which the German exhibits—an aversion to his taste for the Deutschmark and for that worst of all evils, 'the pedestrian precinct'.)

In complete contrast to the hysteria of their elites, the majority of Germans have displayed a measure of insight and reason, in an extremely critical and potentially dangerous situation, that hardly anyone would have believed they were capable of.

Flag-waving parades of patriotic intent, or mass meetings against the threatened Fourth Reich, were not to be sighted in the west of the country, and the noisy minorities who stepped in front of the cameras in the east were at most a sign of the backwardness of a political culture with almost sixty years of dictatorship behind it. On the whole the 'masses' have simply ignored the slogans of the spokesmen with an unshakeable scepticism. Instead they promptly got down to the necessary cleaning-up operations.

After all, it was not the helpless state apparatuses on this side and on the other that realized what had to be done. It was society which, from one day to the next, took things in hand itself: the village mayor who, on his own initiative, had the damaged street surface, the ruined bridge repaired; the joiner who got the broken circular saw on the other side of the border going again; the generous helper and the dubious speculator; the volunteer doctor and the inevitable black-market dealer. As always, it is practical reason that links telephone networks, swaps newspapers, changes money, undertakes journeys and concludes agreements, spontaneously, without regard for ten- or twenty-point plans, and that is precisely why it is effective, even unstoppable. This society could not give a damn which badges of sovereignty are on a cap, which eagle decorates a postage stamp, how many delegations are going to the United Nations, and what Hegel would think of it all, and as far as the symbolic dimension is concerned, the Brandenburg Gate was just about good enough for a collective drinking spree, which was followed the next day by a lasting sobering-up.

The elites who have been left behind look on this spontaneous activity with understandable displeasure; because what comes to the surface is not the anticipated radicalism or the longed-for profundity, but ordinariness. The Germans do not care about the spiritual space of the nation or the idea of socialism, they are not interested in questions of faith at all, but in work, housing, pensions, wages, turnover, taxes, consumption, dirt, air, refuse. What this means is that completely normal, and that means contradictory interests, reservations, fears, complexes and conflicts are finding an outlet.

The prospect that the Germans might eventually become politically mature evidently causes both politicians and intellectuals a great deal of trouble. They will have to reconcile themselves to the banal fact that democracy is an open, productive, risky process which is self-organizing and which evades their control, if not their influence.

And as far as walking without grace is concerned, it was demonstrated most effectively of all by those Germans who, before 9 November 1989, disregarded state power, started out across the border, staggering under the weight of their plastic bags, and upset every prediction. The millennium has not broken out with these runaways—only an everyday normality, which can survive without prophets.

Translated by Martin Chalmers

4

What Does Socialism Mean Today? The Revolutions of Recuperation and the Need for New Thinking

Jürgen Habermas

There has recently been a spate of articles about the end of the socialist illusion, about the failure of an idea, and even about West European or German intellectuals finally coming to terms with the past. In them, rhetorical questions always prepare the way for the refrain that utopian thought and philosophies of history necessarily end in subjugation. The critique of the philosophy of history is, however, old hat. Löwith's *Meaning in History* was translated into German in 1953.[1] So what are the terms of today's debate? How should one assess the historical significance of the revolutionary changes in Eastern and Central Europe? What are the consequences of the bankruptcy of state socialism for political movements whose roots lie in the nineteenth century, or for the theoretical traditions of the West European Left?

I

The revolutionary changes in the Soviet bloc have taken many different forms. In the land of the Bolshevik Revolution itself, a reform process is underway that was introduced from the top, from the upper echelons of the Communist Party. Its results, and, more importantly, other un-intended consequences, condense to form a process of revolutionary *development*, to the degree that changes occur not just at the level of general social and political orientation, but in essential elements of the power structure itself (of particular importance are changes in the mode of legitimation as a result of the birth of a political public sphere, the beginnings of political pluralism and the gradual renunciation of the Party's monopoly on state power). This process is now scarcely control-

lable, and, moreover, is greatly endangered by the national and economic conflicts it has thrown up. Everyone involved recognizes how
much depends on the outcome of this fateful process. It created the
preconditions for the changes in eastern Central Europe (including the
Baltic states' declarations of independence) and in East Germany.

In Poland, the revolutionary changes were the result of the sustained
resistance of Solidarity supported by the Catholic Church, in Hungary
that of a power struggle within the political elite; in East Germany and
Czechoslovakia, the regime was overthrown by peaceful mass demonstrations, in Romania by a bloody revolution; in Bulgaria, the changes
occurred only sluggishly. Despite the variety of its guises, the nature of
the revolution in these countries can be deciphered from what has
happened: this revolution produces its own data. It presents itself as a
revolution that is to some degree flowing backwards, one that clears the
ground in order to catch up with developments previously missed out
on. By contrast, the changes in the home of the Bolshevik Revolution
retain an opacity for which concepts have yet to be found. The revolution in the Soviet Union has, up until now, lacked the unambiguous
character of a recantation. A symbolic return to February 1917, or even
to Tsarist St Petersburg, would be pointless.

In Poland and Hungary, in Czechoslovakia, Romania and Bulgaria—
in other words, in those countries which did not achieve the social and
political structures of state socialism through an independent revolution,
but rather ended up with them as a result of the war and the arrival of
the Red Army—the abolition of the people's republic has occurred
under the sign of a return to old, national symbols, and, where this was
possible, has understood itself to be the continuation of the political
traditions and party organizations of the interwar years. Here—as revolutionary changes gather force and become revolutionary events—is also
where one finds the clearest articulation of the desire to connect up
constitutionally with the inheritance of the bourgeois revolutions, and
socially and politically with the styles of commerce and life associated
with developed capitalism, particularly that of the European
Community. In the case of East Germany, 'annexation' (*Anschluss*) is
literally the word, since West Germany offers to fulfil both desires at the
same time, in the form of an affluent Western society with a democratic
constitution. The voters here have definitely not ratified what the
opposition had in mind when it overthrew the Stasi-oligarchy with the
slogan 'We are the people'; but the vote they cast will have profound
historical effects as it interprets this overthrow—as a revolution of recuperation. They want to make up for all the things that have divided
the Western half of Germany from the Eastern for forty years—its
politically happier, and economically more successful, development.

The revolution of recuperation, in so far as it is meant to make possible a return to constitutional democracy and a connection with developed capitalism, is guided by models that orthodox interpretations consider the revolution of 1917 to have made redundant. This perhaps explains a peculiar characteristic of this revolution, namely its total lack of ideas that are either innovative or orientated towards the future. Joachim Fest has made a similar observation: 'These events gained their hidden, confusing centre ... from the fact that they did not emphasize the element of social revolution that has governed pretty well all the revolutions in modern history.'[2] This is particularly confusing because it seems to remind us of a vocabulary supposedly superseded by the French Revolution: the reformist picture of the return of political regimes following one after another in a continuous cycle like that of the heavens.[3]

It is not surprising, therefore, that the revolutionary changes have been given a variety of mutually exclusive interpretations. I want, in what follows, to set out the six interpretative models that are to be found in discussions. The first three endorse, the other three criticize, the idea of socialism. The two groups can be arranged symmetrically in the following order: Stalinist, Leninist and reform-communist interpretations on the one hand; postmodern, anti-communist and liberal interpretations on the other.

Corrective Interpretations

Stalinist apologists for the status quo are these days few and far between. They deny that the changes are revolutionary, seeing them instead as counter-revolutionary. They force a Marxist explanation that has lost its power on to the anomalous processes of reversal and repair. In Central Europe and East Germany it had become increasingly evident that, in the words of a well-known formulation, those below were no longer willing, and those above were no longer able, to go on in the old way. It was mass anger (and not just that of a handful of imported provocateurs) that was directed at the apparatuses of state security, just as it had once been directed at the Bastille. The destruction of the Party's monopoly on state power could similarly be seen to resemble the execution of Louis XVI. The facts are so irrefutable that even the most die-hard *Leninists* cannot ignore them. Thus the conservative historian Jürgen Kuszynski makes the concession of using the term 'conservative revolution' in order to give the changes the status of a self-purifying reform within a longer-term revolutionary process.[4] This interpretation is, of course, still based on an orthodox history of class struggle whose telos seems to be predetermined. A philosophy of history of this kind is dubious from a purely methodological point of view; but, even setting that aside, it is incapable of explaining the type of social movements and conflicts that rise in, or—as with nationalist and fundamentalist reaction—are provoked by, the structural conditions of the governmental and social systems of state socialism. Moreover, political developments in Central Europe and East Germany have, in the meantime, gone way beyond anything that the idea of state socialism's self-correction might adequately describe.

These developments also form the main argument against the third position so strikingly personified by Dubček's return from internal exile to Wenceslas Square. In East Germany, too, a large proportion of the opposition that started and—to begin with at least—led the revolutionary movement was guided by the ideal of a democratic socialism—the so-called 'Middle Way' between a capitalism curbed by the welfare state, and state socialism. While Leninists believe they ought to correct the mistaken developments that occurred under Stalinism, *reform communists* want to go back even further. In tune with many of the theoretical currents of Western Marxism, they start from the premiss that the Leninist understanding of the Bolshevik Revolution falsified socialism from the start by promoting the nationalization—as opposed to the democratic socialization—of the means of production, and thereby paving the way for increasingly autonomous, totalitarian and bureaucratic power structures. There are other versions of the Middle Way depending on which interpretation of the October Revolution one subscribes to. According to the optimistic reading, shared, among others, by the leaders of the Prague Spring, it should be possible to democratize state socialism radically in order to develop a new social order that is actually *superior* to Western mass, welfare-state democracies. According to another version, the best a Middle Way between the two 'actually existing' systems could achieve would be a radical, democratic reform of state socialism, which, as decentralized control mechanisms produced an increasingly differentiated economy, might at least come to represent an equivalent to the welfare-state compromise that was reached in developed capitalist societies after the Second World War. This search for an equivalent would culminate in a non-totalitarian state, in other words, one modelled on constitutional democracies; but one that, as far as the advantages (relative social security and qualitative growth) and disadvantages (in areas such as the development of the productive forces and innovation) of the system are concerned, would not aim to imitate but rather to *complement* Western forms of society. Even this weaker interpretation relies on the possibility of what has recently been dubbed a functioning 'socialist market'. Some people argue that such a development is impossible on a priori grounds; others think one should find out by a process of trial and error. Even as militant a liberal as Marion Gräfin Dönhoff[5] believes 'that the existing dream of uniting socialism with a market economy could, with a little imagination and a little pragmatism, quite plausibly come true—they correct one another.'[6] This is a perspective that allows for a falliblist type of communist reform that, contrary to Leninist interpretations, no longer makes any claims to be able to predict the course of history.

We can now forget speculation about state socialism's potential for reform and democratic development were it to be revolutionized from within. I suspect that the drastic effects of the legacy of Stalinism (and the growing threat of the Union's disintegration into its constitutive nations) render such speculation unrealistic in the case of the Soviet Union as well. The question of whether or not East Germany could have gone the Middle Way will also have to remain unanswered, if the premisses of my interpretation are correct; for the only way to have found out would have been to undertake a 'pragmatic and imaginative' experiment legitimated by popular consent. The majority of the population has in the meantime, however, decided unmistakably against any such experiment. After forty years of disaster, one can well understand why. The decision deserves respect, particularly from those who would never have been affected by any negative repercussions the experiment might have had. Let us, therefore, turn now to the three interpretative models that are critical of socialism.

Critical Interpretations

The most extreme position on this side has not been very convincingly articulated. For a *postmodern critique of reason*, the basically non-violent upheavals represent a revolution to end the epoch of revolutions; a counterpart to the French Revolution, which does not hesitate to tear the terror born of reason out by its roots. The uneasy dreams of reason, which have produced demons for the last two hundred years, are over. But it is not reason that awakes—reason is itself the nightmare that vanishes as we wake. Here, too, the facts do not quite fit this model of history that takes its idealist inspiration from Nietzsche and Heidegger. According to this account, the modern age is overshadowed by a self-empowering subjectivity. Yet the recent revolutions of recuperation took their methods and standards entirely from the familiar repertoire of the modern age. The presence of large masses gathering in squares and mobilizing on the streets managed, astoundingly, to disempower a regime that was armed to the teeth. It was, in other words, precisely the sort of spontaneous mass action that once provided so many revolutionary theorists with a model, but which had recently been presumed to be dead. Of course, this all took place for the first time in the unorthodox space of an international arena of participating and partial observers, created by the uninterrupted presence of the electronic media. It was, moreover, from the rational legitimacy of appeals to the sovereignty of the people and human rights that the revolutionary demands drew their strength. The acceleration of history thus discredited the image of a posthistorical standstill; it also destroyed the picture, painted by postmodernism, of a universal bureaucracy of crystalline rigidity that had torn itself loose of all forms of legitimation. The revolutionary collapse of bureaucratic socialism seems instead to indicate that modernity is extending its borders—the spirit of the West is catching up with the East not simply as a technological civilization, but also as a democratic tradition.

From an *anti-communist* point of view, the revolutionary changes in the East signify a final victory in the global civil war started by the Bolsheviks in 1917: one more revolution turning against its own origin. The phrase 'global civil war' translates the term 'international class struggle' out of the language of social theory and into that of a Hobbesian theory of power. Carl Schmitt supplied this theoretical metaphor with a historical and philosophical background. In this account, the philosophy of history that came to power with the French Revolution, and shared the utopian charge of its universalist ethics, became the driving force behind a civil war that was first contrived by intellectual elites and then projected on to an international stage. This hypothesis was expanded into a full-blown theory of global civil war at the time when the East–West conflict was just breaking out.[7] Conceived with the aim of exposing Leninism, it remains dependent on it, as a mirror image depends upon the original it inverts. Historical material, however, resists the ideological clutches even of a historian as learned as Ernst Nolte, who recently put forward the thesis that the global civil war has come to an end.[8] For the parties fighting the global civil war are so stylized that it becomes necessary to treat the policies personified by such heterogeneous figures as Mussolini and Hitler, Churchill and Roosevelt, or Kennedy and Reagan, as if they were all made of the same anti-communist clay. The metaphor of the global civil war takes an interpretation that arose during one specific, hot phase of the Cold War and fixes it as a structural description that is then polemicized and made to fit an entire era.

This leaves the *liberal* interpretation, which initially limits itself to the observation that the end of state socialism marks the beginning of the final disappearance of totalitarian government from Europe. An era which started with fascism is drawing to a close. Liberal ideas of social organization have prevailed in the form of constitutional democracy, the market economy and social pluralism. The overhasty prediction of the 'end of ideology' seems finally to have come true.[9] One does not have to subscribe to a monolithic theory of totalitarianism, thereby ignoring important differences between authoritarian, fascist, national-socialist, Stalinist and post-Stalinist regimes, in order to be able to recognize their similarities in the mirror of Western mass democracies. The disintegration of this syndrome in European socialist bureaucracies, as well as in Spain and Portugal, and the accompanying development of a market economy independent of the political system, suggest the idea of a surge in the modernization process reaching out towards Central and Eastern Europe. The liberal interpretation is not wrong. It just does not see the beam in its own eye.

Marx on the Logic of 'Civilization'

There are triumphalist variations on this interpretation, which could have been taken straight out of the first part of the *Communist Manifesto,* where Marx and Engels hymn the revolutionary role of the bourgeoisie:

> The bourgeoisie, by the rapid improvement of all instruments of production, by the immensely facilitated means of communication, draws all, even the most barbarian, nations into civilization. The cheap prices of its commodities are the heavy artillery with which it batters down all Chinese walls, with which it forces the barbarians' intensely obstinate hatred of foreigners to capitulate. It compels all nations, on pain of extinction, to adopt the bourgeois mode of production; it compels them to introduce what it calls civilization into their midst, that is, to become bourgeois themselves. In one word, it creates a world after its own image ... And as in material, so also in intellectual production. The intellectual creations of individual nations become common property. National one-sidedness and narrowmindedness become more and more impossible, and from the numerous national and local literatures, there arises a world literature.[10]

It would be hard to arrive at a better characterization of the mood indicated by the replies that capitalists, eager for investment-opportunities, gave to the last questionnaire circulated by the German Chamber of Industry and Commerce. Only the phrase 'what it calls', qualifying the term 'civilization', betrays reservations. In Marx, this is not, of course, the German preference for a culture (*Kultur*) supposedly superior to civilization (*Zivilisation*), but a more fundamental doubt as to whether a civilization can afford to surrender itself *entirely* to the maelstrom of the driving force of just one of its subsystems—namely the pull of a dynamic, or, as we would say today, recursively closed, economic system which can only function and remain stable by taking all relevant information, translating it into, and processing it in, the language of economic value. Marx believed that any civilization that subjects itself to the imperatives of the accumulation of capital bears the seeds of its own destruction, because it thereby blinds itself to anything, however important, that cannot be expressed as a price.

Today, the agent of the expansion that Marx put so squarely on the map is of course no longer the bourgeoisie of 1848; no longer a class that rules within national limits but rather an anonymous, internationally operating economic system that has ostensibly severed any ties it might once have had with an identifiable class structure. Similarly, the societies of today that have reached the 'economic summit' of this system bear little resemblance to the Manchester whose misery Engels once so tellingly described. For these societies have in the meantime found an answer to the stark words of the *Communist Manifesto* and the tenacious struggles of the European workers' movement: the welfare-state compromise. However, the ironic circumstance that Marx should still offer us the quotation that most aptly describes the situation in which capital scrambles into markets corroded by state socialism, in search of investment opportunities, is just as thought-provoking as the fact that Marx's doubts have themselves been incorporated into the structures of the most advanced capitalist societies.

Does this mean that 'Marxism as critique'[11] is as exhausted as 'actually existing socialism'? From an anti-communist perspective that makes no distinction between theory and practice, the socialist tradition has brought nothing but trouble. From a liberal perspective, everything that was of any use in socialism has already been put into practice during the era of social democracy. Does the annihilation of East European state socialism also dry up the sources from which the West European Left has drawn both its theoretical inspiration and its guiding values? The disillusioned Biermann, whose utopian flair has turned into melancholy, suggests a dialectical answer: 'Give us the spades. Let us finally bury that giant little corpse. Even Christ needed three days underground before he could pull off the trick: pity about the resurrection!'[12] Let's try and find a less dialectical one.

II

The non-communist Left in West Germany has no reason to don sack-cloth and ashes, but equally it cannot pretend that nothing has happened. It does not need to let guilt by association be foisted on it for the bankruptcy of a state socialism that it has always criticized. But it must ask itself how long an idea can hold out against reality.

Those responsible for the coyly pleonastic phrase 'actually existing' socialism seem, in using it, to have retained an obstinate sense of *Realpolitik*: they preferred the bird in the hand. Is it then sufficient simply to point out that the dove on the roof belongs to a different species—and will descend to us one day anyway? Even ideals, the other side replies, require empirical corroboration or they lose their power to orientate action. The idealist can only lose this dialogue, as it starts out from false premises. It assumes that socialism is an idea, abstractly confronting reality, which stands convicted of the impotence of the moral 'ought' (not to mention the total contempt for humanity evident in any attempt at its realization). Of course, there is connected to this concept the normative intuition of a peaceful coexistence that does not provide for self-realization and autonomy only at the expense of solidarity and justice, but rather along with them. However, the socialist tradition ought not to explain this intuition by the direct approach of a normative theory, in order to set it up as an ideal opposing an opaque reality. It should instead be the basis of a perspective from which reality can be critically observed and analysed. During the course of the analysis, this normative intuition should be both developed and corrected, and thus at least indirectly tested against the power of a theoretical description to disclose reality and convey empirical content.

Errors and Defects

Western Marxism[13] has used this criterion since the twenties to subject itself to an unflinching critique that has left little of the theory's original form remaining. While practice was declaring its verdict, reality (in all its twentieth-century monstrosity) was bringing its arguments to bear at the level of theory, too. I would like to review a few of the ways in which it has become apparent how much Marx and his immediate successors, for all their critique of early socialism, remained rooted in the original context and limited scale of early industrialism.

(a) The analysis confined itself to phenomena that can be disclosed from within the horizon of a society based upon labour. The choice of this particular paradigm gives priority to a narrow concept of practice that attributes an unambiguously emancipatory role solely to industrial labour and the development of the technology of productive forces. The forms of organization that arise as the workforce is concentrated into factories are meant to supply the infrastructure for the development of an association of producers, for the raising of consciousness, and for undertaking revolutionary action. A productivist starting point of this sort, however, precludes consideration both of the ambivalences of the increasing domination of nature, and of the potential for social integration within and beyond the sphere of social labour.

(b) The analysis was, furthermore, dependent on a holistic conception of society: class division and, in the modern period, the objectifying violence of capitalist economic processes tear apart and mutilate what was originally an ethical totality. The utopian potential of a society based on labour, spelled out in terms of Hegel's basic concepts, inspires the background assumptions that underlie a critique of political economy undertaken in a scientific spirit. It allows the process of the accumulation of capital to appear as an illusion that, if only it were dispelled, would dissolve into its underlying objective form and become subject to rational control. Theory in this way blinds itself to the resistance inherent in the system of a differentiated market economy, whose regulative devices cannot be replaced by administrative planning without potentially jeopardizing the level of differentiation achieved in a modern society.

(c) The analysis also remained caught up in an over-concrete conception of conflict and social agencies, in so far as it based its calculations on social classes or historical macro-subjects supposedly responsible for the processes of production and reproduction in society. Complex societies in which there are no straightforward connections between the social, subcultural and regional surface structures on the one hand, and the abstract deep structures of a differentiated economic system (intertwined with complementary state intervention) on the other, slip through this net. This same error has produced a theory of the state that no number of supplementary hypotheses can salvage.

(d) The restricted and functionalist analysis of constitutional democracy has had far more serious practical consequences than the defects discussed so far. For Marx, this form of government was embodied by the Third Republic he dismissed so contemptuously as 'vulgar democracy'. Because he understood democratic republics as the final form of the state in bourgeois society—on whose ground the final, conclusive battle of the class struggle was to be fought—he retained a purely instrumental attitude to its institutions. *The Critique of the Gotha Programme* tells us in no uncertain terms that Marx understood a communist society to be the only possible realization of democracy. Here, as in his earlier critique of Hegel's doctrine of the state, freedom consists solely in 'converting the state from an organ superimposed on society into one thoroughly subordinate to it'. But he does not say any more about the way freedom would be institutionalized; he is unable to imagine institutional forms beyond the dictatorship of the proletariat that he predicted would be necessary during the 'period of transition'. The Saint-Simonian illusion of 'an administration of things' reduces the expectation of the need for a democratic forum for resolving conflicts, to such an extent that the spontaneous self-organization of the people, as described by Rousseau, appears to be sufficient.

(e) Finally, the analysis was caught in the Hegelian tramlines of a theoretical strategy that aims to combine the philosophical tradition's claim to infallible knowledge with new historical modes of thought. Historicizing the knowledge of an essence, however, only replaces the teleology of Being with that of History. The secretly normative presuppositions of theories of history are naturalized in the form of evolutionary concepts of progress. This has unfortunate consequences not only for the unexplained normative basis of the theory itself, but also in other areas. On the one hand, a theory of this sort (regardless of its specific content) conceals the margin of contingency within which any theoretically guided practice is bound to move. By abolishing any sense of risk in those who will have to bear the consequences of action, it also encourages a questionable type of vanguardism. On the other hand, a totalizing knowledge of this sort feels in a position to make clinical evaluations of the degree of alienation, or success, of particular forms of life in their entirety. This explains the tendency to see socialism as a historically privileged form of concrete ethical practice, even though the *most* a theory can do is describe the conditions necessary for emancipated forms of life. What concrete shape these take is something for those eventually involved to decide amongst themselves.

(f) A consideration of these errors and defects, present in the theoretical tradition in varying degrees from Marx and Engels up to Kautsky, makes it easier to understand how Marxism, as it was codified by Stalin, could degenerate into the ideology that legitimated what was in practice simply inhuman—'vivisection on a large scale, using live humans' (Biermann). Of course, the step to a *Soviet Marxism*, which Lenin introduced in both theory and practice, cannot be justified by reference to orthodox Marxist doctrine.[14] All the same, the weaknesses we have discussed in (a) to (e) above can be counted among the (of course neither necessary nor sufficient) conditions for an abuse, or even a total inversion, of what was originally intended.

The Price of Social Democracy

Conversely, *social-democratic reformism*, which received important impulses from Austro-Marxists like Karl Renner and Otto Bauer, managed to disengage itself relatively early from a holistic conception of society and embarrassment at the autonomous dynamic of a market system; from a dogmatic view of class structure and the class struggle; from a false evaluation of the normative content of constitutional democracy; and from latent, evolutionist presuppositions. Of course, until very recently, the assumptions underlying day-to-day politics carried the stamp of the productivist paradigm of the society based on labour. After the Second World War, the reformist parties, having uncoupled themselves from theoretical concerns and turned pragmatic, achieved what is indisputably their main success, managing to establish a welfare-state compromise whose effects reach deep into the structures of society. The radical Left has always underestimated how far-reaching this intervention was.

At the same time, however, the social democrats were taken by surprise by the systematic resistance inherent in the state power they had hoped to be able to use as a neutral instrument to universalize civil rights in the welfare state. It was not the welfare state that proved to be an illusion, but the expectation that one could use administrative means to arrive at an emancipated form of life. Moreover, the parties involved in the business of creating social satisfaction through state intervention found themselves increasingly caught up in an ever-expanding state apparatus. The absorption of political parties by the state is accompanied by the displacement of the democratic formation of political will into a largely self-programming political system—something the citizens of East Germany, liberated from the secret police and a one-party state, realized to their amazement as their first election campaign was taken over by Western campaign managers. Mass democracy, in its Western form, is stamped with the characteristics of a controlled process of legitimation.

Social democracy has, then, to pay a double price for its success. It does without radical democracy and learns to live with the normatively undesirable consequences of capitalist economic growth—as well as with the risks inherent in the labour market, which one can cushion, but not altogether eliminate, with welfare policies. This is the price that kept a *non-communist Left*, to the left of the social democrats, alive. This non-communist Left has many guises, and keeps alive the idea that socialism once meant more than state-welfare policies. However, the fact that self-managing socialism remains in its programme is indicative of the difficulty it has in distancing itself from a holistic conception of society, and giving up the notion of a switch from a market-led to a democratically controlled production process. This was the best way of keeping the classical link between theory and practice intact, but also the best way of ensuring that theory became orthodox, and practice sectarian.

As with political practice, the increasing differentiation of institutions caught up with the theoretical tradition long ago. Marxism has become one other, more or less marginal, method of research among the many that make up academic life. This process of academicization has brought about long overdue revisions, and cross-fertilization with other theoretical approaches. The fertile combination of Marx and Max Weber shaped the field of sociological discourse as early as the Weimar period. Since then, the self-criticism of Western Marxism has been completed largely in universities, producing a pluralism mediated by academic discussion. Interesting and conflicting approaches like those of Pierre Bourdieu, Cornelius Castoriadis or Alain Touraine, of Jon Elster or Anthony Giddens, Claus Offe or Ulrich Preuss, indicate how dynamic an intellectual stimulus the tradition begun by Marx still is. As a tradition, its perspective benefits from being stereoscopic: it does not concentrate on purely superficial aspects of the process of modernization, and, equally, is not confined to the rear side of the mirror of instrumental reason, but is sensitive to the ambiguities in the processes of rationalization that plough through society. A plough simultaneously tears up the natural surface and loosens the ground beneath. Many have learnt from Marx, each in his or her own way, how Hegel's dialectic of enlightenment can be translated into a research programme. However, the reservations I enumerated in sections (a) to (e) form the sole basis on which impulses from the Marxist tradition can be taken up today.

Socialism Today: A Purely Moral Standpoint?

If this sketch describes the position in which the non-communist Left found itself when Gorbachev ushered in the beginning of the end of state socialism, how have the dramatic events of the autumn of 1989 changed the scene? Must people on the Left now retreat to a purely moral standpoint, keeping socialism as nothing more than an idea? Ernst Nolte is willing to concede the Left 'an ideal socialism' that is 'a corrective or guiding limit case', and that is even 'indispensable', but he does of course go on to say: 'Anyone who wants actually to realize this limit case, runs the risk of relapsing or collapsing into the "real socialism" we have learnt to fear, however brave his rhetorical attacks on Stalinism may seem to be.'[15] To take this friendly advice would be to defuse socialism and reduce it to a regulative idea, of purely private relevance, that consigned morality to a place beyond political practice. It would be more consistent to stop manipulating the idea of socialism and give it up altogether. Must we then agree with Biermann when he says 'socialism is no longer a goal'?

Certainly, if it is understood in the romantic, speculative sense given it in the 'Paris Manuscripts', where the dissolution of private ownership of the means of production signifies 'the solution to the riddle of history'; or, to put it another way, if it means creating cooperative relations between people so that they cease to be *alienated* from the product of their labour, from their fellow human beings and from themselves. For romantic socialism, the dissolution of private property means the total emancipation of all human senses and qualities—the genuine resurrection of nature, the thoroughgoing naturalism of humanity, the end of the conflict between objectification and self-activity, between freedom and necessity, between individual and species. But we did not have to wait for the most recent critiques of the false totalizations of the philosophy of reconciliation, or for Solzhenitysn, to know better. The roots that bind romantic socialism to its original context of early industrialism have lain bare for a long time. The idea of a free association of producers has always been loaded with nostalgic images of the types of community—the family, the neighbourhood and the guild—to be found in the world of peasants and craftsmen that, with the violent onset of a competitive society, was just beginning to break down, and whose disappearance was experienced as a loss. The idea of the preservation of these eroded communities has been connected with 'socialism' ever since these earliest days; amid the work conditions and new forms of social interaction of early industrialism, the aim was to salvage and transform the forces of social integration of the passing era. The socialism about whose normative content Marx refused to speak is Janus-faced, looking back to an idealized past as much as it looks forward to a future dominated by industrial labour.

The Presupposition of Rationality

In this *concretist interpretation*, socialism is obviously no longer a goal, and, realistically speaking, never has been. Faced as we are with a higher level of social complexity, we must submit the normative implications attached to this nineteenth-century theoretical formulation to a process of radical abstraction. The communicative conditions necessary to the establishment of justified confidence in the institutions of rational self-organization of a society of free and equal citizens become central precisely when one adheres to the critique of naturalized and unlegitimated forms of power. To be sure, solidarity can only really be experienced in the context of the necessarily particular forms of social life we inherit or critically appropriate—and thus actively choose. However, in the framework of a society with a large-scale political integration, let alone within the horizons of an international communications network, mutually supportive coexistence, even conceived on its own terms, is only available in the form of an *abstract* idea; in other words, in the form of a legitimate, intersubjectively shared expectation. Everyone should be justified in expecting that the institutionalization of the process for the non-exclusive formation of public opinion and democratic political will can ratify their assumption that these processes of public communication are being conducted rationally and effectively. The presupposition of *rationality* is based on the normative meaning of democratic processes, which ought to ensure that all socially relevant questions can be taken up and dealt with thoroughly and imaginatively until solutions have been found that, while respecting the integrity of every individual and every form of social life, are uniformly in everybody's interest. The presupposition of *efficacy* touches upon the fundamental materialist question of how a differentiated social system that lacks both summit and centre might still organize itself, once one can no longer imagine the 'self' of self-organization embodied in the form of macro-subjects such as the social classes of theories of class, or the people of popular sovereignty.

The point of conceiving mutually supportive relations abstractly is to separate the symmetries of mutual recognition, presupposed by communicative action, that make the autonomy and individualization of socialized subjects possible in the first place from the concrete ethical practice of naturalized forms of behaviour, and to generalize them into the reflexive forms of agreement and compromise whilst simultaneously safeguarding them through legal institutionalization. The 'self' of this self-organizing society then disappears into the subjectless forms of communication that regulate the flow of the discursive formation of public opinion and political will, such that one can continue to presuppose the rationality of their fallible results. By dissolving into intersubjectivity, popular sovereignty is made anonymous, and then allowed to retreat into the democratic process and the legitimate communicative presuppositions of its implementation.[16] It finds its placeless place in the interaction between a constitutionally established process for the formation of political will and culturally mobilized public spheres. Whether complex societies could ever be enclosed in a tissue of proceduralized popular sovereignty in this way, or whether it is not rather the case that the network of intersubjectively shared and communicatively structured lifeworlds is torn so definitively that the autonomous system of the economy, and, with it, the self-programming processes of state management, will never be brought back within the horizons of the lifeworld—not even by the most indirect types of regulation—is a question one cannot answer adequately at the level of theory, and must therefore reformulate practically and politically. This question was, moreover, fundamental to a historical materialism that did not understand its thesis about the relation between base and superstructure to be an ontological statement about social being, but rather the mark of a seal that must be broken if the forms of a humane interaction are to cease being bewitched by a sociality that has turned into violence.

III

As far as an *understanding* of this intention is concerned, the revolutionary changes taking place before our eyes teach us an unambiguous lesson: complex societies are unable to reproduce themselves if they do not leave the logic of an economy that regulates itself through the market intact. Modern societies separate out an economic system regulated by the medium of money in the same way as an administrative system; the two systems are on the same level, and however their various functions complement one another, neither may be subordinated to the other.[17] Unless something totally unexpected happens in the Soviet Union, we will never discover whether the relations of production under state socialism could have adapted themselves to this condition by following the Middle Way of democratization. But even conversion to the conditions of the international capitalist market does not, of course, mean a return to those relations of production that socialist movements endeavoured to overcome. That would be to underestimate the transformation capitalist societies have undergone, particularly since the end of the Second World War.

The Demobilization and Reconstruction of Industrial Society

A welfare-state compromise that has established itself in the very structures of society now forms the basis from which any politics here has to start. Claus Offe gave us an ironic commentary on the way this is expressed in the reigning consensus over social and political aims when he wrote: 'As the image of actually existing socialism becomes more and more desperate, more and more mournful, we all become "communists" in so far as we are unable finally to get rid of our concern about public affairs and our horror at the possibility of catastrophic developments in global society.'[18] It is not as though the collapse of the Berlin Wall has solved a single one of the problems specific to our system. The indifference of a market economy to its external costs, which it off-loads on to the social and natural environment, is sowing the path of a crisis-prone economic growth with the familiar disparities and marginalizations on the inside; with economic backwardness, if not regression, and consequently with barbaric living conditions, cultural expropriation and catastrophic famines in the Third World; not to mention the worldwide risk caused by disrupting the balance of nature. The social and ecological *curbing* of the market economy is the international formula into which the social-democratic aims of the social curbing of capitalism was bound to be generalized. Even the dynamic interpretation of an ecological and social demobilization and reconstruction of industrial society has support beyond the limited circles of Greens and Social Democrats. This is the basic issue around which argument today revolves. Questions arise about the feasibility, the time scale, and the ways of realizing common, or at least rhetorically endorsed, goals. There is also consensus about a mode of political action that aims to influence the self-regulating mechanisms of the system, whose autonomy must not be disturbed by direct intervention, indirectly and from the outside. As a consequence, the argument about forms of ownership has lost its doctrinal significance.

But the displacement of the struggle from the level of social and political goals to that of how these goals should be made operational, and to that of choosing and executing the appropriate policies, does not stop it having all the characteristics of a fundamental difference of opinion. Just as before, there is an acute conflict between those who use the imperatives of the economic system to set up an embargo on all demands that aim beyond the status quo, and those who would want to hold on to the word 'socialism' until the congenital fault in capitalism— that of shifting the social costs of the system's equilibrium on to the private fate of unemployment—has been eliminated;[19] until women have achieved genuine equality; and the momentum behind the destruction of lifeworld and nature has been checked. From the point of view of this radical reformism, the economic system is not a holy of holies but a testing ground. Even the welfare state, with its ability to take account of the peculiar character of that commodity called labour-power, is the product of an attempt to find out *how much strain* the economic system can be made to take in directions that might benefit social needs, to which the logic of corporate investment decisions is indifferent.

Of course, the project of establishing a welfare state has, in the meantime, become reflexive; the increasingly legalistic and bureaucratic tendencies that arose as side-effects of this project have robbed the supposedly neutral medium of administrative power, through which society was to exert an influence on itself, of its innocence.[20] Now the interventionist state itself needs 'social curbing'. The same combination of power and intelligent self-restraint that marks the political strategies of careful limitation and indirect regulation of capitalist growth needs to be taken back behind the lines of administrative planning. The solution to this problem can lie only in changing the relation between autonomous public spheres, on the one hand, and the areas of activity governed by money and administrative power, on the other. The potential for reflection necessary for such an undertaking is to be found in the form of sovereignty, made fluid by being made communicative, that makes itself heard in the topics, arguments and proposed solutions of free-floating, public communication. It must, however, also adopt the fixed form of decisions made by democratically organized institutions, for the responsibility for decisions with practical consequences needs to be clearly allocated through specific institutions. The power produced through communicative action can exert an influence on the foundations of the evaluative and decision-making processes of public administration, without wanting to take them over altogether, so as to bring its normative demands to bear in the only language that the besieged stronghold understands: it cultivates the range of arguments that, though treated instrumentally by administrative power, cannot be ignored by it, in as much as administrative power is conceived along institutional lines.

Money, Power and Solidarity

Modern societies satisfy their need of regulative capacities from three sources: money, power and solidarity. A radical reformism is no longer characterized by the particular key demands it might make, but rather because it aims to focus on social processes and demand a redistribution of power: the socially integrating force of solidarity should be in a position to stake its claim against the other social forces, money and administrative power, through a wide range of democratic forums and institutions. This expectation is 'socialist' in as much as the valid structures of mutual recognition that we know from relations in everyday life can be transferred to the sphere of legally and administratively mediated social relations through the communicative preconditions of non-exclusive processes for the formation of public opinion and democratic political will. Those areas of the lifeworld that specialize in communicating inherited values and cultural knowledge, in integrating groups and socializing rising generations, have always depended on solidarity. Radical-democratic processes for the formation of public opinion and political will must draw their strength from the same source if they want to have a say in how borders are drawn, and exchange regulated, between the communicatively structured spheres of life on the one hand, and the state and economy on the other.

Of course, whether or not there is still any future in ideas for a radical democracy[21] will depend on how we perceive and define problems—on which way of viewing problems prevails politically. If the only problems that appear urgent in the public arenas of developed societies are those disturbances which threaten the stability of the economic and administrative systems, if this type of problem comes to dominate the descriptions of systems theories, the claims of the the lifeworld, formulated in a normative language, will seem merely to be dependent variables. This struggle over the increasing *de-moralization of public conflicts* is in full swing. This no longer takes place under the sign of a technocratic conception of society and politics; where society has become so complex as to be a closed book, only opportunistic behaviour towards the system seems to offer a way of finding one's bearings. However, large-scale problems actually confronting the developed societies are scarcely such that they could be resolved without a mode of perception sensitive to normative demands, without a reintroduction of moral considerations into the issues under public discussion.

The classical conflict over the distribution of wealth in the society based upon labour was structured against the background of the interests of capital and labour such that both sides were in a position to threaten the other. Even the structurally disadvantaged side could resort, in the last instance, to a strike; in other words, to the organized withdrawal of labour and the concomitant interruption of the production process. Today this is no longer the case. The conflict over the distribution of wealth has been institutionalized by the welfare state in such a way that a broad majority of people in work confront a minority of marginal groupings thrown together to form a heterogeneous mass without the power to set up any similar sort of embargo. If they do not just give up, and resort self-destructively to illness, crime or blind revolt to deal with their burden, the marginalized and the underprivileged can, in the last resort, only make their interests known by means of a protest vote. Without the electoral support of a majority of citizens, asking themselves, and letting themselves be asked, if they really want to live in a divided society in which they have constantly to close their eyes to the homeless and the beggars, to the areas of town that have been reduced to ghettos, to provinces that have been neglected, problems of this nature do not even have enough driving force to be adopted as a topic of broad and effective public debate. A dynamic of self-correction cannot be set in motion without introducing morality into the debate, without universalizing interests from a normative point of view.

Responding to Changing Cultural Priorities

This asymmetrical model returns not only in the conflicts that flare up
over questions of asylum, and the status of minorities, in a multicultural
society. The same lack of symmetry determines the relation of the
developed industrial societies to the developing nations and to the
environment. If the worst came to the worst, the underdeveloped continents could threaten the developed nations with massive immigration,
the hazardous game of nuclear blackmail, or the destruction of global
ecological equilibrium; nature's reprisals, on the other hand, can be
heard only as the quiet ticking of timebombs. This model of powerlessness increases the likelihood of a situation in which a problem that only
gradually increases in urgency can remain hidden, and the search for a
solution be put off until it is too late. These problems can only be
brought to a head by rethinking topics morally, by universalizing interests in a more or less discursive manner in the forums of liberal political
cultures which have not been stripped of all their powers. As soon as we
recognize that we are all still at risk, we will be willing, for instance, to
pay the price of closing down the obsolete nuclear power station at
Greifswald. It helps to perceive the way one's own interests are bound
up with the interests of others. The moral or ethical point of view makes
us quicker to perceive the more far-reaching, and simultaneously less
insistent and more fragile, ties that bind the fate of one individual to that
of every other—making even the most alien person a member of one's
community.

The major problems of today are reminiscent of the problem of the
distribution of wealth in another way; they demand exactly the same
peculiar brand of politics—one that simultaneously restricts and
nurtures. The present revolutions, as Hans Magnus Enzensberger has
pointed out, seem to dramatize this sort of politics. First, the majority of
the population underwent a latent change of attitude, then the solid
ground of legitimation collapsed beneath the feet of state socialism; after
the landslide, the system is left as a ruin to be dismantled or recon-
structed. As a result of the revolution's success, an introverted and
supplicatory politics arises: a politics of demobilization and industrial
reconstruction.

A similar transformation occurred in West Germany during the
1980s in the field from which this metaphor is taken. The deployment of
medium-range missiles was felt to be such an arbitrary imposition that it
became the last straw that persuaded the majority of the population
what a senseless risk the self-destructive escalation of the arms race was.
The summit in Reykjavik (though I do not want to suggest a straightforward connection between the two) then initiated the turn to a politics

of disarmament. To be sure, the change in cultural priorities responsible for the loss of legitimacy did not only occur subcutaneously, as it did in the private niches of state socialism, but could also take place entirely in public, and eventually against the backdrop of the largest mass demonstrations West Germany has ever seen. This is a good example of the circular process by which a latent change of values caused by current events can be linked up with processes of public communication, changes in the constitutional parameters of the democratic formation of political will, and impulses towards new policies of demobilization and industrial reconstruction, which, in turn, feed back into the changing priorities.

The challenges of the twenty-first century will be of an order and magnitude that demand answers from Western societies which cannot be arrived at, nor put into practice, without a radical-democratic universalization of interests through institutions for the formation of public opinion and political will. The socialist Left still has a place and political role to play in this arena. It can generate the ferment that produces the continuing process of political communication that prevents the institutional framework of a constitutional democracy from becoming desiccated. The non-communist Left has no reason to be downhearted. It might well be the case that many East German intellectuals will have to adapt to a situation that the West European Left has been in for decades—that of transforming socialist ideas into the radically reformist self-criticism of a capitalist society, which, in the form of a constitutional democracy with universal suffrage and a welfare state, has developed not only weaknesses but also strengths. With the bankruptcy of state socialism, this is the eye of the needle through which everything must pass. *This* socialism will disappear only when it no longer has an object of criticism—perhaps at a point when the society in question has changed its identity so much that it allows the full significance of everything that cannot be expressed as a price to be perceived and taken seriously. The hope that humanity can emancipate itself from self-imposed tutelage and degrading living conditions has not lost its power, but it is filtered by a falliblist consciousness, and an awareness of the historical lesson that one would already have achieved a considerable amount if the balance of a tolerable existence could be preserved for the fortunate few—and, most of all, if it could be established on the other, ravaged continents.

June 1990
Translated by Ben Morgan

Notes

1. On the relations between ethics, utopian thought and its critique, see Karl-Otto Apel's clear contribution to W. Voßkamp, ed., *Utopieforschung*, Frankfurt am Main 1985, vol. 1, pp. 325–55.

2. *Frankfurter Allgemeine Zeitung*, 30 December 1989.

3. Cf. K. Griewank, *Der neuzeitliche Revolutionsbegriff*, Frankfurt am Main 1973.

4. *Die Zeit*, 29 December 1989.

5. Editor of *Die Zeit*.

6. *Die Zeit*, 29 December 1989.

7. H. Kesting, *Geschichtsphilosophie und Weltbürgerkrieg*, Heidelberg 1959.

8. *Frankfurter Allgemeine Zeitung*, 17 February 1990.

9. Daniel Bell and Ralf Dahrendorf in *Die Zeit*, 29 December 1989.

10. Karl Marx, 'The Communist Manifesto', in D. Fernbach, ed., *The Revolutions of 1848*, Harmondsworth and London 1973, p. 71.

11. This is the title of an essay in which I dealt with Marxism systematically for the first time (1960). It is published in English in Jürgen Habermas, *Theory and Practice*, London 1974.

12. *Die Zeit*, 2 March 1990.

13. Martin Jay gives an overview of it in his *Marxism and Totality*, Berkeley 1984.

14. Herbert Marcuse, *Soviet Marxism*, Harmondsworth 1971.

15. *Frankfurter Allgemeine Zeitung*, 19 February 1990.

16. Jürgen Habermas, 'Volkssouveränität als Verfahren', in Forum für Philosophie, ed., *Die Ideen von 1789*, Frankfurt am Main 1989, pp. 7–36.

17. This is not the 'pragmatic concession' some of my critics on the Left believe it to be, but rather is a consequence of an approach to social theory that has overcome holistic conceptions.

18. *Die Zeit*, 8 December 1989.

19. For ideas of a basic security that was no longer wage-centred, see G. Vobrude, ed., *Strukturwandel der Sozialpolitik*, Frankfurt am Main 1990.

20. Jürgen Habermas, 'Die Kritik des Wohlfahrtsstaates', in *Die Neue Unubersichtlichkeit*, Frankfurt am Main 1985, pp. 141–66.

21. U. Rodel, G. Frankenberg, H. Dubiel, *Die demokratische Frage*, Frankfurt am Main 1989.

5

The 'Woman Question' in the Age of Perestroika*

Maxine Molyneux

Soviet women! Participate actively in the renewal of Soviet society! Rear a strong, worthy successor generation!

CPSU May Day Slogan, 1990

The collapse of 'really existing socialism',[1] and its eclipse as an economic and political alternative to liberal capitalism, has many implications for the populations of the affected countries, not all of them positive. For the half that is female, there will be both losses and gains. As the state retreats from its self-designated role as 'emancipator of women', to be replaced by market forces, civil society and new ideological configurations, vulnerable social groups—such as women—are threatened by the abandoning of old commitments, and by a deepening of existing social divisions and political tensions. At the same time, such groups are now able to form their own organizations and challenge the limited conceptions of citizenship that prevailed under the old state structures.

Although it is too early to predict the outcome of these epochal changes—in some Communist countries it is still possible to talk of 'reforms' under Party rule, while elsewhere it appears that a wholesale move to the free market is in train—the implications for women are momentous. Feminists might view these changes with a degree of ambivalence: on the one hand, welcoming fresh opportunities for debate as state control is relaxed and civil society emerges as a new political terrain; but on the other, fearing that the 'transition from socialism' will lead to a worsening of women's social and economic position, at least in the short to medium term.

Although at this stage any analysis must necessarily be provisional, it is nevertheless possible to discern some changes in the definition of women's social position within this new context. This essay will

47

examine the three most pertinent issues: how those Communist parties that remain in power, or remain competitors for power, have redefined their policies with respect to women; how the socio-economic and political situation of women is likely to be affected by the abandoning of part or all of the orthodox Communist policy package; and how far these new conditions favour the emergence of feminist and women's movements. Whilst the main focus of the discussion will be the Soviet Union and China, where the Communist parties have remained in power, some of the problems and possibilities that can be identified there have also emerged in other parts of the bloc of countries which emulated the Soviet economic model, its social policies and political institutions—not only in Eastern Europe but also in the Communist states of the south. Whereas the USSR waited until after Gorbachev's advent to power in 1985 to introduce major economic and social changes, some of the Third World Communist parties had begun these well before—China after 1978, Vietnam after 1981, Mozambique after 1983. (In Eastern Europe, Poland and Hungary had begun to liberalize—and to rethink policy on women—in the 1970s.) But even where these changes did not always explicitly involve changes in state policy towards women, the new orientations did affect women through their impact on the labour force, population policy and the family. With the launching of perestroika in the USSR after 1985, the great majority of the Communist states became involved in one way or another in this process, and it became increasingly evident that formerly prevalent views on 'the woman question' were being revised, sometimes radically.

The implications for women of these various changes have been of two general kinds. On the one hand, there have been changes in economic policy entailing a revision of earlier commitments in favour of new goals. There is, however, another dimension to reform, so far confined to Eastern Europe: namely, the loosening of state control and the emergence or expansion of civil society. It therefore becomes important to look not just at what state and party leaderships declare, but also at what emerges from civil society itself, as the power of these leaderships recedes or is challenged. Such an analysis has relevance to more than the phenomenon of perestroika: it poses much broader questions about the previous social role of Communist states, and the nature of socialist transformation itself.

Women and the Communist State: Before Perestroika

The starting point in any discussion of the Communist states in relation to gender issues is to establish the significance and meaning of their commitment to women's emancipation. In the socialist tradition and in the practice of Communist parties, the process of women's emancipation was seen as part of the overall socialist revolutionary project, combining ideas of social justice and equality with those of modernity and development. In the classical texts of Engels, Lenin and Marx himself there was a recurrent commitment to the emancipation of women from the bonds of traditional society and the inhumanity of capitalism; and this theme subsequently informed the policies of the ruling Communist parties, committed as they were to social transformation. Emancipation in this context came to mean two things: the mobilization of women into the labour force; and the lifting of traditional social constraints and injustices, thereby enabling them to take part in the effort to develop their societies. A number of classic measures (embodied in the resolutions of the 1920 Congress of the Comintern) were adopted to secure women's 'emancipation', first in the Soviet Union, and later in those states that followed in its footsteps. The most important of these were: the encouragement of women to work outside the home; the introduction of legal equality between men and women; the liberalization of laws on the family and marriage; the promotion of equality of opportunity in education; and the prohibition of sexually exploitative images and writing, and of practices such as prostitution. The earliest declarations of women's rights recognized that women would perform two roles: a 'maternal' function and a role in production. The socialist state was to facilitate this dual function by supplying adequate child-care facilities and provisions for paid maternity leave.[2]

Despite their historical significance and positive aspects, these policies had major limitations. Communist Party officials came to assume—or found it convenient to do so—that the oppression of women consisted almost entirely in their exclusion from paid employment. This, however, ignored both the question of women's inferior position in a segregated, hierarchical workforce, and the stringent demands of their new combined duties. Bolshevik policy on the family, while initially taken with the idea of abolishing the traditional model, soon turned to reinforcing it—while placing it under greater strain—in a way that precluded both a critique of gender roles within the domestic sphere, and consideration of alternative forms of family and interpersonal relationships. From the earliest Bolshevik period, the policies of Communist states towards women and the family were kept subservient to broader economic goals, and changed in accordance with them. Within these authoritarian political systems founded upon centralism and the imposition of orthodoxy, no autonomous women's movement and no feminist critique of socialist theory and policy were allowed. Official women's organizations mobilized women in the service of the economic and political goals of the state, in accordance with a narrowly defined set of 'questions of everyday life'. They did not challenge state policy, or tackle the gender inequalities which survived the substantial social transformations.

The Communist record on 'women's emancipation' is one of some advances coupled with substantial failure—an apparent paradox best understood in the context of the development strategies pursued by these states, rather than as resulting from inadequacies in socialist theory itself. Command economies and authoritarian states of the Soviet variety have attempted to overcome economic backwardness by pursuing policies designed to increase industrial and agricultural output as rapidly as possible. The success of these policies was made dependent on the mass mobilization of the population into various sectors of the economy, changes which had far-reaching consequences both for women and the institution of the family. Women achieved formal legal equality and a limited emancipation from the 'old feudal order'; along with men, they gained access to education, employment, cheap food and heavily subsidized health and housing. Yet the cost of this model was high, and its accumulated failures and distortions fell, as we shall see, especially heavily on the female sex.

This policy orientation prevailed in Communist countries from the 1920s until the late 1980s, and despite the variations of culture, history and politics, the Communist parties exhibited a remarkable degree of consistency in this regard. They proclaimed their commitment to 'the emancipation of women' and were quick to declare that the woman question, like those of the nationalities and unemployment, had been 'solved'. Official discourses stressed Communism's achievements in the realms of legal equality and educational provision, but above all they were proud of their record on employment. High female employment rates were achieved relatively early on in the centrally planned economies. In 1950 in the USSR the female participation rate was over 60 per cent, compared with 32.6 per cent in the USA.[3] In 1980, half the labour force of Eastern Europe consisted of women, compared with 32 per cent in Western Europe; and even as the capitalist states began to catch up, by mid decade only Sweden, Denmark and Finland had higher rates than East Germany (77.5 per cent) and the USSR (70 per cent). The less developed regions under Communist rule also showed significant increases over their capitalist counterparts. Figures for 1980 show that in the Muslim Central Asian republics of the USSR 40 per cent of the labour force was female; in Vietnam 45 per cent; and in North Korea 46 per cent. The average for the Middle East was 20 per cent; for Latin America 22 per cent; and for the Far East (the second highest average after the CPEs), 35 per cent.[4] Although in some cases these gaps were narrowing, they nevertheless remained significant. It was also true that women had entered the professions in substantial numbers—in some cases crossing gender barriers that in the West prevailed to the disadvantage of women. Engineering was a case in point: in the mid eighties, one third of Soviet engineers were female, compared with only 6 per cent in the United States.

Yet despite these advances, it was evident to many outside observers, and to a growing number of people in the Communist states themselves, that women's participation in the economy had brought them neither equality nor emancipation, and that women remained a subordinate social group in both the public and private realms. The realization that women's lot was a harsh one became part of more general criticism of orthodox Communism, and contributed to the rejection of the Communist model by the reform movements.

Pressures from Above and Below

From the 1970s onwards, for reasons unconnected with the emancipation of women as such, policy relating to women was seen to require reassessment. The most pressing issues were demographic, and centred on the birth rate: many states became alarmed at its decline, and took measures to make it easier for women to have more children. This was particularly so in Hungary, the GDR, the USSR, and to an extreme degree in Romania where abortion was outlawed and women were coerced into having a minimum of three children per family. In a few cases—notably China and Vietnam—the opposite consideration prevailed, and coercion and incentives were used to bring down the high birth rate. These demographic considerations were directly linked to the growing preoccupation with an economic performance that was sluggish in comparison with the capitalist states; and in the Soviet Union to the additional fear that the population of the RSFSR would be outnumbered by that of Central Asia. In Yugoslavia, ethnic Albanians were seen to present a similar threat to the Serbian authorities, and 'appropriate' measures were taken to reduce the birth rate in Kosovo.

But other fears, common to these states both in the north and in the south, arose from a perceived disintegration of social life, associated with what some sociologists identified as 'alienation' or 'anomie', and what others linked to the shortage of housing, leisure facilities and consumer goods. The rising rates of divorce, alcoholism and crime were seen as evidence that the state had failed in its duty to support the family. Given the harsh conditions of daily life in most households, it was hardly surprising that families suffered under the pressure; but significantly, the 'decay of family life' was attributed by sociologists and public opinion alike to the pressures on women, especially the 'absent' (that is, working) mother. In the USSR in the first half of the 1980s, theories elaborated by psychologists in the maternal deprivation vein contributed to a general rethinking of policies.[5] The proposal to place a renewed social responsibility on the family would ensure that in practice such responsibility devolved once again upon women. During the 1970s and 1980s throughout the Communist bloc, women's social position became an object of official scrutiny, and the ideological importance given to their role in production was now displaced in favour of their role in the home—a shift which represented a radical departure from the slogans, if not the reality, of the past.

A further link between the crisis of orthodox socialism and the position of women was formed by popular attitudes in these countries themselves. In many cases, the history of Communist Party policy with regard to women was one of a reforming state intervening in society to bring about changes in women's position, often against the wishes and views of a majority of the population.[6] If this was true in the initial revolutionary phase, it remained so throughout the following period. In many cases the result was that the emphasis on 'the woman question' and on the emancipation and promotion of women could too readily be associated with the dead hand of the same distant and bureaucratic centralizing state, to be resisted and rejected along with its other policies. Such rejection was particularly strong when nationalist or religious interests were at stake—for instance, hostility to abortion in Catholic Poland, or the illegal continuation of arranged marriages and of the *kelim*, or betrothal settlement, in Soviet Central Asia.

This resistance to 'emancipation from above' was compounded by conflicts resulting from the policies themselves. In the first place, the very encouragement of women to participate in economic activity generated its own forms of resistance: women were seen as being unfairly forced to take on additional burdens outside the home, and the formal equality such employment bestowed was vitiated by the arduous and sometimes squalid conditions under which they worked at menial jobs in agriculture and industry. Despite a commitment to various forms of protective legislation, such as the exclusion of women from many hundreds of jobs 'to protect their maternal function', this covert paternalism was remarkable for its inconsistency. Women had always performed heavy labour in the countryside, where no laws 'protected' them—even from the hazards of chemical poisoning. In the towns, women performed such work as rubbish collection as a matter of course, and in factories frequently carried far heavier loads than permitted by law, and worked in insanitary, polluted and noisy conditions. In the

USSR, for example, 98 per cent of janitors and street cleaners are women, as are 26 per cent of highway-construction crews. And, although women were formally banned from nightshifts, over 70 per cent of Soviet nightshift workers are female—a result of a loophole in the law that permits women to be employed for short-term emergencies only.[7] Moreover, the gap between the average male and female wage stood at around 30 per cent in most northern Communist states (a gap larger in Vietnam and China), with women concentrated in low-paid jobs in 'feminized' occupations, their distribution in the labour force subject to marked horizontal and vertical segregation.[8] It is little wonder that few women in these circumstances could feel wholly positive about their participation in the labour force, or about government policies in general.

In the political realm, women were excluded even more markedly from positions of power and responsibility, despite a substantial measure of participation at lower levels. Most countries' politburos contained no women, some had a token one, others a few 'candidate members'; and at ministerial level the few women were typically confined to posts in health and education. The policy of establishing quotas for women in political organizations, limited as it was, had its own negative con-sequences: since women were most frequently promoted in those bodies with little authority, such as legislatures, the very formal representation was contradicted by reality. In many cases, from Bulgaria and Romania to China and Cuba, the most prominent women occupied their posts less by virtue of individual merit than by family ties.[9] The official women's organizations, supposedly acting to further women's collective interests, were in most cases strict adherents of the Party line, and in some were moribund, corrupt entities, a fact which only added to women's dis-enchantment with political life.

Mounting Dissatisfaction

Ultimately, it was the failure of the ruling Communist parties to deliver enough of the promised material progress that provided the decisive impetus to reform. This was true for a whole range of social policies, but the emphasis on production to the detriment of consumption, and the elimination of the independent service sector, were failures with special implications for women. The continued scarcity and poor quality of labour-saving equipment for the home made a mockery of Lenin's assault on the drudgery of housework. The shortages of consumer goods, and the many hours spent queueing, more than offset any avail-ability of socialized domestic services. The low standards and variable provision of nurseries; the lack of proper contraception and the consequent high abortion rates of many countries; the appalling conditions in maternity hospitals; the prevalence—especially in the Soviet Union—of male alcoholism as a response to the drabness of social life: all these factors created special problems for women. Official claims made for the superiority of the socialist order rang increasingly hollow among populations who had made their sacrifices and were now impatient for results.

It is useful to distinguish between the actual development and intensification of these problems and the growing intolerance of them by their long-suffering peoples. Taken as a whole, the economic situation of these countries has been, from the late 1960s, one in which growth has slowed down to the point of stagnation. But in the sphere of political life the crisis consisted in a growing awareness on the part of both leadership and population of the failings of the system, even though compared to earlier periods the situation was easing. This growing dissatisfaction had several causes: an extension of the real economic malaise into other areas of life; a greater impatience with the shortcomings of the system as a result of higher levels of education and the relative relaxation of political controls; a decline in the opportunities for social mobility as economic growth slowed down; and, evident in all matters to do with everyday life and social affairs, an increasing sense that the socialist countries were now lagging behind the West. All these factors had their impact on popular attitudes toward gender issues: the slowing down of the economy and the stagnation of output and productivity levels rendered the idea of emancipation through employment less and less plausible; at the same time, and as demand grew, the failures of social services, provisioning, transport and so forth became more evident. The higher levels of education amongst women made some of them less willing to accept the subordinate position they experienced in the home and at work. The sheer difficulty of making ends meet, in terms of both time and money, placed households under acute strain. These material pressures were duly reflected in the rising number of divorces and—in the countries of the north—in the falling or static birth rate.

In addition, the greater visibility of the West produced demands for liberalization that had contradictory implications for women. Their forced participation in the economy was itself said to be an oppression not shared by women in capitalist countries, while the stark contrast with the West in terms of the provision of well-made clothes, domestic appliances, child and baby products, and essential items such as tampons and contraceptives was felt to be increasingly unacceptable. Yet reinforcing this loss of confidence in the Communist record—which came, if not from feminism, then certainly from a general sympathy for women—was a quite different influence from the capitalist world: namely the desire for greater openness in the area of personal life and in the public depiction of women, whether this took the form of egalitarian sexual freedom, prostitution or pornography. The latter became an important—at least an important male—source of interest in the West, producing a situation whereby the restrictions prevailing in Communist societies were seen as imposing a dictatorial puritanism that contrasted with the free sensuality of liberal capitalism.[10]

The Emergence of a Feminist Opposition

A further component of the crisis of orthodox Communism in regard to women was that of explicit opposition to, and critique of, the Soviet model by indigenous women's groups. Feminism has always been a beleaguered force in countries ruled by Communist parties. The world-wide upsurge of feminism in the 1970s did not make much impact in the Communist states, where feminist writings and ideas were officially discouraged. The UN Decade for Women (1976–86) can be credited with making some small inroads by bringing Communist representatives into contact with feminists and feminisms from different parts of the world, and focusing attention on the position of women within the Communist states themselves. For all this, feminists remained isolated and ignorant of the debates going on in the movement outside, and many would-be feminists consequently absorbed the Party line that feminism was a trivial Western irrelevance, one especially unsuited to the different conditions of 'really existing socialism'.

Notwithstanding these unpropitious conditions, however, explicit opposition to Communist Party policy has at times been mounted by women's groups. Autonomous feminist forces had survived in some of the Communist countries prior to the imposition of 'democratic centralist' orthodoxy—notably in Russia (Kollontai, Armand, and others) and in China (Ting Ling). From Lenin onwards, feminism was routinely denounced as 'bourgeois', and seen as a challenge to the orthodox line that it was unnecessary because women had achieved their emancipation under socialism. Yet in the mid 1970s, as part of the global upsurge of women's movements, feminist currents began to emerge in the Communist states.[11] In Yugoslavia a feminist group of teachers, journalists and writers began to campaign for changes in the laws which affected women, focusing on issues such as rape. In 1979 the Leningrad group of writers associated with Tatyana Mamonova published *The Almanac: Women and Russia*. Their club, 'Maria', produced a magazine that combined ideas of women's liberation with mysticism and Christianity. This enterprise provoked charges of anti-Soviet propaganda, and the group was dissolved; four members, including Mamonova, were forced into exile over the following two years.[12] In 1982 in the GDR a women's peace movement associated with Christa Wolf opposed the extension, in times of national emergency, of conscription to women; but although their campaign had some success, the leaders were held for questioning, and at the end of 1983 two of them were imprisoned for six weeks before charges were dropped.[13]

During the same period, active feminist currents arose in some of the countries of the south. In Latin America a continent-wide movement developed, and neither of the two post-revolutionary states in the region were immune to its effects. Cuba's hostility to feminism—expressed in Vilma Espin's regular denunciation of its 'bourgeois' and 'imperialist' character—softened under the impact of changes taking place within socialist movements everywhere. As feminism began to appeal to socialists, so the Cuban leadership began to take note. Members of the *Federación de Mujeres Cubanas* (FMC) began to attend feminist gatherings in Latin America, and so to enter into dialogue with individuals and organizations from different parts of the world.

Nicaraguan feminists had an important influence on Cuba at this time. In the very different political context of the Nicaraguan revolution there emerged in the 1980s a loyal feminist opposition, one that took an active part in debating and formulating state policy on questions concerning women. These feminists came from a variety of social backgrounds, and most of them were active in the FSLN, the women's organization (AMNLAE), or in other mass organizations. This movement was conspicuous in not confining itself to the Leninist agenda or the Party line on women. In a number of cases campaigns were fought to change Party policy, even over sensitive issues such as abortion.[14] From the start, relations between Cuban and Nicaraguan women's organizations were less than harmonious, the differences in approach becoming evident in 1987 at the Fourth Latin American and Caribbean Feminist *Encuentro* in Mexico, at which around forty Nicaraguan feminists argued with three from Cuba. None the less, some of this exposure to other feminisms that were not 'bourgeois' or 'imperialist' had an effect on Cuban attitudes in the 1980s. Feminist concerns began to be reflected in some of the research carried out by social scientists, sometimes conducted under the supervision of feminist scholars from the West. In the early 1980s the *Frente Continental* was founded by the FMC, an initiative which aimed to bring Latin American feminism into line with Cuban priorities and—as one participant saw it—to stop it drifting off into less important issues like sexual politics.[15] Limited though these initiatives were, they none the less marked a significant and positive advance on earlier views. But, in contrast to the Eastern European and Russian cases, there appeared no independent feminist groups, at least none which sought to enter the public realm.

It was such groups, along with writers and film-makers, who, prior to perestroika, began to challenge the orthodox line that the woman question had been 'solved', and in some cases sought to define a programme of reform that was aware of, but not uncritical about, the situation of women in the West.[16] Given the degree to which the West had won favour with popular opinion in the socialist countries, these feminist currents, unimpressed by both socialist and capitalist records, came to represent an important alternative point of reference.

New and Old Soviet Thinking

The transformation of Communist states, epitomized in the Soviet policy of perestroika, has led to the liberalization of both economy and political system, together with reduced confrontation with the West and a loosening of ties between the Comecon states. Initially conceived as an attempt to revitalize socialism in order the better to compete, as a distinct social system, with the capitalist West, it soon became apparent that the prospects for such competition were remote, and that the Communist states were seeking more and more to integrate themselves with the West. Whether in time this would succeed, and whether, if it did, these societies would retain anything distinctive in their mode of political, economic and social organization, remained open questions; what was evident was that these changes involved the sometimes wholesale adoption of certain Western modes of operation, stimulated by reform from above, and in most cases matched by popular pressure from below. One of the hallmarks of the new phase was the abandonment of the old 'internationalist' model, whereby other socialist countries imitated the USSR; but paradoxically it was the changes in the USSR that none the less greatly influenced and accelerated what was occurring in other states, notably the collapse of Communist power in Eastern Europe. This comprehensive revision has implications for women in three main areas: state policy; political representations; and the economy.

The discussion after 1985 of policies relating to women took place against a background of more than a decade of concern in the USSR about a range of social problems relating to family life. The divorce rate was the second highest in the world after the USA; alcoholism, 'hooliganism' and crime were on the rise; the birth rate was falling, infant mortality was rising, and a high number of abortions (seven million per year) were being carried out.[17] The rubric of 'everyday life', used to summarize these problems, implicitly excluded the issues of gender relations and the sexual division of labour at work. When controls on the press were loosened, and the claim that social problems had been 'solved' was dropped, a greater recognition of the depth of these problems was apparent in press and Party statements.

This concern was reflected in the policies that Gorbachev began to introduce in 1985, and which he enunciated in his address to the Twenty-seventh Party Congress in February 1986. Here he restated the orthodox position: 'Socialism has emancipated women from economic and social oppression, securing for them the opportunity to work, obtain an education, and participate in public life on an equal footing with men. The socialist family is based on the full equality of men and women and their equal responsibility for the family.' Gorbachev then went on to itemize the social problems in the USSR, and to outline the changes designed to enable women to combine their 'maternal duties' with involvement in economic activity: 'in the twelfth five-year period we are planning to extend the practice of letting women work a shorter day or week, or to work at home. Mothers will have paid leave until their babies are eighteen months old. The number of paid days off granted to mothers to care for sick children will be increased. The lower-income families with children of up to twelve years of age will receive child allowances. We intend to satisfy fully the people's need for pre-school children's institutions within the next few years.'[18]

Gorbachev's treatment of this issue included, however, a new element: the revival of the women's councils within places of work or in residential areas to 'resolve a wide range of social problems arising in the life of our society'. These women's councils, or *zhensovieti*, mush-roomed in the following years, so that by April 1988 there were reported to be 236,000 in existence, involving 2.3 million women. This emphasis on the political involvement of women was developed later to include the promotion of women within political organizations as a whole. Indeed, Gorbachev's treatment of issues relating to women and the family developed, as did so much of his policy, with an increasing radicalization as glasnost revealed the scope of the problems of 'private life'. By the time of the special Party conference in June 1988, Gorbachev was placing particular stress on the importance of women's political activity as such, beyond the restricted realm of the *zhensovieti* and improvements in 'everyday life': 'Women are not duly represented in governing bodies. And the women's movement as a whole, which gained momentum after the October Revolution, has gradually come to a standstill or become formal (that is, bureaucratized).'[19]

Beyond the policies themselves lay the issue of whether perestroika would succeed, bringing the political liberalization necessary for an effective women's movement to emerge, and consolidating the social services, consumer goods and living conditions that would materially benefit women. This issue would, in the long run, be decisive for women; yet it was precisely here that the contradictory character of the Soviet reforms became clearest. In the political sphere, Gorbachev called for a revival of women's soviets and women's movements. Yet as Soviet writers were soon to point out, the work of the *zhensovieti* required a willingness on the part of Party and employment officials to listen to what they said.

Declining State Power and the Rise of Unofficial Groups

The call for women to be promoted to positions of authority was also compromised by the decreasing power of the state—whatever Gorbachev called for was not necessarily going to occur. In the March 1989 elections to the Congress of People's Deputies the percentage of women elected fell by over half, from 34.5 per cent to 15.6 per cent. (This plummeting representation occurred throughout Eastern Europe. In Poland in January 1988 the number of women holding parliamentary seats fell from 20.2 per cent to 13.3; and after 1989 similar drops were registered in Romania [from one-third of all seats to only 3.5 per cent], in Czechoslovakia [from 29.5 per cent to 6 per cent], and in Hungary [from 20 per cent to 7 per cent].) In the local elections of spring 1990, the percentage of women elected to the RSFSR Congress fell from 35 per cent to just 5 per cent. This was due in large part to the cancelling of previous quota systems which had guaranteed the representation of certain social groups such as workers, peasants and women; under these, women had 33 per cent of the seats in the Supreme Soviet and 50 per cent in local soviets. However, Gorbachev showed that he could and would act in areas under leadership control, such as in the promotion of women to more senior posts. In September 1988, for the first time in twenty-eight years, a woman, Alexandra Biriukova, was appointed a candidate member of the CPSU Politburo, a post she held until the re-shuffle of July 1990. But amidst widespread indifference, and hostility to what was seen as traditional authoritarian imposition of quotas from above, it was an open question how successful any state-led promotion of women's political presence would be. One of the pre-election opinion polls revealed the strength of popular prejudice against women in politics: 'being a man' was the main quality favoured in a candidate.

Outside the formal realm of institutionalized politics, glasnost opened up a new context for political action by unofficial groups—a few within

the socialist tradition, others liberal, nationalist and religious. The years
after 1985 saw a political explosion in the USSR as previously repressed
tendencies erupted into public life. No greater limitations were placed
on the formation of women's organizations and the expression of their
demands than on any other group. All groups still had to ask permission
to exist; not all did. Yet it was striking how, amidst this plethora of
forces, new and old, feminist groups and gender issues appeared to play
such a small role. The religious and nationalist groups paid scant attention to them, beyond routine calls for the end to women's 'involuntary
emancipation' and a return to the 'home and hearth'.[20] The 'informal'
political forces were little better: in the People's Front that emerged in
1989, women's issues were not given any prominence, and women
speakers seemed few and far between in the liberalized political atmosphere. Only five out of 1,256 delegates spoke at the June 1988 Party
conference, and only one of these raised issues pertaining to women.
Ironically, it seemed that socialist state policy on women, which had not
achieved their emancipation, succeeded instead in alienating the population from any serious commitment to a feminist programme.

   The liberalization of the economy had even more contradictory implications for women. Official sources and newspapers were increasingly
admitting that the supposed emancipation of women through participation in economic activity had not occurred. The findings of feminists
and sociologists documenting the double burden of women's lives
appeared in *Pravda, Izvestiya* and *Literaturnya Gazeta*; and the
theoretical journal of the CPSU, *Kommunist*, even published the first
feminist analysis of women's oppression in the USSR.[21] The unhealthy
conditions under which many women worked, the evasions of protective
legislation, women's low pay and their absence in positions of responsibility were all given publicity.[22]

The Social Cost of Economic Rationalization

The priorities of perestroika, involving, at least, rationalization without
technological restructuring, and, at most, severe stabilization measures,
are expected to result in unemployment in the USSR for the first time in
sixty years. Leonid Abalkin, deputy prime minister, told Parliament in
June 1989 that between sixteen and nineteen million redundancies were
expected by the year 2000. Women's representatives have expressed
concern about the effects on women's jobs. Maria Lebedeva, addressing
the plenary session of the Soviet Women's Committee, remarked that
'the scholars make no mention of who these people will be. Let's fill in
the blanks: at least fifteen million of these will be women.'[23] Other

observers have expressed concern that the increased autonomy and cost-effectiveness required of enterprises has meant that managers have become concerned about the social costs of employing women with children, especially after the increased maternity allowances which enterprises were in part responsible for. Zoya Pukhova, while chair of the Women's Committee, argued that 'in trying to exercise their right to have a short working day or a short working week, to have a sliding schedule or additional time off, women involuntarily come into conflict with management and the labour collective of the shop or brigade.'[24]

However, the matter is far from clear cut. The jobs most likely to be affected are in the manufacturing sector, and the most vulnerable workers are the manual unskilled and semi-skilled, and auxiliary clerical staff. But while the first category certainly includes women, the axe could fall even more heavily on men's jobs. Moreover, women in their middle years in both unskilled and auxiliary jobs in industry, while vulnerable to redundancy, are expected to find other work more easily than men in the expanding and already feminized service sector.[25] Women may also find employment in some of the newer light industries being planned. Segregated employment patterns, for all their disadvantages, especially in terms of pay, often serve as protected areas resistant to competition from new labour reserves.

Some female unemployment will occur (as it has already in Hungary and Poland), but one certain outcome is an intensification of gender *segregation* in employment. Working women will find themselves assailed by contradictory messages. On the one hand, economists believe that women are still needed in the labour force, especially if perestroika results in the growth of new light industries and a more developed service sector; while on the other, women are being called upon to take greater responsibility in the home, and to have more children. More than one Soviet commentator has suggested that economic restructuring requiring the loss of labour makes it necessary for women to give up their jobs and return to the home to care for their families. A convenient link between increasing the population and raising productivity is thereby established. Predictably, the group of Russian patriots associated with *Pamyat* welcomes 'modernization' as a 'way to raise production standards and free woman from involuntary emancipation and return her to the family, where she fills the role of mother, keeper of the hearth and bulwark of the nation.'[26] However, this is not exclusively a neo-conservative and nationalist position: Gorbachev, too, has referred to the 'purely womanly mission', investing domesticity and motherhood with an aura of the sacred and natural. Articles in the press frequently appeal for the restoration of a more 'natural' state of affairs 'where men are men and women are women'.

(This has long been a trope in social science literature, which in the seventies and eighties analysed the 'crisis of femininity' as resulting from 'women's emancipation'—that is, overwork.) Henceforth, efforts would be made to restore some balance in women's lives, which meant making it more possible than before for *women* to combine home and work responsibilities, and of course to have more children. A four-day working week for women, and shorter hours for mothers of young children, were seriously considered in 1990 by the USSR Supreme Soviet. But part-time work—the compromise that has evolved in the West—has not been seen as feasible, because of the rigidities in the system. (There are only 700,000 registered part-time workers in the USSR, the majority of whom are female.) But one proposal being debated by Gorbachev's advisers in 1989 was the introduction of higher wages for men to enable them to support their dependent wives at home. This startling about-turn in Communist Party thinking was justified in humanitarian terms by one of Gorbachev's chief advisers as the only way that women would be relieved of the pressure of work and be able to stay with their young children.[27]

The reality for most women is that they will need to work, and that they will probably continue to have few children. Surveys reveal that women have taken advantage of the new maternity-leave provisions introduced selectively since 1981, but expressed little interest in giving up work altogether, even if men's wages were to rise significantly.[28] Unless the USSR is hit by a major recession, it is likely that there will be jobs for women to do and women ready to do them. These factors, together with Gorbachev's proposed reduction in hours, may keep most Soviet women in the workforce, but they will only increase the divisions between men and women workers, both materially and ideologically, as motherhood and household tasks increasingly distinguish men from women as workers with different social attributes and different responsibilities.

The Effects of Economic Liberalization in China

The discussion has so far focused on the implications of perestroika for Soviet women. One of the hallmarks of perestroika was its claim that the Soviet Union no longer acted as the model for other socialist countries, which were now free to pursue different, national, paths of development. In the case of some countries, notably China, this had long been the position. In other countries formerly close to the Soviet model, for instance Cuba, there has been a great resistance to current Soviet policy. Whilst in the USSR perestroika involved a simultaneous liberalization of economic and political life, in some of the less developed countries a measure of economic liberalization proceeded without comparable political change. This was so in China where the democracy movement was brutally repressed, and in Vietnam, Mozambique, Angola and— until its acceptance of political pluralism in late 1989—South Yemen. Cuba, Albania and North Korea, apparently resisting both forms of liberalization, were the exceptions. While recognizing that no single model exists, it is possible to make some observations about the ways in which Communist parties translated the pressure to reform into policies affecting women, focusing on two areas: population policy and economic liberalization.

China and Vietnam are perhaps the clearest instances of how these two policy areas converged. Both states adopted population-control policies in the 1970s as a way of addressing the problem of slow economic growth, and pursued similar incentive packages to encourage a reduction in the birth rate. Both also introduced measures to relax state control over some sectors of the economy. More is known about the Chinese case, where the economic liberalization began earlier and where it converged in 1978 with the adoption of the one-child-family policy. This campaign, aimed at reducing the Chinese birth rate through a combination of incentives and punishments, was more effective in the urban than in the rural areas where production is household based and the availability of family labour is directly linked to economic success or failure.[29] Thus, paradoxically, the economic reforms, which enhanced the importance of the household as a unit of production, have given an unforeseen advantage to those with large families.[30] The tensions generated by the conflict between these state policies have devolved most directly upon the female sex. There has been a rise in female infanticide, and in the abandonment or divorce of women who give birth to daughters; and the toll on the mental and physical health of women who transgress the law is obvious. Many of these problems are exacerbated by the maintenance in China of customary marriage practices which reinforce the preference for sons over daughters. Sons are valued more because they retain responsibility for the natal family when they marry, and this means providing for their parents in their old age. Daughters marry and leave their family of origin and are expected to vest their interests in their husband's kin. The one-child policy, when added to these practices, greatly increases the premium on having a male child: many couples defy the law and suffer the consequences, the women bearing the brunt of social ostracism, late abortion and sometimes involuntary sterilization.

The economic reforms known as the 'four modernizations', which came into effect in 1978, have also affected women directly, with China going further than many other reforming states in liberalizing certain economic activities, and permitting practices previously banned, such as advertising and Western films. China's efforts to modernize and stimulate production have also involved a rationalization of enterprises to put them on a more profitable basis. As in the USSR and Eastern Europe, this has involved tightening up work practices and laying off labour. Evidence suggests that women's work is particularly vulnerable, and it is they who are often called upon to give up their jobs.[31] Discrimination against women at work is also on the increase, and with unemployment high, enterprise managers have no trouble filling vacancies with men. They tend to see women as a more expensive workforce, as a result of paid maternity leave, crèches and earlier retirement; but since it is usually the husband's employer who supplies the couple's accommodation, this should in theory equalize the costs.[32]

Changing Patterns of Discrimination

Testimony to the changes is an increasingly self-confident discrimination against women in China. Amidst the growing criticism of earlier policies—especially the extremes of the Cultural Revolution—prejudice against women occurs in the guise of being realistic about 'natural' differences between the sexes. The famous Iron Girls, once cast in the role of heroines of work, capable of doing men's jobs as well as men, are now openly derided as 'fake men'. There is more talk, even by the Women's Federation, of recognizing sexual difference, and less of denying or minimizing it. Soon after the policy changes of 1978, women began to be transferred out of jobs such as train driving or construction work into lower-paid work as clerks, or into light-industry female ghettos. Others were simply dismissed. Women were openly talked of as being especially suitable for boring, repetitive jobs because they were good at rote learning and were conscientious. Delia Davin has listed the forms of open discrimination typical of the period of reform: 'Factories and other enterprises either demand higher examination scores from female secondary school graduates who apply for employment, or turn them down outright. Technical and vocational schools which take secondary school leavers discriminate against females except for recruitment to training courses in traditional female skills such as nursing, office work and kindergarten teaching. Even university graduates suffer from this prejudice against employing women. Only just over a quarter of students in higher education are female, and China is desperately short of graduates, yet the officials in charge of job assignment report not only that many work units prefer male graduates, but that some reject all women or accept only a tiny number. There have been cases where men with poor marks have been preferred over women with excellent ones, and a notorious instance where members of a laser institute made every effort to recruit a student on the strength of a brilliant graduation thesis, only to change their minds when they discovered her sex. The problem of allocating female graduates is now so serious that some universities have considered reducing the number of female students they will accept.'[33] Although discrimination was rife in the pre-1978 period, it has lately grown on the more fertile soil of the new economic and ideological configurations, and acquired a new boldness.

On the other hand, the relaxation after 1981 of controls over small-scale production has given women forms of income-generating activity, some of which can be highly profitable, and which, because they are usually home-based, can be combined with child care and domestic responsibilities more easily than most forms of waged work. The Women's Federation of China, deploring the conditions most women face in industrial jobs, has even expressed the view that women should keep out of industry if they can, as it places them under too much pressure. It has called on women instead to make 'commodity production'—that is, 'sideline' activities—their favoured area of work. This kind of small enterprise is found equally in the urban and the rural areas. In the former, women more typically work with other members of the family running small businesses providing goods and services. Though women may benefit from sideline production and from the higher standard of living it could bring, there are longer-term dangers inherent in the deepening sexual division of labour that has attended women's re-integration into family-based production and abdication from the public realm of work. Moreover, as feminist scholars have pointed out, although the old work-point system contained its own inequalities, it had the merit of making women's contributions visible, and conferring status on the earner. In the new family-based production systems, the income generated is controlled by the male family head, and the women's contribution is usually invisible.

The new property laws have negative consequences for women. Land has become available to households through the contract system, which is usually made out to male heads of household. As Delia Davin notes, 'a peasant woman's access to the means of income generation ... now depends on her relationship to a man. This contrasts sharply with the collective era when membership of the collective conferred use-rights to the means of production.'[34] This re-inscription of women into the household has been compounded in the countryside by the feminization of agriculture, as men have left to take up more profitable work elsewhere. Although this has placed women in key roles as producers, and sometimes placed them at the head of the household, they are performing work that is unpopular, arduous and usually badly paid.

New Signs of Cultural Oppression

In the industrial sector, economic liberalization in China has brought with it enterprise competition and Western investment; it has also introduced cultural phenomena previously banned. One example is advertising, which appeared in the 1980s for the first time in forty years. Before the massacre in Tiananmen Square, advertising expenditure was growing by more than 30 per cent a year, peaking at US$227 million in 1986, 5–10 per cent of which was accounted for by the multinational corporations. The Women's Federation has protested at the uses being made of images of women models, and has called for government controls. But it is not just imported imagery that has brought about changes in the portrayal of women: by the mid eighties the familiar images of socialist iconography—the smiling woman worker at her machine—were being taken down from public hoardings and factory walls. In their place stood the proud housewife, the new consumer, pictured beside her washing machine.[35]

At the popular level, as in the northern cases discussed earlier, there has occurred a reaction to the old puritanism and what could be seen as the return of a repressed femininity, as young woman attend to the details of hair, clothes and make-up, and grow anxious again about standards of female beauty and shape. In the literature of the past decade, women writers have been free to reflect on the pain of the hard years of work and self-denial, and have returned to the persistent theme of the lost pleasures of motherhood, of the guilt experienced in leaving the children in care, sometimes for months on end, to fulfil the demands of work. Again, some observers have detected an undertow of 'West is best', and the attendant danger that the disillusion with the past becomes a thirst for its antithesis.

In general, it is clear that those able to afford them can now benefit from the wider availability of domestic appliances and consumer goods. In the period before the student protests, greater tolerance of public debate and discussion permitted the expression of views critical of official and more conservative opinion. The Women's Federation, and on occasion independent women, have articulated feminist arguments defending women's place in society as the equals of men. But such feminist movements or networks that might have emerged as part of the democracy movement would find it difficult to mobilize in the atmosphere of fear characteristic of the post-Tiananmen period.

Old Problems, New Struggles

It is evident that perestroika, or economic liberalization, has produced, in a variety of countries, a major shift away from some of the central tenets of Communist Party belief and policy with respect to women. This is as true of official thinking as it is of publicly expressed popular attitudes. If the old policies, based on a combination of some principle and much instrumentalism, had the merit of promoting positive changes in the name of 'women's emancipation', their overall validity, and the legitimacy of their official language, are now in doubt. The 'woman question', a phrase as redolent of old thinking as 'internationalism', may well disappear, and gender issues—if raised at all—will henceforth be formulated in a very different political language.

The paradox of this change is, however, that the underlying problem will endure: the absence in most countries of a strong feminist input into policy—whether from above or below—means that the policies adopted with respect to women will continue to be determined by the overall priorities of the state, whether economic, demographic or social. Questions of social justice, visions of a society in which old privileges and authority patterns have been surpassed, are unlikely to form an integral part of the new direction of economic development, which for the foreseeable future is more likely to be premissed on harsh policies of economic stabilization and adjustment.

As in the pre-reform period, the issue is not so much one of how great the commitment of the state is to women's emancipation, but rather of the very conception of gender relations upon which future policies will be based. The particular issue of gendered divisions in employment and in the home was never seriously tackled by government policies. Instead, in most countries, while the material effects of inequality (women's double burden) were deplored, the divisions them-selves, far from being seen as socially constructed, were increasingly talked of as natural, even desirable, by planners and populace alike, as a reaction to the extremism of earlier years.

Traditional gender divisions were reinforced through the structural and ideological biases inherent in policy and in the organization of society. Scarcity and financial hardship deepened the division of labour and mutual dependency in the family. For many households living on the edge of economic viability, both men and women performed a 'double shift': men took a second job or worked in the informal economy, while women put their remaining energies after a day out at work into managing the household, bartering scarce goods and services, and caring for children and relatives. The family, despite all its tensions, evident in soaring divorce rates, was often regarded as a refuge or as a

site of resistance against the authoritarian state and suffocating public
life. Many women expressed longings to have motherhood and femininity restored to them. These factors taken together implied that reforms
aimed at reinforcing women's ties to the family would find substantial
resonance within the populations of these states, even if their effect was
to intensify gender segregation and inequality.

Meanwhile, the threatened roll-back of women's reproductive rights,
particularly with respect to abortion, gathers pace in a number of
countries as a result of religious, demographic or neo-conservative
pressures. In the USSR this issue has already attracted more attention in
a period of 'openness' and speaking the truth. The high abortion rate
and horrific conditions in clinics (something which Mamonova's group
condemned, and were charged with making anti-Soviet propaganda for
revealing) have been the subject of wide public discussion since 1985.
The fact that the number of abortions exceeds live births is not so much
discussed as a failing of the system's provision of birth-control devices,
than as a moral failing of the society—and, to be more precise, another
symptom of corrupted femininity. In other states, legislative changes
have already been accepted. In Poland, for example, a bill to 'defend the
unborn child' by criminalizing abortion was introduced in June 1989. It
proposes a three-year prison sentence for those infringing the law. An
intense public debate is now under way with the outcome still uncertain.
In Germany, unification under Christian Democracy threatens to
impose restrictions on abortion in the East, to bring it more into line
with the West where it is illegal unless a panel of doctors argues that it is
necessary in order to avoid 'physical or social distress'. Efforts to impose
restrictions on the East were successfully resisted earlier this year by
feminist campaigners who mounted demonstrations in defence of the
existing law. However, there is fear that the current agreement could be
overturned in the future. At present in East Germany, abortion on
demand is legal and free up to the twelfth week of pregnancy.[36]

In the field of political representation, similar limitations recur. The
new commitment—evident at least in the USSR—to a greater political
role for women and to the revival of a women's movement is again
limited by the continuation of traditional assumptions within government circles. Although these are being challenged by more feminist
perspectives, they still have considerable weight. Political liberalization
has, however, opened up a space for autonomous women's movements
and the raising of feminist issues, and it may be that in time these movements will gain strength and emerge as a significant feminist current in
the post-Communist countries. That such movements should be free to
publish and press their demands is a necessary precondition for any real
challenge to prevailing gender inequalities in the social distribution of

power and rewards in these societies. It is also essential that the movements play a part in debates over welfare provision and the negative effects of marketization, and in challenging the simplified view of 'Western' freedom, with its elisions and indulgences of sexism in its various guises.

The Prospects for Soviet Feminism

It is early days yet, but Soviet women, some of them self-proclaimed feminists, have begun to make their voices heard in the period since 1985. Professional women, among them social scientists, lawyers and journalists, have added their criticisms of the social order to the general clamour in their different countries. Women's groups and networks have expanded, with new organizations appearing and gathering strength. In the USSR by the end of the 1980s, women-focused groups and clubs were springing up, predominant among them literary and arts associations like 'Herald', a Moscow club for women writers; 'Women's Creative Effort', organized by Tatyana Ryabikina; and Olga Bessolova's 'Club of Women's Initiatives'—all serving to promote and encourage members' work. Women film-makers and journalists have also established their own clubs, and a Council of Women Writers was set up under the auspices of the existing Writers' Union. The first Gender Studies Centre has recently been established in the Moscow Institute for Socio-Economic Problems of the Population. The objectives of these groups vary, as do their perspectives on women's issues; for example, the 'Transfiguration' (*Preobrazheniye*) Women's Club working in the Academy of Sciences aims to 'enhance women's role and initiative within the socio-cultural spheres'. In Leningrad the human-rights activist Olga Lipovskaya, publisher of the only samizdat magazine for women, *Zhenskoye Chteniye* (Women's Reading), has expressed the view that women's situation cannot be seriously improved without restructuring the entire social system. *Zhenskoye* contains poetry, essays, and even some articles by Western feminists.[37]

Despite a prevailing climate of hostility and ignorance of the women's movement, some women, like Olga Voronina, Anastasya Posadskaya, Valentina Konstantinova and Natalya Zakharova of the 'Lotos' group, have openly identified themselves as 'self-confessed' feminists, and have participated in several international forums bringing women from different countries together for debate. 'Lotos' stands for 'Liberation from social stereotypes', and its members share a commitment to undertaking theoretical work on gender inequalities. Among other issues, they have given publicity to male violence against women, and the rising incidence of rape in some of the Soviet republics. In articles and public meetings, they have also discussed the taboo subject of sexuality, condemning the puritanism and ignorance that surrounds it. Collectively, they have rejected the dominant view of the family crisis, arguing that it results from the as yet incomplete transition from 'patriarchy to egalitarianism', and that Gorbachev's policies aim simply to shore up a system that does not work. Consequently, the group has taken a stand against current attempts to redomesticate Russian women, and has called for the equal sharing between men and women of household responsibilities.[58] On 24 July 1990, they helped to found the Independent Women's Democratic Initiative and to draft its declaration. Two members of 'Lotos' helped to write the *Kommunist* article (see footnote 21), and as a result were invited to submit a position paper to the Council of Deputies, which was later accepted. They now have a role in formulating policy as members of an executive body of the Supreme Soviet which concerns itself with 'the position of women, protection of maternity and childhood, and strengthening of the family'.

Nina Belyaeva, a feminist campaigner, has recently spoken in optimistic terms of feminism's prospects in the USSR, but noted that this was not a common view: 'The women's groups ... I am told, still amount to a drop in the bucket [sic]—and are without clear goals or independence, all of them intellectual clubs.' She added that most women are too exhausted to have the energy for clubs and movements, and speculated that 'perhaps feminism is only for a well-fed society'.[39] If feminism had taken a precarious hold in the Communist states prior to the reforms, on account of state repression, it now addressed equally resistant forces within civil society. More than in any other formerly Communist country, feminism in the Soviet Union faces particularly entrenched opposition. It is derided and caricatured by men and women alike in a social context where anti-feminism draws on motherhood as a powerful cultural symbol to essentialize sexual difference. The writer Tatyana Tolstaya has attacked feminism's 'Western' rationality for misunderstanding Russian womanhood. She counterposes the idea that Russian women are the embodiment of real power in society, a power wielded within the family, 'at times extending to tyranny'. Soviet society, a product of its repressive history and sentimental culture, has, she claims, become almost matriarchal. Soviet women apparently do not need more power than they already have, they do not aspire to equality with men, they do not want to work or participate in politics, they are not oppressed by men (who are poor, weak and broken things, mere 'property' like 'furniture').[40] However problematic and, arguably, unsubstantiated such notions of female 'power' are, Russian feminists have to take account of such pervasive but confused sentiments in their campaigns, if they are to avoid political marginalization.

Feminist Currents in Eastern Europe

Feminist currents—even movements—were active during the 1980s in other Eastern and Central European countries. In Hungary, feminists participated in the opposition movements, and sociologists played an important role by focusing attention on women's particular vulnerability to poverty and overwork. Although most of these currents were composed of educated professional women, there were also signs of working-class discontent and mobilization around concrete women's issues. For the first time, women's sections appeared in some trade unions, with the aim of defending and advancing women's working conditions.[41] In early 1990 a Hungarian Women's Association was formed, and after much debate decided to identify itself as feminist. In Yugoslavia, feminists now speak of the existence of a women's movement, its activists campaigning on issues such as violence against women, for reproductive and gay and lesbian rights, and for policy changes via family laws and party-political involvement.[42] And even in Catholic Poland, where feminism has had very little impact on Solidarity's policies, there were stirrings in 1989 when Polish women demonstrated in their thousands against the proposed bill to criminalize abortion. In October, some of those involved in the campaign for reproductive rights founded the Polish Feminist Association. A feminist newspaper, *Baba Polka*, appeared and campaigned to defend reproductive rights. At government level there were moves to set up a women's group to advise on policy matters.

In East Germany, where feminists initiated the independent peace movement and were sufficiently established to organize demonstrations and meetings, the issues they raised were debated within opposition organizations such as *Neues Forum*. Feminist discussion circles generated a number of political initiatives, including the Berlin-based association known as 'Sophie'. In 1989 a group of feminists from Leipzig left *Neues Forum* because the leadership opposed parity of representation for men and women. They joined the newly founded Independent Women's Association, whose manifesto demanded 'genuine equality and emancipation for women', and called for an end to divisions of labour at home and at work, and shorter working hours for both men and women. In a detailed exposition of its premisses and demands, the Association outlined its social programme, which sought to retain the gains of the past but overcome the 'patriarchal power structures' that oppress and exclude women. Although supporting unification, the Association favoured 'a mutual process of reform' that respected 'the internal sovereignty of both states'. It argued for a society based on a market economy, but with some planning role for the state to guarantee democracy and progressive, ecologically responsible social policies. The Association called for a 'Ministry of Equity' to be established; for a comprehensive revaluation of women's work in the home and economy; and it favoured quotas for women and men in the areas of social life where one sex predominates. It pledged itself to resist the restrictions on abortion threatened by the process of reunification.[43] The Association achieved some political influence in the Modrow government, nominating a Minister without portfolio, and helped to draft the Social Charter and draw up plans for a women's ministry. In a joint campaign with the Green Party it received 2.7 per cent of the vote.[44]

In most northern states these manifestations of feminism were paralleled by a small but growing representation of feminist ideas and concerns in the press, not only by journalists and writers but also in letters from readers. These may not represent the dominant views, but there clearly exists a range of popular opinion that echoes the concern already articulated by feminists on questions of work, discrimination and the 'double burden'.

The manner in which Eastern European and Soviet feminists formulate their political priorities is necessarily shaped by the particular circumstances and cultural conditions in their own regions, as well as by differences of theoretical approach. Yugoslavian feminists have linked women's issues to racial discrimination against the ethnic Albanians, and have opposed sterilization programmes in Kosovo. The same is true of Hungarian feminists in relation to the gypsy population. In East Germany, peace issues have always come to the fore, and the Women's Association has campaigned with other groups for disarmament and demilitarization, in addition to preparing itself for the abrupt, possibly drastic, changes in social provision resulting from unification in 1990. Although a broad consensus exists among feminist groups on the question of abortion and contraception on demand, the need to campaign for social equality, and on issues such as violence and sexuality, there are none the less significant differences of approach and analysis. In Russia, there exists a stronger current of support for ideas of sexual difference than is the case in Hungary, East Germany or Yugoslavia, with Russian feminists like Larisa Kuznetsova arguing that women and men have innately different psychologies, and that women's embody superior ethical values, reflected in their caring and nurturing roles.[45] As women become mobilized as political actors, it is inevitable that differences of politics and perspective will increasingly be reflected both within and between women's movements.

The Future: Emancipation or New Forms of Domination?

So far, five years of perestroika in the USSR have delivered little to women in material terms, and in a number of other countries they are considerably worse off than under the old regime. In Hungary and Poland, many more women than men have been laid off from work, and everywhere the burden of domestic provisioning has increased, as shortages imposed by rationing are replaced by those created by rising prices. Fears of further unemployment grow along with concern over cuts in public expenditure. Russian feminists have pointed out that the deterioration of social life and proliferating violence in the USSR also have gendered effects—as evidenced by the increase in wife battering and in the growing incidence of rape.

Yet were the reforms to succeed, the overall improvement in economic conditions would greatly reduce the everyday pressures to which women are subjected, and thereby in some measure realize the early Bolshevik hope that economic and scientific advance could lessen the burden of household chores on women, principally by altering the sexual division of labour. As long as men are paid higher wages than women, and as long as many men have to perform two jobs in order to gain an adequate income, then gender roles within the family will not be redefined. The preconditions for tackling the sexual division of labour are, on the one hand, a recognition of this goal by the state and organized civic groups, and, on the other, greater employment flexibility in place of the current system which locks men into rigid employment patterns. Women should have the same earning power as men, with both sexes allowed more time for parenting and domestic responsibilities. As Zakharova et al. have said, 'emancipation is a two-way process: men must be given opportunities to participate more in housework and child raising ... We think that men as well as women should be able to combine parenthood and career ... direct and indirect discrimination against women in the workplace and men in the family should be eliminated.'[46] Their call for government measures and a review of existing legislation to help bring this about underlines the importance of women's claims on the institutions of government in a period when their influence and representation remains minimal.

The socialist programme of women's emancipation has always been subordinated to a particular economic model—a result of socialist theory and revolutionary state practice alike. Women's emancipation is certainly dependent upon the direction of economic policy: no programme of social change can be divorced from the general economic conditions in which it takes place. Yet in order to succeed, the policies of perestroika would have to be expanded to include a commitment to establishing real gender equality, coupled with a mobilization of civic support for such a programme. That commitment cannot be derived from, nor formulated to meet, the requirements of economic development alone. In the end, the issue in question is whether the changes being implemented within the centrally planned economies will eventually provide the opportunity to realize a greater degree of emancipation for women, or whether prevailing attitudes will remain unchanged, and women's inequality will be confirmed by the introduction of new forms of discrimination. Either outcome is possible, but the evidence to date provides few grounds for optimism.

September 1990

Notes

* This article is an excerpt from my forthcoming book, *Mobilization Without Emancipation: Women, the Communist State and Its Demise*, Verso, London. Thanks to the many friends here and abroad for help in gathering materials and for comments on earlier versions of this article, especially to Barbara Einhorn, Alistair McAuley, Hilary Pilkington and Anastasya Posadskya.

1. The qualified use of the term 'socialist' prefixed by 'existing' is now an anachronism. No entirely suitable adjective to describe these former states has yet emerged: 'Soviet-type', 'socialist', 'Communist', 'state-socialist', can all be objected to on various grounds. Where, for the sake of brevity, I refer to 'Communist' states or centrally planned economies (CPEs), this is simply a shorthand for those countries which are or were ruled by Communist parties, and claimed allegiance to Marxist doctrine, placing a substantial proportion of their economies under state control.

2. For critiques and assessments of the Communist project with respect to women, see Barbara Wolf Jancar, *Women Under Communism*, Baltimore 1978; Gail Lapidus, *Women in Soviet Society*, Los Angeles 1978; Sonia Kruks et al., eds., *Promissory Notes*, New York 1989; Hilda Scott, *Does Socialism Liberate Women?*, Boston 1984; and my 'Women's Emancipation in Socialist States: A Model for the Third World?' in *World Development*, no. 9/10, 1981. On China, see especially Kay Ann Johnson, *Women, the Family and Peasant Revolution in China*, Chicago 1983; and Judith Stacey, *Patriarchy and Socialist Revolution in China*, California 1983.

3. Labour force calculated as percentage of population aged 15–54. Data from the United Nations Publications *World Survey on the Role of Women in Development*, New York 1986, and *The Economic Role of Women in Development*, New York 1986, and *The Economic Role of Women in the ECE Region: Developments 1974–85*, New York 1985. These figures are lower than those given by national sources, a disparity due to different methods of calculation.

4. *ILO World Labour Report*, Geneva 1985.

5. Author's interview with A.G. Karchev, then head of the Institute of Sociology, Moscow, and leading specialist on the family. For discussion, see my 'Family Reform in Socialist States: The Hidden Agenda', in *Feminist Review*, no. 21, Winter 1985.

6. For a vivid account of the nature of Bolshevik intervention in Central Asia in the 1920s, see G. Massel, *The Surrogate Proletariat: Moslem Women and Revolutionary Strategies in Soviet Central Asia 1919–29*, Princeton 1974.

7. Data from the USSR Central Statistical Administration, reported in *Izvestiya*, translated in *Current Digest of the Soviet Press*, vol. XXXIX, 1987.

8. On the Soviet Union, see Alistair McAuley, *Women's Work and Wages in the USSR*, London 1981.

9. Elena Ceausescu, Vilma Espin and Madame Mao illustrate this point.

10. One of the first acts of the newly liberalized Polish and East German Communist youth magazines was the publication of photographs of naked women, as a sign of their new freedom from orthodoxy. Rupert Murdoch, quick to cash in on the current mood, has launched a new tabloid in Hungary called *Reform*, which, with its 'full-frontal female nudes', has already claimed a circulation of over 400,000 and is expected to produce annual profits of one million dollars. Such images are still outlawed in the Soviet press, but cooperatives are able to produce Pirelli-inspired calendars for sale to the general public. Meanwhile, *Komsomol*, the Communist youth organization, has presented 'beauty contents' which the Russian feminist Olga Voroninov has described as little more than 'porno shows' (*Tageseitung*, 24 November 1989). (In 1989, in a more domestic vein, *Komsomol* organized a 'Wife of the Year' competition.) With respect to pornography, in a context where sex and eroticism were hitherto identified as pornographic, and 'perpetrators' were severely dealt with, it is little wonder that notions of sexual freedom are crudely fashioned, and feminist criticisms dismissed as yet another form of authoritarian intrusion.

11. A definition of feminism is in order here; but such attempts run the risk of being either too broad and inclusive, failing to distinguish between female militancy or solidarity and feminist objectives, or too narrow and based on assumptions that may be sectarian and/or ethnocentric. That there are different feminisms as well as different women's movements alerts us to the heterogeneity of women's interests, and to the varying ways in which they are socially constructed. But what most definitions of feminism agree upon is that as a social movement and body of ideas it challenges the structures and power relations that produce female subordination. Where I refer here to specific groups or individuals as 'feminist', this is because (a) they designate themselves as such; and (b) they conform to the above definition.

12. For a full account, see Alix Holt, 'The First Soviet Feminists', in B. Holland, ed., *Soviet Sisterhood*, London 1986.

13. Barbara Einhorn, 'Sisters Across the Curtain: Women Speak Out in East and West Europe', in *END Journal of European Nuclear Disarmament*, February 1984; and 'Socialist Emancipation: The Women's Movement in the GDR', in Kruks et al., *Promissory Notes*.

14. For details, see my 'The Politics of Abortion in Nicaragua', *Feminist Review*, no. 29, Spring 1988; and 'Mobilization without Emancipation', *Feminist Studies*, vol. II, no. 2, 1985.

15. The *Frente Continental* was established in Cuba after the 1980 UN Decade for Women mid-decade conference in Nairobi.

16. Films and novels by women contributed to the former in no small measure. For the USSR, see especially Natalya Baranskaya, *A Week Like any Other*, now translated and published by Seal Press, 1990.

17. See Hilary Pilkington, 'Abortion, Contraception and the Future of Mother Russia', mimeograph.

18. *Soviet News*, 26 February 1986.

19. *Soviet News*, 19 June 1988.

20. 'Statement of the Bloc of Russian Public Patriotic Movements', in *The Current Digest of the Soviet Press*, vol. XLII, no. 1, 7 February 1990.

21. N. Zakharova, A. Posadskaya and N. Rimashevskaya, 'How We Are Resolving the Women's Question', *Kommunist*, no. 4, March 1989; translated in *The Current Digest of the Soviet Press*, vol. XLI, no. 19, 1989, and discussed by Cynthia Cockburn in *Marxism Today*, July 1989. The authors have now founded a Gender Studies Centre in Moscow.

22. According to Zakharova et al., almost 33 per cent of all women earn less than 100 roubles per month, while the corresponding figure for men is 2 per cent. Some 90 per cent of low-paid employees are women, while 7 per cent of women hold positions of authority compared with 48 per cent of men.

23. See the report by Maria Lebedeva from the plenary session of the Soviet Women's

Committee, in *Izvestiya*, 23 October 1988, p. 6, excerpted in *The Current Digest of the Soviet Press*, vol. XL, no. 43, 1988, p. 23.

24. *Pravda*, 2 July 1988.

25. See Alistair McAuley, 'Perestroika: Implications for Employment', in Martin McCauley, ed., *Gorbachev and Perestroika*, London 1990.

26. 'Statement of the Bloc of Russian Public Patriotic Movements'. This discourse is given particular meaning within nationalist movements, where the reintegration of women within the family is seen as part of the move against the oppressive Soviet legacy. This patriarchal chauvinism is clearly visible, for instance, in the Smallholder's Party of Hungary (slogan 'God, Fatherland and Family') which sees sovietization as responsible for 'denaturing women'.

27. Author's conversation with Tatyana Zaslavaskaya, author of *The Second Soviet Revolution*, London 1989.

28. Polls conducted in the RSFSR have so far shown that less than 20 per cent of women would choose to give up work even if their family incomes remained constant. The picture is very different in Poland and Hungary, where women's responses are more varied, with around 45 per cent preferring to give up work. V. Bodrova and R. Anker, *Working Women in Socialist Countries: The Fertility Connection*, Geneva 1985.

29. Repressive measures are especially prevalent in Tibet. As a national minority, Tibetans are allowed two children, but refugees report mounting pressure (through forced abortions and sterilizations) to have only one. Third children have no claims on welfare provisions or employment.

30. E. Croll, D. Davin and P. Kane, *China's One Child Family Policy*, London 1985; E. Croll, 'The State and the Single Child in China', in G. White, ed., *The Chinese Development State: Change and Continuity*, London, forthcoming; and Delia Davin, 'Gender and Population in the PRC', in Haleh Afshar, ed., *Women, State and Ideology: Studies from Africa and Asia*, London 1987.

31. Marilyn Young, 'Chicken Little in China: Women after the Cultural Revolution', in Kruks et al., *Promissory Notes*.

32. See E. Croll, 'New Peasant Family Forms in Rural China', *Journal of Peasant Studies*, July 1987; Delia Davin, 'Women, Work and Property in the Chinese Peasant Household of the 1980s', in Diane Elson, ed., *Male Bias in the Development Process*, Manchester 1990.

33. Delia Davin, 'Chinese Models of Development and Their Implications for Women', in Haleh Afshar, ed., *Women, Development and Survival in the Third World*, London 1991.

34. Delia Davin, 'The New Inheritance Law and the Peasant Household', *The Journal of Communist Studies*, vol. 3, December 1987.

35. E. Croll, *China After Mao*, London 1984.

36. More than one third of pregnancies ended in abortion in East Germany in 1989; in the West, the International Planned Parenthood Federation estimates that approximately 15–20 per cent of pregnancies end in abortion each year—about 85,000 of which are legal and another 45,000 illegal or performed abroad; *International Herald Tribune*, 15 May 1990.

37. *In These Times*, 21–27 March 1990.

38. From the paper presented to the fifth annual conference of the European Forum of Socialist Feminists held in Sweden in November 1989; and author's interview.

39. *In These Times*, 21–27 March 1990.

40. Tolstaya identifies women as the true soul of the nation—the trope beloved of nationalists and conservatives. See her enthusiastic review of Francine du Plessix Gray, *Soviet Women Walking the Tightrope*, New York 1990, in *New York Review of Books*, 31 May 1990. For a critical response to du Plessix Gray's portrait of Russian women, see the review by K. van den Heuvel in *The Nation*, 4 June 1990.

41. This was also happening in the GDR in 1989. It is interesting to note that Soviet miners striking in Siberia demanded crèches and shorter working hours so that they could fulfil their family responsibilities.

42. Lepa Mladjenovic, 'Summary on Women's Movement in Yugoslavia' [sic],

presented to the workshop on women's movements, Institute of Social Studies, The Hague, May 1990.

43. Programme of the East German Independent Women's Association, translated by Barbara Einhorn and published in *East European Reporter*, vol. 4, no. 2, Summer 1990.

44. Irene Dolling, 'Between Hope and Helplessness—Women in the GDR after "The Turning Point"', mimeograph.

45. Larisa Kuznetsova quoted in *In These Times*, 21–27 March 1990. See also du Plessix Gray, and C. Hansson and K. Liden, *Moscow Women*, London 1980, for ample illustration of the strength of such views among Soviet women. Maternalist and essentializing movements have always posed particular difficulties for feminists, and yet they are among the most common forms of female collective action. In Latin America, for example, women, often in the poorer communities, have been involved in struggles for basic needs provision, citizenship rights, and for other goals such as peace and democracy. Movements of this kind are closely identified with particular social constructions of femininity and motherhood, and the women who participate in these actions often see their politics as a natural extension of their roles in the family, and as based on primordial, intrinsically feminine sentiments. The goals of these movements are usually formulated in altruistic terms rather than as ones designed to advance the particular interests of the actors. In most of these cases, women identify their interests with the household, the welfare of its members, and its conditions of existence in the community. However limited in practice, essentializing movements based on motherhood are not by definition incompatible with all forms of feminism—it depends on their goals, and whether, in defending or celebrating motherhood, they challenge the social devaluation and subordination associated with it.

46. N. Zakharova et al., 'The Women's Question'.

6

The Ends of Cold War

Fred Halliday

The events of the latter half of 1989 represent an earthquake in world politics. They have restated, in a dramatic form, the most neglected facet of political life, one spurned in east as much as in west, namely the capacity of the mass of the population to take sudden, rapid and novel political action after long periods of what appears to be indifference. In their speed and import and the uncertainties they unleash, they can only be compared to a war, in which all established expectations and plans are swept aside, in the face of novel, and irrefutable, realities. Neither Left nor Right can claim credit for this turn of events, even as both seek to claim vindication from it. The Right began in 1989, the year of revolutionary anniversaries, proclaiming that revolutions were a thing of the past. The Left has been confounded by the popular rejection of socialism, and the espousal of nationalism, predominant throughout the eastern bloc states. This is a time not only for major changes in the world situation, but for a re-examination of (often implicit) fundamentals by the socialist movement.

It is in this, comprehensively uncertain and confusing, context that, from both sides of the former divide, voices can be heard saying that the Cold War is over and that we are entering an epoch of greater security and, to use a modish term, interdependence. More attention has been focused on Europe where the initially separate processes of integration in the West, leading up to 1992, and disintegration of the Soviet bloc in the East, have now joined, linked by geography, in the search for a new 'security' architecture and the bridging issue of German unity. Whatever Cold War means, events of the past few months have underlined the fact that, throughout the four frozen decades that have passed, the core issue, the central terrain of rivalry, has been Europe, and the socio-political system prevailing there.

Yet, for all its current European emphasis, this process concerns more than Europe: even in its simplest form, this assertion of an end to Cold War results from more than the collapse of the Eastern European political system and the expectations generated by perestroika. The European 1989 was preceded by another transitional year of perhaps equal importance, the Third World 1988, the year in which, in some dozen conflicts of Asia, Africa and Latin America, processes of nego- tiation, encouraged by the great powers, began to take effect: in Cambodia, Afghanistan, the Gulf, the Horn of Africa, Angola, the Sahara, Nicaragua and elsewhere. The importance of the Third World in this process and in the prospects for East–West relations in the 1990s needs no defence: while Europe has been largely at peace since 1945, over 140 conflicts of an anti-colonial, inter-state, class and ethnic character have raged in the Third World. Trieste and Berlin apart, the major East–West crises have been in the Third World: beginning with Azerbaijan in 1946, through China, Korea, Indo-China, Suez, the Congo, Cuba, down to the 'regional conflicts' of the 1980s. The casualty figures speak for themselves. Over twenty million people are believed to have died in these conflicts. In Europe the only comparably sanguinary encounter was the Greek civil war, in which some eighty thousand lost their lives.

Meanings of Cold War

Before examining these changes and their place in modern history, and before approaching the claim that the Cold War is over, it may be clarifying to pose two anterior questions, namely what the term Cold War means and what its underlying dynamics may have been. Despite its apparently modern, academic and journalistic, provenance, the term actually has a curious prehistory: coined by Don Juan Manuel, a fourteenth-century Spanish writer, to denote the unending rivalry of Christians and Arabs in Spain, it was reinvented by the American financier and diplomat Bernard Baruch, who claimed to have heard it from a vagrant sitting on a bench in Central Park sometime in 1946. This casual origin has not helped precision and has meant that the term 'Cold War' can be used in at least two ways. One is to refer to particular periods of intense confrontation between the two major postwar blocs, and in particular to the years of the late 1940s and early 1950s, the First Cold War, and those from the very late 1970s through to late 1988, the Second Cold War. The other usage of Cold War is to denote the under- lying rivalry of 'Communism' and capitalism itself, which began in 1917 and which, as a result of World War Two, became the dominant, consti- tutive divide in world affairs.

This second usage of the term touches upon much broader questions of interpretation and analysis in international relations. In general terms it can be said that in the literature on Cold War and East–West conflict there are four broad explanations of why the two blocs have conflicted as they have. For one school, associated with conventional 'realist' and strategic thinking, East–West rivalry is but another version of traditional great power conflict, to be explained by balance of power and other considerations. Ideology is seen as only an expression of this strategic interaction, and differences in internal composition of these societies as an analytic irrelevance. A second school, common amongst liberal writers, locates the conflict at the level of policy mistakes, missed opportunities and misperceptions on both sides: in this view, the conflict was avoidable—better communication in the period after 1945 or in the late 1970s could have avoided both Cold War I and Cold War II. A third school argues that what appear to be international rivalries are the product of factors within these societies, that is, of political and economic factors that push the states in question to compete with each other. Many analyses of Cold War II, in particular, stressed the extent to which political factors within the USA and USSR, and the uncontrolled dynamic of the arms race itself, caused this more recent confrontation to mature. The appearance of inter-bloc or inter-systemic conflict masked a homology, with both sides using and benefiting from the contest within their own domains of domination. This, in variant forms, is an argument common amongst left-wing writers critical of both the USA and USSR, such as E.P. Thompson, Mary Kaldor, Michael Cox, Noam Chomsky and André Gunder Frank. For them Cold War itself is a 'system', rather than a competition between two systems.

No one can deny that each of the first three of these explanations can cast light on the course of East–West relations: there were elements of traditional great power rivalry, misperception, and domestic determination. The argument of inter-systemic rivalry has been weakened in its own right because it has been espoused as ideology, in anti-Communist 'freedom' versus 'totalitarianism' form on the right, and in dogmatic 'two camps' form within the Soviet bloc. One of the powerful incentives for critics of Cold War to deny its inter-systemic character has been the desire to break with these competing, but homologous, simplifications. But the argument being suggested here is that on their own the three explanations mentioned are not sufficient to explain the character, duration and depth of the Cold War. What gave it its particular strength, beyond these conventional features of international conflict, was its inter-systemic character, the fact that it expressed the rivalry of two different social, economic and political systems. Each hoped to prevail on a world scale, to produce a homogeneous order within states, and each denied the legitimacy of the other, even as they were compelled to enter into diplomatic and other relations, not least because of the threat of nuclear weapons.

It need not escape mention that if, in the early 1980s, this argument had to be presented at an abstract or at least immanent level, events of the last few years have vindicated it in practice. What follows is a claim that 1989 has been the test of theories of Cold War: the jury is no longer out. The 'end' of Cold War, in the broader sense, was systemic homogeneity, and the target was the socio-economic and political character of the core states of each bloc.

A Triple Historical Context

The claim that the Cold War is over is, therefore, an ambiguous one, depending on the sense in which the term is used. To answer whether and in what sense it is over requires some examination of the three historical contexts within which the changes of 1988–89 may be said to lie. The first, most evident for Third World conflicts and the arms race, is that the detente of the late 1980s marks an end to what has been termed the Second Cold War, that is, the period of intense US–Soviet rivalry and acrimony that began around 1979 and lasted through Gorbachev's advent to power in 1985 until the Iceland summit of 1986. The term 'Cold War' was used in this context, by analogy with the first Cold War of the late 1940s and early 1950s, to denote a period not of hot war, nor of normal peacetime, but of confrontation and alarm, short of all-out military engagement. There are many issues in dispute about Cold War II; but it was arguably comparable to the First Cold War and, like it, involved non-violent confrontation in Europe and multiple and violent conflicts in the Third World.

The second significance of the late 1980s is that they mark an end to the postwar system prevailing in Europe. This applies most obviously to the division of Europe and, by extension, to Germany. The Warsaw Pact and even NATO will have greatly reduced functions, if they survive at all. With reasonable confidence it can be asserted that in the course of the 1990s the current upheavals will produce a new order west of the Soviet frontier. Germany will be reunited, possibly within a matter of months, and functioning multiparty systems and capitalist economies will develop throughout Eastern Europe. Whatever internal uncertainties these countries may face, the international pressures on them—for example, diplomacy, finance—will push them in this direction and steer their transition. The change will be more complicated than it was in the Western European anomalies of the 1970s, Spain and Portugal: alterations of political system are obviously easier than those of socio-economic and ideological structure. But there is little doubt that such a transition can and will occur.

This change in Eastern Europe is accompanied by, and itself compounds, another alteration in the postwar system, namely the end of the bipolar system and in particular of the system dominated by what appeared to be two so-called superpowers. The result of 1989, epitomized in the Malta summit, held amidst the wreckage of the Communist regimes in Eastern Europe, is that there is now only one 'superpower', the USA. The USSR has lost its leverage in Europe, with the collapse of the Warsaw Treaty Organization, is weakened and preoccupied by economic and social crisis, and is not able to compete with the USA or the West more generally in the military and economic spheres. The USSR is now little more than a major continental power, without a supportive alliance system. The illusion of 'rough parity', as Brezhnev liked to call it, is no longer sustainable.

This postwar system is often called that of Yalta, on the assumption that the February 1945 summit in the Crimea actually established it. It is on this basis that those who reject the system have blamed the Western powers for 'agreeing to' Soviet demands. In reality, however, the pattern of peacetime Europe had already been fixed two years earlier, and somewhat to the north-east, in the battles of Stalingrad and Kursk, when the Red Army finally broke Hitler's forces. There was no 'arguing with' Stalingrad: Yalta merely recognized the balance of forces then existing in Europe. Roosevelt and Churchill could no more have altered this than the current British government can guarantee the post-1997 system of government in Hong Kong. Critics of Yalta also tend to overlook the significance of Soviet military power in another respect: the defeat of Hitler not only guaranteed Soviet control of Eastern Europe, but also enabled the re-establishment of democratic government in Western Europe. At a time when all in the Soviet past is being sneered at, not least within the USSR itself, it needs recalling just what the strategic arithmetic of 1944–45 reflected—the 80 German divisions on the eastern front, with only 20 on the western to say nothing of the comparative casualty figures of the Soviet and Western armies. It is on this historic basis that both parts of modern Europe were built. Without Stalingrad a Nazi regime might still be in power, not only in Berlin and Warsaw, but in Paris and Amsterdam as well. All the good things that may now follow—1992, the common European home, the benign oneiric world of the Eurovision song contest—are being constructed on foundations laid by the Red Army.

The Versailles Mould

It is not, however, only the systems and conflicts of the post-1945 period that now appear to be in question, for the upheavals of 1989 have placed in question not only Yalta and Potsdam, but also much of what was agreed at an earlier postwar conference, that of Versailles. As much as anything, the explosion in Europe takes us back to the period of World War One, and in some ways before. There were at least three aspects of Versailles, each of which is now in question. The first, often overlooked today, was the reallocation of colonial territories: two at least of those, Namibia and Palestine, have remained arenas of conflict to the present day. Namibia now seems to have reached a resolution, to become the 170th sovereign state in the contemporary world. The fate of Palestine remains undecided, despite changes in both Israeli and Palestinian opinion. The second significance of Versailles was the establishment of a post-imperial order in Europe itself: four empires lost their European domains—the Ottoman, the Russian, the Austro-Hungarian and, in a separate but none the less conjoined process often forgotten in these islands, the British. The result was the independence of several new European nations, among them the three Baltic states, Finland, Poland, Hungary, Czechoslovakia, Yugoslavia, Albania, Ireland. Germany was subjugated and in part demilitarized. In the mid 1980s it might have appeared that much of that system remained: Germany, which had temporarily broken its bonds in the 1930s, was still subjugated, and those national states that had survived World War Two, that is, all but the Baltic three, were secure.

The upheavals of the late 1980s have altered that: as in other matters, Ireland took the lead, being the first to challenge the post-1918 frontiers with the re-emergence of the Ulster issue in the late 1960s. What Ulster represents in comparative perspective is the failure of a post-World War One settlement to stick and the revival, on the basis of new economic difficulties and fresh political perspectives, of enmities that exploded in that period. Today others have caught up with Ulster in defiance of the verdicts of 1918–20 and with what promise to be even more violent consequences: in Kosovo, Bulgaria, the Caucasus—the latter, for all its remoteness, still part of geographic Europe. Who knows how long it will be before the Fermanaghs and Tyrones of Eastern and Central Europe are once again in the news: Macedonia, northern Epirus, Silesia, eastern Ukraine. From the Falls Road to Rosenheim and beyond, the solemn undertakings of Helsinki, to respect the frontiers of post-1918 and post-1945 Europe, have dwindling purchase.

Versailles was not, however, only concerned with reallocating colonies and redividing the map of Europe. As Arno Mayer has shown so well in his *Politics and Diplomacy of Peace-Making*, Versailles was equally concerned with another legacy of World War One, the Bolshevik Revolution. Much of anti-Communist Western strategy towards the USSR—from the first intervention through the Riga doctrines to postwar containment—was adumbrated at that initial gathering of the imperialist powers. For the collision of two world systems, later to be embodied in the bipolar conflict of the 1940s and beyond, itself had its origins in 1919. Amidst the ruins of the war to end all wars, 1919 saw the constitution of two rival international political systems, each based on a mixture of idealism and calculation: the League of Nations and the Communist International. By constituting a political and social system fundamentally different from and militantly opposed to the capitalist West, Lenin laid down the parameters of the later division of the world and its inherent competitions. That it did not emerge as the dominant feature of the world until 1945 was due to the relative weakness of the USSR up to World War Two. The interwar period was still one dominated by inter-capitalist conflict. But the underlying rivalry of the capitalist and socialist systems was already in place and has continued until the 1980s. Stalin dissolved the Comintern in 1943 to mollify Western leaders; but he did so only when he had in hand an instrument far more effective in spreading Soviet influence abroad, in the shape of the Red Army.

The changes of the last five years appear, however, to have brought this underlying asymmetry of capitalism and 'Communism' to an end, for the retreat of the USSR as a world power has gone together with an increased questioning of its internal system and ideology. The future of the USSR is far less certain than that of Eastern Europe; but a major and probably irreparable breach has been made in the economic and political system prevailing in the USSR since the 1920s. In international policy, Gorbachev has forsaken the commitment to competition with and opposition to the capitalist West, abandoning class struggle in the name of universal human values. Soviet officials now openly deny any conflict between the two systems or the validity of any traditional concept of imperialism. There is, as Fidel Castro so openly regrets, no longer a socialist camp. The semblance of an international Communist movement, which survived the Sino-Soviet dispute of 1960, no longer holds. Soviet policy in the Third World, without wholly discarding previous commitments, has become more and more conciliatory to the West. Soviet officials now tell Third World allies that the term 'solidarity' has been replaced by that of 'mutual interests'. But the internal changes are even more important, not only because they betoken an inexorable Soviet approximation to Western practices and values, and on Western terms, but also because they lock Soviet society and the

Soviet economy more completely into that of the West. In sum, the new course being charted by Gorbachev, however uncertain its future, represents a break with the historical legacy of the Bolshevik Revolution at home and abroad. It amounts to nothing less than the reorganization of the USSR on capitalist lines, socio-economic as well as political; within the space of a generation little may be left of the impact of 1917, beyond a general popular nostalgia for egalitarian distribution and a residual international role. The CPSU, even if it remains the ruling party, may resemble more the Mexican PRI than its previous form.

Class Struggle on an International Scale

It is now possible to return to the question with which we began, namely of whether the Cold War has ended. It is evident that this depends on which sense of Cold War is being used. In the first sense, it would appear plausible to suggest that the Cold War is over. Since the mid 1980s, relations between the USSR and the West have improved to such a point, and across such a wide range of issues, that it is difficult to see how a return to the climate of 1950 or 1983 is possible. There could be a dramatic change of policy in either capital—if Gorbachev is ousted by a nationalist-Brezhnevite coup, or if an unreconstructed Dankworth Quayle were, by some misadventure, individual or electoral, to come to occupy the Oval office. There could also be some major crisis, all the more dangerous for being unanticipated, over a regional issue: a repeat of Suez in 1956, or Cuba in 1962. But the degree of diplomatic and other interaction, and trust, between the two sides is such that even were such a crisis to erupt, perhaps in the Balkans or in Iran, the chances of its being contained would be high, and of its permanently undermining the current detente, and ushering in Cold War III, remote.

When we turn to the second meaning of Cold War, the situation is rather different. Here there appears to be a widespread temptation to recognize that the Cold War is ending, but to see this as a symmetrical, convergent process. Both blocs have faced difficulties in the Second Cold War and have been unable to prevail as they had hoped: the USA, seeking to outspend the USSR in the arms race, has run up the largest budget deficit in history, become the greatest debtor nation in the world, and continued to lose competitiveness to the Japanese and Germans. Equally there are those in the West and in the USSR who suggest that since the differences between capitalism and Communism have diminished, the internal changes within the Soviet bloc accompanying detente are an evolutionary process. Capitalism has changed and will continue to do so. But it is specious to present the outcome as one in which both systems were equally debilitated or in which current changes are symmetrical. For the end of the Cold War, in sense one, and the prevailing climate of detente in Europe and most of the Third World are being achieved not on the basis of a convergence of the two systems, or of a negotiated truce between them, but on the basis of the collapse of one in the face of the other. This means nothing less than the defeat of the Communist project as it has been known in the twentieth century and the triumph of the capitalist. This is so evidently the case that it provides retrospective validation of the inter-systemic interpretation of Cold War. The linkage of international change and relaxation of tension with the internal collapse of 'Communism' and the spread of capitalist relations into the former bloc states illustrates just how the course of inter-state rivalry correlated with internal, systemic difference. The course of recent events should, moreover, underline to those who ever doubted it the degree to which there did exist in the 'Communist' states a system based on different social and economic criteria. If all had been capitalist, or subject to the workings of the international capitalist market, there would have been no need for East–West conflict and no need now for radical reorganization of post-Communist societies.

This process is by no means complete. We do not yet know what the post-electoral map of Eastern Europe will look like, but few can believe that the existing Communist parties will remain in power, or even survive as major political forces: electoral marginalization, at 5 to 10 per cent, would seem their most likely fate. The situation in the USSR is still evolving, but what is striking is not only the USSR's inability to maintain its international alliance system, the erstwhile socialist camp, but also its lack of any plausible future for Soviet socialism itself. Whether the dénouement takes five years or fifty, whether it happens on an 'all-union' basis, within the existing USSR, or through the breakaway of constituent republics, whether it is peaceful or bloody, these we cannot know, although it would not be imprudent to fear the worst. The reality is that the Soviet system has lost its self-confidence, any sense of where it is going, of its own historical and ethical worth, and of its international role. The USSR is engaged in a healthy, long-overdue and public examination of its past and of the problems of Soviet society today. But this is not all. Abject denial of what it did achieve, even in World War Two, a naive overstatement of the virtues of Western capitalism, capitulation to all sorts of regressive ideologies of a nationalist, familialist and religious character, and an abandonment of the internationalist commitments that were one of the brighter sides of the Brezhnevite era, also characterize Soviet policy today. Gorbachev himself is, with great skill and commitment, steering the ship towards a port the character and very location of which he cannot enunciate. He is doing the best he can to give the

Bolshevik Revolution a soft landing: the alternatives—the stony regressions of Ligachev, the vapidities of the demagogue Yeltsin—provide even less of an answer.

In the Third World many states that in the 1970s were seen as socialist or at least 'of socialist orientation' are today imitating the USSR in economy and politics: Gorbachev has given them a contradictory injunction—to follow their own paths to socialism, and, at the same time, to 'learn from the international significance of perestroika'. Today 'states of socialist disorientation' might better describe their condition. At recent count, only five states in the world still adhered in political life to an orthodox model: Cuba, Albania, Vietnam, North Korea, China. All five of these are, of course, distinguished by the fact that they were the sites of indigenous revolutionary movements, with social bases and nationalist character, owing little to the Red Army. The four smaller ones are, however, increasingly on the defensive, unable to take the initiative in the face of increasing pressure from without. Cuba, Albania and North Korea are in political paralysis, of an ominous kind; Vietnam is adjusting and, with a solution in Cambodia, may be able to right itself. It is the last of the five, China, that poses the greatest problems, not least in the wake of Tiananmen Square. It is facile to blame that massacre only on old men, who will soon pass away: the organization, shooting and post-massacre repression have been perpetrated by younger cadres who have a stake in maintaining the system. But China will find it hard to resist international pressure in the long run, especially as its model must now look increasingly discomfited by developments in the USSR. As for those Third World parties espousing orthodox Communism and still not in power, they may be fated either to fail or to adjust: the Filipino New People's Army and Sendero Luminoso, the latter vaunting the imagined virtues of an earlier Mao and an idealized Enver Hoxha, would seem doomed to the first fate, the South African Communist Party and perhaps the Tigre Liberation Front would seem to have chosen the second. In India, the world's largest bourgeois democracy, the CPI(M), initially champion of an independent revolutionary line, has, in saluting the massacre of Beijing, encouraged its demise.

The failure of the Communist model to constitute a viable, internationally distinct bloc, and the historical reversal of the process that began in 1917, do not appear to be in doubt. The Cold War, in its broader historical sense, is continuing, but with the collapse of one of the two protagonists. In this sense, the apparent generosity of Western claims that the antagonism between the two is over conceals a triumphalist undertow. To speak in the language of 'old thinking', what we are now witnessing is class struggle on an international scale, as the superior strength of Western capitalism forces open the societies

partially closed to it for four or more decades. One has only to watch the
swift, decisive and methodical strangulation of the GDR by the python
of West German capitalism to see how this process is working, or the
asset-stripping acquisitions of Hungarian and Polish factories by
Western business.

Complexities of 'Stagnation'

Recognition of this fact does not, however, take us very far towards
answering other questions: what was it that led to this turn in the underlying Cold War and in particular why did it happen when it did? The
conventional answer is to say that the Communist system had 'failed':
that its economy had lost any dynamic, that it lost political appeal
because it was undemocratic, and that it could not match the West in the
range of areas that constitute international competition. There is some
truth in this, but it is important to set this failure in some context. First,
there is, in historical perspective, little correlation between the political
appeal of Communism and its democratic character. The period of
greatest repression in the USSR was not in the 1980s but in the 1930s: it
was then that Stalin killed millions of people, directly and through
neglect. Yet the industrial and military success of the Soviet system was
also achieved in that time, through the mobilization and support of the
Soviet population, and it was then too that Soviet Communism enjoyed
its greatest following in the West. This was also true of the Third World:
witness the revolutions in China and Vietnam in the 1940s. As late as
the 1970s, when 'stagnation' had set in at home, the Soviet model
command widespread support in newly independent African revolutionary states. The historical irony is that Communism has lost its
appeal just at the moment when it has demonstrated a new political
potential, an ability to change that theorists of totalitarianism and many
within the Soviet system had doubted.

At the economic level, a similar problem arises. It is conventional
now to state that the Soviet-style economies are a failure, and Soviet
writers themselves encapsulate this in the terms 'stagnation', *zastoi*, and
'slowing down', *zamedlenie*, applied to the Brezhnev period to cover an
allegedly interlocked range of issues—falling growth rates, technological
inferiority, industrial paralysis, social decay, ecological disaster. Yet this
picture is an overstated one. The fact is that in the postwar period as a
whole growth rates in the USSR, and the provision of a range of social
services, including housing, health and education, have improved
substantially. Overall Soviet living standards doubled between the end of
World War Two and the mid 1970s. By the standards of most people in

the world, the population of the USSR lives comparatively well: it is housed, shod, clothed, transported, cured, amused at standards that are better than those of most of Latin America, let alone Asia and Africa. The populations of Eastern Europe lived even better, in part, of course, through systematic subsidizing of their economies by the USSR.

On the international level, the situation is also mixed. It is worth recalling that when the Second Cold War began in the late 1970s it was common currency in the West that this was a result of a new Soviet strength in the world, manifested above all in greater strategic military power, and in an enhanced situation in the Third World. Soviet missiles, the strategic SS–18 and the intermediate range SS–20, had shifted the balance in Moscow's favour. In the Third World the wave of revolutions of the latter half of the 1970s marked the end of *pax americana* and a new Soviet international reach. Afghanistan was seen as the culmination of this new Soviet power. That many Soviet officials, including Brezhnev, appeared to believe this gave it added credibility. America was weak. The West was on the run. There was much talk of an end to 'US hegemony', on the Left and on the Right. A partial shift in America's relative position in some spheres was turned into an absolute loss of power, both vis-à-vis other capitalist competitors, such as Japan, and vis-à-vis the Soviet Union.

Much of this was nonsense, a deliberate exaggeration of Soviet power and a misrepresentation of developments in the Third World and in the nuclear field, serving to raise alarm and either, on the Left, obscure the continued dominance of the USA, or, on the Right, justify what turned out to be a new Western offensive against the USSR. None the less, the image of growing Soviet international strength in the 1970s was not entirely mythical or imagined: it corresponded to real advances in Soviet capabilities. In historical perspective it was not Khrushchev, Lenin or even Stalin who caused the greatest difficulties to the West outside Europe, but the much maligned Brezhnev. It was Soviet arms and support that enabled the triumph of the Vietnamese, and which greatly facilitated the victories in Mozambique, Angola and, via Cuba, in Nicaragua. Even in the late 1980s the consequences of that inter-nationalist commitment can be seen: despite the last-minute attempts of Western governments to claim credit for it, the dramatic turn of events in South Africa in 1990 owes not a little to long-term military support given to nationalist movements there, against Lisbon and Pretoria, in the 1960s and early 1970s. It is to Brezhnev, as much as anyone else outside South Africa itself, that credit for cracking the racist bloc should go.

The Terminal Crisis

The question therefore arises of why it was in the 1980s, when the
Soviet system was in an apparently sustainable position, that the final
collapse took place. This is an issue that bears on the analysis of Cold
War II produced a decade ago, since it was too rarely seen just how
brittle the overall Soviet position had become. In retrospect, this is, in
my view, the greatest weakness of my own analysis in *The Making of the
Second Cold War*. The assumption was that, even as Western assertions
of a new aggressive Soviet power were unfounded, the Soviet system as
a whole was sufficiently viable that it would continue to reproduce itself
as it then was in the USSR and other bloc countries. In part, this judgement was accurate. The Soviet system did not fail in any absolute sense:
its populations were not in revolt, its economies were providing an
adequate if restricted supply of goods. Levels of economic inequality
and crime were less than in developed capitalist states. Its historical
record was a fair one. It was showing considerable ability to adapt politically. Its international strength was greater than ever before. Yet the
fact is that by the end of the 1980s it was in what appeared to be a
terminal crisis, unable to defy capitalism internationally or to reproduce
itself at home.

As with any such process, and most obviously with the breakdown of
states after long war, it is possible to look back over what seem to be
years of stalemate and divine the sources of later breakdown. Two
obvious reasons for the collapse suggest themselves. The first, the classic
Marxist one that is too easily forgotten in current benign times, was that
in the early 1980s the West launched an offensive to weaken and
paralyse the Soviet Union. In the nuclear field, the USA explicitly went
for 'superiority' over the USSR. The West pushed ahead with its new
programmes, euphemistically described as 'modernization', and Reagan
further turned the screw by propounding and threatening to develop a
system of strategic defence that would have ended the policy of deterrence hitherto prevailing. In the Third World US intervention, at various
levels, ended the wave of revolutions: after that in Zimbabwe, in 1980,
there were no further such upheavals, either as a result of direct
repression, as in El Salvador, or through the diversion of revolutionary
processes by reform candidates, as in the Philippines, Haiti and South
Korea. At the same time, the 'Reagan Doctrine' was developed to justify
pressure on Third World revolutionary states: arms were sent to
guerrillas opposing pro-Soviet regimes in four states—Cambodia,
Afghanistan, Angola and Nicaragua. Washington developed a policy of
eroding Soviet power 'on the margin', meaning by this the Third World
socialist allies. Hundreds of thousands of people died and millions were

displaced from their homes as a result of these counter-revolutionary wars of the 1980s. The outcome of the February 1990 election in Nicaragua was, above all else, a result of such pressure: it represented an exhaustion, after 30,000 people had died at the hands of the *contra*. This counter-revolution was distinct from those in Chile, Guatemala and Indonesia not because it was peaceful, but because the massacres occurred before, not after, the overthrow of the revolutionary regime.

The second argument, found in both Soviet and Western writings, focuses on an internal process, an entropy. This is that in some sense the Communist model ran out of steam in the 1980s, exhausted itself after four to eight decades of dynamism. The most obvious signs of this were the economic gridlock that appeared to have beset the USSR and other Comecon states and the attendant social and ecological problems. The sources of growth previously available had been used up: surplus agricultural populations, initial forms of industrialization, Western loans and selectively applied technology. Contemporary with this economic stagnation, the ecological problems produced by decades of intensive pillage of nature manifested themselves, from the pollution of rivers in southeast GDR to the inexorable contraction of the Aral Sea. Social problems also emerged out of decades of neglect: falling birth-rates, declining life expectancy, growing crime. Above all, there was an exhaustion of political credit: historically, the Communist movement had derived impetus from specific events—the Bolshevik Revolution itself, and the defeat of Fascism. Later successes—the initial lead in space exploration after 1957, the spread of Communist and socialist ideas in the Third World—appeared to confirm this forward march. From the 1960s onwards, however, this prospect of historical advance was checked: the building of the Berlin Wall in 1961, the crushing of the Czechoslovak experiment in 1968 marked the end of that optimism.

It took perhaps two decades or more for it to become evident not just that the 'Communist' system had lost its dynamic but, and this is the crucial point, that it was not going to regain it. The last great expression of Communist optimism was that of Khrushchev, with his triumphalist perspectives on peaceful coexistence proclaimed at the 22nd Party Congress of 1961. Three decades later that vision appears to be empty, based on an exaggeration of the potential of Soviet society, and an unfounded belief in historical determinism. Not only did the 'transition' fail to complete itself, but it was unable to retain the territory it had gained.

An International Failure

These factors alone, subsumed under the Gorbachevian term 'stagnation', cannot, however, provide an adequate explanation of the collapse of 'Communism' in the late 1980s. 'Stagnation' is a simplistic term implying a degree of homogeneity within the 'Communist' states that is invalid. The degree of stagnation was not so great, or so comprehensive, that it would have led to such an outcome. Indeed, on purely internal criteria, it *was* quite plausible to imagine that the Soviet system, in the USSR itself and in the bloc, could have continued for years and decades to come, liberalizing to a degree but retaining the essential features of domestic and international orthodoxy. In other words, endogenous factors on their own cannot account for the final collapse. What was determinant, and what put stagnation into a wholly different light, was the global context, and in particular the relative record of 'Communism' compared with its competitor, advanced capitalism. This, above all, determined the events of the late 1980s.

At the theoretical level, Communist parties had operated with two assumptions that were shown to be fatally flawed: one was of the inevitable crisis and secular decline of capitalism; the other was of the ability of the Communist countries to constitute an alternative, rival and self-contained bloc, independent of the capitalist world. It was on this basis that many Communists who recognized the apparent superiority of capitalism in the postwar epoch could still retain their original optimism, in the belief that capitalist success was either a mirage, a result of 'manipulation' (which certainly exists) alone, or of a temporary penultimate speculative boom: if the socialist camp could hold on long enough, they argued, then the capitalist world would enter its crisis, a new socialist dynamic would emerge, and the initial scenario, long delayed and diverted, would none the less be played out.

In fact, the postwar epoch disproved both assumptions and, in so doing, pointed to what is the central failing of Marxism. It is commonplace to say that Marxism's greatest mistake was the underestimation of nationalism: this is a dubious claim, since liberalism also did this, and it depreciates the justified scepticism about nationalism that runs through the socialist tradition. Marx's scorn for nationalist illusions and Lenin's denunciation of 'nationalist bickering' seem rather apposite today. The greatest mistake of Marxist and socialist thinking was not the underestimation of nationalism nor the overestimation of socialism and its potential but rather the underestimation of capitalism itself, both in terms of its potential for continued expansion and in terms of its lack of an inherent catastrophist teleology: in the apt words of Bill Warren, '"Late capitalism", late for what?' In terms of economic performance, the advanced capitalist countries enjoyed an unparalleled period of growth in the postwar epoch, and the downturns were short-lived and relatively shallow. While income inequalities continued and indeed grew, the majority of the population in these countries enjoyed rising real standards of living. This economic success was matched by political success: the completion, in the postwar epoch, of the extension of universal suffrage in the advanced capitalist states, the acceptance by the overwhelming majority of the populations of these countries of the legitimacy of capitalist democracy, and the shedding, in a remarkably short space of time, of formal colonial control over Asia, Africa and the Caribbean. While capitalism has signally failed to contain the immiseration of a part of the Third World's population, especially in Africa and the Asian sub-continent, the spread of capitalist democracy to much of the Third World has proved another dimension of strength: in addition to the limitations of Third World revolutionary regimes, the evident capacity of capitalist economics *and* politics has served to reduce the appeals of socialism even in those regions where, in the postwar era, it has enjoyed greatest success.

The link between the political and the economic was consolidated by a change in the character of capitalist hegemony itself, that is, in the mechanisms by which the rule of capital was maintained and produced, and in particular in the values and institutions that were seen to embody the legitimacy of the system. As old social barriers and identities eroded, an increasing role came to be taken by forms of activity associated with communications and consumer culture: the power of TV, pop music and fashion was always dependent upon other forms of power, but it none the less acquired a greater relative weight within Western society as a whole. This was an economic-political combination in which the mass of everyday needs appeared to be met by the existing system and in which a degree of choice, exaggerated and massaged as it was, prevailed. The whole image of a socialism 'catching up with and overtaking' capitalism was doubly flawed: first, it was not able to catch up even in the narrowest, most traditional, quantitative terms such as industrial output or food production; but, secondly, the very terms of the competition, the criteria according to which the competition was being judged, not least by the populations ruled over by Communist parties, were themselves changing.

This success within capitalism was therefore one to which 'Communist' society was especially vulnerable. It could not compete economically, in terms of output and technological change. It could compete even less in the newly promoted domains of consumerism and popular culture. Of greatest concern to Soviet leaders was the import of this for the most vital area of competition, above all, military competition:

matching the West in quantity let alone technological quality became harder and harder. 'Communism' could not compete politically, since its initial revolutionary successes failed to develop into functioning, alternative, systems of democracy: 'politbureaucratic' dictatorship, to use Bahro's phrase, prevailed throughout the system. Even less could it compete in the new fields pioneered by capitalist advance: consumer culture on the one hand, the third industrial revolution and the spread of information technology on the other. Nor, and this is in many ways the fatal point, could 'Communist' societies constitute an alternative international bloc. In terms of economic activity, the Soviet bloc never constituted a dynamic trading bloc capable of rivalling the West. It always occupied a defensive, subaltern place in the international economy. It lagged behind, and was condemned to copy, in the field of technology. The Soviet bloc was simply too weak and its internal mechanisms too rigid to allow of such a development.

At the same time, the countries of the bloc could not insulate themselves from the capitalist world. In the most obvious field of all, communications, it became more and more possible for people within Communist states to hear and see what was happening in the outside world. The impact of West German TV in much of the GDR and Czechoslovakia, or of Finnish TV in Estonia, were examples of this. Pop music provided a direct means of reaching the young in the Communist world. With higher levels of education and increasing opportunities for travel the comparison between living standards, and political conditions, in the Communist and advanced capitalist states became more evident. It was this comparative, rather than absolute, failure that provided the basis for the collapse of the late 1980s: not only did it foment discontent with a system that was seen as bankrupt, but it destroyed the belief that in some broader secular sense the Communist system could never catch up with, let alone overtake, the West.

The international determination of this crisis was not, however, only a result of the failure of the Soviet bloc to compete: the very crisis itself had key international dimensions. First, the overthrow of Communist Party rule in Eastern Europe, for all that it was made from below, would have been impossible without the change in Soviet policy propounded in late 1988, according to which the USSR would not intervene to maintain these regimes in power. The old politburos could not go on ruling in the old way: Gorbachev's change of policy was the indispensable precondition for the changes to occur. Secondly, as in other revolutionary situations, the demonstration effect of successful cases was of great importance, with each taking the process a stage further: first, Hungarian liberalization from above, then the election of the Solidarity government in Poland, then the (comparatively) slow erosion of the SED through mass emigration in the summer and later demonstrations, then the much speedier Czech upheaval, and finally the sudden, bloody change in Romania. The international dimension was, moreover, significant in a third and in this case distinctive way, namely in providing a stimulus to the upheavals from the capitalist bloc: most postwar revolutions had taken place against the West, and paid the price of defying the hegemonic bloc; the revolts of 1989 were against the rule of Communist parties, and were facilitated in their course and subsequent stabilization by the encouragement and welcome they received or which the populations believed they would receive from the West, in diplomatic, military and financial terms.

Alternatives, Real and Imaginary

Several consequences follow from this comparative failure of the 'Communist' experiment. The first is that the conventional alternative to Brezhnevite orthodoxy, namely 'socialism with a human face', in the sense in which this was meant by Dubček in 1968 is, and was always, implausible. For what 'socialism with a human face' meant was a maintenance of the Communist Party in power, but pursuing more humane and democratic policies. This belief in democracy plus party control is a constant of liberal communist politics: from Khrushchev and the Prague Spring in the 1960s, to Bahro's *Alternative* in the 1970s, to the initial formulations of perestroika after 1985. In a world where the alternative attraction of a capitalist system, and a functioning capitalist multiparty option, existed, that is, with the possibility of the Communist Party being voted out of power entirely, such an option was a half-way house, an unsustainable compromise. All the talk of mixed economies and the like in the West obscures the fact that political alternation takes place within a relatively unchanged socio-economic system: it is possible to vary the former once every four or five years; it is not possible to reverse out of one socio-economic system to the other in the same way. Either the Communist Party, with a human or inhuman face, had to insist that it alone ruled, or it had to allow the possibility of being removed from power once and for all. The implication of this is that arguments to the effect that the system could have been saved in the 1960s are of dubious validity: if Khrushchev had continued and been more consistent, or if Brezhnev had not invaded Czechoslovakia, the system would still have been subjected to pressures from outside that would have denied it a stable, reformed, Communist trajectory.

The second consequence concerns the fate of 'Communism' outside the Soviet bloc, and in particular in Western Europe. It has long been a claim of liberal or reform Communism that the imposition of political dictatorship in the name of socialism in the East has inhibited the development of Communism in the West. A political opening in the East would, it was claimed, make it easier for Eurocommunist and other currents. The historical record rather contradicts this: as already noted, Communist parties were at the peak of their influence in the West under Stalin, and have suffered a steady erosion ever since, *pari passu* with the liberalizations of Khrushchev and Gorbachev. Indeed the final crisis of Communist orthodoxy in Eastern Europe in 1989 seems to have led to a new round of crisis within the West European Communist parties. The reasons for this paradox are not hard to find. It is not so much that Communist success in the West was based on admiration, covert or overt, for belligerent dictatorship in the East, a frisson of authoritarian identification, though few could deny this played its part, but rather that it rested on the belief in a viable, historically progressive, alternative. It is the destruction of that belief in the 1980s which has undermined the credibility of Communism in the West. The other reason for the apparently paradoxical record of Communist parties is a little harder to specify: it pertains to the fact that an essential precondition for any viable socialism in the West is a degree of combativity towards the very system it is challenging, namely capitalism. Whatever their other faults, the traditional Communist parties embodied that quality. What is most marked about the Communist parties of Western Europe today is not their greater criticism of the Soviet past, but their lack of any radical hostility to capitalism itself.

New Era, Old Problems

This turning point in modern history, and unravelling of the consequences of World War One and World War Two, is being received with almost universal rejoicing, in east as well as west. The end of the Cold War, the onset of a new era of international harmony, even in some neo-Hegelian sense the end of history are being promised. The least that can be said is that if we are to return to a pre-1914 world then there are some obvious dangers. It was that world of inter-capitalist conflict undistracted by the existence of a socialist rival that gave rise to decades of colonial plunder and the great war itself. It ushered in what others have called the European civil war of 1914–45, but which was, as any Chinese or Vietnamese will point out, rather more than that. The anxieties expressed about German and Japanese power hardly promise a calm twenty-first century. More immediately, there is the growing prominence of another, less tractable challenge to international peace, namely ethnic and communal conflict. The collapse of Soviet power has been accompanied by the outburst of nationalism and ethnic conflict throughout Eastern Europe and the USSR itself; simultaneously, much of the post-colonial Third World is riven by ethnic violence that shows no sign of coming to an end. Indeed if one of the hallmarks of the late 1980s has been the ending of Cold War, the other has been the resurgence of nationalist sentiment in much of the developed as well as developing world: from the chauvinist excesses of sporting occasions in Britain to the revival of great power arrogance in the USA, Japan and Germany it has become a commonplace of politics in the developed world. It lurks too in other contexts—from the misplaced indulgence of religious bigotry masquerading as anti-racism shown by sections of the liberal intelligentsia, to the pursuit of 'national traditions' by erstwhile components of the international Communist movement.

Underlying these political conflicts and trends there lies the most fundamental issue of all, one which the Communist movement was founded to confront and which is now placed in question by the end of the Cold War and the suffocation of the 'Communist' bloc attendant upon it. This is the question of political possibilities, and in particular the degree to which the model of advanced capitalism now on the ascendancy is open to criticism in the name of a desirable, and plausible, alternative. The critique of capitalism was the starting point of Marxism and socialism and is the point to which, quite properly, that tradition can now return. It is striking how, amidst the triumph of consumer capitalism and the collapse of 'Communism', the possibility of aberrations is now being submerged in the name of a new international political and cultural conformity; all aspire to, and supposedly endorse, a composite transnational utopia, distilled from, and defined by, the lifestyles of California, Rheinland-Westfalen and Surrey. That this new utopia contains profound structures of inequality, defined on class, sex, race and regional bases, is evident, but repressed in most prevailing public discourses. The determination with which this utopia is projected and defended—from the reporting of events to the presentation of statistics—would alone suggest that it is an artificial and vulnerable construct. Its prevalence means, however, that alternatives are excluded and denigrated.

In the precipitate retreat from orthodox Communism, much that was positive and necessary is being abandoned: a commitment to social justice, insistence on the exclusion of religion from public life, the promotion by the state of equality of men and women, internationalism and solidarity, to name but four. The assertion of a need to intervene to plan and direct economic activity is now almost universally rejected, at a time when the cosmic destructiveness of production has never been more evident. What is occurring on these fronts in the 'Communist' countries is not an advance, but a recidivism of epochal proportions. One can vainly search the columns of a, in other respects, refreshing *Moscow News* to find mention of anything of merit in the Bolshevik record and tradition. In the advanced capitalist world, there has been a disappearance of credible political and social agencies for change. The working class has been to a considerable degree marginalized and fragmented, its organizational and legal powers cut back. The 'new social movements', forces that identified and challenged hitherto denied forms of oppression but whose coherence and potential were much overrated, are now dispersed. New social forces of the radical right, both political and religious, are evident in most of these states. Equally, there is a paucity of ideas as to how contemporary society should and could be organized on a different political and economic basis. Neither from social-democratic parties in the West, nor from Gorbachevite reforms in the East, does a clear and credible critique of present-day capitalism emerge.

This is a curious and ominous development, a triumph of ideological simplification. Capitalism it was, after all, which brought us in the nineteenth century the massacres of indigenous populations on three continents, and two world wars in this century. Capitalism it is which has signally failed to diffuse its wealth so as to reduce the gap between rich and poor on a world scale, and which still conducts its daily business on the basis of adolescent frenzy and inanity in the marketplace, now brought to us every hour in the guise of 'financial news'. The Communist movement was an attempt to present a challenge to that system and to erect an alternative, more desirable and viable, that would replace the anarchy and viciousness of capitalism with a more humane and rationally directed form of economic activity. For seven decades it has presented such a challenge, but in the end it appears to have foundered. In the form in which it emerged, it is, in the eyes of the overwhelming mass of the populations of East and West, neither more desirable nor more viable than advanced capitalism. The relentless flood of young people from the GDR to the West, rejecting an oppression and constriction identified with socialism, contains a momentous historical lesson. Even in the area of greatest success, military competition, it was only able to compete partially and intermittently.

It is perhaps premature to draw up a measured historical materialist assessment of what the Communist experiment has represented. It was a partial, impatient and distorted challenge to the dominant system of our epoch, one whose development and demise only confirm Marx's initial instinct that a challenge to capitalism would have to erupt and consolidate itself on a global level if it were to succeed. In the name of exaggerated economic and political potential, and of a mistaken teleology, the Communist societies presented themselves as being a form of society superior to and historically beyond capitalism. 'Non-capitalist' they certainly were, but 'post-capitalist' they were not: in many respects they resembled forms of early capitalism, with their reliance on military and repressive power, their failure to generate technological change, and their lack of functioning mechanisms of international economic integration. After decades of partial success, they now appear to have succumbed to a mode of production and a political system far stronger than them, and which does not appear to be headed for any predetermined exhaustion or crisis.

What this necessitates, and provides the opportunity for, is a reassessment and realignment not only of Marxism and the socialist movement but of the radical and revolutionary traditions within Western society as a whole. A keen student of political upheavals in Germany, and an unwavering believer in the determinance of socio-economic factors, Marx at least would not have been so surprised by the events of the recent past. After its long and painful historical detour, the Communist tradition can now return to its point of origin, the critique of, and challenge to, capitalist political economy. The central question is whether, and how far, there does exist an alternative to the predominant model of capitalism and, if so, what social agencies can be mobilized democratically to create and maintain it. Much of the reassessment of classical Marxism has taken the form of building or re-establishing links with contemporary forms of resistance hitherto separate from the Marxist tradition—social democracy, cast out in 1914, and currents of the post-1945 epoch, amongst them feminism, ecology and anti-racism. Of equal importance, however, is the recognition of how relevant pre-Marxist radical currents may be, and especially so in the face of the resurgent challenges of the time, clericalism, nationalism and irrationalism. As much as the estranged cousins of the twentieth century, it is important to bring back the supposedly discarded *aufgehobene* ancestors of the eighteenth. If the end of Cold War does nothing else but clarify that question, and emancipate socialism from false and deterministic answers and doomed loyalties, it will have prepared a substantial agenda for the twenty-first century. The task of reflection, theoretical and political, upon the events of the late 1980s has only just begun and analysis of their import must, of necessity, be provisional. The one thing that cannot be underestimated is the challenge that they pose.

7

The Ends of Cold War: A Rejoinder

Edward Thompson

While I sympathize with Fred Halliday's intentions in 'The Ends of Cold War',[1] I must disagree sharply both with its method and execution. No doubt he has been trapped by the pressure to make instant commentary (his lecture on the events of October to December 1989 in Central and Eastern Europe was delivered on 5 March 1990, and presumably written in February), and others (including myself) who were persuaded to commit ourselves too hastily to print may be criticized with equal force. But let us look at the difficulties and also at the silences and theoretical refusals of Halliday's text.

First, in the interest of clarification, I must contest Halliday's simplistic description of four 'schools' of analysis of the Cold War: one, conventional and 'realist'; two, liberal and preoccupied with contingencies; and a third school, with which I am associated, along with Mary Kaldor, Michael Cox, Noam Chomsky and André Gunder Frank (a somewhat disparate group), which is supposed to argue that the 'appearance of inter-bloc or inter-systemic conflict masked a homology, with both sides using, and benefiting from, the contest within their own domains of domination ... For them Cold War is itself a "system", rather than a competition between two systems.' And there is a fourth school, which is Fred Halliday's, which analysed (and analyses) the Cold War in terms of its 'inter-systemic character, the fact that it expressed the rivalry of two different social, economic and political systems.'

This clumpish grouping of 'schools', which are then glossed not in their own language but in Halliday's, is an imprecise method of intellectual argument. We have had too much of this overconfident sorting into supposed 'positions' in the past two decades. I have never used the term 'homology' in my life and I am not sure what it means. The term

which I used several times, both in an article on 'Exterminism',[2] and in
response to critics subsequently,[3] was 'reciprocal' and 'reciprocity'. This
disclosed not a categorical definition but a historical process of mutual
formation: reciprocity (and mutual incitement) in weaponry, ideological
hostilities, internal security, control of satellites and client states, and so
forth.

There are good reasons why this clarification matters. To arrange a
'homology' and 'inter-systemic' conflict as opposed analyses of two
different 'schools' is to confuse the fact that both views can be (although
need not be) compatible with each other. In my own view there have
certainly been inter-systemic conflicts which at a certain point (and in a
concrete historical process) became systematized—perhaps after
1948?—giving rise to a *state* of cold war as itself a 'self-reproducing'
dynamic condition. As I said in my banned Dimbleby Lecture, 'Beyond
the Cold War' (1981), the Cold War 'is about itself'. Borrowing
Pasternak's words, I argued that the Cold War should be seen as 'the
consequences of consequences'; it had 'broken free from the occasions
at its origin, and has acquired an independent inertial thrust of its own'.
But in so far as the Cold War became itself a 'system' (Halliday's term
and not mine), it need not utterly dissolve prior inter-systemic rivalries,
but may incorporate these as part of the very driving force of ideological
incitements. So Halliday's 'schools' are spurious, and we are back with
the need for more precise (and also more empirically informed) analysis.

Categoric Systems or Reciprocal Process?

Halliday supposes that the events of recent months have settled the
argument on his side. He does not tell us exactly what his two 'systems'
are, except that one is capitalism and the other is not-capitalism. He
cannot now use *socialism* or *communism* without embarrassment, but
his major categorical revision of the other system is to place 'Communism' in quotation marks. His article is a 'claim that 1989 has been
the test of theories of Cold War'. And he asserts triumphantly that 'the
jury is no longer out', since the autumn 1989 events prove that the 'end'
(that is, aim) of Cold War was 'systematic homogeneity and the target
was the socio-economic and political character of the core states of each
bloc'. He returns to this argument on page 86 and his position should
be inspected with care: 'For the end of the Cold War ... and the
prevailing climate of detente in Europe and most of the Third World are
being achieved not on the basis of a convergence of the two systems, or
of a negotiated truce between them, but on the basis of the collapse of
one in the face of the other. This means nothing less than the defeat of

the Communist project as it has been known in the twentieth century and the triumph of the capitalist. This is so evidently the case that it provides retrospective validation of the inter-systemic interpretation of Cold War.' Or, as he writes later (notice again the coy quotation marks), 'to speak in the language of "old thinking", what we are now witnessing is class struggle on an international scale, as the superior strength of Western capitalism forces open the societies partially closed to it for four or more decades.'

But I and most of my colleagues in 'school three'—and in the non-aligned peace movement—never predicted the end of the Cold War in a 'convergence of two systems', nor even (except as an interim detente) as a negotiated truce between the antagonists. Indeed the stasis of the Cold War itself relied on a kind of non-dialectical 'convergence' of opposites, who played according to the same rules. We worked for the displacement of the Cold War by altogether new systems of international relations, the breakdown of bipolar confrontation. By proposing the problem in the way that he does, and by glossing our interpretative vocabulary to suit his own ends, Halliday predicates precisely the conclusions he wishes to reach. If we talk about 'homology' and a cold war 'system' (his terms) we may be predisposed to reach his conclusions; if we talk about 'reciprocity', 'inertial thrust', 'self-reproducing dynamic', then we are talking about a real historical process and not categoric 'systems', and the events of the autumn of 1989 may then be seen both as a conclusion to one historical era and the initiation of another. In a logic of reciprocal interaction, if one side withdraws it may have profound effects upon the other, just as the wrestler who suddenly loses an antagonist may fall to the ground.

Secondly, is it not time for me to withdraw my theses about 'exterminism'? Several critics have found these to be overdrawn, and suggest them to have been disproved by events post-1985. In the sense that I allowed in the suggestion that 'exterminism' was a *determined* historical process, some of the criticisms are just.[4] But I should add that this essay was written early in 1980, before a mass peace movement had arisen, and indeed that its bleak and intransigent tone was influenced by this fact and by my desire to challenge what I supposed to be a political 'immobilism' among sophisticated Western Marxists. Of greater significance is the fact that the exterminism theses were put forward as the negative theses, whose positive alternatives were set forth in my 'Beyond the Cold War' lecture of 1981.[5] This lecture never received the attention that 'exterminism' did—least of all in Marxist circles—and yet, looking back from 1990, it may appear to be more prescient and, indeed, to offer a script which prefigures the events of autumn 1989.

I write this not in self-congratulation—after all, if one offers a pessimistic and also an optimistic future scenario, one of them is likely to be nearer the mark than the other—but in order to stress that the argument was never just about 'exterminism' as a doomed structural determinism, but was also always an argument about how to break out of this doomed logic to alternative possibilities. Together with other activists in the nonaligned peace movements I placed a very strong emphasis on the ideological content of the Second Cold War. As I wrote in late 1983: 'It is ideology, even more than military–industrial pressures, which is the driving-motor of the Cold War ... It is as if ... ideology has broken free from the existential socio-economic matrix within which it was nurtured and is no longer subject to any control of rational self-interest. Cold War II is a replay of Cold War I, but this time as deadly farce: the content of real interest-conflict between the two superpowers is low, but the content of ideological rancour and "face" is dangerously high.'[6] Our argument was never confined to some interactionism of weapons systems (especially nuclear), as has sometimes been supposed. The peace movement's work was not only to oppose but also to expose and to demystify the malodorous vocabulary of nuclear weapons, to disclose them as not only weapons but also symbolic rhetoric, for 'the *suppression* of politics ... and the *substitution* of the threat of annihilation for the negotiated resolution of differences'. Hence, the Cold War's arrest of political process, the degenerative stasis of the condition.

Third, if we put the problem back into the terms of our analysis, rather than Halliday's gloss, some large conclusions might follow. The events of autumn 1989, when the ideological barricades of forty years began to break open, might seem to confirm our analysis rather than Halliday's. But the 'jury is still out'. If we replace 'homology' with more dialectical notions of reciprocal process, then this process has only just begun. The test will be in the eventuation of the next four or five years. No one in the nonaligned peace movement ever supposed that events must proceed in lock-step on both sides of the divided globe. But if our analysis had any virtue, we can expect very substantial ideological and political changes to ensue now in the West. Already Western commentators are bemoaning the loss of a convenient enemy 'Other', just as the space and nuclear arms contractors in the USA are complaining that they are 'hurting'. In every presidential election for forty-five years, the Right in America has set the parameters of debate in terms of 'security' and the Soviet threat, and other domestic as well as international issues have been silenced in that deafening propaganda. Already there are premonitions that this kind of suppression of politics cannot long continue in the USA, let alone in Western Europe. At the same time, the political and ideological controls over satellite and client states are weakening in NATO as well as in the Warsaw Pact. If the

Cold War is no longer 'self-reproducing', we can expect other (more traditional, less mystifying and less ideological) pressures to reassert themselves. But let us wait a few months before we decide that it is 'capitalism' which has triumphed *tout court.*

Writing Out the Popular Movements

Fourth, the paragraph which I have just written is a great deal too passive in tone. And Halliday's passivity (in pursuit of supposedly objective analysis) is quite extraordinary. At not one single point, in his relatively lengthy analysis of the ends of the Cold War, does he make even a passing mention of the peace movements. Presumably he sees the Western peace movement as a piece of empty charade (perhaps misdirected) which had no influence upon historical eventuation. Of course, those of us who ate, drank and lived the peace movement obsessively for nearly a decade will not wish to admit our total irrelevance. We have a vested interest in supposing otherwise. We also have a few arguments. I have argued that it was the nonaligned peace movement in the West entering into dialogue and certain common actions with the human-rights movement in the East which gave rise to the 'ideological moment' when the Cold War lock was broken. Mary Kaldor has reminded us that in 1981–83, when millions demonstrated in the capitals of Western Europe, 'the movements were comparable in scale to the democracy movements in Eastern Europe in the late 1980s'—and perhaps influenced the latter.[7] Halliday, who can find space to mention the influence of pop music and of Finnish TV in Estonia, maintains total silence about any movements for peace. Yet in the first half of the decade, the NATO establishments had the fright of their lives and lived through successive emergencies which they negotiated only by exercising every means of media manipulation and political influence—West German, Dutch, Italian and British elections, the NATO referendum in Spain. I remain convinced that NATO's allocation of cruise missiles would have been rejected by Britain if General Galtieri had not come to Mrs Thatcher's rescue.

On the other side, war (1917–20 and 1941–45 and the expectation of invasion in the 1930s) and cold war thereafter were necessary conditions for the historical formation of Stalinism and of its Brezhnevite aftermath: in the exaltation of military priorities, the imposition of command economies and suppression of consumer demand, the enhancement of ideological paranoia, the strengthening of internal security forces, the 'two camps' diplomacies, the outlawing of dissent, and all the rest. This is not to say that there were not strong internal social forces confluent with external pressures—and I find Moshe Lewin's suggestive study *The Gorbachev Phenomenon*[8] especially helpful for the understanding of these—but the current intellectual fashion of attributing a vaguely defined 'generic Stalinism' to the original bad faith of 'Marxism' is as disreputable as was last year's fashionable celebration of the guillotine as the authentic outcome of the Enlightenment. Halliday is never guilty of these follies, except in so far as he can only see the end of the Cold War as a defeat for 'socialism' or for not-capitalism, and not as a reopening of closed possibilities, partly in consequence of popular pressures from both sides.

Why does Halliday keep this extraordinary silence as to the role of popular movements in bringing the Cold War to an end? I suggest that it might be because of an ulterior theoretical refusal. He insists on reducing all analysis to 'two camps' thinking—capitalism versus not-capitalism or 'Communism', as 'systems'—and refuses absolutely to explore the possibility of 'third ways'. They are ruled out of court, categorically. This is an old habit of the editors and contributors who have conducted *New Left Review* so tenaciously since the early 1960s. While they are willing to employ copiously the somewhat empty (and in my view culturally relativist) term 'the Third World', the very possibility of a 'third way'—or a fourth or a fifth—or, indeed, of a reopening field of possibility, in which new variants of social formation and new combinations of old and newer modes of production might be expected to arise, is ruled out of order as a categoric impossibility. Hence Halliday's essay—see especially its penultimate paragraph on pages 98–9 —has to conclude as an obituary upon not only command Communism and 'really existing socialism', but upon any alternative to capitalist society. The profound pessimism of his position is only the other side to the coin of Western capitalist triumphalism, and it shares the same premises.

But we are reminded that this is not only a complex theoretical issue; one that I wish NLR would open to informed debate. It is not just a question of re-examining that moment in 1945–47 when in France, Poland and (subsequently) in Yugoslavia, India and elsewhere, the issue was raised as theory. It is also a question of real movements and of political *practices*. In my view the movements and the practices may now well be ahead of the theorists. In the peace and human-rights movements of the 1980s, and their associated or supportive 'new social movements', the 'third way' emerged on a substantial scale not as theory only but as real social forces: as a historical *fact*.

Observers Only?

And this is my fifth point. Such 'facts' do not only demand intelligent observation and analysis—at which NLR has always been good—but they also require active support. They are sustained by *practices*. I have been impelled to write this comment, not only because I disagree with Halliday's analysis, but also because I think that something more than analysis is called for in 1990. For if we take the 'reciprocity' view of the Cold War, then whether or not the breakdown of that condition is a triumph for aggressive Western capitalism, or is an opportunity for the 'third way' to grow in strength in both East and West, discovering common projects and a common vocabulary, remains undecided and depends upon what we do. The jury will not stay out forever. Nothing is more discouraging than the failure of the Western peace movement and progressive forces to move into the spaces of opportunity which have opened; the failure to hasten on reciprocal process in the West to match the decomposition of Cold War ideological controls in the East. And Halliday's pat return to two-camps thinking (albeit with one camp now prostrate and utterly defeated) signals a retreat to the immobilism of which I accused theoretical Marxism in 1980.

At the same time, one does not have to be an 'expert' to know how bookish are some of the notions of 'market economies' held by dissidents (old-style) in their book-lined apartments in Prague, Budapest and Moscow: obsessively fixated by the profound pessimism of *Nineteen Eighty-Four* and of notions of 'totalitarianism' (which have been refuted in part by their own actions), committed to laughably abstract prescriptions from Hayek, Milton Friedman or American neo-conservatives— prescriptions which have no serious relevance to Western capitalist realities, let alone to the as-yet-undiagnosed ailments of command economies in decomposition.

Some of these dissidents are courageous intellectuals whose teeth have been set on edge by persecution as well as by the horrors of 'really existing socialism', and until very recently I have thought it was more important to listen to them, and to show solidarity with them in their struggle for human rights, than to argue with them. But I think that the argument must now be joined, in as direct and friendly ways as possible. One is irritated only when some of these intellectuals refuse any serious dialogue, refuse to recognize that a significant section of the Western Left has shared their abhorrence of Stalinism and has actively given evidence of their solidarity with them over the decades—when they not only refuse this knowledge but prefer not to know, and prefer to engage in dialogue (as unequal partners) with lavishly funded Western diplomatic and Cold War agencies. This was perhaps the outcome to be expected: the construction of truly internationalist discourse must always be the work of minorities whose voices are lost in the hubbub of money and power's camp followers; and small outfits like END, or European Forum, must patiently start the construction once more.[9]

Yet something has been done in the past that we may build upon: something which Halliday fails even to mention. And there might even be powerful auxiliaries (and more than auxiliaries) coming to our aid from huge circles which have not been involved in earlier exchanges. How can we know yet how political consciousness may be changing 'on the other side', and what struggles over priorities, basic defences of the right to work, housing and health, the allocation of resources, the social control of public wealth, will ensue when working people over there really come to understand what 'free' market forces mean? Already (May 1990) Lech Walesa has put out one fire in the Gdansk shipyards and checked the Polish rail strike; but his one-man fire brigade cannot postpone the crisis for ever. Why should we prejudge the play's last act when the first act is not yet concluded? And who will be the KOS to advise and bring solidarity to the new (Gdansk or Siberian) strikers? And what larger social projects and programmes—as envisaged by Boris Kagarlitsky or Jiri Sabbata—will we soon observe? And will we be observers only, or will we begin to find our way towards common, inter-nationalist programmes?

I ask only that we should take a hand in writing alternative scripts, and should not wait passively for all the scripts to be written by the Western media, politicians and business interests, while we act as a kind of profoundly pessimistic self-flagellant chorus. I hear on every side today fearful warnings as to the growth of 'Fascism' as well as anti-semitism, nationalism, fundamentalism, and so forth, on the other side. And on this side too. And in the 'Third World'. Precisely so. That is what happens in a vacuum, and when no alternative internationalist script or affirmative values are defended. But what worries me almost as much is the profound intellectual distaste (even contempt) of working people which is found equally among Western circles of liberal or (post) modern intellectuals and certain circles of human-rights intellectuals over there. There are real historical reasons for this, in the aftermath of populist reactionary regimes as well as conformist Communist ones. Yet I remain worried less by the manifest crisis of Marxism (which had that deservedly coming to it) than by the loss of conviction, even on the Left, in the practices and values of democracy. But the end of the Cold War has—and on both sides—seen a revival of these practices and a reaffir-mation of these values, in the self-activity of masses who moved outside orthodox ideological and political stockades. And we should still see this as a moment of opportunity, not defeat.

The Third Way

Finally, these last paragraphs are not in fairness addressed to Fred Halliday. Rather they express my own preoccupations, some of which he may share. If I have been a little sharp in contesting (through the case of Halliday's article) a tendency in the NLR to foreclose or to refuse certain issues ever since some of us parted with the Board in the early 1960s, I would like to express my solidarity in other areas. Some of us feared in 1962 that NLR might give way before a sentimental and guilt-stricken Third Worldism (of the Sartre/Fanon variety) which would, in effect, evade the necessary engagements within our own society. This has not proved to be the case, and Fred Halliday's consistent essays in the interpretation of Western capitalist intervention in the Middle East and Asia have contributed positively to the Review's pages for two decades. I share his sense of the total and irrevocable collapse of the orthodox Communist tradition in the events of the past year. Those of us actively involved in the 'border-crossing' work of the peace move-ment in the past decade, theoretical as well as practical, may have been more prepared for this than were others, since we had long sensed that a collapse was imminent. I share also his concern that—in the aftermath of this overdue collapse—there has been in both East and West a 'capitul-ation to all sorts of regressive ideologies of a nationalist, familialist and religious character', some of these in the name of a (post) 'Marxism', or supposedly 'critical' theory. I feel solidarity with Halliday in his attempt to rediscover some vocabulary of rationality and of rehabilitated univer-sals, and his repudiation of the 'misplaced indulgence of religious bigotry masquerading as anti-racism shown by sections of the liberal intelligentsia', and 'the pursuit of "national traditions" by erstwhile components of the international Communist movement'. The causes of rationality and internationalism and some (if not all) of the causes of the Enlightenment now require—in the face of their modish unpopularity—stubborn defenders; and one welcomes Halliday and other NLR contributors among these: they are traditions which the rational Left inherits and can lay claim to, alongside all the mountains of obscur-antism and of bad faith which have been exposed to view (and exposed often by critics from within the Left). I mean only to insist that these are not only theories and traditions. They are also practices and even social movements. They exist in the real worlds of East, West and South; and if we refuse theoretical legitimacy to any third way, we diminish them. We cannot know what spaces the third way might inherit, after the collapse of the Cold War, unless we press in practice beyond the old 'two camps' thinking and find out.

Notes

1. Reprinted above as Chapter 6.
2. NLR 121, May–June 1980.
3. In 'Exterminism Reviewed', in *Exterminism and Cold War*, Verso, London 1982.
4. Constructive articles include: Simon Bromley and Justin Rosenberg, 'After Exterminism', NLR 168, March–April 1988; Michael Sukhov, 'E.P. Thompson and the Practice of Theory', in *Socialism and Democracy*, Autumn/Winter 1989; Martin Shaw, 'Exterminism and Historical Pacificism', in Harvey Kaye and Keith McLelland, eds, *E.P. Thompson: Critical Perspectives*, London 1990. I tried to clarify my views in 'Exterminism Reviewed' in the Verso volume, and I there accepted Raymond Williams's criticism of my metaphor of exterminism as a mode of production. See also my 'Ends and Histories' in Mary Kaldor, ed., *Europe from Below: An East–West Dialogue*, Verso, London 1991.
5. 'Beyond the Cold War' was published as a Merlin/END pamphlet, at the end of 1981, reprinted in *Zero Option*, London 1982, and in the US as *Beyond the Cold War*, New York 1982.
6. *The Heavy Dancers*, London 1985, p. 44.
7. See Mary Kaldor, ed., *Europe from Below*, London 1990.
8. London 1987.
9. For the European Forum, see Kaldor, *Europe from Below*.

8

A Reply to Edward Thompson

Fred Halliday

Despite the evident disagreements between us, and a certain measure of misunderstanding, I find Edward Thompson's comment welcome and stimulating. The overriding issues that confront us all concern the future, on which, as he himself makes clear, there is far more that unites than divides us. There are, however, a number of points he raises where some dissenting reply may be in order. These are: the interpretation of his argument on exterminism; the evaluation of European events over the last few months; the role of the peace movement; the plausibility of a 'third way'.

Thompson disputes my division of theories of Cold War into four broad schools and in particular my inclusion of his 'exterminism' thesis in what I term the internalist school, that is one which sees the Cold War as a product of comparable forces operating within the two blocs, forces for whom the Cold War is in varying respects functional. As I argued in 'The Ends of Cold War' and in *The Making of the Second Cold War*, no one can deny the force of internal factors within the two blocs, but on its own such an argument is misleading in two respects: (1) it understates the degree of contestation and rivalry between the blocs—that is, the degree to which each remained committed to *prevailing* over the other; (2) it overstates how similar the structures were within each bloc, and in so doing failed to see how far Cold War was a product of the very difference, the heterogeneity of socio-economic systems, between them. I do not think, as he seems to do, that the ideological element in East–West relations was separate from the material interests involved.

Thompson may not like the word 'homology' but it is in meaning very similar to the equally un-Anglo-Saxon term 'isomorphism' which appears liberally in his exterminism essay. Both denote a similarity or

identity of structure. 'Homology' is the best I can do to denote the argument that the sources of the Cold War are similar within the two blocs,
and that, in his case, these sources are to be found in a military–social
dynamic which he terms 'exterminism'. The category 'reciprocity' as he
explains it in his comment seems to bear this interpretation out: that the
Cold War was driven by forces within each bloc that, through reciprocal
interaction, more and more came to resemble each other. After all, the
central argument of that text is that whatever differences in social system
may have underlain the Cold War in its inception, the predominance of
the arms race and arms manufacture has produced a similarity: his stress
on 'isomorphism' was in part designed to rebut traditional and apologetic Left arguments about the differences between the capitalist and
non-capitalist systems.

Thompson repeats his view that the Cold War is 'about itself', and it
is this that seems to me to lie at the heart of our disagreement. It was
precisely on this point that a number of us, myself and Mike Davis
included, sought to provide an alternative interpretation of cold war in
the early 1980s based on the view of cold war as an inter-systemic
conflict—that is, a global, ultimately irreconcilable, conflict between two
different kinds of society and political system, within which the arms
race played an important but not determinant role. These differences are
not the result of some current rashness; they have been clear for at least
eight years: the collection of essays, *Exterminism and Cold War*,
published in 1982, to which Thompson, Davis, myself and several others
contributed, was precisely an attempt to debate the arguments of
Thompson's original essay. One of the reasons why the peace movement
shied away from this inter-systemic approach was that it sounded rather
too much like conventional Cold War ideology—either in its Western,
'freedom' versus 'Communism' variant, or in the orthodox, apologetic,
Soviet position of 'socialism' versus 'imperialism'. Thompson tries to
shove me back into such a dogmatic Left box, but in so doing it is he
who is helping to foreclose an intellectual and political space that the
cold warriors also want to keep shut, namely that of seeing in a non-
dogmatic way how different social and economic interests on both sides
are expressed in and through cold war.

My argument about the events of the past few months is that what has
happened is what inter-systemic conflict theory would have suggested:
namely that rivalry of the blocs will end once systemic heterogeneity is
drastically reduced or disappears. What we have seen is not just a reduction in military tension but a prevailing of one socio-economic system
over the other. The collapse of the Communist regimes constitutes
precisely such a process, which is still in train, in so far as the West,
under the rubric of 'conditionality', is making financial and commercial

assistance dependent upon the introduction of capitalist reforms in these countries. It should not be surprising that this is the way things are going. This is the way the capitalist system works.

Here I would argue that Thompson's account of these events retains an element of wishful thinking, although the tone of his comment printed here is rather at variance with his, in my view, more accurate and sober assessment published in the *Guardian* on 3 July 1990. On the one hand, he suggests that the victory of the West may not turn out to be such a victory after all, and compares it to a wrestler who is thrown off balance when his opponent slips. But the real analogy is in Clausewitz's use of wrestling to describe the goal of strategy, which is not to annihilate but *niederwerfen*, to 'throw down' the opponent: the capitalist West has not lost its antagonist, it has subjugated it, nowhere more so than in the takeover of the GDR by Bonn. There has not been reciprocal interaction, but a victory of one side over the other. On the other hand, he suggests that what the peace movement proposed was 'new systems of international relations': this *is* what the peace movement proposed, but it is not what it got. What we have is a strengthening of the institutions of one side in the face of the collapse of those on the other. NATO and the EC have become more accommodating, but as a function of their new strength. The Warsaw Pact, for all current piety, is as dead as the League of Nations, and Comecon may follow suit. Of course, assessment of what the outcome is depends on what one is looking at: if inter-bloc military tension is the sole focus, then there has been reciprocal but unequal reduction of threat; if socio-economic and political competition is the issue, then one side can be seen to be the winner.

Thompson chides me for ignoring the role of the peace movement, and he is, in one sense, right to do so: much as it pains me to say it, I do not think that the peace movement played a major role in bringing about the end of the Cold War. Here I can only quote the telling sentence from the end of Thompson's own exterminism essay: 'The end of politics is to act, and to act *with effect*' (EPT's italics). The question is what the effect was. In the conclusion to *The Making of the Second Cold War*, written in early 1983, I argued that, for all the mass mobilizations and appeals across party lines involved, the goal of a peace movement had to be to influence political processes: this meant elected or established governments. Beyond generic statements of influence, one has to look at what actually happened in Western Europe in this period. In no country within NATO was a government elected that opposed the deployment of Cruise and Pershing, let alone opposed continued membership of NATO: the nearest was in the German elections of March 1983, but Kohl was returned, the SPD retreated, and the Greens later lost their momentum. Later, in Holland, the peace movement almost got a majority against Cruise deployment, but in the end that failed too. These were close-run things, but the reality is that NATO proceeded with its policies on INF deployment, there was no concerted opposition to SDI, and few even seriously raised the key issue, that of leaving NATO. Thompson's interpretation of the British possibilities had there not been a Falklands War may or may not be valid—I doubt it. What was most striking throughout the height of the peace movement was that, while many in Britain expressed doubts about Cruise deployment, this happened, the Thatcher government that carried it through was re-elected and even regarded this issue as a vote winner, and there was never more than a small minority in favour of leaving NATO—hence the equivocations of CND on this issue. The fate of the freeze movement and of SANE in the USA was little different.

It may be said that the peace movement played a role in another respect, namely in influencing developments in the East. Quoting Mary Kaldor, Thompson says that the peace movements of the West 'perhaps' influenced those of the East. Thompson and Kaldor can evaluate this better than I: there is no doubt that the movements of the East were influenced by some aspects of the movements in the West—concerning democracy, human rights, environment, and, in the GDR at least, feminism. But whether the Western peace movements had an influence on the issue of peace—that is, deployment of arms—itself is more debatable: many in the East, not least those most opposed to their own Communist regimes, wanted the West to stand firm on INF—there were plenty of such voices within Solidarity. The process of disarmament that began in earnest in 1987 came as a result of state-to-state relations, not of pressure from below within the USSR or anywhere else; the democratic turn in the East has been a great advance, but it has not involved a two-sided, reciprocal, rejection of both systems, so much as a transition from one to the other. Those who have propounded a third way, as in East Germany, have, quite simply, been swept aside by the combined pressures of their own populations and Western state and financial intervention.

The one area where Western peace movement thinking did find an echo was in theories of 'minimal deterrence' and 'defensive defence'; yet these ideas did, as developed within the USSR, imply the retention of some nuclear weapons and, while their enunciation in the early 1980s was to be found in the West, their previous formulation had, of course, been within the USSR, by Khrushchev in the early 1960s. Thompson puts the words 'empty charade' into my mouth to describe the peace movement: this is to confuse the issue, one of sober historical assessment. This must, in my reluctant view, show that the peace movement, for all its great exertions, was, in the political terms in which its success has to be evaluated, defeated.

So much for the past. Thompson regards my analysis as passive and defeatist. Here, apart from calling me 'coy', is perhaps the largest misunderstanding in his comment. Let me restate my concluding argument, not one of defeatism but of realism: the starting point for a future politics has to be the critique of existing capitalist society and the laying out of alternatives to it that are both desirable and plausible. Thompson himself talks of a 'third way': yes, but no society embodying such a third way has been produced in the contemporary world despite many attempts to do so, and much of what masqueraded as 'third' was in reality one or other of the first two in disguise. The term 'nonaligned' which he uses is not quite as solid as might appear: what is striking about the 'nonaligned movement' is that it has found only a marginal support in Europe (Yugoslavia, Malta, Cyprus) and the majority of European neutrals preferred an atomized, low-key, approach to international issues, not the constitution of a third bloc.[1] All these countries were, moreover, in political and socio-economic terms not 'third' at all, but estranged members of one or other bloc. If this third alternative is to be elaborated, and if it is to command the political support needed democratically to implement it, then it has to avoid much of the woolly thinking about economic, political and military matters that has characterized so much Left analysis in the past. Those of us involved in NLR in the 1960s and 1970s could be taxed with having contributed at least as much to voluntarism as to fatalism; a sober, but combative, assessment of the end of Cold War may help us all to avoid both in the future.

Note

1. I have gone into this in greater detail in 'European Neutralism and Cold War Politics: A Harder Look', Sheffield Papers in International Studies, Department of Politics, University of Sheffield, Sheffield S10 2TN.

9

Goodbye to All That

Eric Hobsbawm

What is the historical significance of 1989, the year in which Communism collapsed in Eastern Europe, suddenly and presumably irrevocably, anticipating the collapse of the existing regime in the USSR and the break-up of its multinational structure? Instant diagnosis is a dangerous game, almost as dangerous as instant prophecy. The only people who dive into it without hesitation are those who expect their diagnoses and prophecies to be instantly forgotten (like journalists and commentators) or not to be remembered after the next election or two (like politicians). Still, there are times when events concentrated into a short space of time, whatever we make of them, are plainly historic and immediately seen to be such. The year of the French Revolution and 1917 were such times and 1989 was equally clearly another. So what do we make of it?

It is much easier to see 1989 as a conclusion than as a beginning. It was the end of an era in which world history was about the October Revolution. For over seventy years all Western governments and ruling classes were haunted by the spectre of social revolution and Communism, eventually transmuted into fear of the military power of the USSR and its potential international repercussions. Western governments are still coming to terms with the collapse of an international policy entirely designed to meet a Soviet threat, both political and military. Without the belief in such a threat NATO has no sense at all. That there was never any reality in this Western image of a Soviet Union poised to overrun or nuke the 'free world' at a moment's notice only proves how deep the fear of Communism was. For over seventy years international politics has been waged by one side as a crusade, a cold war of religion, with a brief intermission for confronting the more real dangers of the Berlin–Tokyo axis.

On the other side it had long been clear that it was no such thing. It is true that Lenin and the Bolsheviks saw October as the first phase of the world revolution which would overthrow all capitalism. The early generations of Communists (including the present writer) still joined what we thought of as a disciplined army to fight and win the world revolution. Nikita Khrushchev, the only peasant ever to rule Russia (or for that matter any important state), still sincerely believed that Communism would bury capitalism, though not by revolution. And the dramatic extension of both anti-imperialist and Communist revolution after World War Two seemed at first sight to confirm the prospect.

Nevertheless, it is clear that from the early 1920s onwards the USSR's policy was no longer designed to achieve world revolution, although Moscow would certainly have welcomed it. In the era of Stalin, who actively discouraged bids for power by any Communist party and distrusted Communist parties who made revolution against his advice, Soviet policy was cautious and essentially defensive, even after the stunning victories won by the Red Army in World War Two. Khrushchev, unlike Stalin, took risks and lost his job for it. Whatever Brezhnev wanted to do, spreading Communism all over the world, let alone invading the West, were neither within his power nor on his agenda.

After 1956, when the international Communist movement visibly began to disintegrate, various groups outside the Moscow orbit claimed the original Marxist-Leninist or at least the world-revolutionary inheritance. On a world scale, neither the fifty-seven varieties of Trotskyists, Maoists, revolutionary Marxists, neo-anarchists and others, nor the states nominally committed to their support, amounted to anything. Even within particular countries their impact, except for brief moments, was usually marginal. The most systematic attempt to spread revolution along these lines, the Cuban revolutionary export drive of the 1960s, did not even begin to look like getting anywhere. Unlike the first revolutionary wave of 1917–19 and the second wave which followed World War Two, the third wave, coinciding with the world crisis of the 1970s, even lacked a unified ideological tradition or pole of attraction. The most important social upheaval of this period by far, the Iranian revolution, looked to Muhammad and not to Marx. The Communists, though central to the ending of the last hold-overs of the European Fascist era, were soon side-lined in post-Salazar Portugal and post-Franco Spain by what claimed to be social democrats.

But if there was no significant movement to overthrow capitalism worldwide, revolutionaries still hoped that its contradictions and those of its international system made it vulnerable—perhaps one day fatally vulnerable—and that Marxists, or at any rate socialists, would provide the alternative to it. If Communist power did not look like expanding much except in small Latin American countries and, nominally, African states of little international significance, the world was still divided into the 'two camps', and any country or movement which broke with capitalism and imperialism tended to gravitate or to be notionally absorbed into the socialist sphere. Ex-colonies which did not claim in some sense to be 'socialist' or which did not look in some way to the Eastern model of economic development were rare birds indeed in the generation or two after 1945. In short, world politics could still be seen, even on the Left, as the working out of the consequences of the October Revolution.

All this is now over. Communism in Eastern Europe has dissolved or is dissolving. So is the USSR as we have known it. Whatever China will be like when the last of the Long March generation is dead, it will have little to do with Lenin and less with Marx. Outside the former regions of 'real socialism' there are probably not more than three Communist parties with genuine mass support (Italy, South Africa and the regionally concentrated CP-Marxist of India), and one of them wants to rejoin international social democracy as fast as it can. We are seeing not the crisis of a type of movement, regime and economy, but its end. Those of us who believed that the October Revolution was the gate to the future of world history have been shown to be wrong. What was wrong about Lincoln Steffens's 'I have seen the future and it works' was not that it failed to work. It worked in a rackety way, and it has great and in some cases astonishing achievements to its credit. But it turned out not to be the future. And when its time came, at least in Eastern Europe, everyone including its rulers knew this, and it collapsed like a house of cards.

How did it happen that the fear, or the hope, or the mere fact of October 1917 dominated world history for so long, and so profoundly, that not even the coldest of cold war ideologists expected the sudden, virtually unresisted disintegration of 1989? It is impossible to understand this, that is, the entire history of our century, unless we remember that the old world of global capitalism and bourgeois society in its liberal version collapsed in 1914, and for the next forty years capitalism stumbled from one catastrophe to the next. Even intelligent conservatives would not take bets on its survival.

A simple list of the earthquakes that shook the world during this period is enough to make the point: two world wars, followed by two bouts of global revolution, leading to the wholesale collapse of old political regimes and the installation of Communist power, first over one-sixth of the world's surface and later over one-third of the world's population; plus the dissolution of the vast colonial empires built up before and during the imperialist era. A world economic crisis brought even the strongest capitalist economies to their knees, while the USSR seemed to be immune to it. The institutions of liberal democracy virtually disappeared from all but a fringe of Europe between 1922 and 1942 as Fascism and its satellite authoritarian movements and regimes rose. But for the sacrifices of the USSR and its peoples, Western liberal capitalism would probably have succumbed to this threat and the contemporary Western world (outside an isolated USA) would now consist of a set of variations on authoritarian and Fascist regimes rather than a set of variations on liberal ones. Without the Red Army the chances of defeating the Axis powers were invisible. Perhaps history, in its irony, will decide that the most lasting achievement of the October Revolution was to make the 'developed world' once again safe for 'bourgeois democracy'. But that is of course to assume that it will remain safe...

For forty years capitalism lived through an era of catastrophe, vulnerability and constant instability, with a future that seemed entirely uncertain. Moreover, during this era it faced, for the first time, a system claiming to provide an alternative future: socialism. In the most traumatic years of this era, the early 1930s, when the very mechanism of the capitalist economy, as hitherto known, apparently ceased to function and Hitler's triumph in Germany dealt a body-blow to liberal institutions, the USSR appeared to make its most dramatic advances. In retrospect it seems amazing that liberal and conservative politicians (not to mention those of the Left) went to Moscow to learn lessons ('plan' became a buzz-word across the Western political spectrum), or that even socialists could have sincerely believed that their economies would outproduce the Western system. In the days of the Great Slump it did not seem absurd at all.

On the contrary, what was entirely unexpected, not least by governments and businessmen anxious about postwar ruin and possible depressions, was the extraordinary surge of global economic growth after the Second World War. This turned the third quarter of the present century into the all-time golden age of capitalist development: the 'Thirty Glorious Years' in the French phrase. So unexpected was it, that the existence of this super-boom was only slowly recognized, even by those who benefited from it—'You never had it so good' did not become a British political slogan until 1959—and was fully recognized only in retrospect, after the boom had come to an end in the early 1970s. Initially it did not look like a specifically capitalist triumph, since both 'camps'—at least in Europe and Asia—were busy recovering from the ravages of war, and the rate of growth of the socialist economies during this period was generally considered to be as fast, if not faster, than the rest.

However, from some time in the 1960s it became patent that capitalism had surmounted its era of catastrophe, although it was not yet so evident that the socialist economies were running into serious trouble. Nevertheless, in material and technological terms the socialist camp was clearly no longer in the race.

Somehow the heritage of the age of catastrophe was surmounted, or at least buried. Fascism and its associated forms of authoritarianism were destroyed and liquidated in Europe, and variants of liberal democracy once again became the normal political regimes in the metropolitan countries. (In what now came to be called the Third World this was notably not the case.) The colonial empires of the imperialist era, notoriously the Achilles heel of their metropoles, were politically decolonized. Both processes, decisively initiated in 1945–48, were essentially completed in the 1970s.

War, which had twice swept through the developed world, and especially Europe, was eliminated from this region, partly by being transferred to the Third World. There the years from 1945 to 1990 have probably seen rather more bloodshed and destruction than any other period of comparable length in modern history.

Peace in the developed world was probably not maintained simply by the fear of nuclear war, and by mutual deterrence, that is, in practice by the deterrent effect of the Soviet nuclear arms on the USA after the end of the shortlived and extremely dangerous period of US nuclear monopoly.[1] It was also due to three factors: a world politics simplified into a game for two players; the Yalta agreement, which in practice demarcated each superpower's zone in Europe, from which neither tried to break out; and, eventually, the unquestionable prosperity and stability of the developed capitalist countries which eliminated the possibility, let alone the likelihood, of social revolution in this region. Outside Europe major wars (without nuclear weapons) were not, of course, eliminated.

Most important of all, capitalism learned the domestic lessons of its age of crisis, both in economics and in politics. It gave up the sort of free-market liberalism which Reaganite America and Thatcherite Britain, alone among developed Western countries, have tried to restore in the 1980s. (Both, not coincidentally, are capitalist economies on the slide.) The original stimulus for this change was almost certainly political. Keynes himself made no bones about the fact that his aim was to save liberal capitalism. After 1945 the enormous expansion of the socialist 'camp' and the potential threat it presented concentrated the minds of Western governments wonderfully, not least on the importance of social security. The intention of this deliberate break with free-market capitalism was not only to eliminate mass unemployment (which was then regarded as automatically likely to radicalize its victims) but also to stimulate demand. From the mid 1950s it became clear that both these aims were being achieved. Expansion and prosperity made welfare capitalism affordable. It reached its peak in the 1960s, or even in the 1970s, before a new world crisis provoked a fiscal backlash.

Economically, therefore, the turn to a Keynesian mixed economy paid off dramatically. Politically it rested on the deliberate partnership between capital and organized labour under the benevolent auspices of government, which is now known and usually derided as 'corporatism'. For the age of catastrophe had revealed three things. First, that the organized labour movement was a major and indispensable presence in liberal societies. Indeed sometimes, as in Central Europe after the 1918 defeat, it emerged briefly as the only state-sustaining force to survive the collapse of empires. Second, it was not Bolshevik. (Comintern exclus- ivism actually forced most socialist sympathizers with the October Revolution back into the reformist camp, and kept Communists in a minority in the countries of the old Second International until the period of anti-Fascist resistance.) Third, that the only alternative to buying working-class loyalty with (expensive) economic concessions was to put democracy at risk. For this reason, even the fanatical economic neo- liberalism of Thatcher's type has so far not actually been able to dismantle the welfare state, or to cut down its expense.

The political consequences of leaving populations naked to fend for themselves in the blizzards of genuine neo-liberal capitalism are too unpredictable to risk—except by graduates of business schools advising Third World and formerly socialist countries from local Hilton hotels. (Even the International Monetary Fund has discovered that there are limits to the sacrifices that can be imposed on remoter peoples.)

However, social Keynesianism, New Deal policies and 'corporatism' visibly bore the birthmarks of the era of capitalist troubles. The world capitalism that emerged from the 'Thirty Glorious Years' and (in the developed world) sailed through the economic gales of the 1970s and 1980s with surprisingly little difficulty was no longer in trouble. It had entered a new technological phase. It had restructured the world into a substantially transnational economy with a new international division of production.

The two main pillars of the social-Keynesian era, economic manage- ment by nation-states and a mass industrial working class, especially one organized by traditional labour movements, did not so much crumble as slim down. Neither was any longer capable of carrying such heavy loads as before. Both Keynesian policies and the (mainly social-democratic) parties most firmly identified with them were clearly in difficulties, even though the essential foundation of any flourishing capitalism remained as before: a mixed public–private 'social market economy' (that is, profits plus a welfare state and social rights), an interweaving of private enterprise, public enterprise and a good deal of public control. To this extent the past fifteen years have seen the fading away of another part of the heritage of the era from 1914 to the early 1950s.

However, a major symptom and product of that era remained: the third of the world under 'really existing socialism'. It did not 'fail' in any absolute sense, in spite of the growing sense that these economies required fundamental reforms, and the failure of the various attempts to reform them. Probably people in the USSR and in most of Eastern Europe were better off in the 1970s than ever before. But three things were increasingly clear.

First, socialism was incapable of moving fully into, let alone generating, the new hi-tech economy, and was therefore destined to fall ever further behind. To have constructed the economy of Andrew Carnegie was no good unless one could also advance further into the economy of IBM—or even of Henry Ford, for socialism signally failed to achieve the mass production of consumer goods.

Second, in the society of global communications, media, travel and transnational economy, it was no longer possible to insulate socialist populations from information about the non-socialist world, that is, from knowing just how much worse off they were in material terms and in freedom of choice.

Third, with the slowing down of its rate of growth and its increasing relative backwardness, the USSR became economically too weak to sustain its role as a superpower, that is, its control over Eastern Europe. In short, Soviet-type socialism became increasingly uncompetitive and paid the price. What is worse, it has so far proved incapable of adapting and reforming. In this it differs from Chinese socialism, whose economic reforms succeeded spectacularly—at least in the rural sector—but at the cost of seriously worsening social conditions; and which has so far fended off political unrest in the cities because the countryside is still predominant. Nor do these weaknesses apply to social-democratic mixed economies.

The Scandinavian countries and Austria have remained in the vanguard of economic and technical development and prosperity while keeping unemployment down and maintaining their ambitious welfare system in good order.

Who has won? Who has lost? And what are the prospects? The winner is not capitalism as such, but the old 'developed world' of the OECD countries,[2] which form a diminishing minority of the world's population—say 15 per cent today as against 33 per cent in 1900. (The so-called Newly Industrializing Countries, or NICs, in spite of striking advances, still average only between a quarter and a third of the

OECD's average per capita GDP.) The bulk of the world's population, whose governments have pursued economic development since 1917 if not before, without Communist regimes, hardly encourage shouts of triumph from the Adam Smith Institute.

Unlike the former 'socialist camp', the non-socialist world contains regions that have actually reverted to local subsistence economy and famine. Moreover, within 'developed' capitalism it is certainly not the Thatcherite free-market utopia that has won. Even its intellectual appeal has been limited to ultras in the West and to despairing intellectuals in the East who hope that the South Pole is warmer than the North Pole because it is its polar opposite.

Nevertheless, it is undeniable that capitalism, as reformed and restructured during its crisis decades, has once again proved that it remains the most dynamic force in world development. It will certainly continue to develop, as Marx predicted that it would, by generating internal contradictions leading to periodic eras of crisis and restructuring. These may once again bring it close to breakdown, as happened earlier this century. However, the current such period of crisis and restructuring has brought disaster to parts of the Third World, and to the Second World, but not to the First.

Who or what has lost, apart from the regimes of 'really existing socialism', which plainly have no future? The main effect of 1989 is that capitalism and the rich have, for the time being, stopped being scared. All that made Western democracy worth living for its people—social security, the welfare state, a high and rising income for its wage-earners, and its natural consequence, diminution in social inequality and inequality of life-chances—was the result of fear. Fear of the poor, and the largest and best-organized bloc of citizens in industrialized states— the workers; fear of an alternative that really existed and could really spread, notably in the form of Soviet Communism. Fear of the system's own instability.

This concentrated the minds of Western capitalists in the 1930s. Fear of the socialist camp, so dramatically extended after 1945 and represented by one of two superpowers, kept them concentrated after the war. Whatever Stalin did to the Russians, he was good for the common people of the West. It is no accident that the Keynes–Roosevelt way of saving capitalism concentrated on welfare and social security, on giving the poor money to spend, and on that central tenet of postwar Western policies—and one specifically targeted at the workers—'full employment'. As it happens this bias against extreme inequality served capitalist development well. The showpiece countries of postwar economic growth, Japan, South Korea and Taiwan, have enjoyed unusually egalitarian income distributions until recently, partly assured by postwar land reforms by occupying powers determined to counteract revolution.

Today this fear, already reduced by the diminution of the industrial working class, the decline of its movements and the recovery of self-confidence by a flourishing capitalism, has disappeared. For the time being there is no part of the world that credibly represents an alternative system to capitalism, even though it should be clear that Western capitalism represents no solutions to the problems of most of the former Second World, which is likely to be largely assimilated to the condition of the Third World. Why should the rich, especially in countries such as ours, where they now glory in injustice and inequality, bother about anyone except themselves? What political penalties do they need to fear if they allow welfare to erode and the protection of those who need it to atrophy? This is the chief effect of the disappearance of even a very bad socialist region from the globe.

It is too early to discuss long-term prospects for the future. What a Hungarian historian has called 'the short twentieth century' (1914–90) has ended, but all we can say about the twenty-first is that it will have to face at least three problems, which are getting worse: the growing width of the gap between the rich world and the poor (and probably within the rich world, between its rich and its poor); the rise of racism and xeno-phobia; and the ecological crisis of the globe which will affect us all. The ways in which they can be dealt with are unclear, but privatization and the free market are not among them.

Among the short-term problems, three stand out. First, Europe has returned to a state of instability, as between the wars. Hitler's triumph briefly produced a 'German order'. Yalta and superpower duopoly produced forty-five years of European stability, which are now at an end. Since Russia and the USA have ceased to be able, jointly, to impose their order as before, the only alternative hegemonic force on our continent, as between the wars, is Germany. That is what everyone is afraid of, not because 'Germans are Germans'—there will certainly be no return to Hitler—but because German nationalism has dangerous unfinished business: the recovery of the large territories lost in 1945 to Poland and the USSR.

And the new instability, as the Middle Eastern crisis proves, is not only European, but global. No longer held back by the fear that a sudden move by one superpower or its associated states into the other's zone of influence would provoke a direct confrontation between East and West, adventurism is once again on the agenda. What kept the world order in being since 1945, including most of the sixty sovereign mini-states with populations of less than 2 million (the Gulf is full of such political artefacts), was largely the fear of global war. But if the nuclear world holocaust is no longer an immediate danger, a world in which medium-sized gangsters no longer hesitate to take over small neighbouring territories is not safer from war than before. Nor is one in which a superpower rushes blithely into the Middle Eastern explosives store ready to fire, knowing that those whose missiles could reach New York will no longer do the same. Is it an accident that, within barely half a year of the collapse of the Warsaw Pact, we find ourselves facing a major war crisis in the Gulf?

The second development reinforces this world instability. For Central and Eastern Europe are relapsing into something like the post-First World War zone of nationalist rivalries and conflicts. In fact *all* the burning problems of this kind date back to the interwar years. They posed no major headaches before 1914.[3] What makes the situation more explosive is that today the last of the pre-1914 multinational empires is in disintegration. For it was the October Revolution which saved the tsar's domains from the fate of the Habsburg and Ottoman empires and gave them another seventy-odd years of life as the USSR.

The dangers of war in this situation are serious. Already the demagogues of Great Russian nationalism are talking lightly about a possible 'civil war in which our situation would be a nuclear one'.[4] One day soon we may look back with melancholy on the days when nuclear triggers were under the control of the two superpowers.

Lastly, there is the instability of the political systems into which ex-Communist states have rushed: liberal democracy. So did the new states in 1918. Twenty years later only Czechoslovakia was still democratic. The prospects for liberal democracy in the region must be poor, or at least uncertain. And the alternative, given the unlikelihood of a return to socialism, will most likely be military or right-wing or both.

So, let us wish Eastern Europe and the world luck as it ends an old era and is about to enter the twenty-first century. We shall need luck. And let us commiserate with Mr Francis Fukuyama, who claimed that 1989 meant 'the end of history', and that henceforth all would be plain liberal, free-market sailing. Few prophesies look like being more short-lived than that one.

October 1990

Notes

1. The most dangerous period since the war was undoubtedly 1946–53, during which Attlee specially travelled to Washington to dissuade Truman from using nuclear bombs in Korea. Probably the only time when the USSR appears to have seriously believed that war might be imminent was 1947–50.

2. If we leave out Turkey, Greece, Spain and Portugal, which were included only on political grounds, the OECD consists of Austria, Belgium, Canada, Denmark, Finland, France, Iceland, Ireland, Italy, Japan, Luxembourg, the Netherlands, Norway, Sweden, Switzerland, the UK, the US and West Germany. Australia is partly associated.

3. Among the problems which did not exist or were of very minor political significance before 1914: Croats versus Serbs; Serbs versus Albanians; Slovaks versus Czechs; the Transylvanian imbroglio; the three Baltic nationalisms; Byelorussia; Moldavia; Azerbaijani nationalism; not to mention the former German territories east of the Oder–Neisse line.

4. Edward Mortimer, 'Bolshevism At The Mercy Of The Republics', *Financial Times*, 31 July 1990.

10

Marxist Century, American Century*

Giovanni Arrighi

In the closing paragraphs of the first section of *The Communist Manifesto*, Marx and Engels advance two distinct arguments why the rule of the bourgeoisie will come to an end. On the one hand, the bourgeoisie 'is unfit to rule because it is incompetent to assure an existence to its slave within its slavery, because it cannot help letting him sink into such a state that it has to feed him, instead of being fed by him. Society cannot live under this bourgeoisie; in other words, its existence is no longer compatible with society.' On the other hand: 'The advance of industry, whose involuntary promoter is the bourgeoisie, replaces the isolation of the labourers, due to competition, by their revolutionary combination, due to association. The development of Modern Industry, therefore, cuts from under its feet the foundation on which the bourgeoisie produces and appropriates products. What the bourgeoisie, therefore, produces, above all, is its own gravediggers. Its fall and the victory of the proletariat are equally inevitable.'[1] It will be my thesis here that these two predictions represent both the strength and the weakness of the Marxian legacy. They represent its strength because they have been validated in many crucial respects by fundamental trends of the capitalist world economy in the subsequent 140 years. And they represent its weakness because the two scenarios are in partial contradiction with each other and—what is more—the contradiction has lived on unresolved in the theories and practices of Marx's followers.

The contradiction, as I see it, is the following. The first scenario is of proletarian helplessness. Competition prevents the proletariat from sharing the benefits of industrial progress, and drives it into such a state of poverty that, instead of a productive force, it becomes a dead weight on society. The second scenario, in contrast, is of proletarian power. The

advance of industry replaces competition with association among proletarians so that the ability of the bourgeoisie to appropriate the benefits
of industrial progress is undermined.

For Marx, of course, there was no actual contradiction. The tendency
towards the weakening of the proletariat concerned the Industrial
Reserve Army and undermined the *legitimacy* of bourgeois rule. The
tendency towards the strengthening of the proletariat concerned the
Active Industrial Army and undermined the capacity of the bourgeoisie
to appropriate surplus. Moreover, these two tendencies were not
conceived as being independent of each other. To the extent that the
capacity of the bourgeoisie to appropriate surplus is undermined, two
effects concerning the Industrial Reserve Army follow. The means available to the bourgeoisie to 'feed', that is, to reproduce, the Reserve Army
are reduced, while the incentive to employ proletarian labour as a means
to augment capital also decreases and, *ceteris paribus*, the Reserve Army
increases. Hence, any increase in the power of the Active Industrial
Army to resist exploitation is translated more or less automatically into a
loss of legitimacy of the bourgeois order.

At the same time, any loss of legitimacy due to inability to assure the
livelihood of the Reserve Army is translated more or less automatically
into a greater (and qualitatively superior) power of the Active Army.
For in Marx's view the Active and the Reserve Armies consisted of the
same human material which was assumed to circulate more or less
continuously from the one to the other. The same individuals would be
part of the Active Army today and of the Reserve Army tomorrow,
depending on the continuous ups and downs of enterprises, lines and
locales of production. The bourgeois order would thus lose legitimacy
among the members of the Reserve and Active Armies alike, thereby
enhancing the tendency of whoever happened to be in the Active Army
to turn their association in the productive process from an instrument of
exploitation by the bourgeoisie into an instrument of struggle against the
bourgeoisie.

The Three Postulates

The power of this model lies in its simplicity. It is based on three postulates. First, as Marx was to state in Volume 3 of *Capital*, the limit of
capital is capital itself. That is to say, the evolution and the eventual
demise of capital are written in its 'genes'. The dynamic element is 'the
advancement of industry', without which capitalist accumulation cannot
proceed. But the advancement of industry replaces competition among
the workers, on which accumulation rests, with their association. Sooner

or later, capitalist accumulation becomes self-defeating.

This deterministic view, however, applies only to the system as a whole and over long periods of time; the outcome at particular places and at particular times is left entirely indeterminate. There are defeats and victories of the proletariat but both are necessarily temporary and localized events and tend to be 'averaged out' by the logic of competition among capitalist enterprises and among proletarians. The only thing that is inevitable in the model is that in the very long run capitalist accumulation creates the conditions for an increase in the number of proletarian victories over proletarian defeats until bourgeois rule is displaced, replaced or transformed beyond recognition.

The time and modalities of the transition to a post-bourgeois order are also left indeterminate. Precisely because the transition was made to depend on a multiplicity of victories and defeats combined spatially and temporally in unpredictable ways, little was said in the *Manifesto* about the contours of the future society, except that it would bear the imprints of proletarian culture—whatever that culture would be at the time of the transition.

A second postulate is that the agents of long-term, large-scale social change are personifications of structural tendencies. Competition among individual members of the bourgeoisie ensures the advancement of industry, while competition among individual members of the proletariat ensures that the benefits accrue to the bourgeoisie. The advancement of industry, however, means an ever-widening cooperation within and among labour processes, and at a certain stage of development this transforms the proletariat from an ensemble of competing individuals into a cohesive class capable of putting an end to exploitation.

Consciousness and organization are reflections of structural processes of competition and cooperation which are not due to any individual or collective will. The multiple struggles waged by proletarians are an essential ingredient in the transformation of structural change into ideological and organizational change, but are themselves rooted in structural changes. This is the only 'understanding' that can be usefully 'brought to' the proletariat from outside its condition:

> The Communists do not form a separate party opposed to other working-class parties.
>
> They have no interests separate and apart from those of the proletariat as a whole.
>
> They do not set up any sectarian principles of their own, by which to shape and mould the proletarian movement.
>
> The Communists are distinguished from the other working-class parties by this only: 1. In the national struggles of the proletarians of the different countries, they point out and bring to the front the common interests of the

entire proletariat, independently of all nationality. 2. In the various stages of development which the struggle of the working class against the bourgeoisie has to pass through, they always and everywhere represent the interests of the movement as a whole.[2]

The third postulate of the model is the primacy of the economy over culture and politics. The proletariat itself is defined in purely economic terms as 'a class of labourers, who live only as long as they find work, and who find work only so long as their labour increases capital. These labourers, who must sell themselves piecemeal, are a commodity, like every article of commerce, and are consequently exposed to all the vicissitudes of competition, to all the fluctuations of the market.'[3]

The Proletarian Condition

To be sure, Marx's entire work was to disclose the fiction involved in treating labour as a commodity like any other. Being inseparable from its owner, and hence endowed with a will and an intelligence, the commodity labour-power was different from all other 'articles of commerce'. Yet in the Marxian scheme this appeared only in the struggles of the proletariat against the bourgeoisie, and even there only as an undifferentiated proletarian will and intelligence. Individual and group differences within the proletariat are minimized or dismissed as residuals of the past in the process of being eliminated by the laws of market competition. The proletarian has neither country nor family:

> Differences of age and sex have no longer any distinctive social validity for the working class. All are instruments of labour, more or less expensive to use, according to their age and sex.[4]

> [Modern] subjection to capital, the same in England as in France, in America as in Germany, has stripped him of every trace of national character...
> National differences and antagonisms between peoples are daily more and more vanishing, owing to the development of the bourgeoisie, to freedom of commerce, to the world market, to uniformity in the mode of production and in the conditions of life corresponding thereto.[5]

In the Marxian scheme, therefore, the proletarian is either an atomized individual competing with other (equally atomized) individuals over the means of subsistence, or a member of a universal class struggling against the bourgeoisie. Between the universal class and the atomized individual there is no intermediate aggregation capable of supplying security or status in competition with class membership. Market competition makes all such intermediate aggregations unstable and, hence, transient.

Similarly, the Marxian scheme reduces power struggles to a mere reflection of market competition or of the class struggle. There is no room for the pursuit of power for its own sake. The only thing that is pursued for its own sake is profit, the principal form of surplus through which historical accumulation takes place. Governments are instruments of competition or class rule, simply committees 'for managing the common affairs of the whole bourgeoisie'. Once again, it is market competition that forces governments into this mould. If they do not conform to the rules of the capitalist game, they are bound to lose out also in the power game:

> The cheap prices of [its] commodities are the heavy artillery with which [the bourgeoisie] batters down all Chinese walls, with which it forces the barbarians' intensely obstinate hatred of foreigners to capitulate. It compels all nations, on pain of extinction, to adopt the bourgeois mode of production; it compels them to introduce what it calls civilization into their midst, i.e., to become bourgeois themselves. In one word, it creates a world after its own image.[6]

In sum, the Marxian legacy originally consisted of a model of bourgeois society which made three strong predictions. 1. Bourgeois society tends to polarize into two classes, the bourgeoisie itself and the proletariat, understood as a class of workers who live only so long as they find work, and who find work only so long as their labour increases capital. 2. Capitalist accumulation tends to impoverish and, simultaneously, to strengthen the proletariat within bourgeois society. The strengthening relates to the role of the proletariat as producer of social wealth, the impoverishment relates to its role as more or less commodified labour-power subject to all the vicissitudes of competition. 3. The socially and politically blind laws of market competition tend to merge these two tendencies into a general loss of legitimacy of the bourgeois order which provokes its supersession by a non-competitive, non-exploitative world order.

In order to assess the extent to which these predictions have been borne out by the subsequent history of capitalism, it is useful to break up the 140 years that separate us from 1848 into three periods of roughly equal length: 1848 to 1896; 1896 to 1948; and 1948 to the present. This periodization is meaningful for many of the problems at hand. They all correspond to a 'long wave' of economic activity, each comprising a phase of 'prosperity' in which relations of cooperation in the economy are predominant (A phases) and a phase of 'depression' in which relations of competition predominate (B phases). Besides that, each fifty-year period has its own specificities.

Between 1848 and 1896 market capitalism and bourgeois society, as analysed by Marx, reached their apogee. The modern labour movement was born in this period and immediately became the central anti-systemic force. After a protracted struggle against rival doctrines, Marxism became the dominant ideology of the movement. In the period 1896 to 1948 market capitalism and bourgeois society as theorized by Marx entered a prolonged and ultimately fatal crisis. The labour movement reached its apogee as the central anti-systemic force, and Marxism consolidated and extended its hegemony over anti-systemic movements. However, new divisions appeared within and among anti-systemic movements, and Marxism itself was split apart into a revolutionary and a reformist wing. After 1948 corporate or managerial capitalism emerged from the ashes of market capitalism as the dominant world-economic structure. The spread of anti-systemic movements increased further but so did their fragmentation and reciprocal antagonisms. Under the pressure of these antagonisms, Marxism has been thrown into a crisis from which it has yet to recover and, indeed, may never recover.

I THE RISE OF THE WORLD LABOUR MOVEMENT

The major trends and events of the first period (1848–96) conformed to the expectations of the *Manifesto*. The spread of free-trade practices and the transport revolution in the 20–25 years that followed 1848 made market capitalism more of a world-wide reality than it had ever been before. World-market competition intensified and industry expanded rapidly for most of the fifty-year period. The proletarianization of intermediate strata became more pronounced, though not as widespread and irreversible as it is often claimed. Partly because of the contraction of the intermediate strata, partly because of a widening gap between the incomes of proletarian and bourgeois households, and partly because of the greater residential concentration and segregation of the proletariat, the polarization of society into two distinct and counterposed classes seemed an indisputable tendency, though more so in some countries than in others.

The tendency of capitalist accumulation simultaneously to impoverish and strengthen the proletariat was also in evidence. The greater concentration of the proletariat associated with the spread of industrialization made its organization in the form of unions much easier, and the strategic position of wage-workers in the new production processes endowed these organizations with considerable power, not only vis-à-vis capitalist employers, but vis-à-vis governments as well. The successes of the British labour movement in the course of the mid nineteenth century A phase in limiting the length of the working day and in extending the franchise were the most visible but not the only expressions of such power. Yet the proletariat was also being impoverished. Each victory had to be sanctioned by market forces which narrowly constrained the capacity of workers to resist the economic and political command of the bourgeoisie. It was in this period that unemployment acquired qualitatively and quantitatively new dimensions which curtailed the improvements in the proletariat's working and living conditions and intensified competitive pressures in its midst.

Finally, as predicted by the *Manifesto*, the two opposing tendencies of impoverishment and strengthening jointly undermined proletarian consent for bourgeois rule. A relatively free circulation of commodities, capital and workers within and across state jurisdictions spread the costs and risks of unemployment among proletarian households. The consequent loss of legitimacy led to an entirely new degree of political autonomy of the proletariat from the bourgeoisie. Only now did the era of working-class political parties begin. But whether or not such parties had come into existence, wage-workers in all core countries shook off their traditional subordination to the political interests of the bourgeoisie and began to pursue their own interests autonomously from, and if necessary against, the bourgeoisie. The most spectacular (and dramatic) expression of this political emancipation was the Paris Commune of 1871. In the Commune, the proletariat for the first time held political power 'for two whole months' (as Marx and Engels wrote enthusiastically in the preface to the 1872 German edition of the *Manifesto*). Although defeated, the Paris Commune was hailed by Marx as exemplary of the future organization of the proletariat as the ruling class.

The close fit of the trends and events of 1848–96 with the predictions of the *Manifesto* goes a long way towards explaining the hegemony that Marx and his followers established over the nascent European labour movement. Their success came only after protracted intellectual struggles over whether proletarianization was historically irreversible— and so formed the proper ground on which to carry forward the struggles of the present for the society of the future as theorized by Marx—or whether proletarians could historically recover their lost economic independence through one form or another of cooperative production. The latter view had been propounded in earlier periods by the Owenites in England the the Fourierists in France but lived on in new and different forms among the followers of Proudhon and Bakunin in France, Belgium, Russia, Italy and Spain, and of Lassalle in Germany.

The First International was little more than a sounding board of this intellectual struggle which saw Marx on the side of British trade-unionists (the only real representatives of an actually existing industrial proletariat) against a mixed bag of revolutionary and reformist intellectuals (some of working-class extraction) from Continental Europe. Even though Marx largely ran the show, he never won a clear-cut victory and, when he did, the impact on the real movement was illusory. The moment of truth came with the Paris Commune. The conclusions that Marx drew from that experience (the need to constitute legal working-class parties in each country as the presupposition of socialist revolution) alienated, for opposite reasons, Continental revolutionaries and British trade-unionists alike, and the end of the International was sealed.[7]

Towards a New International

Just as the First International was disintegrating with no winners and many losers around 1873, the mid century phase of 'prosperity' turned in the late century Great Depression, and the conditions were created both for the labour movement in its modern form to take off and for Marxists to establish hegemony over the movement. Intensifying competitive pressures widened and deepened processes of proletarianization and multiplied the occasions of conflict between labour and capital. Between 1873 and 1896, strike activity on an unprecedented scale developed in one country after the other, while working-class parties were being established throughout Europe along the lines recommended by Marx in 1871. By 1896 a new International, this time based on working-class parties with a broad unity of purpose, had become a reality.

The success of the *Manifesto* in predicting the broad contours of the subsequent fifty years was and is quite impressive. Yet not all the relevant facts fitted into the Marxian scheme—most importantly, proletarian politics itself. For the only major attempt by the proletariat to constitute itself as the ruling class along the lines theorized by Marx, the Paris Commune, was almost completely unrelated to the kind of tendencies which, according to that theory, were supposed to bring about such a revolutionary takeover. It was not the outcome of structural factors (a strengthening of the proletariat, due to the advancement of industry, combined with its growing impoverishment, due to commodification) but mainly the result of political factors: the defeat of France by Prussia and the harsh conditions created by the war. That is to say, the proletariat attempted a political revolution not because of a growing contradiction between its increasing exploitation and its increasing power in production processes, but because the bourgeois state had proved to be incompetent in 'protecting' French society in general, and the Parisian proletariat in particular, from or against another state.

It might be argued that defeat in war was only the detonator of structural contradictions which were the real, that is, deeper, cause of the explosion. It is certainly true that where structural contradictions were most developed (in England throughout the period under examination, in the United States from the late 1870s onwards) the level of direct class warfare between labour and capital (as gauged, for example, by strike activity) was indeed much higher than elsewhere.[8] The problem is, however, that labour unrest in these countries showed no propensity whatsoever to turn into political revolution. If the British industrial proletariat (by far the most developed as a class in itself, and the most prone to strike activity, around 1871) had had the slightest propensity in this direction, its representatives in the First International would have taken a more positive attitude towards the Paris Commune than they actually did. Their negative attitude was in fact symptomatic of a major problem with the Marxian scheme, and probably played a role in inducing Marx to abandon his active involvement in labour politics.

The disjunction between direct and more roundabout forms of the class struggle was confirmed after the Paris Commune in a different way. As we have seen, the coming of the late nineteenth-century Great Depression coincided with a major upsurge in strike activity (the most direct form of class struggle) and the formation of national working-class parties (a roundabout form of class struggle). Even though these two tendencies seemed to validate the predictions of the *Manifesto*, their spatial separation could not be fitted easily into the Marxian scheme. The countries that were leading in strike activity (Britain and the USA) were the laggards in the formation of working-class parties, while the reverse was the case in Germany. Generally speaking, the formation of working-class parties seemed to have little to do with economic exploitation, working-class formation and structural conflict between labour and capital. Rather, the main determinants seemed to be the actual and perceived centrality of the state in social and economic regulation, and the struggle for basic civil rights (rights to assembly and to vote in the first place) of and for the proletariat. In Germany, where the state was highly visible and a growing industrial proletariat was denied basic civil rights, the class struggle took the roundabout form of the organization of a working-class party. Only at the end of the Great Depression, above all in the subsequent A phase, did the class struggle take the form of a direct clash between labour and capital. In Britain and the USA, where the state was less centrally organized and the proletariat had already secured basic civil rights, the class struggle took the form of strike activity and trade-union formation, and only much later (in Britain) or never (in the USA) were attempts to form nationally significant working-class parties successful.

These differences will be further discussed in the next section. For now let us simply note that the history of the class struggle in the first fifty years after the publication of the *Manifesto* provided *both* strong evidence in support of its main predictions *and* some food for thought on the validity of the relationship between class struggle and socialist revolution postulated by Marx and Engels. More specifically, the socio-economic formation of the industrial proletariat led to the development of structural forms of class struggle, but did not lead to the development of political, let alone politically revolutionary, tendencies within the proletariat. The attitude of the proletariat towards political power remained purely instrumental *unless*, as in Continental Europe, political conditions themselves (relations among states, and relations between states and their subjects) prompted a more direct, and if necessary revolutionary, participation in political activity. In the huge late-century advances of the labour movement (and of Marxism within it), these anomalies must have looked like details unworthy of much consideration. Moreover, it was still reasonable to expect that the invisible hand of the market would take care of national discrepancies, and make the labour movements of all countries converge towards a common pattern of struggle, consciousness and organization. As it turned out, what had been a minor anomaly became in the next half-century a major historical trend which split the labour movement into two opposite and antagonistic camps.

II GLOBAL WARS, MOVEMENT AND REVOLUTION

Between 1896 and 1948 the orderliness of world-market rule for political and social actors broke down, and Marx's expectation of ever more homogenized conditions of existence in the world proletariat went unfulfilled. Following nineteenth-century liberal ideology, Marx had assumed that the world market operated over the heads rather than through the hands of state actors. This proved to be a major misconception because the world market of his time was first and foremost an instrument of British rule over the expanded European state system. As such, its effectiveness rested on a particular distribution of power and wealth among a multiplicity of ruling groups whose continuing consent, or at least acquiescence, was essential to the continuation of British hegemony.

The Great Depression of 1873–96 was both the high and the terminal point of world-market rule as instituted in the nineteenth century. A major aspect of the Depression was the arrival in Europe of massive and cheap overseas (and Russian) grain supplies. The main beneficiaries were the overseas suppliers (the US in the first place) and the hegemonic power itself, which was the main importer of overseas grain and controlled most of world commercial and financial intermediation. The main loser was Germany, whose rapidly rising wealth and power still relied heavily on the domestic production of grain and very little on the organization of world commerce and finance. Threatened by the new developments, the German ruling classes responded with a further build-up of their military–industrial complex in an attempt to displace or join Britain at the commanding heights of the world-economy. The result was a generalized and open power struggle in the interstate system which took two world wars to resolve.

In the course of this struggle world-market rule was impaired and, during and after the First World War, suspended. The demise of world-market rule did not stop the 'advancement of industry' and the 'commodification of labour'—the two tendencies which, in the Marxian scheme, were supposed to generate a simultaneous increase in the social power and the mass misery of labour. On the contrary, global wars and their preparation were more powerful factors of industrial advancement and mass misery than market rule had ever been. But the demise of the world market meant that the social power and the mass misery of the world proletariat came to be distributed among its various segments far less evenly than they had been before.

Generally speaking, in the periods of war mobilization the size of the Active Industrial Army increased (both absolutely and relative to the size of the Reserve Army) in most locations of the world-economy—including countries not directly involved in the war. Moreover, the increasing 'industrialization of war' in the late nineteenth and early twentieth centuries had made the cooperation of industrial recruits as important as (if not more important than) the cooperation of military recruits in determining the outcome of war efforts. The social power of labour thus grew in step with the escalation of the power struggle in the interstate system.

But global wars also absorbed a growing amount of resources, while disrupting the networks of production and exchange through which resources were procured. As a consequence, the overall capabilities of the ruling classes to accommodate labour's demands decreased or did not rise as rapidly as the social power of labour. World wars thus created that combination of proletarian power and proletarian deprivation which, in the Marxian scheme, was supposed to bring about an intensification of the class struggle and the eventual demise of the rule of capital.

Both world wars did in fact generate global waves of class struggle. Overall strike activity declined in the opening years of the two wars only to escalate rapidly in their closing years. The resulting peaks in world labour unrest had no historical precedent, and have remained unmatched to this day. And each peak was associated with a major socialist revolution—in Russia and then in China. Though these waves of class struggle did not bring the rule of capital to an end, they did bring about fundamental changes in the way in which that rule was exercised. These changes proceeded along two radically different and divergent trajectories which correspond quite closely to the opposite stands taken by Bernstein and Lenin in the course of the so-called Revisionist Controversy.

In one of its final resolutions, the International Socialist Congress of 1896 predicted an imminent general crisis which would put the exercise of state power on the agenda of socialist parties. It therefore impressed upon the proletariat of all countries 'the imperative necessity of learning, as class-conscious citizens, how to administer the business of their respective countries for the common good'. In line with this resolution, it was decided that future congresses would be open only to representatives of organizations that worked to transform the capitalist order into a socialist order and were prepared to participate in legislative and parliamentary activities. All anarchists were thereby excluded.

Movement and Goal

The end of the old controversy between the followers of Marx and Bakunin marked the beginning of a new controversy among the followers of Marx themselves. While the goal of working towards the socialist transformation of the capitalist order was stated in terms sufficiently vague and ambiguous to suit all shades of opinion among Marx's followers, the very definition of a common political objective for the proletariat of all countries posed some fundamental theoretical and practical problems. Eduard Bernstein was the first to bring these problems out into the open.

Even though Bernstein has gone down in history as the Great Revisionist of Marxian thought, his declared revisionism was actually very mild, particularly in comparison with some of his 'orthodox' opponents. In line with the principles of *scientific* socialism, he sought validation/invalidation for Marx's theses of a secular increase in the social power of labour and of a simultaneous secular increase in its misery. And like Marx, he thought that the best guide to the future of the labour movement in Continental Europe in general and in Germany in particular was the past and present of the movement in Britain. He accordingly focused his attention on trends in the latter.

Starting from these premises, Bernstein found plenty of evidence in support of the first thesis but little in support of the second: not only had there been significant improvements in the standards of life and work of the industrial proletariat, but political democracy had been expanded and transformed from a tool of subordination into a tool of emancipation of the working classes. Writing at the end of the Great Depression of 1873–96 and at the beginning of the *belle époque* of European capitalism, he saw no reason why these trends should be reversed in the foreseeable future. The liberal organizations of modern society were there to stay, and were sufficiently flexible to accommodate an indefinite increase in the social power of labour. As in the past, all that was needed was 'organization and *energetic action*' (emphasis added, GA). A socialist revolution, in the sense of a revolutionary dictatorship of the proletariat, was neither necessary not desirable.[9]

Bernstein summed up his position in the slogan 'The movement is everything, the goal nothing.' This sounded like a provocation to Marxist reformists and revolutionaries alike. It was in fact a reformist (Karl Kautsky) who led the onslaught against Bernstein's revisionism. Kautsky argued, essentially, that all economic and political gains of the proletariat were conjunctural, that a general crisis was inevitable and indeed in-the-making, and that in such a crisis the bourgeoisie would try to win back forcibly whatever economic and political concessions it had had to make previously to the proletariat. Under these circumstances, everything would be lost unless the proletariat and its organizations were prepared to seize and to hold, if necessary through politically revolutionary means, the commanding heights of the state and of the economy. Thus, although Kautsky retained all of Marx's ambiguities concerning the relationship between the present struggles of the proletariat (the 'movement' in Bernstein's slogan) and the ultimate objective of socialist revolution (the 'goal'), his position at this time was a short step away from the conclusion that the goal was everything and the movement nothing.

Kautsky himself never took this step. It was left to Lenin, who had sided with Kautsky against Bernstein, to carry Kautsky's argument to its logical conclusion. If only a socialist seizure of state power could save/ expand all previous achievements of the movement, then the former had clear priority over the latter. It also followed that the achievements of the movement were deceptive. For one thing, they did not take into account the future losses that the movement, left to itself, would inevitably encounter. In addition, they only reflected one side of the proletarian condition. By adding new emphasis to the thesis of the 'labour aristocracy', Lenin implicitly dismissed Marx's view that the best guide to the future of the labour movement in Continental Europe and elsewhere was the present and the past of the labour movement in Britain. The increasing social power of labour in Britain was a local and short-term phenomenon connected with Britain's position at the commanding heights of the world economy. The present and the future of the proletariat of Continental Europe in general and of the Russian Empire in particular was one of increasing mass misery and continuing political oppression, notwithstanding the presence of highly energetic and well-organized labour movements.

Two conclusions followed. First, the achievements (or for that matter the failures) of proletarian movements created the wrong kind of perceptions among their leaderships and rank-and-file. Consciousness of the necessity and the possibility of socialist revolution could only develop outside the movements and had to be brought to them by a professional revolutionary vanguard. Second, the organizations of the movements had to be transformed into 'transmission belts' capable of conveying the commands of the revolutionary vanguards to the proletarian masses. In this theorization, the movement was truly nothing, mere means, the goal everything.

A Contradictory Balance

Looking back at the actual evolution of the labour movement over the entire period 1896–1948, we find plenty of evidence validating either Lenin's or Bernstein's positions but very little validating the intermediate Kautskian position. It all depends where we look. Bernstein's prediction/ prescription that organization and energetic action were sufficient to force/induce the ruling classes to accommodate economically and politically the secular increase in the social power of labour associated with the advancement of industry captures the essence of the trajectory of the labour movements of the Anglo-Saxon and Scandinavian worlds. Notwithstanding two world wars and a catastrophic world-economic crisis, which Bernstein failed to predict, the proletariat in these locations continued to experience an improvement in economic welfare and governmental representation commensurate with its increasingly important role in the system of social production.

The most spectacular advances occurred in Sweden and Australia. But the most significant advances from the point of view of the politics of the world-economy took place in Britain (the declining hegemonic power but still the dominant colonial power) and in the USA (the rising hegemonic power). A marginal and subordinate force in the national politics of both states in 1896, organized labour had become by 1948 the governing party of Britain and a decisive influence on the US government. All this was achieved precisely along the path predicted and prescribed by Bernstein—the path, that is, of energetic and well-organized movements capable of exploiting whatever opportunity arose to transform the increasing social power of labour into greater economic welfare and better political representation. In this context, the goal of socialist revolution never became an issue, and revolutionary vanguards of the proletariat found few followers.

Yet, 1896–1948 was also the period of the greatest successes of socialist revolution, the period when self-proclaimed revolutionary vanguards of the proletariat took control of the means of rule over almost half of Eurasia. Though different in many respects, the experiences of the proletariat in the Russian and former Chinese empires presented important analogies. Vigorous movements of protest (in 1905 in the Russian empire, in 1925–27 in China) had failed to improve the conditions of existence for the proletariat: increasing mass misery, rather than increasing social power, was its overwhelming experience. Moreover, the escalation of the interstate power struggle ('imperialism' in Lenin's theory of revolution) had further lessened the ability of the ruling classes to provide the proletariat with minimal protection.

Under these circumstances a vanguard of dedicated revolutionaries, trained in the scientific analysis of social events, trends and conjunctures, could take advantage of the disruption of national and world power networks to carry out successful socialist revolutions. The foundation of the power of this vanguard was the impoverishment of the increasingly extensive exploited masses, regardless of their precise class locations. For increasing mass misery transformed the vast majority of the population into actual or potential members of the Industrial Reserve Army and, at the same time, prevented whoever happened to be in the Active Industrial Army at any given time from developing a separate class identity from that of other subordinate groups and classes. In this context, the movements of protest that did develop within the transient and precarious condition of the wage-labour force provided neither an adequate foundation for a continuing movement, nor a direction to political action oriented towards the socialist transformation of the existing social order. The ways and means of that transformation had indeed to be developed outside of, and often in opposition to, the spontaneous movements of protest of the proletarian masses.

The most striking feature of these divergent tendencies—the development of the social power of labour in some locations and of socialist revolution against mass misery in others—is that, taken together, they demonstrated the historical imperviousness of the industrial proletariat to socialist-revolutionary ideologies and practices. Where the social power of the industrial proletariat was significant and growing, socialist revolution had no constituency; and where socialist revolution had a constituency, the industrial proletariat had no social power. As we saw above, the negative correlation between the social power of labour and its socialist revolutionary predispositions had already appeared in embryonic form at the time of the Paris Commune, and it was probably the most important single cause of the disbanding of the First International. Faced with a choice, both theoretical and political, between a strong but reformist labour movement in Britain and a revolutionary but weak labour movement in France, Marx chose not to choose and left the issue up in the air.

Fateful Choices

As Marxism turned into a political institution, against Marx's and Engels's original intentions, a choice had to be made, particularly in view of the fact that the disjunction between the social power and the revolutionary predispositions of the proletariat was increasing instead of decreasing. Bernstein posed the problem and chose to side with the social power of labour (the 'movement'); Lenin chose to side with the revolutionary predispositions that grew out of increasing mass misery (the 'goal', in Bernstein's antinomy); and Kautsky, like Marx thirty years earlier, chose not to choose. This indeed was his only legitimate claim to 'orthodoxy'.

This choice not to choose had disastrous political implications. Whereas Bernstein's choice was validated by the subsequent successes of labour movements in the Anglo-Saxon world and Scandinavia, and Lenin's choice by the subsequent successes of socialist revolution in the former Russian and Chinese empires, Kautsky's choice not to choose was invalidated as a political strategy by the subsequent successes of counter-revolution in Central and Southern Europe. For the rise of Fascism and National Socialism can be traced at least in part to the chronic inability of the relevant working-class organizations to choose between energetic reformist and energetic revolutionary action.

To be sure, this chronic inability to choose was related to the more complex social situation which labour organizations faced in these regions—a situation, that is, characterized by a combination of increasing social power of labour and of increasing mass misery rather than by the predominance of one or the other tendency. The contradiction was real and localized. This combination generated within the industrial proletariat significant revolutionary predispositions alongside

more reformist predispositions—a combination that left the leadership of
the movement in a permanent dilemma. Kautsky's choice not to choose,
and the impressive theoretical and political apparatus that backed it up,
provided plenty of justifications for a leadership which, instead of tilting
the balance in a specific direction, reflected passively the divisions that
tore apart the movement and thus compounded political confusion and
disorientation.

We shall never know whether a more energetic reformist or revolutionary action on the part of German Social Democracy would have
made any difference to subsequent German and world history. But just
as the historical responsibilities of German Social Democracy (or for
that matter of Italian Socialism) in paving the way to National Socialism
and Fascism should not be belittled, they should not be exaggerated
either. For the hegemonic successes of reactionary elites in seizing power
in countries as diverse as Germany, Japan and Italy had world-systemic
as well as local causes. The world-systemic causes were the joint
processes of disintegration of world-market rule and escalation of the
interstate power struggle outlined at the beginning of this section. These
processes put a premium on war-preparedness, which in the twentieth
century had come to mean first and foremost expansion and modernization of military–industrial complexes, on the one hand, an exclusive or
privileged access to the world-economic resources required for that
expansion and modernization, on the other hand. In states affected by a
structural disequilibrium between an overgrown military–industrial
apparatus and a narrow domestic economic base, revanchist ideologies
had a strong appeal to all kinds of social groups, including non-
negligible fractions of the industrial proletariat.

Under these circumstances, the political indeterminacy engendered
by the contradictory predispositions of the industrial proletariat towards
reform and revolution contributed to undermine the legitimacy of
organized labour, regardless of its actual role in compounding the
indeterminacy. Whatever its causes, the rise of National Socialism in
Germany became the decisive event in precipitating a new round of
generalized war and class struggle. It was in the course of this round that
organized labour became a decisive political influence on the great
powers of the Anglo-Saxon world and that the domain of socialist-
revolutionary regimes came to include almost half of Eurasia.

It is important to note that this prodigious expansion of the political
power of elected and self-appointed representatives of the industrial
proletariat took place in the context of an almost complete disappearance of autonomous revolutionary predispositions on the part of the
industrial proletariat itself. Nowhere during and after the Second World
War did the industrial proletariat attempt to take state power into its

own hands through 'communes' or 'soviets'—not even in defeated countries, as it had done in France in 1871, in Russia in 1917, in Germany and Austria–Hungary in 1919–20. The expansion of the domain of socialist revolutionary regimes was essentially due to armies defeating other armies—a proletarian version of Gramsci's 'Piedmontese Function'.[10]

In Eastern Europe, Communist regimes were established by the Soviet Army, substantively if not formally. Elsewhere, as in Yugoslavia, Albania and, most importantly, China, Communist regimes were established by indigenous armies raised and controlled by revolutionary political elites and cadres who had taken the lead in the struggle of national liberation against Axis Powers. Even in Italy and France, where Communist parties won hegemony over significant fractions of the industrial proletariat, this hegemony was largely the result of previous leadership in the armed struggle against German Occupation. Rejected by the labour movement of core countries, socialist revolution found a new and highly responsive constituency in national liberation movements.

III US HEGEMONY AND THE REMAKING OF THE WORLD LABOUR MOVEMENT

In 1948 a simple extrapolation of the main social and political trends of the previous half-century pointed towards an imminent termination of the rule of capital. Each round of generalized war and class struggle had resulted in major advances of socialist revolution in the periphery and semiperiphery of the world-economy and in major advances in the social and political power of the industrial proletariat in core countries. Were the trends not reversed, the only question that remained open was not whether capitalism would survive but by what particular mix of reforms and revolutions it would die.

But the trends were reversed, and in the next twenty years capitalism experienced a new 'golden age' of unprecedented expansion. The single most important development was the pacification of interstate relations and the reconstruction of the world market under US hegemony. Up to 1968, the reconstruction of the world market remained partial and heavily dependent on US military and financial capabilities. Then, between 1968 and 1973, the collapse of the Bretton Woods system and the defeat of the US in Vietnam showed that these capabilities in and by themselves were no longer either sufficient or necessary for the ongoing process of world-market reconstruction. For it is precisely from 1973 onwards that the world market seems to have become within limits an 'autonomous force' that no one state (the US included) can control. In concert, states, corporations and administering agencies can, and do, construct and manage the limits of the world market, but not without difficulty and unintended consequences. As a matter of fact, it would seem that at no time in capitalist history has the rule of the world market per se approached Marx's limiting ideal type as much as it has in the last 15–20 years.

Today, the social foundations of the world market are quite different from what they were in the nineteenth century. At the end of the war, the US did not set out to re-establish the same kind of world market that had collapsed over the previous fifty years. Quite apart from the historical lessons of that collapse and the structural differences between nineteenth-century British capitalism and twentieth-century US capitalism to be discussed presently, the power and influence gained by organized labour in the US and Britain and the successes of socialist revolution in Eurasia made such a re-establishment neither feasible nor advisable. The most enlightened factions of the US ruling classes had long understood that no return to the strictly bourgeois order of the nineteenth century was possible. A new world order could not be built on the social power and aspirations of the world bourgeoisie alone; it also had to include as large a fraction of the world proletariat as, in their view, was possible.

A most important aspect of this strategy was US support for 'decolonization' and for an expansion/consolidation of the system of sovereign states. Like Wilson before him, Franklin D. Roosevelt implicitly shared Lenin's view that the struggle over territory and population among core capitalist states was a negative-sum game that created a favourable environment for socialist revolutions and the ultimate demise of the world rule of capital. If the tide of socialist revolution in Eurasia was to be stopped before it was too late, this struggle had to be brought to an end and the right to self-determination of the weaker fractions of the world bourgeoisie and of the world proletariat had to be acknowledged.

A secondary yet highly important objective of Roosevelt's world-hegemonic strategy was to accommodate the social power of labour at home and to expand it abroad. This policy had a number of advantages for the coalition of interests that had come to rule the US. From the point of view of corporate capital, it would create in Europe and elsewhere 'domestic' mass markets similar to the one already existing in the US and thus pave the way for its further transnational expansion. From the point of view of organized labour, it reduced the threat of competitive pressures originating in the lower standards of returns for effort obtaining almost everywhere else in the world. Last and most important, from the point of view of the government, a policy of accommodation at home and expansion abroad of the social power of labour meant that the US could present itself, and be widely perceived, as the bearer of interests, not just of capital, but of labour as well. It was this policy, together with support for decolonization, that transformed US military and financial supremacy into a true world hegemony.[11]

American military and financial power thus became the vehicle through which the ideology and practice of the primacy of the movement over the goal, typical of the US labour movement, was exported as far as that power reached. The transplant was most successful in those defeated states (West Germany and Japan) where the US Army by itself or in collusion with its allies held absolute governmental power and, at the same time, industrialization had proceeded far enough to provide organized labour with a firm social base. Even where it was most successful, however, this restructuring of class relations from above by a foreign power would have come to nothing had it not been followed, as it was, by the reconstruction of world-market rule and a rapid spread of the structures of accumulation on which the social power of labour in the US rested.

In the previous section, the labour movement in the United States was dealt with as part of a wider Anglo-Saxon model in which the 'movement' had primacy over the 'goal'. Yet in the interwar period it had come to exemplify better than the labour movement in any other country the social power that the accumulation of capital puts in the hands of labour. Elsewhere—particularly in the UK, Australia and Sweden—strong labour movements had found expression in the rise of Labour Parties, which remained under the control of the movement but could act as substitutes for and complements of the movement if and when the need arose. In the USA no such development had taken place. At most an existing party had become the principal political representation of organized labour. The movement went forward or foundered as its capabilities of self-mobilization and self-organization succeeded or failed.

New Structures of Accumulation

These capabilities were the unintended consequence of the structural transformations undergone by US capital over the previous half-century. Also in this respect, the Great Depression of 1873–96 had been a decisive turning point. It was in that period that US capital had created vertically integrated, bureaucratically managed structures of accumulation that corresponded to the full development of Marx's 'production of relative surplus value'.[12]

As painstakingly demonstrated by Harry Braverman, the creation of these structures of accumulation was associated with a shopfloor recomposition such that as the labour processes became more complex the skills required of each participant became fewer and less difficult to master (his 'de-skilling'). This reworking of the technical division of labour undermined the social power of the comparatively small class of wage-workers (primarily craftsmen) who controlled the skills necessary to perform the complex tasks. However, the decreasing social power of craftworkers was only one side of the coin. The other side was the greater social power that accrued to the comparatively much larger class of waged operatives who came to perform the simpler ('semi-skilled') tasks.

'De-skilling' was in fact a double-edged sword which eased the valorization of capital in one direction only to make it more problematic in another. The valorization of capital was eased because it was made less dependent on the knowledge and skills of craftworkers. But this was associated with a major expansion of managerial hierarchies (Galbraith's 'technostructures') whose valorization depended on the speed of production processes and, therefore, on the willingness of a large mass of operatives to cooperate with one another and with management in keeping production flows moving at the required speed. This greater importance of the productive effort of a large mass of operatives for the valorization of complex and expensive technostructures provided the social power of labour with a new and broader foundation.

This new and broader foundation became manifest for the first time in the course of the long wave of strikes and labour unrest that unfolded in the United States between the mid 1930s and the late 1940s. The strike wave began as a spontaneous response of the rank-and-file of the industrial proletariat to the attempts by capital to shift on to labour the burdens of the Great Slump of the early 1930s.[13] The main and indeed the only pre-existing organization of the industrial proletariat of any significance (the AFL) did nothing to initiate the strike wave. It became active in organizing and leading the movement only when the latter had proved capable of standing on its own and of generating alternative organizational structures, which became the CIO.

The struggles were most successful in the period of war mobilization which, as argued earlier on, tended to inflate the social power of labour. McCarthyism notwithstanding, most of the wartime gains were then consolidated in the period of de-mobilization, and for a decade or two the US industrial proletariat enjoyed unprecedented and unparalleled economic welfare and political influence. But the social power of labour in the US was also contained. The most effective forms of struggle were delegitimated, conflict was routinized, and the pace of corporate expansion abroad experienced a sudden acceleration.

The predisposition of US corporate capital to expand its operations transnationally long preceded the strike wave of the 1930s and 1940s. It was built into the processes of vertical integration and of bureaucratization of management which brought it into being in the late nineteenth century and constituted its essential form of expansion. In the 1930s and 1940s, however, the escalation of the interstate power struggle seriously hampered US direct investment in Europe and its colonies precisely at a time when the increasing social power of labour at home was making expansion abroad more profitable and urgent. It should be no surprise, therefore, that as soon as Washington had created conditions highly favourable for corporate expansion in Western Europe (primarily through the Marshall Plan), US capital seized the opportunity and set out to remake Europe in its image and according to its likeness.

American corporate capital was not the only actor involved in this remaking of Europe. European governments and businesses joined eagerly in the enterprise, in part to catch up with the new standards of power and wealth set by the US and in part to meet the competition brought into their midst by the US corporate invasion. The result was an unprecedented expansion of production facilities which embodied the new structures of accumulation pioneered in the US in the first half of the century. With the new structures of accumulation came also a massive increase in the social power of European labour, signalled in the late 1960s and early 1970s by a strike wave that presented important analogies with the US of the 1930s and 1940s. First, this wave also was largely based on the capacity for self-mobilization and self-organization of the rank-and-file of the industrial proletariat. Pre-existing labour organizations, regardless of their ideological orientation, played no role in initiating the struggles and became involved in leading and organizing the militancy only when the latter had proved capable of standing on its own and of generating alternative organizational structures. Often, the new movements and labour organizations came into conflict with one another as the latter tried to impose on the former their own political objectives and the former struggled to retain their autonomy from objectives that transcended the proletarian condition.

Second, the foundation of the self-mobilization and self-organization of the industrial proletariat was wholly internal to the proletarian condition. Self-mobilization was a spontaneous and collective response to the attempts of capital to shift the intensifying competitive pressures of the world-economy on to labour by curtailing rewards for effort (primarily by demanding greater effort). And self-organization was the use of the technical organization of the labour process so as to coordinate scattered acts of insurgency.

Third, the movement was highly successful, not only in the pursuit of its immediate objectives, but in inducing the ruling classes to accommodate the social power demonstrated by labour in the struggles. Between 1968 and 1973, rewards for effort skyrocketed throughout Western Europe bringing them close to North American standards. At the same time or shortly afterwards, the formal or substantive restrictions on the civil and political rights of the industrial proletariat still in force in many Western European countries began to crumble.

The Transnational Expansion

Finally, the accommodation of the social power of labour was slowed and then halted by re-orienting the expansion of production processes towards more peripheral locations. Up to 1968, the transnational expansion of production processes, as measured for example by direct investment abroad, was primarily a US-based phenomenon, while European-based counterparts were a remnant of earlier colonial operations and experiences. Capitalist enterprises originating in small and wealthy countries, such as Sweden and Switzerland, had also engaged in this kind of expansion but the enterprises of the larger and more dynamic core countries, such as Germany and Japan, were conspicuous by their absence in the construction of transnational networks of production and distribution.

Then, between 1968 and 1973, there occurred a sudden acceleration in direct foreign investment in which previous laggards, Japan in particular, played a leading role. By 1988 control over transnational production and distribution networks had become a common feature of core capital of all nationalities, with Japanese capital close to overtaking US capital in extent and scope. Japan's leadership in the sudden acceleration of direct foreign investment in the 1970s and 1980s has not been just a matter of exceptionally high rates of growth. Accompanying, and indeed underlying, these growth-rates was an anticipation of, and a prompt adjustment to, world-economic trends in labour–capital relations. As soon as domestic strike activity and labour costs began to rise, Japanese capital promptly relocated abroad the production processes that were most dependent on an ample supply of cheap labour. What is more, at least in its initial stages the transnational expansion of Japanese capital, unlike that of US capital, was oriented primarily towards a reduction in costs rather than an expansion of revenues.[14]

Japanese leadership in the transnational expansion of capital of the 1970s and 1980s was built on an anticipation of the difficulties created for the accumulation of capital by the generalization of the structures of corporate capitalism to the entire core zone. As long as corporate capitalism was almost exclusively a US phenomenon, US corporations could pick and choose among a wide range of locations where to seek the valorization of their managerial hierarchies. This lack of competition was the single most important reason why US corporate capital in the 1950s and most of the 1960s could simultaneously expand its productive base abroad and at home, accommodate the social power of labour that went with that expansion, and increase the mass of profit under its control. By the late 1960s and early 1970s, the greatly expanded managerial hierarchies of US capital were no longer alone in seeking valorization outside their original domain. Western European and Japanese capitalist enterprises had developed the same kinds of capabilities and propensities, while the number of locations offering comparable opportunities of profitable expansion had decreased. Western Europe, which had been a prime location for the valorization of US capital externally, was itself seeking a profitable outlet for its own overgrown technostructures. Opportunities for foreign direct investment in the rest of the world were narrowly constrained, either by centralized state controls over production and distribution (as in all Communist countries) or by mass misery (as in most Third World countries) or by a combination of the two.

The cost-cutting race of the 1970s and 1980s has its deeper roots in this situation of overcrowding—that is, a situation in which too many corporate structures 'chased' too few locations offering profitable opportunities for expansion. In the 1970s, attempts by states and corporations to sustain the expansion of productive facilities and to accommodate the increasing social power of labour that went with it simply resulted in an accentuation of inflationary pressures. These pressures, in turn, enhanced the profitability of cost-cutting and the attractiveness of speculative activities which, in the 1980s, have accordingly drawn to them increasing monetary resources and entrepreneurial energies.

Financial speculation and cost-cutting activities are thus reflections of the growing inability of corporate capital to adjust to the increasing social power of labour that goes with corporate capital's own expansion. Their main impact has been a limited but none the less very real spread of mass misery to the core zone. The phenomenon has taken different forms: falling real wages (primarily in the US), rising unemployment (primarily in Western Europe), and an increasing effort-price of proletarian incomes in almost all core locations.

This increase in mass misery has not been associated with a proportionate decrease in the social power of labour. Financial speculation reflects the emergence of an incompatibility between corporate expansion and the increasing social power of labour. It cannot stop the latter without stopping the former. Its main effect is to undermine the social consensus on which the rule of capital has rested since the Second World War.

Cost-cutting

As for cost-cutting activities, they have taken three main forms: (a) a substitution of cheaper for more expensive sources of wage-labour *within* each and every core state—the feminization of the waged labour force being the most important aspect, and the use of first-generation, often illegal, immigrant labour its secondary aspect; (b) a substitution of cheaper for more expensive sources of wage labour *across* state boundaries, particularly between core and more peripheral regions—plant relocation and substitution of imports for domestic production here being the most important aspects; and (c) a substitution of intellectual and scientific labour-power for proletarian labour-power in production processes—automation and the use of science-based technologies being its most important aspects.

The first two kinds of substitution have been by far the most important in spreading mass misery to the proletariat of core countries. Yet neither of them involves a reduction in the overall social power of the world proletariat. What they do involve is a transfer of social power from one segment of the world proletariat to another. Substitution within core states transfers social power from male to female and from native to immigrant members of the industrial proletariat; and substitution across state boundaries transfers social power from the proletariat of one state to the proletariat of another state. Either way, social power changes hands but remains in the hands of the industrial proletariat.

Automation and science-based technologies, in contrast, involve a reduction in the social power of the proletariat as presently constituted. By transferring control over the quality and quantity of production from subordinate wage-workers to managers, intellectuals and scientists, this kind of substitution transfers social power from substantively proletarianized workers to workers who, at best, are proletarianized only in the formal sense of working for a wage or salary. However, the stronger this tendency and the larger the size of the managerial and scientific labour force in the overall economy of production processes, the stronger also the tendency for capital to subject this labour force to its rule, and thus make its proletarianization more substantive than it has been thus far. In this case, therefore, there is a transfer of social power out of the hands of the industrial proletariat, but only as a prelude to a future enlargement of its size and power.

It follows that the deteriorating living standards of the proletariat in core countries have been associated not so much with a loss as with a redistribution of social power within its present and future ranks. Social power and mass misery are no longer as polarized in different segments of the world proletariat as they were in the middle of the twentieth century. Mass misery has begun to spread to the proletariat of the core, while social power has begun to trickle down to the proletariat of the periphery and semiperiphery. In short, we are approaching the scenario envisaged by Marx and Engels in the *Manifesto*—a scenario in which the social power and the mass misery of labour affect the same human material rather than different and separate segments of the world proleteriat.

To be sure, social power and material deprivation are still distributed extremely unevenly among the various components of the world proletariat. Insofar as we can tell, such unevenness will remain for a long time to come. Yet the tendency of the first half of the twentieth century towards a spatial polarization of the social power and mass misery of labour in different and separate regions of the world-economy has begun to be reversed. Between 1948 and 1968, the social power previously enjoyed almost exclusively by the industrial proletariat of the Anglo-Saxon world spread to the industrial proletariat of the entire core zone, which had come to include most of Western Europe and Japan, while mass misery continued to be the predominant experience of the proletarianized and semi-proletarianized masses of the Third World. From circa 1968, however, this polarization became counterproductive for the further expansion of corporate capital. In core regions, the enlarged social power of labour began to interfere seriously with the command of capital over production processes. In peripheral regions, the enlarged mass misery of labour undermined the legitimacy of the rule of capital, impoverished markets, and interfered with the productive mobilization of large segments of the proletariat.

Faced with these opposite and mutually reinforcing obstacles to its further expansion, corporate capital has been trying ever since to overcome its difficulties by bringing the mass misery of the proletariat of the semiperiphery and periphery of the world-economy to bear upon the social power of labour in the core. The attempt has been eased by the ongoing reconstruction of the world market which, from 1968 onwards, has become increasingly independent of specifically US interests and power. This reflects, among other things, the ever widening and deepening transnational organization of production and distribution processes through which corporate capital regardless of nationality has been trying to bypass, contain and undermine the social power of labour in the core.

Reshuffling of the Proletariat

The result has been a major reshuffling of the human material that constitutes the Active and Reserve Industrial Armies. In comparison with twenty years ago, a far larger proportion of the world Active Industrial Army is now located in the periphery and semiperiphery of the world-economy, while the Active Army in the core contains a large number of female and immigrant recruits in its lower ranks and of formally proletarianized intellectuals and scientists in its upper ranks. This reshuffling has put considerable pressure on the native male workers of the core employed in the lower and middle ranks of the Active Army to accept lower standards of reward for effort or else be squeezed out of that Army.

Resistance against this deterioration of living standards in the core has thus far been rather weak and ineffectual mainly because the segments of the industrial proletariat that have experienced it most directly have also been affected by a loss of social power, while the segments that have been gaining social power have not yet experienced a major deterioration in living standards. In the case of the women and immigrants that have come to occupy the lower ranks of the industrial proletariat, two circumstances have softened the impact of the deterioration. On the one hand, standards of reward for effort in their previous occupations were in many instances even lower than standards obtaining in the lower ranks of the Active Industrial Army to which they have been recruited. On the other hand, often they still consider their rewards as a supplement to other sources of income and their efforts as temporary additions to their usual workload. Low rewards for effort are thus borne with greater patience than, one would imagine, they would be if rewards were perceived as the sole or principal source of income and if the efforts were perceived as a permanent addition to their workload.

Both circumstances are inherently transitory. Over time, standards of rewards for effort are formed by present rather than past conditions. In addition, the more widespread becomes the use of female and immigrant labour in the lower ranks of the Active Industrial Army, the more low rewards turn into the main source of income and high effort turns into a lifetime condition. As this happens, acquiescence gives way to open rebellion in which the social power of women and immigrants is turned against the rising tide of mass misery in the core. Even in the 1970s and 1980s women and immigrants in core states have shown a strong predisposition to rebel and make use of their social power; but we have yet to see a major wave of industrial conflict focused specifically on their grievances. If and when it occurs, this kind of wave will interact positively and negatively with movements of protest originating in the upper ranks of the Active Industrial Army.

These upper ranks are increasingly occupied by intellectuals and scientists who are taking over an ever widening range of productive tasks. For now, they are the main beneficiaries of the ongoing cost-cutting race which inflates the demand for their labour-power and provides them with comparatively inexpensive luxuries. But the more their weight in the cost structure of capital increases, the more they will be targeted as the main object of the cost-cutting race. At that point, these upper strata of the Active Industrial Army can also be expected to mobilize their social power in movements of protest to prevent mass misery from spreading to their own ranks.

These are the movements of the future of the core. But in the semi-periphery the future has already begun. The 1980s have witnessed major explosions of labour unrest in countries as far apart as Poland, South Africa and South Korea—just to mention the most significant cases. Notwithstanding the radically different political regimes and social structures, these explosions present important common features, some of which resemble those attributed earlier to the waves of class struggle of the 1930s and 1940s in the US and of the late 1960s and early 1970s in Western Europe. In all instances, industrial conflict has been largely based on the capabilities of self-mobilization and self-organization of the rank-and-file of the industrial proletariat. The foundation of these capabilities has been wholly internal to the proletarian condition and has consisted of a fundamental disequilibrium between the new social power and the old mass misery of the industrial proletariat.

The resemblances in these respects are striking. Nevertheless, the differences between this latest wave and the earlier waves have been as significant as the similarities. These movements have been as hard to repress as the earlier ones; but they have been far more difficult to accommodate. The reason lies not in the grievances themselves, which are far more basic than the grievances of the earlier waves, but in the limited capabilities of states and capital in the semiperiphery to adjust to even the most basic of grievances. The result might well be a situation of endemic social strife of the kind envisaged by Marx and Engels in the *Manifesto*.

IV THE CRISIS OF MARXISM IN
WORLD-HISTORICAL PERSPECTIVE

The argument that the predictions of the *Manifesto* concerning the world labour movement might be more relevant for the next 50–60 years than they have been for the last 90–100 years may seem to be contradicted by the current crisis of organized labour and Marxist organizations. There is no denying that over the last 15–20 years labour unions, working-class parties and states ruled by socialist governments, particularly of the Communist variety, have all been under considerable pressure to restructure themselves and change their orientation or face decline. This pressure, however, is not at all incompatible with the argument developed here. On the contrary, it provides further evidence in its support.

Like all other social organizations, proletarian organizations (whether Marxist or not) pursue strategies and have structures that reflect the historical circumstances under which they have come into existence, and most continue to retain the same sort of strategy and structure long after the circumstances of their origin are finished. The proletarian ideologies and organizations that are now under pressure to change or face decline all reflect the historical circumstances typical of the first half of the twentieth century—a period in which the capitalist world-economy departed in fundamental ways from the scenario sketched in the *Manifesto*. To the extent that the capitalist world-economy once again begins to match more closely that scenario, it is only to be expected that all organizations whose strategies and structures reflect the historical circumstances of a previous epoch would be challenged fundamentally and be faced with the prospect of decline. Some may be able to stave off the decline, even prosper, through a simple change in strategy. Others can attain the same result but only through a process of thorough self-restructuring. And others again can only decline, no matter what they do.

More specifically, Marx had assumed that market rule would constantly reshuffle within and across the various locations of the capitalist world-economy the increasing social power and the increasing mass misery of labour. In actual fact, for a long time this did not happen. In the first half of the twentieth century the escalation of the interstate power struggle first impaired and then totally disrupted the operation of the world market. The social power and the mass misery of labour increased faster than ever before but in polarized fashion, with the proletariat in some regions experiencing primarily an increase in social power, and the proletariat in other regions experiencing primarily an increase in mass misery. As Marx had predicted, this accentuation of the tendencies towards an increasing social power and an increasing mass misery of labour gave a tremendous impulse to the spread of proletarian struggles, ideologies and organizations. But the polarized fashion in which the two tendencies materialized made proletarian struggles, ideologies and organizations develop along trajectories which Marx had neither predicted nor advocated.

The assumption that the two tendencies would affect the same human

material across the space of the capitalist world-economy was an essential ingredient in Marx's theory of the socialist transformation of the
world. Only under this assumption would the everyday struggles of the
world proletariat be inherently revolutionary, in the sense that they
would bring to bear on states and capital a social power which the latter
could neither repress nor accommodate. Socialist revolution was the
long-term, large-scale process whereby the ensemble of these struggles
would force upon the world bourgeoisie an order based on consensus
and cooperation instead of coercion and competition.

Within this process the role of revolutionary vanguards, if any, was
supposed to be moral and educational rather than political. According
to the *Manifesto*, truly revolutionary vanguards ('communists') were not
supposed to form separate parties opposed to other working-class
parties; they were not supposed to develop interests of their own
separate and apart from those of the proletariat as a whole; and they
were not supposed to set up sectarian principles by which to shape and
mould the proletarian movement. Rather, they were supposed to limit
themselves to express and represent *within* proletarian struggles the
common interests of the entire world proletariat and of the movement as
a whole (see the passage quoted above). The most striking fact about
this list of what revolutionary vanguards were not supposed to do is that
it is a list of what Marxists actually did do in becoming collective historical agents.

The formation at the end of the nineteenth century of separate parties
competing with and often opposed to other working-class parties was
the first thing that Marxists did. As a matter of fact, this formation of
separate political parties marks the very act of birth of Marxism as effective historical agency and shared ideological identity. Soon thereafter,
the Revisionist Controversy purged Marxism of the idea that the movement of concrete proletarian struggles had primacy over the principles
(socialist or not) set up by revolutionary vanguards. This development
was a tacit invitation to set up particular principles as criteria of pro-
letarianism and, hence, as working guidelines for a vanguard's shaping
and moulding of actual proletarian movements—something that
happened right away. When one version of this path brought to Marxism
its first territorial base (the Russian Empire), the Leninist theory of
supremacy of the revolutionary vanguard over the movement became
the core of Marxist orthodoxy.

Finally, having acquired a territorial domain, Marxism as an orthodoxy developed interests of its own—interests not necessarily nor
evidently coincident with those imputable to the world proletariat. The
internecine struggles that followed the seizure of state power in the
Russian Empire redefined Marxism as coercive rule (of the Party over

the state and of the state over civil society); the aim was not so much to achieve proletarian liberation as such as to keep up or catch up with the wealth and power of the core states of the capitalist world-economy. This strategy turned the USSR into a superpower and helped bring about a phenomenal expansion of the territorial domain of Marxist rule. Coercive rule plus industrialization became the new core of orthodoxy.

Party, State and Class

Notwithstanding this progressive negation of Marx's legacy, Marxism continued to claim representation of the common interests of the entire world proletariat and world labour movement. This claim, however, was increasingly emptied of substance by a constant redefinition of the common interests of the world proletariat to match the power interests of Marxist organizations (states, parties, unions). Right from the start, the common interests of the world proletariat were redefined, one, to exclude the material interests of those segments of the world proletariat (so-called 'labour aristocracies') that rejected the necessary role of Marxist parties in the pursuit of their emancipation and, two, to include the power interests of Marxist organizations regardless of their participation in actual proletarian struggles. Then, as Marxist organizations came to include the USSR, the common interests of the world proletariat were redefined to give priority to the consolidation of Marxist power in the USSR and of the USSR in the state system. Finally, as the USSR became a superpower engaged in a struggle for world hegemony with the USA, the common interests of the world proletariat were redefined once again to match the interests of the USSR in that struggle.

This trajectory of successive and cumulative negations of Marx's legacy by individuals, groups and organizations who, none the less, continued to claim allegiance to that legacy, does not describe a 'betrayal' of Marxism, whatever that might mean. Rather, it describes Marxism for what it is, a historical formation that conforms to the actual unfolding of the Marxian legacy under circumstances unforeseen by that legacy. Or to rephrase, Marxism was made by bona fide followers of Marx but under historical circumstances that were neither prefigured for them nor of their own making.

The escalation of the interstate power struggle and the concomitant breakdown of world-market rule imposed upon Marx's followers the historical necessity of choosing between alternative strategies which for Marx were not alternatives at all. As argued in section II above, the choice in question was to develop organic links either with the segments of the world proletariat that experienced most directly and systemati-

cally the tendency towards increasing mass misery, or with the segments
of the world-economy. Marx thought, and hoped, that this division,
cally the tendency towards increasing social power. The choice was
imposed by the increasing division of the two tendencies over the space
of the world-economy. Marx thought, and hoped, that this division,
already observable in embryonic form in his own days, would decrease
over time. Instead, the escalation of the interstate power struggle
strengthened both tendencies and increased their spatial division.
Hence, the necessity to choose, and to choose promptly.

When Bernstein raised this issue and proposed to develop organic
links with the stronger segments of the world proletariat, Marxists
almost unanimously rejected his proposal, regardless of their revolutionary or reformist predispositions. The actual reasons for this almost
unanimous rejection, which set the course of Marxism for decades to
come, fall beyond the scope of this essay. All we need to point out is
that they can be imputed to motivations that in no way contradict the
letter and the spirit of the Marxian legacy.

Organic links with the weaker rather than the stronger fractions of the
world proletariat presented a double advantage for Marxists. First, it
appealed to their sense of moral outrage at the mass misery of the world
proletariat, which no doubt had been a major motivation for many of
them to follow in Marx's footsteps. Second, it appealed to their sense of
self-esteem—the sense, that is, that there was something they could
personally do to overcome the mass misery of the world proletariat,
which no doubt also played a role in inducing them to engage in
working-class politics.

Bernstein's choice was disadvantageous from both points of view. If
the accumulation of capital provided the proletariat with the social
power necessary to stave off mass misery, Marxists—or at least most of
them—were left without motivation or function: moral outrage was
unjustified because mass misery was a passing phenomenon, and self-
esteem was out of place because the proletariat had all the power it
needed to emancipate itself. It is plausible to assume that this was an
unstated but important reason why Bernstein's 'choice' was rejected and
historical Marxism was constituted both theoretically and practically on
the foundation of the increasing mass misery of labour rather than on its
increasing social power.

A Double Substitution

Whatever the motivations, this was a fateful decision, not just for
Marxism, but for the world proletariat, the world labour movement and

the capitalist world system. It imposed on Marxists a double substitution which greatly enhanced their power to transform the world but also made them depart more and more radically from the letter and spirit of the Marxian legacy. At first, it imposed on Marxists the historical necessity of substituting organizations of their own making for the mass organizations that reflected the spontaneous acts of revolt of the proletariat and other subordinate groups and classes. Then, once in power, it imposed on Marxist organizations the historical necessity of substituting themselves for the organizations of the bourgeoisie and other dominant groups and classes in performing the unpleasant governmental tasks which the latter had been unable or unwilling to do.

The two substitutions (the first primarily associated with the name of Lenin, and the second with the name of Stalin) complemented each other in the sense that the first prepared the second and the second brought to completion, as best the actors could, the work initiated by the first. But whatever their mutual relations, both substitutions were rooted in the previous decision of Marxists to choose as the social foundation of revolutionary theory and action the increasing mass misery rather than the increasing social power of labour. Increasing mass misery was a necessary condition for the success of Lenin's strategy of the revolutionary seizure of power. But as soon as state power had been seized, mass misery turned into a serious constraint on what Lenin and his successors could do with that power.

The inability or unwillingness of previous ruling classes to provide basic protection (military protection in the first place) to the proletariat and other subordinate groups and classes in a situation of escalating interstate violence had been the primary factor in their downfall. Marxist organizations could thus hope to stay in power only by providing the proletariat and other subordinate groups and classes with better protection than that provided by previous ruling groups. In practice, this meant—or so it seemed to all actors involved in the consolidation of Marxist power—catching up or at least keeping up with the military–industrial complexes of the great powers of the state system.

The alleviation of mass misery was accordingly subordinated to the pursuit of this objective. Since military–industrial backwardness had been a major, if not the major, cause of the increasing mass misery of the proletariat in the Russian Empire, it seemed quite reasonable to those involved in the consolidation of Marxist power in the USSR to assume that the alleviation of mass misery itself would begin with heavy industrialization. This assumption, however, did not seem so reasonable to a large number of Soviet subjects (including a great variety of proletarian subjects) whose ways of life were disrupted by the stepping up of heavy industrialization under conditions of mass misery. Given this opposition, coercive rule became the necessary complement of heavy industrialization.

The success of the USSR in becoming one of the two superpowers of the interstate system and, at the same time, in actually alleviating the chronic mass misery of its proletarian subjects turned coercive rule plus industrialization into the new core of Marxist theory and practice. Marxism thereby became even more closely identified than before with the mass misery of the world proletariat, and thereby enhanced its hegemonic capabilities in the periphery and semi-periphery of the world-economy. But, for that very reason, it lost most if not all of its residual appeal for those segments of the world proletariat whose predominant experience was not increasing mass misery but increasing social power.

The rejection of Marxism by the proletariat of core countries and the suppression of actual proletarian struggles in the theory and practice of historical Marxism went hand in hand. The more historical Marxism came to be identified with increasing mass misery and with the bloody struggles through which Marxist organizations attempted to overcome the powerlessness that went with mass misery, the more it became alien, nay repugnant, to the proletarians of core countries. And, conversely, the more proletarian organizations based on the increasing social power of labour in core countries succeeded in obtaining a share of the power and wealth of their respective states, the more they came to be perceived and presented by Marxists as subordinate and corrupt members of the dominant social bloc that ruled the world.

This mutual antagonism was a historical development which no one had willed or, for that matter, anticipated. Once in place, however, it provided the world bourgeoisie with a valuable ideological weapon in the struggle to reconstitute its tottering rule. As we have seen, US hegemony after the Second World War relied heavily on the claim that the experience of the US proletariat could be duplicated on a world scale. Let the expansion of corporate capitalism proceed unfettered—it was claimed—and the entire world proletariat will experience sufficient social power to eliminate mass misery from its ranks.

American and World Labour

As we now know, this claim (like all hegemonic claims) was half true and half fraudulent. As promised, the global expansion of corporate capitalism, which followed from and secured the establishment of US hegemony, did in fact spread the social power of labour to the entire core, most of the semiperiphery, and parts of the periphery of the world-economy. And, as promised, the segment of the world proletariat with sufficient social power in its hands to stave off mass misery has expanded, if not in relative terms, certainly in absolute terms.

But the claim that the world labour movement could be remade in the image of the United States has turned out to be also half fraudulent. The increase in the social power of labour has not resulted in a proportionate decrease in the mass misery of labour, as happened in the US. The more corporate capitalism expanded, the less capable it became of accommodating all the social power that its own expansion put in the hands of labour. As a consequence, expansion has slowed down and the cost-cutting race of the 1970s and 1980s has set in.

The unravelling of the fraudulent aspects of US hegemony has been a major factor in precipitating its crisis in the late 1960s and early 1970s. Yet neither organized labour nor Marxist organizations have been able to take advantage of the new situation. On the contrary, both have been affected by a crisis as structural as that of US hegemony.

The previous strength of organized labour in core countries was rooted in a situation in which a particular segment of the proletariat had considerable social power while states and capital had the capability of accommodating that power. Organized labour, as presently constituted, developed and expanded by delivering social peace to states and capital and greater returns for effort to its proletarian constituencies. The ongoing cost-cutting race, however, has made states and capital more reluctant or less capable to grant labour greater returns for effort and has transferred social power into the hands of proletarian segments (women, immigrants, foreign workers, etc.) with whom existing labour organizations have weak or no organic links. Organized labour has thus lost its previous social function or its social base or both.

The strength of Marxist organizations, in contrast, was rooted in a situation in which their proletarian constituencies had little social power and in which states and capital were incapable of providing such constituencies with minimal protection. Marxist organizations, as presently constituted, grew on the basis of their capacity to provide such constituencies with a better protection than previous ruling classes had been able or willing to provide. However, the strategy of keeping up and catching up with the most powerful military–industrial complexes of the interstate system, through which Marxist organizations consolidated and expanded their power, was vitiated by a fundamental contradiction.

On the one hand, this strategy required that, wittingly or unwittingly, Marxist organizations put in the hands of their proletarian constituencies a social power comparable to the social power enjoyed by the proletariat of the core. Over time, this increasing social power was bound to interfere with the capability of Marxist organizations to pursue interests of their own at the expense of their proletarian constituencies. The longer they waited to adjust their strategies and structure to the increasing social power of their proletarian constituencies, the more serious the subsequent adjustment would have to be.

The reconstruction of world-market rule under US hegemony has aggravated this contradiction in more than one way. Interstate relations came to be pacified and war as a means of territorial expansion was delegitimated. This change undermined the capacity of Marxist organizations to mobilize consent among their proletarian constituencies for a strategy of coercive industrialization. In the situation of generalized preparation for war and of actual war in the 1930s and 1940s, this strategy probably reflected a genuinely and deeply felt proletarian interest. But with the establishment of US hegemony it came more and more to reflect the self-serving interests of Marxist organizations and of their political clienteles. At the same time, the growing division of labour in the rest of the world economy associated with the reconstruction of market rule heightened the comparative disadvantage of coercive industrialization in the race to keep up with the standards of power and wealth set by core capitalist states. As a consequence, Marxist states became increasingly incapable of keeping up with those standards or of adjusting to the increasing social power of their proletarian subjects or both.

The Shape of the Crisis

The crises of organized labour and of Marxist organizations are thus two sides of the same coin. The crisis of organized labour is due primarily to its structural inability to stop the spread of mass misery to the proletariat of the core, while the crisis of Marxist organizations is due primarily to their structural inability to prevent the spread of social power to their actual or prospective proletarian constituencies. But the crisis is the same because each kind of proletarian organization is ill-equipped to cope with a situation in which labour has greater social power than existing economic and political institutions can accommodate.

Under these circumstances, the old opposition between the 'movement' and the 'goal', which underlay the dual development of the world labour movement in the course of the twentieth century, no longer makes any sense to the protagonists of the struggles. As Marx had theorized, the simple exercise of the social power that has accumulated or is accumulating in the hands of labour is in and by itself a revolutionary act. An increasing number of proletarian struggles since 1968 have demonstrated the incipient recomposition of 'movement' and 'goal'.

The recomposition was presaged and explicitly advocated in the slogan 'practicare l'obbiettivo' ('putting the objective into practice') coined by Italian workers at the height of the struggles of the late 1960s. Under this slogan, various practices of direct action were carried out. Even though practices of direct action were nothing new, their socially revolutionary effects were. The social power deployed in and through these struggles imposed a major restructuring of economic and political institutions, including Marxist and non-Marxist working-class organizations, to accommodate the democratic and egalitarian thrust of the movement.[15]

More compelling evidence of an incipient recomposition of 'movement' and 'goal' has come from Spain in the 1970s and from South Africa and Poland in the 1980s. In Spain, a persistent and long-drawn-out movement of proletarian struggles, which the Franco dictatorship could neither repress nor accommodate, was the single most important factor in the demise of that dictatorship and the subsequent rise of social democracy. In less clear-cut fashion, the same pattern can be identified in the later crises of dictatorships in Brazil, Argentina and South Korea. It can also be recognized in the ongoing struggles of the proletariat in South Africa and Poland. In these two cases, however, the labour movement presents specificities which enhance their significance.

The special significance of the labour movement in Poland is that it was emblematic of the contradictions and current crisis of historical Marxism as ideology and organization of the proleteriat. The movement was based primarily, if not exclusively, on the social power that had been put in the hands of labour by the strategy of coercive industrialization pursued by Marxist organizations. The deployment of this social power in pursuit of livelihood and basic civil rights was as inherently subversive of existing political and economic relations in Poland as it is or has been in all the other countries mentioned above. No distinction between the goal of social revolution and the actual unfolding of the movement was necessary or indeed possible—as witnessed, among other things, by the kind of leadership and organization which the movement has generated.

The irony of the situation was that, in struggling against a Marxist organization, knowingly or unknowingly Solidarność followed Marx's prescriptions for revolutionary vanguards more closely than any Marxist organization ever did. It restrained itself, (1) from forming a political party opposed to existing working-class parties; (2) from developing interests of its own separate from those of the world proletariat; and (3) from setting up sectarian principles by which to shape and mould the proletarian movement. Moreover, as advocated by Marx, its function was more moral than political, though its political implications were truly revolutionary.

The fact that a Marxist organization was the stage counterpart to this most Marxian of proletarian organizations should not surprise us. Indeed, the *Solidarność* experience provides vivid evidence in support of the two main theses of this essay: the thesis that Marx's predictions and prescriptions are becoming increasingly relevant for the present and the future of the world labour movement; and the thesis that historical Marxism has developed in a direction that in key respects is antithetical to the one foreseen and advocated by Marx.

But by bringing to the fore the role of religion and nationality in the formation of a distinctive but collective proletarian identity, the *Solidarność* experience does more than that. Together with other contemporary proletarian struggles—the South African experience in the first place—it warns us against excessive reliance on the Marxian scheme in charting the future of the labour movement. For in one major respect the Marxian scheme itself remains seriously defective—namely, in the way in which it deals with the role of age, sex, race, nationality, religion and other natural and historical specificities in shaping the social identity of the world proletariat. Consideration of such complex issues lies beyond the scope of this essay,[16] but their importance for the future of the world labour movement forces me to mention them by way of qualification and conclusion of what has been said so far.

To be sure, the cost-cutting of the last 15–20 years has provided new and compelling evidence in support of the observation that *for capital* all members of the proletariat are instruments of labour, more or less expensive to use according to their age, sex, colour, nationality, religion, etc. However, it has also shown that one cannot infer, as Marx does, from this predisposition of capital a predisposition of labour to relinquish natural and historical differences as means of affirming, individually and collectively, a distinctive social identity.

Whenever faced with the predisposition of capital to treat labour as an undifferentiated mass with no individuality other than a differential capacity to augment the value of capital, proletarians have rebelled. Almost invariably they have seized upon or created anew whatever combination of distinctive traits (age, sex, colour, assorted geo-historical specificities) they could use to impose on capital some kind of special treatment. As a consequence, patriarchalism, racism and national-chauvinism have been integral to the making of the world labour movement along both of its twentieth-century trajectories, and live on in one form or another in most proletarian ideologies and organizations.

As always, the undoing of these practices, and of the ideologies and organizations in which they have been institutionalized, can only be the result of the struggles of those who are oppressed by them. The social power which the cost-cutting race is putting in the hands of traditionally weak segments of the world proletariat is but a prelude to these struggles. To the extent that these struggles succeed, the stage will be set for the socialist transformation of the world.

May 1989

Notes

* I am indebted to Terence K. Hopkins and Beverly J. Silver for comments and criticisms on earlier drafts of this chapter.

1. Karl Marx, Friedrich Engels, *The Communist Manifesto*, Harmondsworth 1967, pp. 93–4.

2. Ibid., p. 95.

3. Ibid., p. 87. In this definition, which I shall adopt throughout, there is no indication that workers must be engaged in particular occupations ('blue collar', for instance) to qualify as members of the proletariat. Even expressions like 'industrial proletariat' must be understood to designate that segment which is normally employed by capitalist enterprises engaged in production and distribution, regardless of the kind of work performed or the branch of activity in which the enterprise operates.

Marx's definition is ambiguous, however, with regard to the upper and lower boundaries of the proletariat. At the upper end we face the problem of classifying workers who do sell their labour-power for a wage, but from a position of individual strength that enables them to demand and obtain rewards for effort which, other things being equal, are higher than those received by the average worker. This is most clearly the case of the upper echelons of management, but a great variety of individuals (so-called 'professionals') work for a wage or salary without being proletarianized in any meaningful (that is, substantial) sense of the word. In what follows, all such individuals are implicitly excluded from the ranks of the proletariat unless they are explicitly referred to as being only formally proletarianized.

At the lower end we face the opposite problem of classifying workers who do not find a buyer for their labour-power (which they would be more than willing to sell at prevailing rates) and therefore engage in non-waged activities that bring rewards for effort which, other things being equal, are lower than those received by the average wage-worker. This is indeed the case with most of what Marx calls the Industrial Reserve Army. As a matter of fact, the entire Reserve Army is in this condition except for the small minority of individuals who qualify for unemployment benefits or can otherwise afford to remain fully and truly unemployed for any length of time. In what follows, all non-wage workers in the above condition will be implicitly included in the proletariat—in its Reserve Army, to be sure, but in the proletariat none the less.

4. Ibid., p. 88.

5. Ibid., pp. 92, 102.

6. Ibid., p. 84.

7. Cf. Wolfgang Abendroth, *A Short History of the European Working Class*, New York 1973.

8. All the statements of fact concerning labour unrest contained in this article are based on research conducted by the World Labor Research Working Group of the Fernand Braudel Center, State University of New York at Binghamton. The main findings of this research will be published in a special issue of *Review*.

9. Eduard Bernstein, *Evolutionary Socialism*, New York 1986, pp. 163–4.

10. Antonio Gramsci, *Selections from the Prison Notebooks*, New York 1971, pp. 104–5.

11. As this sentence implies, I use the term 'hegemony' in the Gramscian sense of a domination exercised through a combination of coercion and consent. See ibid., pp. 57–8.

12. Cf. Alfred D. Chandler, Jr., *The Visible Hand: The Managerial Resolution in American Business*, Cambridge, Mass. 1977, and Michel Aglietta, *A Theory of Capitalist Regulation*, NLB, London 1979.

13. A more exhaustive account of what follows in this section can be found in Giovanni Arrighi and Beverly Silver, 'Labor Movements and Capital Migration: The United States and Western Europe in World Historical Perspective', in C. Bergquist, ed., *Labor in the Capitalist World-Economy*, Beverly Hills 1984.

14. Cf. Terutomo Ozawa, *Multinationalism, Japanese Style: The Political Economy of Outward Dependency*, Princeton, NJ 1979.

15. Cf. Ida Regalia, Marino Regini, Emilio Reyneri, 'Labor Conflicts and Industrial Relations in Italy', in C. Crouch and A. Pizzorno, eds, *The Resurgence of Class Conflict in Western Europe since 1968*, vol. 1, New York 1978.

16. But see Arrighi, Hopkins, Wallerstein, *Anti-Systemic Movements*, Verso, London 1989.

11

Radical as Reality

Alexander Cockburn

They said Tuesday that the line in front of Lenin's tomb was longer than
it had ever been, country folk visiting Moscow to catch a glimpse of the
old fellow before they clear the mausoleum, pending conversion to a
trade mart, Pizza Hut or some kindred symbol of the new dawn.

When Lenin was in exile in Zurich during the First World War,
before the sealed train brought him back to Russia in 1917, he used to
visit a restaurant frequented by bohemian types, Dada painters and
poets, and low-lifers of one sort or another. A young Romanian poet
called Marcu later wrote an account of a chat he had with Lenin there.

'You see,' he said, 'why I take my meals here. You get to know what people
are really talking about. Nadezhda Konstantinovna (Lenin's wife, Krupskaya)
is sure that only the Zurich underworld frequents this place, but I think she is
mistaken. To be sure, Maria is a prostitute. But she does not like her trade.
She has a large family to support—and that is no easy matter. As to Frau
Prellog, she is perfectly right. Did you hear what she said? Shoot all the offi-
cers!'

Then Lenin said to me, 'Do you know the real meaning of this war?'

'What is it?' I asked.

'It is obvious,' he replied. 'One slaveholder, Germany, who owns one
hundred slaves, is fighting another slaveholder, England, who owns two
hundred slaves, for a "fairer" distribution of the slaves.'

'How can you expect to foster hatred of this war,' I asked at this point, 'if
you are not in principle against all wars? I thought that as a Bolshevik you
were really a radical thinker and refused to make any compromise with the
idea of war. But by recognizing the validity of some wars, you open the doors
for every opportunity. Each group can find some justification of the particular
war of which it approves. I see that we young people can only count on
ourselves ...'

Lenin listened attentively, his head bent toward me. He moved his chair closer to mine. He must have wondered whether to continue to talk to this boy or not. I, somewhat awkwardly, remained silent.

'Your determination to rely on yourselves,' Lenin finally replied, 'is very important. Every man must rely on himself. Yet he should also listen to what informed people have to say. I don't know how radical you are, or how radical I am. I am certainly not radical enough. One can never be radical enough; that is, one must always try to be as radical as reality itself.'

That last line has always been one of my favourites, and I hope to be using it long after the last bust of the man Reagan insisted on calling Nikolai has been ground down to talcum powder.

Those coup makers who now await trial, or who have committed suicide (or had their suicides involuntarily administered; a lot of people 'committed suicide' during the purges too), had certainly ceased to be as radical as reality. So too had Gorbachev. Somewhere in these last six years there surely was a chance for a Third Way, leading neither back to the lost world of the coup makers nor to the neo-liberal agenda now shaping up.

But probably Gorbachev never had a chance, because after Khrushchev was ousted the long narcolepsy of the Brezhnev years irretrievably wrecked the Soviet Union's hopes of establishing any successful rendezvous with a modernized socialist economy. At the very moment in the 1970s and 1980s that capitalism was learning to be hyperflexible—to the great cost of workers and peasants the world over—the Soviet Union became more rigid and inflexible. As I once remarked, to the great rage of many, the Brezhnev years were a Golden Age for the Soviet working class. Indeed they were, in terms of economic advance (just as the fifties and sixties were for its white North American counterpart), but they couldn't last, and now those workers' sons and daughters will face diminishing expectations as neo-liberal market norms take them by the throat. And why did narcolepsy thus extinguish hope? Because, long since, the Communist Party had become the expression of a corrupted elite, a spoils allotment system. Just as the allocation system presided over by Gosnab (dismembered by Yeltsin in the Russian Republic at the start of this week) had become hopelessly unwieldy and choked up, so too had the party suffocated initiative and creativity.

'The heritage of the great Lenin is lost', Stalin cried out when he was informed of the German invasion of 1941. Twenty million Soviet lives later that heritage, already mangled by the horrors of the 1930s, had been saved. After the Second World War Soviet industrial growth ran at an average of just under 10 per cent a year through the 1950s. By 1956 Khrushchev was telling the West, 'We will bury you', and the words did not seem lunatic. A decade later the Soviet economy began to slow, and

the gravedigger leaned ever more heavily upon his spade, in a premoni-
tion of the exhaustion that came with the seventies. Now comes accelerating Balkanization of what was formerly the Union, strife between the
republics, looting of resources by foreign powers, and extension of
German influence up to the Urals meeting the Japanese coming the
other way. In Russia presidential ukase will stifle trade unions and representative institutions. A year or two from now Boris Yeltsin may be able
to stand atop the converted mausoleum and view the parade of new
times: Soviet lumbermen under the command of Georgia Pacific and the
Japanese; oil drillers bearing the standard of Conoco; long battalions of
unemployed under the discipline of the Chicago School.

The weekend that Gorbachev resigned as party leader and plumes of
smoke began rising from party archives across the country I was at a
conference on anticorporate environmental strategies, hosted in Los
Angeles by the Labour/Community Watchdog. There were plenty of
intelligent, radical people there. There was much talk and analysis of the
victory of Salinas de Gortari and the PRI in Mexico, about the need for
internationalism and building of ties in the new era of the *maquiladora*
and the unending corporate search for cheaper labour and laxer laws. I
barely heard the Soviet Union or the collapse of the Communist system
mentioned until I brought up the matter myself in the course of some
remarks on the last day. A friend who'd gone that weekend to a conference of the Union of Radical Political Economists in upstate New York
said the same thing happened there. The Soviet Union's disintegration,
the end to what electrified the world and horrified capital three-quarters
of a century ago, didn't seize the imagination of these conference-goers
(or maybe, for some in the older crowd, it was a matter of just preferring
to talk about something else, because there wasn't too much to say).
    Like any other fifty-year-old born into a Communist family I felt sad.
The Soviet Union defeated Hitler and fascism. Without it, the Cuban
Revolution would never have survived, nor the Vietnamese. In the
postwar years it was the counterweight to US imperialism and the terminal savageries of the old European colonial powers. It gave support to
any country trying to follow an independent line. Without it, just such a
relatively independent country as India could instead have taken a far
more rightward course. Despite Stalin's suggestion to Mao that he and
his comrades settle for only half a country, the Chinese Revolution
probably would not have survived either.
    It was Communists who spearheaded the fight for civil rights for
black people in the United States in the 1930s; and without the threat of
the Soviet model in the competition for the loyalties of the Third World,
Truman probably would not have felt the pressure to desegregate the

Army when he did, though of course there were domestic pressures on him too. Without the threat of the Soviet Union there would have been no Marshall Plan. There wouldn't have been ... Well, write your own list. There wouldn't have been the International Brigades, the workers who had crossed the Atlantic or ridden the rails across Europe to Spain.

But I could see too why the young folk at the conference felt the way they did. As long as half a century after Spain and after the heroism of the Communist-led resistance movements of the Second World War, the Soviet Union offered dwindling allotments of inspiration, however many barrels of oil it gave to the Cubans, or guns to the Vietnamese. And besides, Soviet distintegration stands well back in the sequence of disasters that have overtaken the Third World in the past two decades. The people in Los Angeles were discussing the havoc wrought by hyperflexible capitalism: runaway plants on the Mexican border standing amid pools of poisonous waste; cholera in Peru and malnutrition and disease across the Southern tier; environmental regulations at the local, state and federal level in the USA facing annulment by the provisions of the US–Mexico free-trade agreement. The Soviet Union's future will be a familiar chapter.

Outside a few enclaves of state-assisted capital around the world the trendlines are now all down, as the tensions and desperation rise. For the future of Lenin's heritage we need only study what has been happening in Yugoslavia and fear those horrors on a far vaster and more savage scale.

A couple of days into postcommunism a friend of mine said he was off to the hypnotist to stop smoking. While he was at it, he said, he might as well get the whole Communist era wiped out as well. It would be soothing, a straight transition from Kerensky and the Duma to Yeltsin and the Russian parliament, with everything in between a blur. Whatever happened to that nice Czar Nicholas? Collectivization, what's that? Joseph who?

Russians, hauling down the statues and cleaning out the mausoleum, seem keen on wiping out their history all over again, just as they have so many times in this century—very much the reverse of what Boris Kagarlitsky remarked to me in Moscow in 1987 as we chatted underneath a statue of a czarist general, a hero of Pamyat: 'People are crazy about history and eager to get the empty parts of the past filled in.' Four years later it seems to be ending with more chunks of history being sent off to the cellars.

Almost since the moment the Bolshevik-led soldiers of the Petrograd garrison, sailors from Kronstadt and the workers' Red Guards stormed the Winter Palace in the early night hours of 8 November 1917, tens of thousands of books—many of them covertly subsidized by the state—

have been written in the capitalist West dedicated to the proposition that it was all a very bad idea, a detour from the proper course of history. This is an inane game. To say that the Russian Revolution was a bad idea is also to say that the First World War was a bad idea. In the latter case it was, but it happened; and because it happened, the revolution happened. The revolution wrought some bad things, but some good things too.

My father often talked to me about the If Only fallacy. Discussing the pact between the Soviet Union and Germany in 1939, he wrote in his memoir *Crossing the Line*, 'Nobody can judge whether an historical event, an order to an army, a diplomatic manoeuvre, was a catastrophe or otherwise unless he is prepared to say at the same time what *would* have happened if that thing had *not* happened. And since nobody is in a position honestly to make such a statement about what the alternative would have been, the question is in the nature of things unanswerable and otiose.'

It all happened, and at this juncture I'm reminded again of what the Vietnamese Dr Vien recently wrote, 'If a world front of capital is being founded, its counterweight, the democratic popular front on a world scale, is also in formation.' We have a history to carry forward, so long as we remember what Lenin said to the young poet in Zurich seventy-five years ago.

24 August 1991

PART II

The Implications for the Future

12

Fin de Siècle:
Socialism after the Crash*

Robin Blackburn

As we enter the last decade of the twentieth century the ruin of
'Marxist-Leninist' Communism has been sufficiently comprehensive to
eliminate it as an alternative to capitalism and to compromise the very
idea of socialism. The débâcle of Stalinism has embraced reform
Communism, and has brought no benefit to Trotskyism, or social
democracy, or any socialist current. Mummies of Lenin and Mao are still
displayed in mausoleums in Moscow and Beijing as emblems of an old
order which awaits decent burial. But today's moribund 'Great Power
Communism' is not a spectre stalking the globe but an unhappy spirit,
begging to be laid to rest.

Yet a socialism willing to confront history and to engage with the
most penetrating critics of the socialist project could enable a new
beginning to be made. There still exist significant anti-capitalist movements, some influenced by the Communist tradition, but they lack a
programme which could take us beyond capitalism. There are surviving
regimes which call themselves Communist or Socialist but whether or
not they can point to real achievements (as could, say, Cuba in the fields
of public health and education) there can be no doubt that they too
require an even more thoroughgoing renewal and reorientation—one
aimed not just at constructing a genuinely democratic culture and polity
but also at discovering a new and viable socialist model of economy.

Problems of Capitalism and Anti-capitalism

As we address the death-throes of the former Communist world we
should not forget the different, but very serious, ills of the capitalist

world. The globe is now more firmly within the grip of the processes of capitalist accumulation—we should be all the more attentive to the price exacted by these processes, their harvest of mayhem and misery, destruction and neglect, division and irresponsibility. In the 1980s the workings of capitalism were associated with an obscene process whereby huge populations in the poorest countries found their prospect of development blocked by their debts to the richest and by the latter's exclusion of their products. The distribution of economic and political power in much of the capitalist Third World proved compatible with widespread famines and epidemics of curable disease. Attempts by movements based on the poor to challenge this state of affairs were often met by merciless repression and death squads. Indeed there can be no doubt that the loss of human life, and extent of physical suffering, in the capitalist Third World in the 1980s greatly exceeded that experienced in the countries ruled by Communist bureaucracy—a dismal comparison which does nothing to justify the stifling tyranny exercised by the latter but does put it in perspective. Meanwhile the workings of capitalism in the metropolitan regions were marked by fundamental instability, mass unemployment, a buoyant arms trade, an escalating crisis of social provision and, most serious of all, a gathering and global ecological crisis. While the Communist states have a terrible ecological record, their very economic failures have set some limits on the damage they have done. Capitalism, with its uncontrolled momentum and heedless rapacity, has brought humanity to a point where its powers of intervention in nature risk the destruction of the habitability of the globe.

The destructive and exploitative dynamic of capitalism, and its implication in an unfree social and political order, helps to provoke movements of contestation. But it is still hard to discern the outlines of a noncapitalist model. Anti-capitalist movements can do valuable work checking particular manifestations of the divisive or destructive logic of capitalist organization. But if they won sufficient support, what could they offer at the level of regional or national government? And if they are dissatisfied with the world pattern presided over by the Group of Seven, what would they have develop in its place? Answers to these questions will emerge, if they emerge at all, in large measure through impulses derived from the experience and reflection of anti-capitalist movements in the historic zones of capitalist accumulation in both the First and the Third Worlds. But the anti-capitalist Left will have no credibility unless it can account for the dire experience of Communism since 1917. In some ways this is a tribute to Communism since, for good or ill, its impact on the history of the twentieth century has been a huge one. Indeed the political movements and orders claiming allegiance to 'Marxism-Leninism', though now foundering on all sides, have been second only to liberal capitalism as protagonists and shapers of the age in which we live, ahead of fascism and colonialism, and capable of subsuming at least some of the appeal of nationalism and religion— again, for good or ill. While Communism was able to attract impressive organizers and intellects in the First World it was generally less influential than the social-democratic variant of socialism. In the Third World, Communism was generally far more effective than social democracy and the same could be said for the respective record of these two currents in the resistance movements of occupied Europe and Asia in the Second World War.

Someone as little suspect of sympathy for Communism, or any sort of socialism, as Ludwig von Mises was to describe the broad socialist tradition as the 'most powerful reform movement that history has ever known, the first ideological trend not limited to a section of mankind but supported by people of all races, nations, religions and civilizations'.[1] This must be read as a tribute to Communism as much as to the largely Eurocentric social-democratic tradition. It is neither desirable nor possible to pass by the Communist experience as something without significance to those who would construct an alternative to capitalism. Nor should critical reflection content itself with simply denouncing the evident denial of democracy, including socialist democracy, that is the hallmark of Stalinism. If all that was lacking in these Communist regimes was democracy then its introduction would solve everything. But, however welcome moves towards democratization are, or would be, in the Communist, or formerly Communist, states it is already clear that this is far from solving all their problems and is certainly far from yielding an advance beyond both Stalinism and capitalism. There were always socialists and Marxists who denounced the repressive features of Communism and who sought to identify the basic flaws in its conception of the socialist project.

Bolshevism and Backwardness

It is interesting to recall Kautsky's first reaction to the Russian Revolution. This is now he later summarized it:

If they [the Bolsheviks] succeeded in making their expectations and promises come true, it would be a tremendous accomplishment for them and for the Russian people and, indeed, for the entire international proletariat. The teachings of Marxism, however, could then no longer be maintained. They would be proved false, but, on the other hand, socialism would gain a splendid triumph, the road to the immediate removal of all misery and ignorance of the masses would be entered in Russia and pointed out to the rest of the world. How gladly I would have believed that it was possible ... The most powerful, best founded theory must yield when it is contradicted by the facts. However, they must be facts, not mere projects and promises ... [M]y expectant benevolence did not last long. To my chagrin, I saw ever more clearly that the Bolsheviks totally misunderstood their situation, that they thoughtlessly tackled problems for the solution of which all conditions were lacking. In their attempts to accomplish the impossible by brute force, they chose paths by which the working masses were not raised economically, intellectually or morally, but on the contrary, were depressed even deeper than they had been by Tsarism and the world war.[2]

Kautsky, writing this in 1931, could certainly dispute Stalin's empty boast to be constructing 'socialism in one country' in the name of orthodox Marxism. In *The Communist Manifesto* and in other writings, Marx and Engels famously insisted that a genuine socialism could only be built on the basis already laid by capitalism; in *The German Ideology* they had observed that socialism would require social overturns in at least several of the most developed countries. From this classic Marxist conviction it followed that it was a complete delusion to attempt to 'build socialism' in one large backward country, or, as was subsequently to be attempted, in a string of backward countries. By this Kautsky did not mean that nothing at all should be done and that Russia should simply be handed over to the Whites. His Menshevik friends were quite prepared to form a government in Georgia where they had majority support, and to promote social reforms. It was the specific abuses of party dictatorship and so-called War Communism, and their latter systematization and intensification under Stalin, that he attacked. Kautsky was on firm ground in arguing that Marx had insisted on the primacy of the struggle for democracy, and had outlined his notion of a 'dictatorship of the proletariat' in terms that were irreconcilable with a narrow party dictatorship. Kautsky is sometimes chided for 'economism', yet his critique of Bolshevik strategy was centred upon its ominous implications for the cultural and political development of the toilers. He warned that conspiratorial, secretive and hierarchical organization 'may be rendered necessary for an oppressed class in the absence of democracy, but it would not promote the self-government and independence of the masses. Rather it would further the Messiah-consciousness of leaders, and their dictatorial habits.'[3]

The would-be socialist revolutions of the twentieth century have all taken place against a background of war-devastation and capitalist failure and each has had to struggle with a heavy weight of socio-economic backwardness as well as military encirclement. In each revolutionary process there have been primitive elements of democracy, as hitherto excluded and suppressed layers of the population asserted their elementary interests, but in each case a centralizing political and military apparatus, while giving stability and direction to the revolution, has also foreclosed democratic development. The palpable threat of bloody counter-revolution has often appeared to justify the curtailment of democracy and diversity within the revolutionary camp, as happened in Russia with the outbreak of civil war in 1918. But, significantly enough, Bolshevism took a fateful step towards Stalinism only after victory in the civil war. Besieged by famine, fearful of demoralization and believing that counter-revolution could easily stage a comeback, the leaders of the post-revolutionary state responded by banning rival parties and decreeing the formal suppression of factions within the ruling party. However it was not until the severe economic crisis of the late twenties that monolithic and totalitarian principles of party organization and leadership over society were generalized. The practices and principles of 'high Stalinism' acquired added prestige both inside and outside Soviet borders in the aftermath of World War Two. Stalingrad consecrated Stalinism—paradoxically, since Soviet victory was hugely assisted by that wartime relaxation depicted in Grossman's *Life and Fate*.

The Responsibility of Marxism

These days we are often told that the Russian Revolution was a 'Marxist experiment' and that it shows the perils of any socialist policy. Kautsky's reaction, and that of other Marxists to be considered below, shows this to be a very partial and one-sided judgement. But for Marxists to disclaim any responsibility whatever for the October Revolution and the state which issued from it would be wrong. It would be wrong because the leaders of the Soviet state from Lenin to Gorbachev have appealed to Marx, have sought to organize political support for this state on the basis that they were Marxists, and, at the subjective level, have believed that, in a difficult and unexpected situation, they acted in furtherance of the socialist cause as they understood it. Until quite recently the political credentials of the Soviet leaders were accepted by a powerful international movement. It would also be wrong because the Soviet system has appeared to implement key aspects of the classical Marxist and socialist programme, implicating, in some degree, any politics which chooses public ownership as a means and popular welfare as a goal. The

economic order of the Soviet Union was centrally based on state ownership and planning while an insistent workerist ideology pointed—not
always mendaciously—to achievements in the sphere of health and education, and to the social promotion of those of proletarian extraction.
That Stalin was to be horrendously callous and a cynical traducer of
Marxism is also true. But we must take political doctrines and systems of
belief as we find them not only at their face value; historical materialists
should be the last to object to such a method. For example, Christianity
cannot only be judged by the doings of the saints but should also accept
some responsibility for the actions of Christian governments and more
generally the impact of Christian Europe on the world. To say that the
Atlantic slave trade or the Jewish Holocaust reveal to us the essence of
Christianity would be grotesque. But, nevertheless, some connection can
be found between Christian doctrine and these events, or otherwise
Christians would not have helped to bring them about. One such
connection would simply be the traditional portrayal of heathens and
Jews in popular Christianity.

Likewise, Western liberalism cannot just be judged on the basis of the
ideas and intentions of Adam Smith, Immanuel Kant, Marie-Jean
Condorcet, and Alexis de Tocqueville. The responsibility of liberal
states for war or colonialism or famine would have to enter the picture
as would the characteristic blindspots of liberal thought. So with
Marxism the gaps, errors and inadequacies in what Marx had to say
about, for example, the rule of law, or the rights of the individual, or the
need for checks and balances in political structures, or the abolition of
commodity–money relations, do not constitute the essence of Marxism,
as some would like to claim; but they may have some responsibility,
direct or otherwise, for the practices of what used to be called 'actually
existing socialism'.

Kautsky wrote *Dictatorship of the Proletariat* and *Bolshevism at a
Deadlock* partly because he felt some responsibility, as Lenin's teacher,
for what was happening in Russia. His critique was not solely directed at
political repression but rather insisted that repression was itself the result
of refusing to compromise with other forces and forcing the pace of
economic socialization, first under 'War Communism' and later in the
period of collectivization and the Five Year Plan. Some might dismiss
Kautsky's critique on the grounds that the Austrian Social Democrats,
who were more inclined to follow his advice, failed to prevent a different
sort of disaster—the victory of clerical reaction and Nazism. Alterna-
tively one could question the record of Kautsky's Menshevik friends in
Georgia or Russia itself. And the positions he had adopted in 1914 on
the war certainly damaged his moral standing. However, the point here
is not retrospectively to endorse Kautsky's position, another element of

which will be considered below, but to insist that his ideas must be evaluated on their merits, and to contradict the myth cultivated by Stalin, and accepted by many anti-Communists, that the Soviet state was the only valid living embodiment of the Marxist programme. Kautsky was indeed struck by the fact that Leninism and Stalinism, far from being a realization of Marx's ideas, represented, to a significant extent, an atavistic return of the conspiratorial, Jacobin and doctrinaire strains within socialism which Marx had spent much of his early political life combating.

Thus while Marxism cannot escape implication in the fate of the Russian Revolution, neither should it be ignored that many of the most notable Marxists of the day—not only Kautsky, of course, but also Rosa Luxemburg—repudiated the practice of the party dictatorship right from the beginning. If Luxemburg had lived, she would certainly have developed the remarkable and prescient observations contained in her last writings on the Russian Revolution. Some supporters of the new Soviet state recognized the revision of Marxism implied by Bolshevik strategy. Antonio Gramsci, sympathizing with the voluntaristic element in the October Revolution, described it as 'the Revolution against "Capital"' (that is, Marx's *Das Kapital*).[4] The subsequent history of the Soviet Union has been marked by successive critiques from Mensheviks, Social Democrats, Austro-Marxists, Council-Communists, Liberal Socialists, Left Oppositionists, Right Oppositionists, East European revisionists, Western Marxists, New Leftists, Euro-communists, and so forth down to the most recent writings of such as Rudolf Bahro and Boris Kagarlitsky. This criticism and rejection has related in different ways both to the basic strategic line of march and to particular crimes and errors perpetrated along the way. Most of these critics have situated themselves squarely within the Marxist tradition. They have appealed to a Marx who bitterly attacked press censorship and the arbitrary exercise of state power, who insisted that the battle to win democracy must have priority, and who supported the accountability of political representatives. Marx's writings on Jacobinism and Bonapartism were animated by deep hostility to political formations that sought to usurp social forces. As twentieth-century Marxists have grappled with the modern horrors of total war and totalitarianism, they have certainly had to develop new concepts, but without jettisoning the standpoint of historical materialism. Within this literature is to be found a critical self-reflection which extends and develops Marx's ideas in areas where they had remained sketchy, ambiguous and open to abuse. To refer back to the examples given previously, the Christian and liberal record also includes, to a lesser or greater extent, courageous, in some cases prophetic, opposition by a minority of Christians and liberals to militarism or slavery or religious and racial persecution. A doctrine's capacity for integral self-criticism and self-correction is as important as the starting point since the latter is anyway bound to be mistaken or inadequate in various ways.

In recent times it has also become fashionable to decry Marxism as a utopian and messianic doctrine. Of course Marx himself explicitly rejected 'utopian socialism' and there is an absence in his work of elaborate programmes or proposals as to how the future socialist society should work. In *The Communist Manifesto*, Marx and Engels conclude with a lengthy critique of prevailing socialist doctrines arguing that they have an ideological and doctrinaire character. While it is often pointed out that Marx and Engels paid an extraordinary tribute to capitalism in the *Manifesto*, it is less often noted that this work is, in fact, a polemic against all then-existing conceptions of socialism. Marx insisted that socialism should arise from the real movement and not be cooked up by thinkers in their studies. Marx was, in general, far more committed to pursuing the materialist method in history than he was to particular programmatic notions. Reflecting this impulse, Marxist research in history, sociology, cultural studies and economics has given rise to a variety of schools imbued with a critical, sceptical and realist spirit. This is not to say that Marx did not enunciate important principles for judging whether or not the 'real movement' was in fact a movement towards human emancipation and self-realization. He wrote that 'the free development of each is the condition for the free development of all', or stipulated that the goal of communism was 'to each according to their need, from each according to their ability'—the first from the *Manifesto* being, I think, his own coinage, though it has echoes of Spinoza and Lessing, the second being an adaptation of a French socialist slogan.

Socialism as Simplification—or Complex Development?

The late twentieth-century fate of Marxism and socialism lends a quite proper retrospective interest to the study of its earlier programmes and proposals. In Marx, and more generally in the Marxist tradition, there is often a tension between what might be called a *simplifying* assumption and a *developmental* assumption. The simplifying assumption implies that once capitalism is swept away the problems of production, or of law, or of political organization will be easily manageable. Lenin's peremptory theses in *State and Revolution* would be a good example here. But in Marx, and in the tradition more generally, there is also a strong, possibly stronger, commitment to the idea that human social powers are cumulative, dialectical and various, and that in a socialist society some forms of complexity may be removed but others will be added. Thus Marx insisted that before the workers' movement was ready to be the (temporary) leading force in society, it needed to develop parties, trade unions, cultural associations, newspapers and so forth.[5] Marx favoured support for struggles over the extension of the suffrage, or over specific items of legislation such as the eight-hour day, both for their own sake and because it would strengthen the capacity of the movement. The classical Marxism of the early twentieth century argued for a rule of law (Karl Renner), for a democratic state and for a plurality of forms of representation (despite their many disagreements neither Luxemburg nor Kautsky subscribed to a monolithic or simplified notion of working-class interests, while with Gramsci the developmental thesis is given further impetus). Some of Lenin's later writings, such as *Left-wing Communism*, also contradict the simplifying approach.

In some famous passages Marx uses a rhetoric which implies that in economics too the 'simplification' thesis holds—everything will be transparent and readily understood after capitalism has been suppressed. This is certainly one of the messages conveyed by the strange proletarian 'Robinsonade' towards the end of the section on the fetishism of commodities in the first chapter of *Capital* Volume I, where the world working class, as a collective entity, is compared to Crusoe on his island.[6] The *Critique of the Gotha Programme* outlines general principles of individual and collective provision but has little useful to say about the coordination and socialization of production.

On closer inspection, Marx's contention in these passages is not that economic calculation becomes redundant after the expropriation of the expropriators, but that the rationality of applying labour to social need will become readily apparent once the veil of commodity entitlements has been lifted. Since Marx favoured a sweeping socialization of production in several of the most advanced capitalist states, it is difficult to think that he really envisaged a world planning authority deciding how much of everything should be produced. He was content to see positive references to cooperatives inserted into the programmatic declarations of the International Working Men's Association so long as they were not identified as the sole or privileged route to socialism. Another fact worth noting is that the *Critique of the Gotha Programme* did not offer the principle 'to each according to their work' as the *sole* principle of distribution in the initial or lower stage of socialism, but also argued for public provision for education, health and welfare. Among the chief purposes of this text was a challenge to propagandistic but misleading claims—the contention that labour is the sole source of all wealth is met by insistence that nature is just as important, and the claim that workers should receive the full fruits of their labour is met by itemization of the prior charges that should be made for investment. Notwithstanding such points, it must be conceded that Marx never sketched out exactly how the socialist economy would function. In all probability the unmet human need which he could see around him required no very complex assessment while the major industrial processes still had a fairly rudimentary character.

Marx's excessive restraint was not, of course, practised by others. Popular interest in the ideas of Eugen Dühring probably derived from the fact that he happily speculated on the economic shape of a future when autonomous economic communes would be ruled only by principles of social justice and communal cohesion. Many of Dühring's ideas were half-baked, and some highly obnoxious (he was, for example, an anti-semite). Engels's determination to combat his influence is understandable. But why did he feel the necessity to imitate Dühring's misguided system-building and 'world-schematism' rather than concentrate on the central political issues of economic prescription and programme? Newton, Lavoisier and Darwin scarcely needed to be defended; what did need attention was the economic and social programme of the workers' movement, yet in this area Engels's broad-brush phrases took matters little further forward.[7]

Mention should also be made of August Bebel's work *Woman in the Past, Present and Future* (1879) because of the author's importance in the founding of the German Social Democratic Party and because of the book's great popularity in the early socialist movement. Bebel's book drew a vivid contrast between the miseries of capitalism and the beauties of socialism. The discussion of the advent of socialism perfectly illustrates the approach of the 'simplifying' tradition, studded as it is with remarks to the effect that demand will be established 'with ease', production will go 'like clockwork' and 'everything will be simplified to a very large degree'. But Bebel's book is redeemed by some attractive and relevant passages—thus he indicts congested urbanism and industrial capitalism for its destruction of forests, poisoning of rivers and squandering of natural resources, leading him to urge the harnessing of water power to generate the electricity which he sees as vital to the society of the future.[8] With its strengths and its weaknesses, Bebel's text could be seen as a precursor of Magnitogorsk or of the Greens, according to taste. While its author came to think of himself as a Marxist, this book is redolent of the innocence of early socialism; John Stuart Mill and Fourier are cited no less respectfully than the author of *Capital*. The leitmotiv of the book is, of course, the need to ensure real political and social equality for women.

Criticism in Retrospect

The contemporary fate of Communism lends a new interest and topicality to the early critics of Marx or of socialism, such as Bakunin or J.S. Mill. Bakunin rejected what he saw as Marx's state socialism. While he admired *Das Kapital* and approvingly quoted Marx's dictum to the effect that the emancipation of the workers can only be carried through by the workers themselves, he was worried that Marx had too narrow a conception of who was a worker and he feared that Marx's notion of a revolutionary state would simply lead to the 'reign of scientific intelligence, the most aristocratic, despotic, arrogant and contemptuous of all regimes'. He observed:

> The State is government from above downwards of an immense number of men, very different from the point of the degree of their culture, the nature of the countries and localities they inhabit, the occupation they follow, the interests and aspirations directing them—the State is the government of all these by some or other minority; this minority, even if it were a thousand times elected by universal suffrage and controlled in its acts by popular institutions, unless it were endowed with the omniscience, omnipresence and omnipotence which the theologians attribute to God, it is impossible that it could know and foresee the needs, or satisfy with an even justice the most pressing interests in the world.[9]

Yet a close reading of Bakunin reveals that his real target was Lassalle and his notion of the *Volksstaat*; in fact Bakunin's criticisms goaded Marx to produce his own rejection of the statism of the German Social Democrats in the *Critique of the Gotha Programme*, as Daniel Guèrin has pointed out.[10] Bakunin may have been prescient in his remarks on state socialism, but his own antidotes were not appropriate and were in fact close to those espoused by the simplifying tradition referred to above.

Whereas Bakunin had no economic system of his own, the same cannot be said of Proudhon, who went further than Marx in outlining an alternative productive organization. Instead of proposing the statification of society he argued for a social economy, established by free and equal contracts between autonomous producers' associations, which should simply absorb and displace the tasks of government. Proudhon has been acclaimed as a precursor of market socialism, in that he sought to harness rather than suppress economic competition. He also had a greater sensitivity than Marx to the significance of petty production and exchange. As Gustav Landauer, one of the leaders of the Munich Revolutionary Council of 1918, was to write in 1914: 'Karl Marx and his successors thought they could make no worse accusation against the greatest of all socialists, Proudhon, than to call him a petit-bourgeois and petit-peasant socialist, which was neither incorrect nor insulting, since Proudhon showed splendidly to the people of his nation and his time, predominantly small craftsmen and farmers, how they could achieve socialism without waiting for the tidy progress of big capitalists.'[11] While Landauer was not wrong in identifying a strain of Marxist arrogance towards the small producers, his point would have been far stronger if he had explored the basis for their alliance with other social forces, including workers, rather than promoting the voluntaristic notion of a small-producer socialism. Both the 'late Marx' and the mature Kautsky did strive to get beyond dismissive condescension towards supposed 'rural idiocy' and to identify ways in which the labour movement could champion the cause of peasants.[12] While the Marxist tradition sometimes wrongly depreciated the small producers, they were not wrong in supposing that they would be unable to stem the advance of capitalist accumulation. Proudhon's own economic ideas were themselves wrong-headed in various ways. Like some Marxists, he rejected the need for a rate of interest, while his proposed central bank, lacking criteria for investment, would have found its substance drained by the soft-budget constraint. Proudhon's notion that economic organization made political democracy redundant drew from Engels the criticism that it would lead to an unaccountable and intensified state centralization, despite its author's mutualist or anarchist phrases.[13]

J.S. Mill expressed cautious enthusiasm for a decentralized socialism but also showed some insight when he warned that it would not be practical let alone desirable for the state to take charge of the whole life of society. He asserted that 'the very idea of conducting the whole industry of a country by direction from a single centre is so obviously chimerical, that nobody ventures to propose any mode in which it should be done'.[14]

Mill was not specifically addressing the ideas of Marx or Marxists, but as socialist movements grew in influence they naturally attracted the critical attention of sociologists and economists. Towards the close of the nineteenth century, it began to seem possible, as it scarcely did before, that socialists or social democrats might be in a position to lead the government in one or another of the major European states. There was commonly a feeling, detectable in the writings of Emile Durkheim, Wilfredo Pareto and the pre-war Max Weber, that the socialists should become more responsible and more ready to accept the realities and disciplines of power.[15] This line of criticism tended to encourage rather than contest the statist elements in socialist thinking. On the other hand, there were critics who challenged the coherence of Marx's account of capitalism—the most famous of these being the Austrian Böhm-Bawerk and such Russian Legal Marxists as Tugan-Baranovsky. But challenges to Marx's value theory or reproduction schemas did not explore their programmatic implications and did not question the economic rationality of planning or public ownership.[16]

The political and economic thinking of the German Social Democrats now occupied a special position in Marxist thought and was marked by a rejection of the 'state socialism' associated with Vollmar. The programme adopted at Erfurt in 1891 by the German Social Democrats was to become a classical reference point. The first section, written by Kautsky, constituted a vigorous indictment of the exploitation, instability and inhumanity of the capitalist system. The latter was held to be preparing the ground for its own demise because of the social polarization it promoted and because of its own readily identifiable tendency towards more socialized production. The second part of the programme, written by Eduard Bernstein and concentrating on immediate issues, centred on a call for the democratization of the German state—to include universal suffrage, broad civic liberties and trade-union rights. It is worth noting that this programme contained proposals, such as votes for women and proportional representation, that were in the vanguard of democratic politics; while Engels was very happy with this, the first 'Marxist programme', he would have liked to see a further commitment to republicanism and federalism.

The subsequent electoral successes of the German Social Democrats and the outbreak of the controversy over Bernstein's proposals led to some further elaboration of the programme. While Bernstein did not challenge the viability of socialization—indeed he rather argued that it was already happening under capitalism—his celebration of reformism helped to elicit from Kautsky a more thoughtful discussion of the problems of socialist production than had hitherto been offered by any socialist—or for that matter anti-socialist—thinker. In 'The Day After the Revolution' (1902) he registered the very considerable problems which a workers' government bent on socialization would face. He pointed out the organizational difficulty involved if 'in Germany the state is to become the director of production of two million productive plants and to act as the medium for circulation of this product, which will come to it partly in the form of the means of production and partly as means of consumption to be distributed to sixty million consumers, of which each one has a special and changing need'. While not discounting the possibility that means could be found to achieve this feat, he did reject any project for 'regulating the necessities of humanity from above ... assigning to each one, barrack-fashion, his portion'. Such a crude solution would return civilization 'to a lower stage'. Under prevailing conditions, money, wages and market prices could not be dispensed with. Socialist regulation would be principally realized through the larger enterprises, of which there were some 18,000, and it would be made easier because the patterns of consumption and the rhythms of production had a definite constancy or statistical regularity. Nevertheless the problem of coordination would be 'the most difficult which will come to the proletarian regime and will furnish it with many hard nuts to crack'. He concluded by insisting that there would be no need to do everything at once: 'As with money and with prices it is necessary to connect with that which is historically descended and not to build everything from the ground anew but only to broaden out at some points or to restrict at others.'[17]

Kautsky's tentative and exploratory remarks might have encouraged the Marxist economists to address the problem of what should be done when 'the necessity for regulating production by the exchange of equal values will cease'. Instead it was to be a small number of economic critics of socialism who were to concern themselves, in either a friendly or hostile spirit, with probing the practical presuppositions of a socialist society and economy. In these exercises the intellectual attraction of establishing the requirements of different forms of economy are allied to a conscious or unconscious intention of showing that such categories as price, rent, interest or saving would have their equivalent in any economic system. Among those who undertook such demonstrations were Friedrich von Wieser, Enrico Barone and N.G. Pierson. Though there was much that was interesting and pertinent in these critiques, they sometimes attributed over-simplified positions to Marx—both Barone and Pierson foist on Marx the notion that workers should receive the full fruit of their labour; a view which, as pointed out above, Marx and Engels had vigorously rejected in the *Critique of the Gotha Programme*. However, Barone was the first person to seek to identify the mathematical schema required for calculating values in a planned economy. He sought to demonstrate that this would involve many difficulties unsuspected by the advocates of socialism and that it would oblige them to reinvent 'bourgeois' categories. Nevertheless, if some seventy thousand equations could be solved then the 'Socialist Ministry of Production' could do the job required of it. Technically impressive though it was, Barone's essay was not as practical and realistic as Kautsky's thoughts on the subject had been.[18]

The critiques offered by Pierson and Wieser were less formalistic and static, and more relevant to Marxism—a variant of socialism which had, after all, not defined itself by a radical refusal of all economic categories. Pierson was encouraged by Kautsky's lecture on 'The Day After the Revolution' to press for further elaboration of how the Social Democrats proposed to run a publicly owned economy; a notable feature of this critique, which went unanswered so far as I am aware, was that it posed the question of how prices would be arrived at for 'trade' between different socialist states. Wieser's critique was both the most suggestive and, it seems, the least hostile in intent. While evincing some sympathy for, as well as interest in, socialism, Wieser questioned the appropriateness or even possibility of central state direction of economic activity:

> The one will or command which, in war or for legal unity, is essential and indispensable as the connecting tie of the common forces, detracts in economic joint action from the efficacy of the agency. In the economy, though it has become social, work is always performed fractionally ... Part-performances of this sort will be executed far more effectively by thousands and millions of eyes, exerting as many wills; they will be balanced, one against the other, far more accurately than if all these actions, like some complex mechanism, had to be guided and directed by some superior control. A central prompter of this sort could never be informed of countless possibilities, to be met with in every individual case, as regards the utmost utility to be met with in given circumstances or the best steps to be taken for further advancement and progress.[19]

The mainstream of Marxist economics did not take up the challenge of these programmatic critics but instead claimed that finance capital itself was refining techniques of economic calculation and control which could be inherited by a workers' government when the time was ripe. At this stage the nation-state was not yet established as the sole or privileged locus and agent of public ownership and planning. The existence of influential socialist municipalities, cooperatives and trade unions made for a more variegated, albeit hazy, vision of the future socialist economy.

The developing socialist movement needed ways of imagining the future and a common mode was the utopian (or, with Jack London, dystopian) novel, such as Edward Bellamy's *Looking Back* (1887), William Morris's *News from Nowhere* (1890) and Theodor Hertzka's *Freeland* (1876, 1890). Bellamy's book, which was to go through many editions, projected a peaceful evolution to collectivism on the basis of trends already present in late nineteenth-century capitalism which were seen as counter to the wasteful and anarchic features of capitalist competition—the formation of trusts and syndicates and the activities of municipal reformers. However, in Bellamy's view, state control of the whole economy would result to a significant extent from the fact that the public sector would prove to be vastly more effective as a provider, and popular as an employer, than the remaining private sector. William Morris found Bellamy's vision repugnant. Bellamy's portrait of happily regimented workers provoked from Morris the remark: 'If they brigaded

me into a regiment of workers I'd just lie on my back and kick.'
Bellamy's socialistic order was to have been introduced by popular
consent when 'public opinion had become fully ripe' but its central institutional expression was to be 'a single syndicate representing the whole
people'. Morris believed that this was inimical to the variety and self-
government which should be defining features of a genuine socialist
society. Seeing a link between Bellamy's utopia and the work of the
Fabians, with their identification of socialism with statification, he wrote:

> For the rest I neither believe in state socialism as desirable in itself, nor,
> indeed, as a complete scheme do I believe it to be possible. Nevertheless some
> approach to it is sure to be tried, and to my mind this will precede any
> complete enlightenment on the new order of things. The success of Mr
> Bellamy's book, deadly dull as it is, is a straw to show which way the wind
> blows.[20]

Morris's own utopian novel, *News from Nowhere*, was written partly
in opposition to Bellamy. Although work is given an important role in
the novel, specifically economic mechanisms, beyond a generalized
invocation of gift-markets, are not described. In this respect, Hertzka's
Freeland, in many ways less appealing and less socialist than *News from
Nowhere*, did attempt a more detailed picture of how free associations
of producers might regulate their affairs. For example, it addressed the
problem of how an overall equality was to be guaranteed in a competitive system of production and exchange. There was free movement of
workers who could demand that more successful, better-paying collectives take them on. Original members of the successful collective
received a modest seniority premium but had to share their prosperity
with newcomers. The device proposed by Hertzka did have a definite
technical ingenuity, as A. Chilosi has shown. We should, however, note
that Hertzka's utopia took the form of a colonizing fantasy, set in Africa,
and complete with attempts to reform the morals of the native; in this
and many other ways *Freeland* is scarcely a vision which contemporary
socialists would wish to embrace.[21]

In so far as the Second International parties elaborated a vision of the
future, it was to remain that outlined by Engels, by Kautsky and by
Bebel. The Marxist economists preferred to study, and argue about, the
workings of capitalism. The 'revisionist' Bernstein and the orthodox
Hilferding both argued that the advance of capitalist trustification and
financial cartelization were unwittingly creating the instruments of a
future socialist order. Kautsky was to develop a strong reservation about
the possible implications of this type of argument: 'This comfortable
conception of an imperceptible transition to the state of the future,
caused by the diligent activities of the capitalists themselves, leads

merely to this: the main task of the proletariat would then be to support the capitalists, for to do so would be to foster the liberation of the proletariat itself.'[22]

Leninism and Stalinism

With respect to mainstream Marxism, Lenin's Bolshevik current came to represent a species of political voluntarism. His concept of the revolutionary party was criticized for its Jacobinism and commandism by Luxemburg and Trotsky as well as by the Mensheviks.[23] But in the context of an incoherent autocracy Lenin's cult of party organization and discipline made sense to many militants.

Subsequently, the industrial carnage of the First World War, and its devastating impact on the lives of some hundreds of millions of people, could appear to justify not only the Bolshevik seizure of power but also the ruthlessness with which they defended this seizure. The Bolsheviks were scarcely disposed to take lessons in humanitarianism from those who bore responsibility for the hetacombs of Ypres and the Somme, or used starvation to cow central Europe in 1918–9, or from statesmen who savagely repressed the aspiration to colonial independence.[24]

On the other hand, the Bolsheviks of 1917 were impressed—probably overimpressed—by the workings of the German war economy, which was seen as demonstrating the effectiveness of physical planning; however, neither Switzerland nor the sealed train were good vantage points from which to make this assessment. In *The State and Revolution* Lenin wrote of how the economy could be organized as a single syndicate, echoing traditional socialist views about the achievements of trusts. The outbreak of civil war in March 1918 and the pressure of famine led to the institution of what was later called 'War Communism', with far-reaching attempts to replace all exchange by requisitioning. While this was effective militarily it cast a blight on small-scale production in this backward country. It was also associated with an intensified and hardened Bolshevik sense of destiny which would brook no opposition.[25]

Victory brought no political relaxation. In 1921 Bolshevik messianism was stepped up to justify an increasingly pervasive and truculent monopoly of power. Within the space of a few months, the remnants of pluralism in the Soviets were suppressed, the ban on factions within the Party adopted, Menshevik Georgia invaded, the revolt of the Kronstadt sailors suppressed militarily and Makhno's 'green' partisans hunted down. The stage had been set for Stalin.

Lenin certainly does not carry full responsibility for Marxism-

Leninism—a doctrine unknown to him. Lenin, though not a systematic thinker, in some ways developed a greater grasp than Marx of the necessary complexity of both politics and economics. Together with some other Russian Marxists, notably Bogdanov, Lenin developed a sense of the necessarily if partially autonomous significance of political organization. The voluntarism of his earlier writings was thus not devoid of real intuition. It was not until his last years that he appreciated the very double-edged discovery he had made, helping to fashion a political force that could be used for purposes of which he did not approve. His last writings, attacking the autonomy and arrogance of the new Soviet bureaucracy, reflect this painful realization. But as Marxist historians like Isaac Deutscher and Moshe Lewin have shown, he was just beginning to display some sense of the real dangers when he was overwhelmed by the practical and historical context, and struck down by illness.[26]

This is not to say that either Lenin or Trotsky can escape the charge of having themselves in some degree prepared the ground for Stalin by their often ruthless practice of a party dictatorship. One of Lenin's worst texts from the revolutionary period, 'How to Organize Competition' (1918), bristles with ill-considered and extreme formulations. For some reason Lenin decided not to publish it, but it was lying in the archives ready for publication in *Pravda* in 1929, allowing Stalin to claim Leninist credentials for his pitiless ferocity.[27] In a careful assessment of the period *Before Stalinism*, Samuel Farber has recently demonstrated how prophetic Luxemburg was in her 1918 indictment of Bolshevik practice. Indeed Farber shows that the Bolsheviks even violated their own claimed attachment to Soviet authority and legality. Within months of the Revolution, the Party organs usurped the Soviets, curtailed or suppressed pluralism within the revolutionary camp, manipulated elections, permitted or encouraged lawless repression, prevented the development of an independent press or system of justice, and reinstated one-man management in industry. Farber's detailed and documented account distinguishes between early Bolshevik rule and Stalinism but connecting threads are clearly established. If this work has a weakness it is that it does not quite give sufficient weight to the terrible domestic and international context with its pressures of war and famine—though Farber does argue that the latter was inadvertently compounded by 'War Communism'.[28]

Lenin and Trotsky themselves came to acknowledge that the economic policies of 'War Communism', whatever their militarily rationale, had contributed to a wrenching economic dislocation. In Russia, as in the rest of Europe, the imposition of a war economy, so far from furnishing an ante-chamber to socialism, did not stave off, and may even have aggravated, famine and epidemic. The failures of economic policy compounded the political problem, setting the scene for popular protest and what Farber calls 'surplus repression'. Bertrand Russell, after a visit to Russia in 1920, published a critique of the Bolsheviks which argued that many of the most regrettable and repressive features of Bolshevik rule were associated with economic failure. While he readily acknowledged the role played in this failure by foreign blockade, he insisted that the Bolsheviks must share some of the blame for the collapse of agriculture, because of the literally counter-productive effect of their insistence on seizing peasant produce rather than simply setting a tax.[29]

Inside the young Soviet republic, Martov, the Menshevik leader, came to accept the October Revolution as a fait accompli and urged that it should be defended against its enemies. But he vigorously attacked the 'political terrorism' and 'economic utopianism' of Bolshevik policy. Since 1905 Martov had argued that soviets and trade unions should make an independent contribution to the vitality of civil society—their independence within the larger process of bourgeois-democratic revolution should be championed by Marxists. Consistent with this position, Martov opposed dissolution of the Constituent Assembly in 1918 while still favouring an independent role for the soviets and trade unions. Elections showed this to be a popular view within the Russian working class and the Mensheviks recovered much support they had lost to the Bolsheviks in 1917. Martov, unlike Kautsky, tried to establish a modus vivendi with the Bolsheviks during the civil war but both men agreed that war had provided extremely adverse conditions for any socialist or democratic project. Appointed President of the Socialization Commission in 1919, Kautsky was appalled at the state of economic collapse and argued that priority would have to be given to restoring production; he urged that a system of workers' and consumers' control, rather than 'centralized bureaucracy', would attain that end. For his part, Martov opposed the European war more consistently and radically than did Kautsky. He argued that imperialist war had disrupted and divided the working class, swelling a deracinate and desperate lumpen proletariat that was vulnerable to any demagogy. Martov wrote of the new Soviet republic that 'here is flourishing ... "trench army" quasi-socialism based on the general "simplification" of the whole of life'. While Bolsheviks expressed the extremism of this layer so did the Black Hundreds; Martov reluctantly conceded a preference for the former over the latter. But he believed that the Bolsheviks, through their policy of armed requisitions, were digging a gulf between themselves and the direct producers in either the town or the countryside.[30]

Justifying the New Economic Policy in October 1921, Lenin himself acknowledged: 'We made the mistake of trying to change over directly to Communist production and distribution.' As is well-known, Lenin's subsequent economic thinking made large concessions to the need not only for internal markets and petty-commodity production but also for foreign investment.[31]

The Moment of Communism

The attempts made by Lenin and Trotsky to answer Kautsky and other socialist critics, including in Trotsky's case defence of the invasion of Menshevik Georgia, belong to their most unhappy and unconvincing exercises in polemic, since they insisted on justifying measures of repression which were not military necessities and which actually weakened the legitimacy of the Soviet republic. Yet their later justifications of the original Bolshevik seizure of power did contain one powerful refrain. They argued that the Bolshevik Revolution was simply a holding operation, staving off the terrible prospect of counter-revolutionary victory in Russia and securing a base that might assist the advance of movements that challenged the ruling classes of the advanced countries— whether labour movements or national liberation movements. Today we know the appalling cost of Stalinism and the often negative impact of the Soviet 'example'. However, we do not know what bloody consequences would have flowed from a victory by the Whites. While the peoples of the Soviet Union have good cause to rue the horrendous cost of Stalinism, the survival of the Soviet Union has had huge, and often positive, implications for those outside Soviet borders—most obviously the immense and irreplaceable Soviet contribution to the defeat of Nazism but also the real, though less quantifiable, Soviet contribution to persuading Western ruling classes to cede ground to anti-colonial liberation movements and to make concessions to their own domestic labour movements. Though other factors are certainly at work, it is interesting to note that welfare and social provision were often at their most generous in those European states bordering the former Soviet bloc, and were often introduced at a time when the prestige of the Soviet Union was at its highpoint, in the early postwar period. In Western Europe today we are still enjoying the fruits of 1945, in the form of enlarged democratic rights and more generous social provision for education and welfare. Similarly the great arc of postwar decolonization owed much to the challenge and competition supplied by the fact that the West had to contend with a global rival.[32] To point out such facts is not to justify Stalin's callousness and criminality, since the great purges and famines for which he was responsible weakened rather than strengthened the Soviet Union.

In a letter to a Russian correspondent, Marx wrote that he did not intend to impose a *marche générale* upon history such that each people had to pass through the sequence of feudalism, capitalism and socialism as laid out in the *Communist Manifesto*. With the collapse of the Communist alternative it can seem, however, that capitalism has itself imposed a *marche générale*, even if one which no longer terminates in socialism. However it should be remembered that the perspective of Marx's historical materialism principally concerned itself with the broad development of civilization in the world as a whole and not with necessarily subordinate developments within one or another nation-state, however large. From this standpoint, both the advent of a non-capitalist social order, the Soviet republic, and its prospective disintegration today, should not be seen in isolation, but rather as major shifts within the larger pattern of world politics and economics. The Bolshevik victory of 1917–20 or the Soviet role in the victory of 1945 did not put socialism on the agenda, even in Russia, but, in conjunction with antagonisms internal to the leading capitalist nations and empires, they did help to bring about a new global order, both limiting and threatening prevailing forms of capitalist and imperialist power.

A Hybrid Formation

The very distorted and costly achievements of the Soviet Union as a non-capitalist power, and the more or less faithful reproduction of the central features of the Soviet system throughout the Communist world, give some support to the idea that it represented a wholly distinct and rival political and social order to capitalism. But it is now clear, something few suspected before, that this rival order fell short of dynamic integration as a full-blown alternative system to capitalism. The Soviet economy was always a socio-economic hybrid and often failed to find a way to exploit the contradictions of the dominant capitalist world order—its only hope of undermining that dominance and ensuring its own complex development. But the Soviet polity was sufficiently densely structured to have a considerable margin of manoeuvre vis-à-vis the global ascendancy of capitalism. Stalin's forced collectivization and industrialization programme were driven forward by a quasi-military mobilization of cadres who, in a hostile world, saw Stalin's 'general line' as essential to the survival of their Party and the state it controlled. The Party apparatus inhabiting and dominating the state used a combination of military-style planning from above and cadre mobilization from below to impose the construction of a command economy. But the pressures of the global capitalist environment could not be entirely evaded, nor could the residues of capitalist social relations be entirely suppressed. Both Victor Serge and Leon Trotsky pointed to the 'totalitarian' logic by which Stalinism intensified invigilation, mobilization and repression in Soviet society in order to mask old and new forms of social differentiation and fragmentation. In evident contrast to the later use of this concept, Trotsky saw the totalitarian features of both Fascism and Stalinism as an extraordinary and non-sustainable political form which could only gain a temporary ascendancy because of the depths of social disorganization and crisis.[33] Trotsky's analysis implied that the totalitarian dictators were far less powerful than they seemed and that they were doomed to be ground between, on the one hand, the superior strength of the leading capitalist nations, and, on the other, the popular resistance that their rule inevitably engendered.

Was Leninism inherently totalitarian? Many have answered affirmatively, and there is certainly a case to answer. Luxemburg's famous indictment of the early phase of Bolshevik rule describes a party dictatorship, not a full-blown totalitarian system:

> With the repression of political life in the land as a whole, life in the soviets must also become more and more crippled. Without general elections, without unrestricted freedom of press and assembly, without a free struggle of opinion, life dies out in every public institution, becomes a mere semblance of life, in which only the bureaucracy remains as the active element. Public life gradually falls asleep, a few dozen party leaders of inexhaustible energy and boundless experience direct and rule. Among them in reality only a dozen outstanding heads do the leading and an elite of the working class is invited from time to time to meetings where they are to applaud the speeches of the leaders, and to approve resolutions unanimously—at bottom then a clique affair—a dictatorship, to be sure, but not of the proletariat, however, but only of a handful of politicians, that is, a dictatorship in the bourgeois sense, in the sense of the rule of the Jacobins.[34]

While ominous enough, this does not quite add up to totalitarianism. A totalitarian system is one in which the rulers forcibly impose a single imperative system on the whole of society and criminalize even the thought of any alternative. The Party member and citizen is not allowed to be lifeless but must show signs of enthusiasm or risk a harsh penalty. Lenin's practice of a Party dictatorship was not fully totalitarian for a number of reasons. Until 1921 there were different factions and tendencies within the Bolshevik Party and there were different legal parties. Lenin himself contributed to the maintenance of a de facto pluralism within the Party and the leadership both by provoking disagreements and by his preparedness to ally with former opponents. While he urged Bolsheviks to be self-critical, he never demanded recantations or sought to impose monolithic unanimity. The discipline that was demanded was supposedly justified by struggle against the class enemy and did permit the Party member to play some formal role in electing leaders and voting on policies. In Lenin's day the Party members' role was small but at least there were some real choices to be made. The Extraordinary Commission engaged in arbitrary acts against the regime's political opponents but it was not used to purge the ranks of the Bolsheviks or to maintain routine labour discipline. Non-Party organizations like trade unions were, at least in theory, meant to enjoy autonomy from the Party. Votes at Party congresses reveal many narrowly contested issues and radically differ from the Stalinist and post-Stalinist pattern.[35]

Victor Serge was to write:

> It is often said that 'the germ of all Stalinism was in Bolshevism at its beginning'. Well, I have no objection. Only, Bolshevism also contained many other germs—a mass of other germs—and those who lived through the enthusiasm of the first years of the first victorious revolution ought not to forget it. To judge the living man by the death germs which the autopsy reveals in the corpse—and which he may have carried with him since his birth—is this very sensible?[36]

Serge saw the statification of the economy as conducive to totalitarian tendencies but for something like a decade neither process was either complete or uncontested. In the early years of the Soviet republic there were many residues of the revolutionary self-management which had erupted in 1917. Educational and cultural institutions, including journals and publishing houses, enjoyed some autonomy and as late as 1925 'free competition' of different schools was declared to be the appropriate cultural policy. Regional and municipal soviets exercised some economic initiative and in the textile industry a species of workers' control survived, perhaps because the predominantly female workforce was not disrupted and dispersed by conscription as happened in other industrial sectors. The policy of 'land to the tiller' was bound to create an element of economic pluralism, even if War Communism sought drastically to curtail it. Lenin's hostility to Great Russian chauvinism and his insistence that Finland and the Baltic states should be allowed to exercise a sovereign right of self-determination are policies which do not conform to a totalitarian project. Twentieth-century totalitarianism has often allied itself to nationalism, since the latter helps it to make good on its promise to furnish a total identity penetrating to the soul of each citizen. Lenin's practice was not always fully consonant with his principles, but even in the case of Georgia it is clear that he saw Stalin's arrogant and heavy-handed conduct as quite sufficient grounds for disqualifying him as General Secretary.

Rosa Luxemburg is undoubtedly a more attractive example of a socialist politician than Lenin, entirely lacking the Bolshevik leader's streak of intolerance and ferocity. On the other hand, she failed to see the importance of either the policy of distributing land to the peasants or of the principle of national self-determination. Her draft for a pamphlet on the Russian Revolution vigorously attacks Lenin on both these points.[37]

The years, between 1927 and 1931 saw the installation of a totalitarian system with forced collectivization, a frenzied cult of the leader, criminalization of all opposition, the pervasive influence of the secret police and the imposition of a monolithic Marxist-Leninism on all areas of life. Economic dislocation and crisis made a powerful contribution to the radicalization of the Stalinist regime and its totalitarian *fuite en avant*. Forced collectivization was itself a response to the peasants' refusal to deliver grains on a scale, and at a price, that would meet urban needs. Peasant recalcitrance, in its turn, reflected the failures of urban industry and services. The trial of engineers and specialists reflected the ruling bureaucracy's frustration and anger at its weak ability to control the economy. The Five Year Plan was soon accompanied by recourse to Stakhanovism and a crude mixture of intimidation and bribery in the mobilization of urban workers. This period was a sort of reprise of 'War Communism' and involved an emphatic re-militarization of all aspects of social relations. The totalitarian regime thrived on crisis and a siege climate.

The Great Purges completed the process of subjecting all institutions and persons to a monolithic and unified regime. While an irrational paranoia was in evidence, so too was a remorseless totalitarian logic that shattered and remoulded any institution with a potential for independence, including the Stalin faction itself, the officer corps and the political police. Lenin had introduced commandist and centralist principles to the organization of the Party and had urged the Party activists to supply leadership in every field. His terroristic methods, directed mainly outwards at a real enemy, were designed to promote revolutionary solidarity. Lenin's notion of tactics and strategy was designed to win over whole social groups. The Leninist Party was based on the notion that the individual on joining would henceforth owe it their primary loyalty; but note that the Party was defined by a programme and joining it was a voluntary act. Stalinism demanded of every citizen the sort of political commitment and discipline which Lenin had demanded of the Party member; together with the suppression of the remnants of intra-Party democracy this was an essential element in the totalitarian project. Stalin's terror broke up social groups, serializing all social relations such that each individual saw in every other individual the potential representative of the ruling power. Once the system was established, quite small doses of terror could keep it going, though Stalin was rarely satisfied with only small doses. Despite the extraordinary power which he exercised, Stalin was to display signs of frustration down to his last days at the fact that the political machine he wielded continually spawned new forms of bureaucratic inertia and cunning.

The category of bureaucracy used by many Marxist critiques in the analysis of Stalinism refers us both to macro-social processes of rationalization, of which the bureaucracy was supposedly the bearer, and to a separation between mental and manual labour, with the functionary being the expression of the domination of the latter by the former. These connections were explored in various ways by anarchosyndicalist writers and by Herbert Marcuse, T.W. Adorno and other members of the Frankfurt School. Someone influenced by both these traditions and a former follower of Trotsky, the Trinidadian revolutionary C.L.R. James, gave sharp expression to this line of analysis when he wrote: 'In Russia by 1928, from a revolution exhausted and desperate, and seeing in the world around it no gleam of hope arose the same soviet type ... administrators, executives, organizers, labour leaders, intellectuals. Their primary aim is not world revolution. They wish to build factories and power stations larger than all others which have been built. They aim to connect rivers, to remove mountains, to plant from the air, and to achieve these they will waste human and natural resources on an unprecedented scale. Their primary aim is not war. It is the Plan. In pursuit of what they call planning the economy they have de-populated Russia of tens of millions of workers, peasants and officials so that it seems as if some pestilence sweeps periodically across the country.'[38] In James's view the bureaucratic approach to planning expressed a besotted faith in the powers of intellect and a necessarily totalitarian logic. While James acutely analysed the Plan as the ideological expression of bureaucratic power he did not really explain what made the Soviet economy function nor how the intellectual workers secured a degree of everyday compliance from those who carried out orders.

Distortions and Defects

Kautsky's critique of the Bolshevik regime and of Stalinism did not lead him to invent a new political category, though he did compare the Soviet state of circa 1930 to a species of proletarian Absolutism in which an urban working-class cadre played the pitiful role of a prostrate minor nobility, shackled by fear and petty privileges to a political order over which it had no control. He failed to produce a concept which properly seized the modernity of the Soviet system, but did identify limits to the modernization that was being attempted. Kautsky believed that Stalinist dictatorship and bureaucracy, despite its workerist and productivist propaganda, would bar the road to the sort of economic development that required a creative and self-confident workforce. In his unjustly neglected, if also one-sided, critique of Soviet economic forms in the twenties and thirties, Kautsky pointed out that they lacked the requisite social basis and capacity for true socialization and sustained, diversified economic growth. He did not deny that a certain primitive industrialization had been achieved but observed 'all its successes are in spheres where military methods can be applied.'[39]

Kautsky argued that it was simply beyond the competence of the Soviet bureaucracy to administer a complex modern economy, and that instead it would sponsor only that type of development which corresponded to its own narrow interests and capacities. Kautsky himself considered that the Soviet state had an essentially bureaucratic-capitalist relationship to the peasantry, and, incipiently, to all direct producers. Democratic rights and controls were required to ensure the quality of industrial advance and a harmonious collaboration between peasants and proletarians, workers by hand and workers by brain. He advocated not only a 'democratic revolution' but also a path of economic development that gave assistance to small property holders as it encouraged voluntary forms of cooperation, and would oblige the public sector to prove its superiority in competition with a continuing private sector.

Despite all the claims made for the first Five Year Plans, Stalin himself recognized the limits of his own administrative model by retaining elements of a money–commodity economy that were associated with capitalism. Indeed it can now be seen that in most of the Soviet-style regimes such institutions retained a key role: money has been the main medium of exchange, wages the essential reward for labour, petty production common in the agricultural sector, foreign trade of significance for important branches, and so forth. According to a particular type of Marxist orthodoxy, whether simple utopianism or bureaucratic voluntarism, these economic mechanisms have been identified as elements of capitalism (though nearly every one of them actually long preceded the rise of capitalism). Although the Communist states have often been tempted by strategies of national autarchy, this has usually led to stagnation and heightened repression—in the end they usually signalled the abandonment of such autarchy by blatant concessions to capitalism, as in China in the 1970s.

Stalin sometimes appeared to recommend and practice such autarchic models of development—especially after 1945 in the context of the enlarged, but still backward, 'socialist camp'. But research into Soviet economic development shows that it was at its most rapid in the thirties and forties when there were extensive exchanges with the West. It is an extraordinary fact that in the early thirties more than half of UK and US machine exports were destined for the Soviet Union. In some branches the figures were over 90 per cent. It was the massive import of Western technology in the thirties and forties that laid the basis for Soviet growth up to the end of the fifties.[40] We should not forget that the Cold War policies of the West—from Cocom to other forms of economic and military blockade—were successfully designed to cut the Soviet Union off from Western technology and also forced Soviet planners to waste huge resources on military expenditures. In the thirties and forties Stalin was able somewhat crudely to exploit contradictions within the world capitalist system because these took the form of clashes between the most powerful capitalist states. In the period after 1945 the capitalist world became increasingly politically unified and thus afforded few openings to Soviet diplomacy. An alternative approach would have been to seek potential allies within the leading capitalist states, in the shape of labour and social movements. But Stalin's recourse to repression and political isolation within the Soviet Union made it impossible for him to pursue this line with any success. Soviet insistence that Marshall Aid should be rejected by the new 'People's Democracies' betrayed a costly nervousness of the perils of capitalist encroachment.

As more reliable Soviet data become available it will be possible to establish the contribution made by Stalin's repressions—either forced collectivization or the Gulag system—to Soviet 'primitive accumulation'. It is quite possible that the overall balance-sheet will show a deficit in purely economic as well as human terms. Though more surplus was for a time seized from the peasantry, agricultural output was permanently damaged. It is true that the wretched inmates of the Gulag opened the frozen Far North; they built power stations and railway lines in terrible conditions that no free workers would have tolerated. But typically these projects were poorly planned and executed in a way that was extremely wasteful of valuable materials and machines as well as lives. The repressive apparatus was a costly, parasitic growth. Even in the Kolyma gold mines it seems that free labour is more productive today than the forced labour of the past. Apart from anything else, the increasing propensity of forced labourers to revolt, as in Vorkuta in 1953, became disruptive. When millions were released from the Gulag in the fifties, the reason was partly social pressure—but perhaps also partly that the forced labour system was proving cumbersome, expensive and inefficient.[41]

Plan, Market and Democracy

But was there an alternative? As an opponent of 'socialism in one country' Trotsky attempted to show that there was. Some of his best ideas in this area are also the least well known. Thus in 1930 Trotsky came up with a bold plan to achieve a double objective: firstly, to help the Soviet Union break out of economic isolation, and, secondly, to promote the cause of the West European working-class movements. He proposed that the Soviet government should invite the West and Central European Social Democrats to join it in devising and implementing the Five Year Plan. He pointed out that the Soviet Union desperately needed to buy machinery. He also pointed to the growing scourge of unemployment in the rest of Europe. In such a situation the internationalist—or, as Marx would have put it, 'cosmopolitan'—approach would be to draw up a programme of economic and social advance between the Soviet government and such other European governments as would be willing to join in—those of Austria, Germany and Britain, for example, where the workers' parties were in government or could hope to form a government. Trotsky saw this proposal as the economic counterpart to the principled strategy of proposing a United Workers' Front.[42] He did not fear that economic collaboration on the Plan between the Soviet government and social-democratic governments would 'contaminate' the rationality of the transitional economy by the admixture of capitalist elements, since the Soviet economy inescapably had to incorporate capitalist elements, the only choice being whether they derived from advanced or backward forms of capitalism. Though Trotsky favoured planning, he did not see this as a comprehensive or self-sufficient social process. In *The Revolution Betrayed* (1937) he acknowledged that heavy industry was advancing rapidly, but he argued that many of the vaunted achievements of the Five Year Plans were illusory. He pointed to the lasting damage wreaked by forced collectivization and stressed the poor quality of much that was produced by industry. At several points his economic critique echoed the analysis of the Left Oppositionist Christian Rakovsky. According to Rakovsky, the Soviet economic system was in fact characterized by an all-out advance on its chosen objectives and did not involve intricate coordination. He also argued that quality control was almost entirely lacking: 'we are not dealing with individual defects but with the systematic production of defective products.'[43]

In *The Revolution Betrayed* Trotsky attacked what he described as Stalin's 'totalitarian' delusions. Around the same time he wrote that Soviet society was not—nor could any society be—structured like a great brain, controlled from some all-knowing centre. He argued this in an article in 1932 in terms which are worth quoting in full:

> If a universal mind existed, of the kind that projected itself into the scientific fancy of Laplace—a mind that could register simultaneously all the processes of nature and society, that could measure the dynamics of their motion, that could forecast the results of their interactions—such a mind, of course, could a priori draw up a faultless and exhaustive economic plan, beginning with the number of acres of wheat down to the last button for a vest. The bureaucracy often imagines that it has such a mind at its disposal; that is why it so easily frees itself from the control of the market and of Soviet democracy. But, in reality, the bureaucracy errs frightfully in its estimate of its spiritual resources. In its projections it is necessarily obliged, in actual performance, to depend upon the proportions (and with equal justice one may say the disproportions) it has inherited from capitalist Russia, upon the data of the economic structure of contemporary capitalist nations and finally upon the experience of the successes and mistakes of the Soviet economy itself. But even the most correct combination of all these elements will allow only the most imperfect framework of a plan, not more. The innumerable living participants in the economy, collective and individual, must serve notice of their needs and of their relative strength not only through the statistical determinations of plan commissions but by the direct pressure of supply and demand. The plan is checked and, to a considerable degree, realized through the market. The regulation of the market itself must depend upon the tendencies that are brought out through its mechanism. The blueprints produced by the departments must demonstrate their efficacy through commercial calculation. The system of the transitional economy is unthinkable without control by the rouble.[44]

Thus while Trotsky believed that Soviet democracy should embrace 'the living regulation by the masses of the structure of the economy', he also insisted that a reborn Soviet democracy would use the market to check on the adequacy and rationality of planning, since, as he explained, 'economic accounting is unthinkable without market relations'.[45]

Bukharin's advocacy of the use of the market and of the need for a long-term alliance with small producers is well known. But Trotsky had been the first Bolshevik leader to question 'War Communism',[46] and, as Alec Nove has pointed out, Trotsky and the Left Opposition opposed the delusions of the administrative-command system. As early as 1922, Trotsky had pointed out at the Fourth Congress of the Comintern that 'in the course of the transitional epoch each enterprise and each set of enterprises must to a greater or lesser extent orient itself independently on the market and test itself through the market. It is necessary for each state owned factory with its technical director to be subject not only to control from above—by state organs—but also from below through the market, which will remain the regulator of the state economy for a long while to come.'[47]

By 1933, Trotsky was arguing that the role of money and of commodity turnover would grow as the Soviet economy became more advanced: 'The methods of economic and monetary calculation developed under capitalism are not rejected but are socialized', he wrote.[48] It is true that in some fairly remote future, beyond the transitional economy, money and markets would cease to be necessary instruments of social planning, or would be subsumed within some new economic mechanism, but Trotsky gave no intimation of how economic rationality would then work, beyond insisting that it would have to operate at a global level.

The construction of a socialist economy had to be continually oriented to the advancing forces of world economics, hence Trotsky's advocacy of joint planning with social-democratic governments in Central and Western Europe. On the one hand, Trotsky's proposal would allow Soviet development to tap the superior technology of the West; on the other, it would allow Western labour movements to come up with practical and transitional objectives to deal with the problem of mass unemployment.

While Stalin never adopted Trotsky's proposal, he did promote economic collaboration with the advanced countries in the thirties and in the war years. The cruel and costly 'successes' of the Stalin period derived partly from this fact, partly from the simplification of economic tasks during the early phase of industrialization and wartime, and partly from the sacrifices which the CPSU was still able to demand from its cadres, members and supporters. The need to meet threats of foreign intervention and to realize the promise of a happy future were enough to persuade even such a man as Andrei Sakharov to give of their best and to weep when Stalin died.[49] But the contribution of all these factors diminished over time. The protracted Cold War imposed an increasingly stringent technological blockade and contributed to incipient stagnation. The tasks of economic coordination became more complex as industrialization advanced and the 'socialist camp' grew.[50] Access to Western technology ceased. Cocom proved stronger than Comecon. The ideological motivation of the cadres and activists was dimmed by repeated frustrations and disappointments. Cynicism and corruption spread.

The closing up of access to Western technology was thus only one feature of the slow-down in Soviet growth. And furthermore the question has to be asked, why did the Soviet Union, once a certain threshold had been reached, not generate its own technology? And why has it so often made bad use even of that technology it has been able to import, such as the advanced computers given to many large Soviet enterprises in the early seventies? In answering these questions it will be worth briefly considering the basic problem of economic calculation in a planned or collectivist economy.

The Calculation Debate

The twenties, thirties and forties witnessed a debate on 'socialist calculation' between the leading members of the Austrian school, Ludwig von Mises and Friedrich von Hayek, and socialist economists, such as Oskar Lange and H.D. Dickinson, which sharply posed the question of the criteria that could govern the allocation of resources to a multiplicity of ends once the market mechanism had been suppressed. In fact Mises claimed in his first contributions in 1920 and 1922 that calculation would be impossible in a planned economy because there would be no *numéraire* available to evaluate alternative uses of labour and resources. He believed that calculation in terms of labour time, even if it could be done and some way found of attributing different values to different types of skill, would still not yield rational results because, in default of a market, there would be no way of arriving at the complex pattern of demand for final and intermediate goods. He was similarly unimpressed by Otto Neurath's claim that it would be possible to elaborate an ecological economy based on physical and natural coordinates such as the quantity of coal needed for smelting iron ore. Once again, such a method could not evaluate final demand (in all its complexity) nor arbitrate between rival uses of raw materials and intermediate products (in all *their* complexity).[51]

While Mises's original critique seemed to imply that a planned economy would simply grind to a halt, he later developed the argument that third-rate solutions, or solutions at odds with the proclaimed goals of socialists, could be arrived at. For example, the planners could use prices derived from the capitalist world or the capitalist past in making their calculations. Likewise the existence of money, wages and a restricted market for consumer goods would allow a botched semblance of economic rationality. If the workers were allowed to run the enterprises in which they worked, then a species of 'syndicalist capitalism' might develop. Mises also developed the point that a planned economy, lacking general criteria, would necessarily foster special interests of a spuriously 'natural' character, such as those based on national or ethnic categories. And, of course, the government could simply usurp the functions of consumers and entrepreneurs only if it was prepared to impose authoritarian solutions. Even elected governments would behave in this way because their programmes would always be an arbitrary abridgement and simplification of social needs, and one which, even supposing it made sense at one moment, would soon be overtaken by the ever-changing flux of circumstance, fortune and taste.

Mises argued that capitalism allowed for a much broader participation in decision-making than that permitted by the cult of nationalization and planning: 'The distinctive mark of socialism is the oneness and indivisibility of the will directing all production activities within the whole social system. When socialists declare that "order" and "organization" are to be substituted for the "anarchy" of production, conscious action for the alleged planlessness of capitalism, true cooperation for competition, production for use for production for profit, what they have in mind is always the substitution of the exclusive and monopolistic power of only *one* agency for the infinite multitude of the plans of individual consumers and those attending to the wishes of the consumers, the entrepreneurs and capitalists.' Mises rejected the criticism that the market was a social mechanism which acted behind the backs of the agents active within it while planning expressed conscious social control: 'The truth is that the alternative is not between a dead mechanism or a rigid automatism on one hand and conscious planning on the other hand. The question is whose planning? Should each member of society plan for himself, or should a benevolent government alone plan for them all? The issue is not *autonomism versus conscious action*; it is *autonomous action of each individual versus the exclusive action of the government.*'[52]

Most of the Left chose to ignore this critique, pointing to the palpable evidence of capitalist failure and the apparent Soviet success in rehabilitating the Russian economy and embarking on the road to industrialization. However, a few socialist economists did see that there was a significant case to be answered and were provoked by Mises's confident ascriptions to insist that he had not considered the best socialist solutions. Mises's original critique had drawn a response from Eduard Heimann, a Social Democrat who had served on Kautsky's Socialization Commission, and both he and Karl Polanyi, the social historian, developed market socialist models in the twenties.[53] In the thirties, further efforts were made to adapt market mechanisms to socialist purposes by the English 'liberal socialist' H.D. Dickinson, by a group of Polish socialists including Oskar Lange, and by A.P. Lerner, who was to make a decisive contribution to welfare economics. The economic models proposed by Heimann and the Polish socialists envisaged a system of workers' councils, each of which would be responsible for a given industry; the market was to coordinate relations between these industries, each of which was to be organized on monopolistic lines. The socialist critique of capitalism stressed the wastefulness of competition so it seemed only natural to propose unified groups in each major industrial branch—footwear, iron and steel, coal, textiles, and so forth. In their unsophisticated form these models could not claim to answer all the problems posed by Mises. But Dickinson, Lange and Lerner elaborated complex mathematical models, drawing on neoclassical equilibrium theory, which appeared more capable of withstanding the Austrian assault. Thus Lange responded to Mises's challenge by conceding that planning, even carried out by the most democratic of governments, would lack proper economic criteria. To prevent a relapse into crude and authoritarian solutions he and Dickinson proposed that socialist planning authorities could develop a simulated market, with a system of shadow prices which would be used to compare different paths of development. Moreover, Lange and Dickinson pointed out that the planners would be able to start from past price schedules and then use trial and error to refine and improve them, this latter process being described as a species of *tatonnement*. Thus if not enough of a given product was sold then prices would be lowered, and if shortages occurred they would be raised. The profits made by enterprises would also furnish an indicator. The financial authority would use the rate of interest as a regulator and would pay out a social dividend to every individual on a regular basis. While these socialist models embodied new concepts and involved virtuoso displays of mathematical economics, they were institutionally centralist, by comparison with, for example, the account of a socialist economic order earlier elaborated by Oskar Lange and Marek Breit, which had allowed a greater margin of autonomy both to working collectives and to individual workers.[54] Abba Lerner himself noted that models of this sort were too static and, in a dynamic world, Lange had become 'dazzled by the picture of equilibrium'.[55]

Hayek took it upon himself to respond to these new socialist models and to develop the Austrian critique further. In essays published in 1940 and 1945, he argued that Lange and Dickinson had failed to register the indispensable role of entrepreneurship in seizing opportunities and 'creating' price relationships which were not simply given. Their notion of a socialist central bank advancing funds to enterprises failed to register that the banking authorities would lack specifically economic guidelines for backing one project rather than another; enterprises bidding for funds could promise unrealistic returns with no fear of the consequences. One of Hayek's refrains was that collectivist ownership would erase responsibility for investment decisions by distributing them indistinctly between the central authority and the enterprise managers. 'It will rest with the central authority to decide whether one plant located at one place should expand rather than another plant situated elsewhere. All this involves planning by the central authority on much the same scale as if it were actually running the enterprise. And while the individual entrepreneur would in all probability be given some definite contractual tenure for managing the plant entrusted to him, all new investments will be necessarily centrally directed. This division would then have the result that neither the entrepreneur nor the central authority would be in a position to plan, and that it would be impossible to assess the responsibility for mistakes. To assume that it is possible to create conditions of full competition without making those who are responsible for the decisions pay for their mistakes seems to be pure illusion.'[56]

With his essay on 'The Uses of Knowledge in Society' published in the *American Economic Review* (1945), Hayek drew attention to the inescapably fragmented and dispersed character of economic knowledge. The real economic potential of a resource or commodity depended on exactly where and when it was available. While a multitude of entrepreneurs might be able to spot new possibilities and relationships, and back their hunches at their own cost, the planners simply could not know this mass of dispersed and discrete information, much of it strictly unintelligible or meaningless outside its given context.[57]

The Fallacy of the Single Mind

If Hayek's critique of Lange and Dickinson succeeded in sowing real doubts as to the effectiveness of a make-believe, simulated market, it also reinforced the case against full-blooded planning developed by Mises. Thus Hayek answers the argument that so long as consumers' preferences are established then this will imply the need for the appropriate producers' goods, with these observations: 'It is evident, however, that the values of the factors of production do not depend solely on the valuation of the consumers' goods but also on the conditions of supply of the various factors of production. Only to a mind to which all these facts were simultaneously known would the answers necessarily follow from the facts given to it. The practical problem, however, arises precisely because these facts are never so given to a single mind, and because, in consequence, it is necessary that in the solution of the problem knowledge should be used that is dispersed among many people.'[58] Hayek's argument significantly parallels some of the points quoted above from Trotsky. Both authors point to the fallacy of a single mind directing an economy; indeed Hayek himself quotes from Trotsky's 1932 essay on 'The Dangers Facing the Soviet Economy', in this same article.[59]

The 'calculation debate' petered out in the forties without achieving resolution, but many issues were left hanging since the critical points made by both sides were generally stronger than their positive proposals. From a non-Marxist perspective sympathetic to planning, Joseph Schumpeter argued in his influential work *Capitalism, Socialism and Democracy* (1943) that Hayek and Mises had failed to sustain their case. Hayek's 1945 essay was as much directed at Schumpeter as at the Marxists. The socialist side of the debate did argue that a capitalist market would reflect the unequal and irrational structure of economic power. Dobb warned that recourse to an uncontrolled market could lead to mass unemployment. He pointed out that the broad planning of economic development meant that large-scale projects could be undertaken which would never have seemed justified according to the atomized calculation of market actors. While Dobb did not engage with Hayek's argument concerning planner's ignorance, the latter's account of entrepreneurial knowledge shows that he had developed his own position through his encounter with the socialist economists.[60]

On the other hand, neither Mises nor Hayek addressed themselves to the syndicalist market socialism originally put forward by Lange and Breit, understandably since it had been abandoned by Lange himself (Breit died in the war). The syndicalist strain within socialism was particularly weak in the forties and belief in the big battalions was particularly strong. So far as I am aware, no one pointed out that Hayek's argument from the dispersed nature of knowledge could also be deployed against a narrow capitalist entrepreneurialism by advocates of social and worker self-management. Of course, the argument from dispersed knowledge would not justify an indiscriminate and incoherent populism since the development of democratic expressions of intersubjectivity is as difficult as it is vital to achieve in a world in which the structures of social life are more thoroughly collective and interwoven than ever before.

While respect for individual choice must be the starting point for politics and economics, many facilities in a modern economy are inescapably collective in character. That collective decisions can never match the apparent lucidity and self-sufficiency of the choice of an individual is a source of inescapable complexity. But this does not require us to outlaw the hope that better collective arrangements could furnish all with a greater real possibility of self-determination. Socialists are committed to the view that a range of consciously concerted measures are either desirable or unavoidable, and that everyone should have broadly the same claim on society's material resources. The Austrians rejected equality on the grounds that there was literally no way of measuring the wishes of one individual against those of another. They rejected all interventions in the system of free (capitalist) exchange, or 'catallaxy', other than those designed simply to guarantee and protect the 'spontaneous order' brought about by the clash of individual wills and dispositions. The mildest reformism was as unjustified as the most sweeping revolutionism. While they reasonably denied that society could be made to function with the synoptic logic of a single mind, they unreasonably contended that there is no area of economic life where collective decisions could be validly made outside the market itself. Simple-minded socialism, or a socialism adapted to simple conditions, has imagined that the logic of social choice can be just as intelligible and definitive as an individual's decision to slake their thirst by drinking a glass of water. But without at all abandoning socialism it is quite possible to recognize that social need and public good have to be arrived at by complex, tentative and negotiated ways—indeed this could be seen as the very essence of genuine socialism. Without abandoning the ideal and touchstone of individual self-determination, or falsely projecting it on to the collective, socialists have contended that: (1) a broad equality of material condition will be most conducive to generalized self-determination; (2) the intimate structures of individuality are constructed out of a social fabric which should consequently be as rich as possible; (3) there are common conditions of human existence which require collective attention and sustenance; (4) a variety of processes of democratic self-determination are required to achieve such outcomes. Production, consumption and, of course, communication all rest on social presuppositions. Socialism postulates the necessity of developing forms of social life which will allow for conscious human control of economic processes, with the aim of banishing want, furnishing every individual with the material means for self-realization, preventing class division and ensuring a sustainable relationship with the natural environment. What is implied is not a single mind but institutions that will encourage a meeting of minds. The Austrian position denies equality, restricts the social dimension of individuality, argues that the common conditions faced by humanity can take care of themselves and minimizes the scope for collective deliberation and determination.[61]

A number of such points were made by the socialists who contributed to the 'calculation debate'. Polanyi, in his classic work, *The Great Transformation* (1944)—which can be read as a sustained riposte to Mises and Hayek—argued that the market did not protect the lifeworld which made it possible. He did not deny the efficacy of market calculation in relation to real commodities, but urged that capitalism allowed market forces to escape their proper limits and treat labour and nature as if they were no more than goods to be sold. Dickinson itemized market failures and Lerner identified criteria for public welfare and social cost. Otto Neurath also developed arguments that were never really addressed by Mises or Hayek, perhaps because Neurath was a philosopher rather than an economist. He had observed that the market reflected the interests and needs of those now living but not those of future generations; economic resources would thus tend to be exploited in a short-sighted and unrenewable way. Neurath also stressed that it was not the job of economists to pre-empt democratic debate; they should therefore produce rival scenarios of possible futures. Neurath argued that neither a market nor a *numéraire* were appropriate in assessing social needs and public goods, many of which were intuitive and indivisible. He argued that just as generals do not deal in 'war units', so governments should not aim at achieving or maximizing 'instruction units' or 'health units', but should rather aim to furnish whatever resources are needed to ensure a healthy population educated to whatever level the citizens found desirable. Thus Neurath did argue that society could develop a 'common mind', in the sense of a majority view, on the desirable provision of welfare and public goods; doctors and clinics would not need a market to inform themselves of the ailments of their patients.[62] In the further elaboration of the Austrian position it is notable both that it has remained vulnerable to arguments from ecology and is consistently minimalist in its view of public goods. Moreover, Hayek has been drawn to advocate a drastic narrowing of the scope of democratic government.[63] However, although Neurath posed questions which the Austrians never satisfactorily answered, his own belief that it was possible to entirely suppress the market was quite wrong-headed, for some of the reasons indicated by Mises. Dickinson and Lerner did not espouse this fantasy and argued for the adaptation of the market for socialist purposes. But for their part, the market socialists did not establish that they had put forward a fully workable model, rather than particular mechanisms and concepts which could be used to modify the workings of either a market or a planned economy. In particular, they did not respond to the Hayek/Mises arguments of the forties, with their vindication of entrepreneurship, risk-taking, innovation and the need to make economic agents responsible in the use of resources.

The Austrian critique could only really have been met by a case for socialist self-management and public enterprise which based itself on the dispersed character of economic knowledge and refused the tempting delusion of totally planned outcomes. At the time, the arguments of the Austrians could be more easily ignored since they were rejected en bloc by mainstream neoclassical and Keynesian economists as much as by socialists. Hayek's specific policy recommendations in the early thirties had been disastrously wrong.[64] By the mid forties Hayek was arguing that the problems of the thirties should not be blamed on capitalism but on inept government intervention and regulation. Today's socialists can take some comfort from Hayek's defiant belief that genuinely liberal capitalism did not yet exist, and therefore had not failed, since this is what we would say about genuine socialism. The socialist can also be encouraged by Hayek's view that human nature, formed in millennia of primitive collectivism, is predisposed towards socialist thinking.[65]

On the other hand, the ideas of Dickinson, Lange and Lerner played a part in the elaboration of British wartime and postwar economic and welfare policy, where they seemed popular and effective. Lord Beveridge and Evan Durbin drew directly on this work while Abba Lerner's *The Economics of Control* (1944) was to become a classic text in the field of welfare economics. The 'market socialism' of this period, with its important concepts of social cost and equity, could be absorbed in a reformist and technocratic mode. Dickinson envisioned a non-capitalist society, but his model did not incorporate any element of worker representation within the productive enterprise. Both Lange and Dickinson were concerned to show that a socialist economy was compatible with, indeed necessary to, the functioning of political democracy, the safeguarding of individual liberties and the satisfaction of consumer needs. They were influenced by Lerner's critique of Dobb, notably Dobb's espousal of an authoritarian model and preparedness to discount consumer wishes in favour of supposedly far-sighted planning authorities.

Neither Dickinson nor Lange celebrated consumerism. Indeed Dickinson veered in the opposite direction, as in the following recommendation, which also illustrates his technocratic bent: 'The powerful engine of propaganda and advertisement, employed by public organs of education and enlightenment instead of by the hucksters and panders of private profit-making industry, could divert demand into socially desirable directions while preserving the subjective impression of free choice. If the meretricious but effective arts of the salesman and the publicity expert were placed at the disposal of impartial and disinterested bodies of experts—dietitians, architects, heating engineers, textile specialists, orthopedists, psychologists—what an improvement in the standard of food, houses, clothes, footgear, and toys would result!'[66]

This cheerful paternalism was soon to be amplified on a national scale by Britain's wartime Ministries of Food, Information and Aircraft Production. The British economy was soon more collectivized than that of Nazi Germany, where private car production was to continue until as late as 1944. In Britain the Ministry of Food suppressed branded goods in several fields and supplied consumers with their due ration of a standard, medically approved diet, sharply reducing the incidence of rickets and other signs of malnutrition. Hayek's *Road to Serfdom* (1944) was written against this background. While there were certainly unappealingly statist features of the social reforms embarked on in these years, they did not turn out to have the dire implications of which Hayek warned in this highly charged polemic.[67]

The Left economics of this period was prone to be much impressed by the power of big business as well as big government. The Austrian faith in the market seemed blind to the ways in which monopoly and oligopoly distorted, and dictated to, the market. The new market-sensitive Left economists no longer held up the supposed economic rationality of cartels and trusts as a model for socialism, but they were prone to exaggerate the power and durability of monopoly forms. A more satisfactory account of the dynamics of capitalist competition could, it is true, be found in Schumpeter's notion of the gale of 'creative destruction' that was entailed by capitalist social relations. But the notion of 'state monopoly capital' was propagandistically more congenial and perhaps made 'state monopoly socialism' seem more acceptable. In war-devastated Eastern Europe the tasks of reconstruction did indeed probably require large-scale state initiative. As the Cold War closed in and Stalinism asserted itself in Poland, Oskar Lange himself abandoned his schematic dream of a democratic market socialism.

The notion of a dispersed social initiative and of the potential of the direct producers did not entirely disappear from Marxist writing—but now it cropped up in debates about the past. Thus Maurice Dobb in *Studies in the Development of Capitalism* (1946) and in the subsequent 'transition debate' drew on Marx's work to illuminate the ways in which productive organization from below, working through the mechanism of competition not mercantile monopoly, had been the really revolutionary path to industrial capitalism. Though Dobb insisted on the early successes of Soviet planning, he was later to note that such planning had been quite narrowly focused in the thirties and was to face quite different problems in the aftermath of postwar reconstruction. He pointed out that the Second Five Year Plan had only mentioned about 300 specific products while that of 1960 had to deal with 15,000 different products, produced by 200,000 enterprises, with all the signs suggesting that complexity was growing at an exponential rate.[68]

The critics of Stalinist economics had been almost too devastating in their arguments. If rationality was so totally lacking, if quality and coordination was so bad, how did the population of the Soviet Union actually get fed and how was it that Soviet output grew so rapidly? The Austrians and the Left Oppositionists could argue in their different ways that totalitarian political methods could be used to mobilize society for a few simple objectives. And they could also call in question the validity of Soviet statistics, as Rakovsky and Trotsky certainly did by pointing to the problem of quality and appropriateness, and stressing the terrible cost of Soviet advances. Writing in this tradition, David Rousset published one of the first studies of the large-scale use of forced labour in the Soviet Union in 1949. But the Soviet Union of Khrushchev's day, with its Sputnik and official de-Stalinization, seemed both economically more successful and headed towards a more humane order. By the late fifties even Hayek seemed slightly to qualify, but not abandon, his argument: 'The conspicuous successes which the Russians have achieved in certain fields and which are the causes of the renewed interest in the deliberate organization of scientific effort should not have surprised us and should give us no reason for altering our opinion about the import- ance of freedom. That any one goal, or any limited number of objec- tives, which are already known to be achievable, are likely to be reached sooner if they are given priority in a central allocation of all resources cannot be disputed.'[69]

Despite the acuteness of the theoretical critique developed by Mises and Hayek, they did not follow it up either by empirical investigations of the workings of the Soviet economy, nor did they extend it to consider other socialist economic models, beyond planning and the simulated market. In the sixties and seventies, leading economists in the Soviet Union, Eastern Europe and Cuba conducted their own debate on the best way to improve the functioning of their economic systems. While important issues were certainly at stake in these debates, the prevailing single-party state model furnished a restricting context and the argument itself was settled by party diktat, or even tanks.[70]

The researches and theoretical arguments of Alec Nove have furnished a new twist to the debate about socialist economics in the seventies and eighties. While he drew copiously on the experience and debates of the Communist world, he was in a better position to integrate the political moment—favouring democracy without seeing it as, by itself, the solution to all or most economic problems of socialism. Nove accepted the relative efficiency of market mechanisms in allocating routine investment, but disputed their distributional and ecological logic in a world of scarcity. He rejected the view that markets could only work on the basis of private property. In his empirical work, Nove gave many examples both of the absence of an effective measure of economic performance in the Soviet planning system and of the now multi-million complexity of basic decisions that had to be taken simply to keep the economy going.[71] If the Prague Spring had been allowed to flourish, this sort of thinking would have developed openly in the East itself, but instead debate on rival models of socialism was suppressed.

The Lessons of Soviet Stagnation

In the seventies and eighties, capitalism, despite its own problems and injustices, proved itself productively superior to the Soviet-type econ- omies. What were the specific brakes and blockages developed by these economies? What bearing do they have on any project for a socialist economy?

The ferocious negation of socialist democracy must certainly count as one factor which inhibited innovation and the creative development of working collectives, especially in the era of information technology. At best Stalinism inhibited that free interchange between skilled workers and scientific investigators which so often characterizes the frontiers of technical development, while at worst it led to the terroristic imposition of the technical fantasies of pseudo-scientists like Lysenko. But this argument by itself does not explain the full measure of Soviet stagnation, since states such as South Korea, Taiwan and Singapore have derived productivity advantages from new technology while operating systematic censorship, suppressing political dissidents, and so forth.

Rapid economic development in Southeast Asia has thrown up social forces which demand greater democracy. Relative prosperity allows the rulers to extend some democratic concessions. The economic failings of the Soviet-type economies, by contrast, have created most unpropitious conditions for political reform and democratization.

The critical failing of Soviet-type economies would appear to be the crudity of the links between micro-decisions and macro-decisions—or, to put the same point a different way, the absence of a well-calibrated system for determining socially necessary labour time. (However, note that, in the nature of things, the social necessity of labour expended in production is only validated *post festum*, in the act whereby consumers confirm through their purchases that the product in question really did meet a socially effective need. And because technique changes, the notion of socially necessary labour time is neither fixed nor preordained, which is why the problems faced by planners are not algorithmic.)

Soviet-type economies are most able to meet 'consumer' need in those sectors where there is a single large customer, which can place specific orders and reject the product if it is not of acceptable quality. Thus Soviet arms production often achieves global competitiveness, because the Soviet arms procurement ministries monitor the production process and have the power to reject sub-standard equipment. The ordinary Soviet consumer is not in that position, as we know, and has no effective institutional representation. Gorbachev's attempts to remedy this deficiency in the late eighties by enforcing effective quality control (*gospriemka*) ran aground, encountering opposition from both workers and managers.[72]

The problem, however, relates as much to the minimization of costs for a certain output as to the satisfaction of demand. Even Soviet military production, or the successes of the industrialization drive, have been achieved at excessive cost. Where there were only a few basic inputs, and little possibility of substitution, then the problems of planning and calculation were at least manageable. With traditional heavy industry the number of inputs were relatively few and the main variable was simple human effort.[73]

In Soviet-type economies the enterprises do not confront many problems which demand fine calculations of alternatives. Soviet enterprises have found no use for computers because they exist in an economic climate where they face either too much or too little regularity. In principle they have been told exactly what to produce and what their inputs would be. In practice shortages will occur and informal contacts will have to be used to remedy the gap. The skills required are not those of a rational entrepreneur, acting as the bearer of an economic logic, but rather those of a fixer. Those running different enterprises trade favours, weaving a complex web of mutual personal obligations. Because the enterprise managers are eager to be allotted an easy plan target, they will not give the centre a true picture of costs and capacity—the result is a 'slack' rather than 'taut' plan. There is no scope for finding the cheapest supplier, nor for monitoring the response of the consumer, since both are given in the plan. Neither the enterprise nor the planning authority can make those comparative and marginal cost calculations, and those estimates of demand elasticities, which are yielded by market competition. Let us take the question of by-products as an example. A Western manager will not be averse to finding a profitable sale for the by-products of an enterprise—the Soviet manager works for one ministry and is unlikely to discover that his industrial waste could be a vital input for another branch. For its part, the ministry is also likely to give priority to its sectional interest. This fact, compounded by negligent social control and the fetishism of *val* (value-added)—without any proof that what has been added is indeed of social value—is one factor contributing to the poor ecological record of the Soviet-type economies. Such considerations help to explain why the so-called 'waste products' emitted by the Siberian oil fields poison the atmosphere and soil rather than serve as the basis for a plastics industry.

The Soviet experience with management computers revealed the crudity of the calculations required by the administrative command system. In the event the powerful computers which had been purchased with scarce hard currency in the seventies were never used by Soviet management for anything except calculating the wage packets of the enterprises' employees. If a Soviet manager has surplus resources these will be invested in such a way as to promote the self-sufficiency of the enterprise, building ever larger buffer stocks, opening component factories and catering to the needs of a precious workforce. Thus a large Soviet combine will not only make most of its components, it will also

SOCIALISM AFTER THE CRASH

run farms, cattle ranches and brick-making kilns so that it can directly meet the needs of its workforce without recourse to an unreliable and ineffective market. This method of organization has a certain weird economic logic of its own, but it is not conducive to, or regulated by, a wider rationality. Formally more socialized than capitalist production, it is in practice much less so.[74]

The Soviet enterprise is either 'under orders' or 'on its own'. In the first case the effective socialization of management is limited by the planners' inability to know or control any large, complex economy, while, in the latter, plant autonomism is unabashed. By contrast, the elementary mechanisms of market competition compare the use of resources made by one enterprise with the use made of similar resources by others. Capitalist entrepreneurs and managers do not know their competitors' costs with any exactness, but they do know what they are selling at what price, and can usually make an informed guess about changing techniques and sources of supply. When purchasing inputs, they can compare the prices offered by different suppliers and can also consider the advantages of supplying the input themselves.

Until very recently, most Soviet planning was conducted in physical terms. To a ruling bureaucracy which lacked rational criteria, beyond that of defending its own power, this seemed at least to promise growth. But it could and did result in manifest absurdities, with enterprises producing unnecessarily heavy equipment since their targets were specified in tonnes. Transport organizations, similarly, would find their efforts measured by tonne-miles, giving them no incentive to ensure the shortest journey. At the root of such problems was the failure to develop a rational pricing system. Of course products could be assigned prices, but the latter had an inert character, not altering however much or little of the good was produced and not bearing any clear relationship either to productivity or to the prices of other goods. As a consequence, market gardeners in the Caucasus could find that it made sense to fly to Moscow with their produce (because air travel is cheap relative to fresh produce) or collective farmers could find that it made sense to feed their pigs with subsidized bread.[75]

Rejecting or denying market prices, and also lacking any rationale for departing from market price, the Soviet-type economies have tended to form stagnant pools cut off from the mainstream of the world economy. In the fifties this was not so clear because of the exceptional nature of postwar reconstruction. But it was to be pointed out in a lucid, indeed prescient, article by Che Guevara in February 1964:

> The starting point is to calculate the socially necessary labour required to produce a given article, but what has been overlooked is the fact that socially

necessary labour is an economic and historical concept. Therefore, it changes
not only on the local (or national) level but in world terms as well. Continued
technological advances, a result of competition in the capitalist world, reduces
the expenditure of necessary labour and therefore lowers the value of the
product. A closed society can ignore such changes for a certain time, but it
would always have to come back to these international relations in order to
compare product values. If a given society ignores such changes for a long
time without developing new and accurate formulas to replace the old ones, it
will create internal interrelationships that will shape its own value structure in
a way that may be internally consistent but would be in contradiction with the
tendencies of more highly developed technology (for example in steel and
plastics). This could result in relative reverses of some importance, and, in any
case, would produce distortions in the law of value on an international scale,
making it impossible to compare economies.[76]

Interestingly Guevara here assumes that economic planning should
make use of the 'law of value', itself an expression of market relations,
and that there can be a succession of partially segmented markets. This
suggests the need for an acceptance of complexity if economic regulation is to be effective and a willingness to check results against what is
happening elsewhere.

Measures of Efficiency

In *Capital* and in other works, Marx gives a marvellously intricate
account of the operations of the law of value under capitalism. But at
the same time he makes it clear that the juggernaut of capital accumulation simplifies the problems it sets itself by ignoring certain human and
ecological costs which achieve no representation upon the capitalist
market. One would have thought that the workings of a socialist
economy would inescapably be *just as complex as* those of capitalism.
Yet, puzzlingly, socialist economists have often been so preoccupied
with making propaganda for the cause that they have barely paused to
acknowledge or investigate the fact, instead falling back on the simplification thesis discussed earlier. Of course the unavoidable complexity of
the modern economy does not have to involve obscurity if a variety of
mechanisms are found for allowing decisions to be made in the light of
relevant information, by those best-placed to make them, and under the
influence of democratically determined and effective social norms.

Does Marx encourage a blindness to the role of the market in trans-
mitting information, and does socialism necessarily inhibit the initiative
of many economic actors? It is sometimes thought that for Marx market
relations are seen as mere surface phenomena concealing the workings

of the real mode of production and relations of appropriation. Yet, in his own account, competition between different capitals shapes and structures the processes of production and distribution at the most fundamental level. Marx's argument that the 'specific labour' of the worker is governed by socially necessary 'abstract labour' refers us directly to the workings of competition and the market. Similarly Marx's argument could be extended to show that each specific concentration of capital has to justify itself in terms of the norms of 'abstract capital'. Indeed it is difficult to deny that in Marxist terms the market must be seen as an aspect of the forces of production rather than as simply an epiphenomenon of the relations of production.[77]

Marx's insight into the complexity and dynamism of capitalism should presumably infuse our understanding of what planning and socialization might mean. It should be a conception of planning and socialization which builds upon, and gives a new direction to, the forms of economic coordination achieved by, for example, the multinationals, the banks, the credit card agencies, and bodies like the European Community. Some may contest the notion that a socialist economics should seek to emulate the sort of efficiency that is promoted by market competition. In a socialist pattern of economy the overall distribution of demand would be very different from that in a capitalist society and so would be the context and capacity of public regulation. The automatism of the accumulation process—growth for growth's sake—would not be there, nor would the encouragement to a greedy consumerism. Social costs and 'externalities' would be rendered more visible. But both productive and transactional efficiency would still be vital.

The more productive and resource-efficient are the various enterprises in the economy, the more they can contribute, and the more legislation and taxation can oblige them to contribute, to egalitarian and socially responsible goals. While the market is certainly blind to many social costs, and may entail unnecessary expenditure on promotion and management, it does require enterprises to minimize costs of production; likewise the capitalist market is not good at registering social benefits which might outweigh identified costs, but, once again, this does not mean that production costs can be discounted. In a capitalist context such costs will refer either to raw materials, labour or capital equipment; from either a socialist or 'green' perspective it will generally make sense to minimize the use of raw materials, the using up of equipment or the expenditure of labour for a given level of output—though since labour will not be a commodity whose price is determined by the market, the inclination to save labour will never take the form of depressing wages, as it can do in capitalism. While capitalist efficiency and socialist efficiency are quite different concepts, there is some overlap between them.

Socializing the Market

One of the key institutional problems to be solved is that of developing
socialist micro-economics—mechanisms which encourage the enterprise
in a socialist economy to take full and adequate measure of social need
and social cost rather than simply pursue its own path in an egoistic or
purblind fashion. For the foreseeable future this must include what
Diane Elson called 'Socializing the Market'.[78] Using the market a
socialist economy could both encourage and regulate the activity of the
millions of economic actors—including small cooperatives and partnerships—which any modern economy requires. Taxes and subsidies can be
finely adjusted to meet social objectives and to promote the conservation
of natural resources. A law on enterprises could require disclosure of the
commercial data lying behind managerial decisions on prices, profits and
investment. Elson suggests that Price Boards could help to lend visibility
and responsibility to the workings of the market, whose often costly or
counter-productive proclivities she documents.[79]

The need to monitor optimization with the use of market indicators is
a lesson of Soviet and Chinese experience which can certainly not be
ignored by socialists who wish to suppress capitalism in its global
strongholds. The critique of Soviet 'War Communism' by Trotsky,
Lenin and Bukharin, the later critique of Stalinist planning and industrialization by Trotsky and Bukharin, not to speak of the more recent
critiques of hyper-centralization by Alec Nove or Su Shaozhi, actually
have more force the more complex the economy. An advanced socialist
economy would have to tackle a planning and regulation problem of
formidable complexity—institutionalize the power of consumers, allow for
democratic consultation at the local, regional, national and international
level, consider ecological costs as well as alternative uses, harmonize
the activity of millions of autonomous economic agents, and so forth.

A socialist system of economy which genuinely embraced democracy,
social responsibility and self-management would not possess the
enforced, and often illusory, simplicity and predictability of the
administrative-command system. Thus in any modern economy each
enterprise depends upon a host of suppliers and outlets. Each working
collective needs some room to experiment and improve; but at the same
time, if the whole ensemble is to retain coherence, there must be a
provisional—adequate—system of constraints, rewarding more effective
and responsible work. The 'internal market' techniques used by some
multinationals and public bodies to simulate the workings of the market
can help identify excessive costs; though they should not be used to
substitute for public choice.

Another technique employed by the modern enterprise which seems well suited to a socialist production system is the celebrated 'can ban', or reverse-flow system of ordering parts, pioneered by Japanese electronics companies. In principle such a system makes the consumer the planner, issuing orders upstream from supplier to supplier at each different stage in the production process. Note that this is a device for coordination within a given economic space that does not require the different agents to represent different propertied interests. Though it is oriented to the market, it is itself a non-market mechanism of coordination.[80]

The Communist experience offers powerful support to the view that economic innovation requires some form of competition. The Soviet economy was not so bad at registering a purely quantitative growth. Indeed by the 1980s the Soviet Union was the world's largest producer of coal, steel, electricity and cement. But the human purpose of such gigantic expenditure of energy and resources had been lost. Labour productivity was still very low, waste of every sort high, and a capacity to use these products in a socially useful way almost entirely lacking. Soviet 'planning' simply imposed a thoughtless incrementalism, with each plant or enterprise seeking to increase its output of goods or services compared with the previous period.

In some cases it may be that the calculations of an ecologist or technician will reveal the necessity of ending production of a given item without recourse to specifically economic calculation. But competitively established prices, in so far as they reflect material scarcities, will assist the subsequent search for benign substitutes and alternatives. The real costs and benefits of a project cannot always be established in advance and some vital calculations will concern the best use of resources rather than (or as well as) absolute indications one way or another. Thus ecological calculation might set an absolute limit on the use of a particular technique or raw material but economic calculation might still be needed to indicate best use. If real market competition is allowed then various conclusions follow. There should be mechanisms for monitoring and minimizing avoidable market failure of the sort itemized by Elson. But we should be aware that some costs are unavoidable and that a heavy price would be paid for shunning all risks. While the innovation permitted, and indeed stimulated, by economic competition can lead to vital productivity gains, it will certainly produce winners and losers. The context furnished by a socialized market could steer innovation in one direction rather than another—for example towards the better use of scarce materials rather than the maximization of output. It could also set limits on winnings and losses, by safety net provisions, so long as it did not erase the responsibility of economic agents for the consequences of their decisions.

It should be borne in mind that economic innovation is not quite the same as technical innovation. The Communist economies adapted some technical innovations quite successfully but had a very poor record of meeting social need through economic innovation. The entrepreneur who spots that people would like a fresh, oven-hot bread roll or croissant in their lunch break may be making an economic discovery though the ovens used are quite conventional, or even technically inferior to those of the large bakers. Austrian economics sets great store by such entrepreneurship and rightly argues that it will not be found in a command economy. But a risk-taking socialized market system could encourage economic innovation of this sort. There would, however, then be a problem, this time caused by success not failure. How to stop the entrepreneur becoming a wealthy capitalist? In a capitalist economy the development of innovations is financed by the enterpreneur's bank or the idea is bought out by a large corporation which might then employ the innovator. In the socialized market economy there could be a ceiling on the turnover of private firms, after which they would be obliged to find a public financial institution, or socialized enterprise, to back further development and, assuming ownership, reap the extra rewards or losses that this might entail.

The Austrian contention that economic responsibility in investment, or successful entrepreneurship, requires private ownership is contradicted by the performance of some enterprises even in the capitalist economies. The workings of the Mondragon Group of cooperatives in the Basque country suggest that non-capitalist ownership can produce effective economic performance. In Emilia-Romagna (Italy), in Jutland (Denmark) and in Kerala (India) local authorities have sponsored a mixed economic complex combining collective facilities with cooperative and small-scale private property. Some 'ethical' investment trusts, like Friends' Provident, and some state concerns, such as Volkswagen, Renault, ENI, the New Zealand Dairy Board, or Taiwan's state banks, show that private enterprise has no monopoly on social innovation and economic efficiency. Then there is the example of large concerns such as Zeiss in Germany and the John Lewis Partnership in the UK which are owned by their employees. Then again, public-service broadcasting has identified and met needs ignored by the commercial media. There are different models and combinations here—for example that of the BBC, making most of its own programmes, and that of the publicly owned Channel Four, which contracts for programmes from a multitude of independent producers. Because of the pressure of context, all such examples furnish only a very partial notion of what a non-capitalist entrepreneurialism might look like. In a socialist economy a variety of socially owned financial institutions—state and regional banks, pension funds and philanthropic trusts—could offer funds in a competitive context to enterprises that would have to wax or wane according to how effectively they applied them. Taxation and social insurance, and a guaranteed minimum (and legal maximum) income, could prevent class-like inequalities resulting. While some elements of a contemporary capitalist economy might prefigure some features of 'socialist entrepreneurialism', the critical absence in the latter would be the momentum of capitalist accumulation, and its propensity to plunder and divide.

The argument here is not at all that any type of market reform is to be welcomed, nor that the market plus state ownership furnishes the answer. The market reforms that have been, and are being, introduced in some still-Communist states have often managed to get the worst of both worlds. They generate inequality and unemployment without yielding the productivity and (selective) consumer friendliness of an advanced capitalist system. This has been the Yugoslav and Soviet experience. Where there were a large number of modestly sized enterprises, market reforms have at least succeeded in their own terms—for example in China this is so in both agriculture and light industry, but not in heavy industry. In China the advance of output in the marketized sector in the eighties was quite dramatic, generating economic inequality but also meeting the needs of its population more successfully than most large capitalist Third World states.[81] The growth of Chinese GNP and exports, 70 per cent of them now industrial goods, has matched that of South Korea and Taiwan for more than a decade. The dynamic sector of rural industry is publicly owned but not controlled by the Beijing ministries. However the Chinese experience is exceptional.

A critical failing from the standpoint of market rationality was that the Communist power system worked in such a way as to prevent the operation of competition in the vital sphere of the allocation of productive resources. Loss-making enterprises were protected by Kornai's famous 'soft-budget' constraint. Political influence ensured that large enterprises would not simply be condemned to bankruptcy. In this way the capitalist mechanism for ensuring the reallocation of productive assets was stifled. It came to seem to many market reformers, including Kornai, that only thoroughgoing privatization could introduce real efficiency in the allocation of investment. The capitalist restructuring of the seventies and eighties appeared to lend substance to this view.

The capitalist growth of the most recent period has by no means been concentrated only in large corporations. The mechanisms of competition allowed a plethora of small and new companies to build a position for themselves and to force transformations upon the dinosaurs of the rust-belts. This capitalist restructuring was not matched by the Soviet economy because the latter had no mechanism for ensuring that

resources were channelled to the most efficient and innovative enterprises. Indeed, with few exceptions, the larger the Soviet enterprise the
more political influence it wielded, and therefore the more subsidies it
could command. The ruling parties in the Communist states gave no
democratic representation to workers, but generally the rulers found it
prudent to seek to organize the workers in the workplace; the Party
apparatus and cadres in the industrial sector had a vested interest in
defending the given industrial pattern, with its bias towards large-scale
plants. In Poland the large factories retained enough influence to
prevent the closing down of loss-makers up to and beyond the collapse
of Communist rule.

Having pointed out the role of competitive mechanisms in promoting
productivity in capitalism, we should note that they nowadays rarely
involve outright bankruptcy in the large enterprise sector. Takeovers
and mergers play a more important part in the reorganization of assets,
though bankruptcy remains significant in the small business sector. The
sanctions of takeover and bankruptcy are unusual in the large corporation sector of the dynamic Southeast Asian capitalist economies. Thus
in Japan the banks play an active role in monitoring and protecting their
clients. The prevalence of interlocking shareholdings between different
large companies in distinct sectors constitutes a defence mechanism
against the corporate raider. Because these *keiretsu* straddle various
sectors they are not so vulnerable to downturns. The banks believe that
if a particular management is underperforming then it should be re-
organized and removed without the generalized disruption of a bankruptcy. This is, in fact, more rational than the classic laissez-faire
approach, which can disperse an entire productive ensemble because of
the failings of particular managers rather than confine its effects simply
to the latter. The Japanese or Korean approach also contrasts with the
high incidence of takeovers and mergers in the United States and
Britain, often motivated by asset stripping or a desire to impress
investing institutions with no long-term commitments.[82] Presumably a
socialist central planning authority could also devise effective, but
socially less disruptive and painful, substitutes for bankruptcy and
unemployment. The organization of publicly owned regional and
industrial groups could help to ensure that social costs and benefits of
economic restructuring were shared equally. Retraining on full pay and
legislation establishing a narrow gap between maximum and minimum
incomes would also help.

There is a risk with 'self-management socialism' or 'market socialism'
that the notion of social ownership becomes too weak and diffuse,
leading either to slackness and inefficiency or to selfish exploitation of a
privileged position or access to privileged resources. Large-scale pri-

vatization, leading back to capitalism, may reduce inefficiency but would aggravate the problem of inequality and injustice. What is needed are forms of social property that make the direct producers really accountable for the effective use of the resources entrusted to them. In a capitalist economy the private owners—shareholders—have professional companies of auditors to check on management. There are also rules, though rather lax ones, concerning the publication of business information. While self-management should give working collectives a stake in efficiency and profitability, laws on disclosure of information (about, say, costs and prices) and the institution of a periodic 'social audit' could check tendencies to excessive and self-reproducing privilege, and could monitor infringements of ecological and egalitarian norms.

New Models of Market Socialism

In the wake of Alec Nove's work a British school of 'market socialists' has developed within the Fabian Society. Its members are at pains to insist that they are not simply 'social democrats' tinkering with capitalism, but advocate policies that would lead to an economy where social ownership predominated and where there would be a variety of laws and institutions which would promote enterprise democracy and social equality. On the other hand, they wholeheartedly embrace the market as an institution not only compatible with, but necessary to, these objectives. Their efforts are both complemented and questioned by the work of Wlodzimierz Brus and Kazimierz Laski, *From Marx to the Market* (1989). The highly qualified support given by Brus and Laski to market socialism, and the knock-about critique of Anthony de Jasay, recall key themes of the 'calculation debate'.[83]

The new models of 'market socialism' share with the similar, though not identical, concept of the 'socialized market' a notion of economic institutions which is not monist. On the one hand, this means that no single economic institution is expected to guarantee all socially desirable outcomes; and on the other, it means that there will be a variety of public funds, holding companies or banks undertaking investment in competition with one another within a shared framework of legislation. Thus a broad social equality will be achieved partly by suppressing large-scale private property but also by income supplements and taxation. The general aim would be to secure the allocative advantages of the market with respect to investment while removing its distributional injustices with respect to income.

But can proposals like this meet the classic Austrian objection that without capitalist ownership and inequalities entrepreneurs will not be sufficiently motivated to innovate nor sufficiently responsible in the handling of the assets entrusted to them? While entrepreneurs are indeed motivated in capitalism by pecuniary considerations, there is no one-to-one quantitative relationship between entrepreneurial innovation and financial reward. Not all entrepreneurs are owners. While they may gain greatly from displays of entrepreneurial skill, the main gainers will normally be the real owners. Even if the former Guinness chief executive, Ernest Saunders, author of a—for the company's owners—highly lucrative takeover of the Distillers Company, was not in jail, he would not have been the main gainer. Indeed the hired executive, the banker and stockbroker are all, in principle, economic agents who do not fully share in the gains or losses for which they are responsible. The owners of assets find that they can hire entrepreneurial skill in a reasonably competitive market. If such mechanisms help to solve the 'principal/ agent' problem in capitalist conditions, why would they not be available to market socialism as well?

Why could not publicly owned banks hire investment specialists or managers just as banks or pension funds do in today's capitalism? The successful socialist entrepreneur, whether investment banker or manager, would not, of course, be able to claim the hypothetical 'full fruit' of the results of his or her expertise, but neither does the professional today. They would be able to derive intrinsic satisfactions from their job and they could easily be offered well above the average rate of pay if this was found necessary to their motivation. In a generally egalitarian socialist society quite small differences of pay could be quite highly valued by certain individuals. And it might even be discovered that there were potential entrepreneurs who had been deterred by the morally obnoxious consequences of successful management under capitalism, such as depriving others of a livelihood by closing down a plant. And even in a pattern of socialist economy which encouraged worker-participation and enterprise democracy there would still be 'positional goods'; the elected manager, indeed, might obtain satisfaction from the discharge of his or her responsibilities rather more legitimately than the owner-appointed manager. If the more acceptable motives failed to work, would not the recourse to differential economic rewards recreate class division? A principled realism might allow that if incomes vary only modestly, and are prevented from being invested in ownership of productive property, then this could permit some incentive element without allowing social differentiation to acquire class-like self-reproducing dimensions and forms.[84]

The banks or holding companies could be encouraged to make a proportion of their funds available for more risky investments or for socially desirable investments by tax breaks. They could be encouraged to display responsibility as well as initiative by linking them to corporate entities based on pension funds or municipal development boards. The social in social ownership should not be derived from one privileged economic agent—the nation-state—but from a plethora of differently constituted but accountable public bodies. The exact nature of the bodies will no doubt itself reflect the route to socialization. Thus in Sweden the original version of the Meidner plan based socialization on the sharply increasing importance of pension funds. It conferred on these funds more concentrated economic powers in given regions— making them owners of enterprises rather than passive rentiers, the preferred role of Anglo-Saxon institutional investors. It might be objected that where concerns like this fail, blameless sections of the population would lose pension rights. But there are two responses to this. Firstly, individuals would have several revenue sources—a guaranteed basic and occupational income—and pensions themselves could be spread between two or three funds as a legal minimum. Gains and losses would not thereby be wiped out but they would counteract one another. Secondly, it seems that mature capitalist economies are anyway moving in the direction of creating an ever larger institutional sector of investment, characterized by a situation where the supposed beneficiaries enjoy only a very inferior species of ownership. This sector is prey either to under-performance or to scandal as it becomes obvious that the agents are not giving good service to the nominal principals (the recent US savings and loan scams being only the latest example). Facing up to the real problems encountered in this area, market socialism or the socialized market would greatly increase public visibility and accountability.

In a different, but possibly complementary, approach a further 'market socialist' model has been proposed by Ortuño, Roemer and Silvestre. In this, a variety of socially owned enterprises are regulated by means of a central bank, or set of financial institutions, which lend money to enterprises, charge interest to enterprises, and pay out the proceeds in the form of an equal social dividend to every citizen. This model allows for a greater degree of central planning than do the Fabian 'market socialists'. They show that public funding agencies charging differential interest rates would have a powerful lever for promoting equality, efficiency and welfare.[85] In this conception democratic planning, whether at local, national or international level, would consist in setting the terms on which credit would be available, steering resources towards those sectors that were favoured on, say, ecological or egalitarian grounds. However, within such constraints the decision whether or not to invest would be taken by enterprises independently. Presumably the financial authorities would also have some discretion in deciding whether or not to foreclose on enterprises that failed to service loans; but even if they did foreclose, the former employees would have the social dividend to fall back on, as well as social insurance. The authors describe this social dividend in terms of a 'social surplus' which should be shared amongst all equally in token of equal civic rights—and also, perhaps, of the fact that the social context of combined labour is the secret of its productivity—the latter should not be attributed to individuals taken in isolation.

Green politics, with its frequent insistence on the small-scale and on the need for decentralization, might seem to have little or nothing to learn from the débâcle of Communism. Yet some varieties of Communism—Maoism for example—also had their variants of these watchwords while Green politics itself has already produced minority currents displaying authoritarianism and misanthropy. There are radical or deep ecologists who insist that humanity is a plague species and that its numbers have to be reduced by some means from five thousand million to five hundred million. Such notions are often accompanied by advocacy of sweeping plans for the radical simplification of all social and economic processes. The experience of twentieth-century Communism should be one cautionary example to consider when evaluating such proposals.

On the other hand, many of the main Green parties have adopted a perspective generally compatible with the 'socialized market'. They favour the construction of integrated local economies, combining public services with a plethora of modestly sized cooperatives and partnerships, financed by banks with selective investment criteria. They support, as an immediate demand, the call for a guaranteed basic income for all citizens. This latter demand has also been adopted by a number of Europe's 'New Left' parties, notably the newly launched Left Alliance in Finland. It is argued by supporters of guaranteed basic income that it would provide a far more flexible and less bureaucratic route to a universal welfare system, dispensing with the need for cumbersome and intrusive means tests. While this measure would immediately tackle the primary poverty of the homeless and destitute, some advocates believe that it would inaugurate a progressive alleviation of the dependency of workers on employers (involving, in some conceptions, progressive 'deproletarianization'). Clearly, to have such effects the guaranteed basic income would have to be set at a generous level. This proposal links up with the classic market socialist concept of the 'social dividend', as outlined by Oskar Lange and as recently refined by Ortuño, Roemer and Silvestre.

An attractive feature of some of these arguments is that they readily link up today's movements and struggles with ultimate objectives. In a similar way there is a new conception of trade unionism which links conventional struggles over pay and conditions to campaigns for a shorter working week and for ecological and feminist goals.[86] There are also adjuncts to, or variants of, social ownership and control, which have emerged from the experience of left-wing or 'red–green' municipalities. These include the insistence that any enterprise benefiting from a public contract adhere to certain employment and ecological norms. Such municipalities have also experimented with forms of 'entrepreneurial socialism' in which working collectives put in a competitive tender to lease facilities for a specified period, at the end of which they have to give an accounting of their activities.[87] Such conceptions help to constitute a bridge between today's struggles and the goal of a socialized market.

As this article has undertaken to defend the necessity of the socialized market, I should, perhaps, make it clear that such a market should incorporate and institutionalize the quite justified suspicion of market processes which has marked the history of capitalism and which has led to repeated, but only partially successful, attempts to curb the relentless processes of capitalist accumulation that have dominated it. Thus André Gorz has argued in his *Critique of Economic Reason* that the Austrian cult of the 'free' market menaces the integrity of the lifeworld upon which the economy itself rests; it promotes heedless consumerism and stifles enterprise democracy. He points to the way in which successive social struggles—against slavery and the slave trade, for the eight-hour day, for trade-union rights, against ecological degradation or the yawning gap between North and South—derive from widespread distrust of the market.[88] Gorz's ideas are reminiscent of the approach of Karl Polanyi in *The Great Transformation*, published in 1944. While Polanyi vigorously contests the commodity status of labour, land and money, he sees a subordinate and regulated market as quite acceptable.[89]

An important socialist tradition, stretching in Britain from William Morris to Raymond Williams, has opposed the corrupting and destructive logic of pervasive commercialization and passive consumerism. Yet the market itself, in and through the reactions to it, also broadens the potential scope of human solidarity. Thus the market should be socialized not only 'from above', through the action of the state, but also 'from below', through the pressures of working collectives and communities. Thus in the capitalist market information about products and services is provided either by those who supply them or by media which rely on such interested advertising. In a socialized market the more wasteful types of advertising could be minimized and resources given to bodies and media representing the consumers.

The Economic Success of Impure Capitalism

But, the Hayekian critic could object, all such attempts to revise or improve upon the market, whether piecemeal or wholesale, will ultimately have disastrous effects. By sapping efficiency they will ultimately ensure that we are all worse off. Yet in the capitalist world today it is by no means clear that obeisance to the market is the royal road to success even in capitalist terms. Thus Southeast Asian capitalism departs widely from free-market prescriptions.

Indeed if we compare South Korea and Taiwan with the Communist states we are faced by a paradox. The successes of these states are often explained by factors which parallel the Communist experience: (1) land reform, eliminating the old landlords and guaranteeing farmers' income by government subsidy; (2) state planning, and state ownership of key industrial sectors; (3) government manipulation of the economy, including 'getting prices wrong'; (4) a conformist ideology, stressing hard work and deferred gratification; (5) a tough regime, repressing popular opposition; (6) worker involvement, through 'quality circles' and the like. The fit is remarkably close, while the economic results are so different. The paradox is sharpened if we register the extent to which the Southeast Asian states have avoided the extremes of wealth and poverty found elsewhere in the capitalist world; while economic egalitarianism is rarely cited as a factor in Southeast Asian success, it is often cited as a factor of Communist failure. Yet *The Economist* recently noted: 'Unlike most developing countries, Taiwan and Korea grew fast and sharply reduced income inequalities at the same time. In 1970, when Korea's GNP per head was still only about $1,300 in today's money, by one measure it had a more equal income distribution than Japan or the United States. In 1952 the income of the best-off 20% of Taiwanese households was 15 times the income of the lowest 20%; by 1980 the multiple was only 4.2. The equivalent in America that year was 7.5, in Sweden a year later 5.6, in Japan a year earlier 4.4. For much of the past two years Taiwan has been the world's most egalitarian society, as well as one of the half-dozen fastest-growing ones.'[90]

Why does this surrogate 'bourgeois Stalinism' work so much better than the real thing? Clearly it is significant that these two states received large and sustained aid packages from the United States—and even more significant that they could trade reasonably freely with the more advanced countries. (Soviet performance in the thirties and forties and Chinese dynamism today both reflect similar trading advantages.) Consequently the Southeast Asian strategy of 'governing the market' was geared to exports while the Communist states, giving priority to local development, treated trade as an optional extra. While the East Asian states were market-oriented at one level (oriented to the export market), at another they were quite prepared to use the segmentation of markets, in particular the disjuncture between the internal and external market, to subsidize and protect their economic growth. Their industrial strategy was based on investment in consumer goods industries, in contrast to the Soviet emphasis on producer goods.[91] As Japan pioneered the Southeast Asian pattern while respecting bourgeois democratic norms, it does not seem that military dictatorship is a vital ingredient in the mixture that has yielded economic success. It would probably be more to the point to explore historical conditions which opened the West, broke the resistance of traditional elites, but enabled traditional sources of social cohesion, discipline and motivation to be tapped. Yet, at all events, the market mechanism plays only a subordinate part in the story.[92]

The relative economic successes of Germany or Sweden would also be hard to explain in terms of dedication to laissez-faire. Of course socialists would not be content with Taiwanese-style equality any more than they would stop at Korean- or Japanese-style worker-participation or German-style *Mitbestimmung* or Swedish-style welfarism. None the less, these societies are amongst the most prosperous and successful in the world and perhaps a part of the reason for this is that in some small but not insignificant particular they do not conform to a purely capitalist logic or form of organization. Beyond the features already mentioned, each of these societies gives huge public funding to the formation of 'social capital', in the shape of education, research and training. While this investment has reaped an impressive societal return, it has not been subordinated to narrow commercial criteria.

These experiences suggest that an 'impure' capitalism works better, in capitalist terms, than undiluted private enterprise. Even if we consider the heart of capitalist private property, conundrums and contradictions seem to be of the essence. For example, the threat of takeover and the so-called 'market in management' seemed to give back to shareholders a means of making managers attentive to their interests. Jasay argues that: 'The owner-manager, who has absolute security of managerial tenure, is potentially more inefficient than the professionally-run corporation, since he is much freer not to "maximize", and can indulge his fancies— as the history of so many family-owned firms and of capricious robber barons demonstrates.'[93] While this praise of the market in management may seem reasonable, it does not capture the way that corporations actually function in the United States or Britain, where the market in corporate control operates most vigorously. In these economies there is now every sign that managers can bid up their salaries and perks to levels which hugely outstrip company performance. Thus between 1980 and 1989 US company profits broadly stagnated, output and wages grew by about a half, but chief executives' remuneration grew by 160 per cent.[94] In these two countries institutions are responsible for a large slice of capital formation. These institutions, mainly insurance and pension funds, buy or sell shares purely with an eye to short-term financial performance, producing the phenomenon of what *The Economist* calls 'punter capitalism'. The professionals who run the institutions tend to be indulgent to managers, while the policyholders who supply the cash enjoy a third-rate type of ownership. By contrast, in Japan and Germany, up until fairly recently, bank debt furnished the major source of finance for large industrial companies. As these banks could not simply 'sell' debts owing to them, they were forced to take a more long-term and intimate interest in the fate of the concerns that they were financing.[95]

The point being made here is somewhat Hayekian, as the focus is on the responsibility with which economic agents make decisions, rather than the more narrowly conceived notion of individual motivation. On the other hand, it is anti-Hayekian in so far as the requisite degree of economic discipline has been produced not by ownership but by credit. This would seem to vindicate the market socialist proposal to use credit as a regulatory mechanism to encourage the efficient use of resources. Does this mean that 'socialist banks' might have the power to deny credit or to remove elected managers? And if a rival socialist bank or holding company was willing to take on an enterprise which its original sponsor found excessively risky, or poorly managed, who is going to discipline the banks and holding companies? *Quis custodet ipsos custodies*? And how should credit be distributed on an international basis, and subject to what international regulatory principles? While there are problems here, they are far from being irresolvable in principle by socialists; nor, as the Third World debt and the 'principal/agent problem' show, have they all been solved by capitalism, even by its own standards.

The Challenge of Global Poverty and Ecology

In a global market system some economies will be bound to do better than others. If this inegalitarian momentum was checked in too crude a fashion—siphoning most of the surplus away from the most efficient—it would make everyone worse off. But if international financial agencies promote, even 'create', purchasing power in poorer countries, and penalize rich-nation protectionism, then this could have an evening-up rather than levelling-down logic. Today the industrial and agricultural protectionism of the advanced countries is a major barrier to development in the Third World and former 'Second World'. And, consequent upon the Third World debt mountain, the almost complete drying up of credit compounds the problem, leaving the poor countries reliant on the narrow-minded, stingy treasuries of the rich countries.

Socialists cannot afford to ignore Hayek's taunt that their schemes only ever extended to the favoured few: 'What socialists seriously contemplate the equal division of existing capital resources among the people of the globe? They all regard the capital as belonging not to humanity but to the nation—though even within the nation few dare to advocate that the richer regions should be deprived of some of their capital ... to help the poorer regions.'[96] The yawning inequalities in the world cannot be removed at a single stroke; such a move would be politically impossible and might even make everyone worse off. But that does not mean, as Hayek might imply, leaving the poor countries to the tender mercies of the 'free market'. (However, note that Hayekian liberalism is not the worst offender here, inasmuch as Austrian economics does not defend First World protectionism.)

The overall aim should be continually to improve the absolute position of the worst-off, consistent with transition to a new model of production and consumption based on sustainable growth. The revenue from tariffs and taxes on the employment of scarce resources could be devoted to funds for developing the poorer regions, employing benign technologies that were not subject to such taxation. Such funds could also be the beneficiaries of exploitation of the sea-bed, to be conducted with rigorous ecological safeguards. The market socialists rightly argue that political democracy, giving every individual an equal vote, is more egalitarian than the market, which privileges purchasing power. Thus both nationally and internationally democratic institutions must be used to check on market performance.[97]

The massive scale of global poverty and the global threat to ecology help to constitute powerful arguments for public enterprise and planning at a world level. But the very fact that these problems are posed at their most acute at the level of the world as a whole should remind us that the answer cannot be a global command economy. As I have already pointed out, some types of planning actually inhibit the micro-calculation that can promote recycling. Of course, the initiative of a planning authority could give decisive encouragement in vital areas—for example, to developing alternatives to fossil fuels as an energy source. But market regulation will also provide means of promoting ecological responsibility that cannot be achieved by relying on simple administrative fiat. Thus a heavy tax on fossil fuels can both inhibit use and promote the search for renewable and less deleterious sources of energy—which does not mean that research and investment into the latter could not also be promoted by other, more direct, means. We should also be keenly aware of the point made by Diane Elson that there are widely different sorts of markets, reflecting different social settings and forms of regulation. The capitalist market stimulates an insatiable pattern of consumption which is incompatible with the constraints of scarce resources. It would be vital to ensure that the socialized market did not have the same results, and there is some reason for supposing that this would not be so since the impulses of competition would be monitored and constrained in different ways.

The critique of socialist planning has relevance for any project for a non-capitalist economy. Those who shun the term socialist but still aspire to suppress the insatiable momentum of capitalist accumulation have to confront many of the same obstacles and objections that have been noted above. The ecological crisis certainly lends a new interest to Otto Neurath's argument for intergenerational responsibilities, for an economy attentive to natural limits and for pluralist planning. There is now an overwhelming case for one or several international planning agencies tracking both the use of scarce resources and the likely effects of production decisions and consumption trends on global ecological systems. Such agencies could be given information-gathering powers and even emergency veto powers. While they should have resources to conduct their own educational campaigns, it would not be appropriate for them to have the power actually to prescribe patterns of production 'down to the last button'. The socialist contributors to the 'calculation debate' of the thirties argued for planning authorities to use a 'simulated market' to guide their actions. It would be more appropriate if governments and electorates had available to them 'simulated plans' which could be used to devise, and modify, the regulation of the socialized markets.

International trade is now so extensive and important that the institutions of the 'socialized market' in one country, or group of countries, could help to extend its principles to others. Thus in a submission to the Socialist Group of the European Parliament on textiles, 'Working Women Worldwide' proposed that there should be 'social regulation' of the textile trade such that no garment, wherever produced, should be marketed in the Community unless it met certain quality standards with respect to the conditions of its production. It explained: 'Absolute standards for conditions of production should include health and safety; rights of workers to overtime pay, redundancy pay, maternity pay, sickness benefit; rights of workers to organize; facilities of workers to organize.' However, to prevent covert protectionism, the proposal adds: 'Different levels of economic development mean that it is not feasible to set absolute standards for hours of work or wages. Relative standards for hours of work and pay would need to be set related to each country's norms. The standards would need to be met at the enterprise level. It is no use just examining what legislation a country has on the statute books ... Much more stringent labelling requirements could be introduced so that consumer products carry not just a brand name but also the name of the parent firm, the country of origin, whether the conditions of production just meet or exceed the standards set.'[98]

In order to meet familiar risks of market failure, the whole sector of agriculture and primary production is today covered by extensive national and international regulation. Sometimes privileged special interest finds a nesting place in such regulation. However, the answer is not wholesale deregulation but an attempt to identify and root out the defence of privilege. It is often the case that agricultural and primary production concerns the whole livelihood and integrity of a given community; so in such cases there are excellent grounds for closely considering social costs before allowing market factors to operate.

An international socialist planning body would have plenty to do in ensuring that prevailing regulations and interventions really did encourage social equality, ecological responsibility and civic fulfilment without undertaking responsibility for the entirety of global production. If some of Marx's rhetoric now seems overly simple, this emphatically does not apply to the previously cited aphorism which sums up his vision of the principle which should govern the future society: that the precondition for the free development of each would be the free development of all. The question I have been addressing is really that of discovering economic mechanisms which embody this principle in both a dispersed and concentrated way throughout the entire pattern of a global economy. The harsh contrasts of wealth and poverty in the modern world—and the spectre of ecological catastrophe—demand global and regional planning but they also require a framework of economic cooperation which encourages responsible initiative and innovation in a myriad of citizens.

The Dynamic of Communist Collapse

My advocacy of the 'socialized market' may appear ill-judged just at the moment when the populations of the former Communist states are discovering the appalling social costs of their experiment in laissez-faire shock therapy, attempted privatization and doctrinaire ultra-liberalism. The elaboration of a socialized market requires vigorous and various forms of social ownership, not privatization. It also requires an authoritative, competent and democratic set of local, national and regional state bodies. As the peoples of Eastern Europe and the Soviet Union are now discovering, a lively civil society and a coherent market both require a strong framework of public authority and support. The vital areas of communication, culture and education invariably require public subsidy. The imposition of narrow commercial criteria menaces the integrity of civil society and hands the initiative to rapacious commercial interests, such as the media empires of Rupert Murdoch and Robert Maxwell.[99]

Thus opposition to laissez-faire and privatization should not mean support for given state structures, many of which are quite compromised and discredited. In the Soviet Union today there is a widespread social revolt against the centre, which could lead either towards 'self-managed' capitalism or 'self-managed' socialism. It is a striking fact that the Soviet 'New Left' opposes privatization but does not offer blanket opposition to 'the market'.[100] Neither do the more politically active and leftist Soviet workers—at a meeting of factory committees in Togliatti in September 1990 those assembled demanded the ending of ministerial control. While they offered no proper economic alternative of their own, it is clear that economic revival would be facilitated by the exist- ence of a state and property system whose legitimacy was widely accepted. So far as the state is concerned, this must mean full accep- tance of democracy. And so far as the property system is concerned, it may rule out large-scale private ownership since this does not yet enjoy wide backing from the Soviet public.

In *The Great Transformation* Polanyi argues that it is fatal to allow the market to dispose of the fate of what he called 'fictional com- modities'—that is, entities like labour, land or, in Polanyi's view, money— which, since they were not brought into existence through commercial production, should, likewise, not be used up like a commercial product. In the Communist and formerly Communist states huge cultural, infra- structural and productive resources exist which are far from lacking in all social value, though in hard-currency terms they are worthless. They were not built in conformity with market criteria and the societies in which they subsist anyway lack the most rudimentary market facilities. While some sectors, like health and education, should be largely exempt from market pressures, the export sector and those areas relating to individual consumption are likely to benefit from a market orientation. An attractive feature of the Soviet Union or China today, compared with ten or twenty years ago, is the new function of large popular open- air markets, enabling energies to be tapped and needs to be met. But encouraging developments of this sort is very different from allowing the sort of devastation to take place that was witnessed in East Germany following its assimilation by the Federal Republic—especially bearing in mind that other post-Communist societies are not nearly so favourably placed for eventual recovery as the Eastern *Lande.*

Socialists are, not without reason, suspicious of the ideological forces generated by the capitalist market; I have suggested above some ways in which a socialized market could prevent or discourage wasteful or irresponsible invitations to consume. But it should also be acknowledged that the pattern of nationalized property in the Communist states also produces unlovely ideologies—notably an intolerant nationalism and an excessively tolerant attitude towards traditional patriarchy. This is partly because the nationalized command economy tended towards national self-sufficiency, and reduced the variety of contacts between those of different national groups. It is also because it encouraged its citizens to see economic distribution in very tangible, zero-sum terms. In practice many goods are acquired through a network of favours and obligations that all too easily reflect and reinforce ties of kinship and ethnicity. While the impersonality of the capitalist market hides too much— including social costs and human exploitation—the non-market aspects of the Communist command economies foster a pernicious and pervasive personalism, such that satisfaction of the most trivial personal needs involves tedious obligations and the negotiation of an informal conspiracy against other citizens. For their part the state authorities, lacking other sources of legitimacy and aware of their economic failures, often seek to exploit nationalism and communalism.

In the account I have offered of the crisis of Communism I have placed great emphasis on its failings at the economic level. I have done this because economic failure exercised an ultimately fatal constraint, not because I regard the other grave failings as of little account. The denial of democracy, of individual rights and of rights of free association themselves intersect in complex ways with the economic, as Martov, Kautsky and Trotsky all insisted. One might add that the conformism and stupor of so much of the official culture of the Communist states has also made a contribution to their collapse. The cultural inertia of the Communist states is not only a by-product of their denial of democracy, though there is certainly a link here too. While Communism was capable of arousing a messianic fervour it was also, like Christianity and Islam in their heyday, capable of inspiring significant cultural achievement. The best work of the recipients of the Prizes handed out in Stalin's time— Eisenstein, Pudovkin, Ehrenberg, Sholokov—or the work of the fellow travellers in other lands—Brecht, Neruda, Hikmet, McDiarmid, Aragon, Picasso, Chaplin, and so forth—was not exactly Stalinist but it certainly was not robustly anti-Stalinist. It would be a fallacy to suppose that bad politics always produces bad art. Of course, the impact of Stalinism on the built environment was generally dreary and oppressive. However, the Moscow metro system is not only clean and efficient but a genuinely

impressive and exuberant example of the use of public space, to which
even the unabashed elements of kitsch make their own contribution; the
metro, unlike other prestige projects, was of immediate utility to the
mass of the population, a circumstance which may have made it easier to
realize. The best work of the immediate post-Stalin period was certainly
anti-Stalinist, though very often, as Lukács pointed out in the case of
Solzhenitsyn, it could be interpreted as a species of critical realism. In
the seventies and eighties the cultural inertia of the Communist states
made them vulnerable to the cultural vitality of the non-Communist world.
The Communist authorities could not insulate their populations from
the cultural products of the West, and on occasion actively promoted
them; in East Germany the GDR authorities actually relayed Western
television to parts of the country, such as Dresden, which had difficulty
in receiving signals from the Federal Republic. Of course the vitality of
popular culture in the West or South is not capitalist, drawing as it
frequently does on a variety of impulses, some of them utopian or resistant. But as the theorists of the 'society of the spectacle', or of the postmodern, have pointed out, the cultural logic of late capitalism has been
able to ally itself with the electronic media in ways that proved to be
beyond the post-Stalinist command economies. As Eastern publics
lacked any purchasing power, their appropriation of 'Western' culture in
the East was greatly facilitated by the diffusion and reproduction of
music or images in ways that owed little or nothing to the commodity
form. Radio broadcasts and 'pirated' tapes played a vital part in
dissolving the ideological monolith. Unofficial and oppositional
balladeers like Vygotsky, Bierman and Siem Reap underlined the failings of bureaucratic culture.

The defeat of Communism has thus been the defeat of a type of social
formation which gave too little scope for popular initiative and
pluralism, or self-recognition and self-activity (whether collective or
individual), either in economic life, politics or culture. This defeat was
inflicted on Communism partly by internal forces, such as Solidarity in
Poland or Charter 77 in Czechoslovakia, and partly through the tremendous external pressure of a species of capitalism which had compromised in various ways with popular interests and energies. The method
of historical and cultural materialism itself would recommend that we
seek the West's superiority in the realms of political economy, understood in the broad sense indicated above. The Communist crises of
1989–90 can be distinguished from those centred in the Hungarian
uprising of 1956, or the Prague Spring of 1968, by the greater salience
of this 'external' pressure of systemic competition—though the whole
point is that the external had become the internal; for, as Gorbachev
told the United Nations in 1988, consciously or unconsciously echoing

Che Guevara's observation of 1964, a 'closed society' is not possible in the modern world.

If we had to specify this revolutionary transformation in terms of social agency it would be difficult to contest that we here face a bourgeois revolution. The Marxist historians have for some time been telling us that the classic bourgeois revolutions were not purely or simply pro-capitalist in character, even if their more or less remote consequences were conducive to the growth of capitalism. It is a striking fact that demonstrations by town-dwellers in the major Communist cities played a vital part in the crises of 1989–90, and that the old order retrenched, in so far as it was able, often by falling back on support in the countryside, the stronghold both of the 'conservative' factions of the Chinese and Russian ruling group and of former ruling parties in Eastern Europe. While working-class forces were undoubtedly mobilized in the cities, the not-yet-capitalist middle classes of liberal professionals and administrators were able to assert leadership of the movement by holding out the tempting prospect of joining the system with a proven track record, capitalism, rather than exploring some third way. That this transition to capitalism will not be easy or uncontested is already clear. The countries of the 'Second World' do not have a viable system and need to develop more extensive exchanges with the capitalist world and to import some of the latter's more advanced institutions. But it is difficult to see these countries joining the 'First World' very quickly, while there could be widespread resistance if they have imposed on them the capitalism of the Third World. Democratization is, as yet, far from consolidated in Eastern Europe, while in China and the Soviet Union a political and military bureaucracy still holds sway. The sheer size of the Soviet and Chinese economies rules out any speedy conquest of these societies by capitalism, even though the bureaucratic order is both vulnerable and incompetent in both these states. While democratic movements are more strongly embedded in Soviet society the comparatively far more successful Chinese economy offers a more favourable terrain to any renewal of reform Communism. In the decade or so in which such possibilities are worked out it is not impossible that some new hybrid will be elaborated, perhaps in conjunction with anti-capitalist formations elsewhere, in which democratic socialist movements and institutions might make a belated appearance.

Some reform Communists are now inclined to resurrect the old Menshevik argument that it is neither possible nor desirable to skip the bourgeois-democratic stage and that their countries need to pass through the school of modern capitalism before they could hope to build socialism. Such an argument does need to be seriously addressed. But the conjuncture in each part of the world reflects to some degree devel-

opments in the world as a whole. China and the Soviet Union will
certainly have to absorb economic lessons from the capitalist world,
relating not only to technology but to modes of organization and calculation. These countries also badly need to develop democracy and the
rule of law, though institutions of this sort by no means come with
capitalism as part of some preordained package. Together with elements
of capitalism the post-Communist societies will need to develop socialist
antibodies: a democratic public opinion and movements against new
types of inequality and ecological degradation. It would not be right to
exclude in advance that some more or less democratic socialist solution
can still be negotiated in these lands, though the odds are certainly now
against this happening.

Socialism and Social Forces

The crisis of socialism and Marxism has been considered here as a crisis
of its inherited programmes. These programmes are by no means wholly
useless, and some precariously survive through popular support even
within today's capitalism. But the crisis of socialism is also reflected in
the weakness of the social forces which might sustain these programmes.
The traditional Left parties have been weakened by a combination of
electoral decline and, at a more fundamental level, a decline in the
activity, enthusiasm and social embeddedness of their supporters. The
old style of leftist national-liberation movement is also almost defunct.[101]

Yet, on the other hand, there are what might be called new proletarian
movements and New Left movements. In the South these might include
the Brazilian Labour Party (PT), the Mexican Revolutionary Democratic Party (PRD), South African UDF/ANC or the South Korean
opposition, which all have a strong relationship to trade unions without
conforming to the old labourist model. At their best these movements
have embodied popular aspirations to democracy and social justice. The
link to the world of labour allows for the construction of political and
social identities which cross the boundaries of particular ethnic and
religious communities. In Europe a thoroughgoing programmatic
renewal of Left parties has produced new formations of significant size
in Finland, Norway, Denmark, Spain, Turkey and the Netherlands,
while Green and feminist ideas have a pervasive influence. These 'New
Left' formations typically define themselves in relation to regional,
continental and global issues rather than mainly to the sphere of national
political life: ecology, migrant labour, anti-racism and anti-militarism
being key concerns. In the post-Communist states there are already the
first stirrings of social resistance to the imposition of the 'unsocial'

market and of a form of privatization that favours the old *nomenklatura* and mafia.[102] There is a large and often well-educated working class in the Communist and post-Communist states. In some cases reform Communists under some new name are trying to establish credentials as the defenders of workers' interest, winning a tenth or more of the popular vote. And former oppositionists who now find their hopes traduced by the socially regressive and undemocratic features of the new order are discovering that a vital civil society is being devastated by free-market experiments, and democratic values by a resurgent national populism. These new social forces are already transforming the historic programmes of the Left. Almost no one is nostalgic for the command economy. While there are many different elements that might help to constitute an alternative—new concepts of trade unions, of self-management, of cooperative and municipal enterprise, of contract compliance and basic income, of market socialism and the socialized market, of egalitarian and ecological responsibility—it is probable that they do not yet comprise a fully comprehensive and coherent package that could replace the logic of capitalism. But there are here a variety of models, measures and movements from which an effective programme promises to develop. There is an evident connection with the values of the traditional Left just as there are major issues which were scarcely identified by the traditional movements. Kautsky, for all his virtues, was undoubtedly one of the more stolid and less imaginative traditional Marxists. Yet he had no hesitation in declaring that 'Socialism as such is not our goal, which is rather the abolition of every kind of exploitation or oppression, be it directed against a class, a party, a sex, or a race.'[103] While creditable, such a declaration does not address today's ecological crisis, which undoubtedly calls for a new model of consumption and production as well. Those socialist thinkers who did address ecological issues—for example, Morris or Bebel—often inclined too much to the notion that social life could be drastically simplified. The future belongs only to a diversified socialism, a 'socialism without guarantees', or even to some new concept more adequately embodying the goals of the Left and the creative impulses of anti-capitalist movements. In this connection, Raymond Williams's reflection on industrial capitalism retains all its force: 'We want more, much more, in its place than a chaotic breakdown or an imposed order or the mere name of an alternative. The challenge is therefore to a necessary complexity. I have been pulled all my life ... between simplicity and complexity, and I can still feel the pull both ways. But every argument of experience and of history now makes my decision—and what I hope will be a general decision—clear. It is only in very complex ways, and by moving confidently towards very complex societies, that we can defeat imperialism and capitalism and begin that

construction of many socialisms which will liberate and draw upon our
real and now threatened energies.'[104]

January 1991

Notes

* I would like to thank the following for their written comments on an earlier draft: Perry
Anderson, G.A. Cohen, Diane Elson, Gunder Frank, Monty Johnstone, Marcel Van der
Linden, Branka Magaš and Peter Wiles. I wish also to thank Tariq Ali, R.W. Davies, Meghnad
Desai and Mel Leiman for bibliographical guidance. Of course none of the foregoing bears any
responsibility for my arguments or mistakes.

1. Ludwig von Mises, *Planned Chaos*, Irving-on-Hudson, NY 1947, p. 124.

2. Karl Kautsky, Introduction to *Bolshevism at a Deadlock*, London 1931, pp. 17–
18, trans. amended.

3. Kautsky, *Dictatorship of the Proletariat*, Ann Arbor 1964, p. 20. Kautsky's
response to the Bolshevik Revolution is much illuminated by Massimo Salvadori, *Karl
Kautsky and the Socialist Revolution, 1880–1938*, London 1979, pp. 218–25, 251–93.

4. David Forgacs, ed., *A Gramsci Reader*, London 1988, pp. 32–6. Unlike other
enthusiasts for the Revolution, Gramsci was aware from the beginning that in Russian
conditions it would mean a sharing of misery and want. See G. Fiore, *Gramsci: A Life*,
London 1990, pp. 111–13.

5. These aspects of Marx's thought are emphasized, perhaps overemphasized, but
certainly not invented, in my essay, 'The Theory of Proletarian Revolution', NLR 97,
May–June 1976. (Reprinted in Robin Blackburn, ed., *Revolution and Class Struggle*,
London 1977.

6. Karl Marx, *Capital* Volume I, London 1990, pp. 171–2. The reference is at least
half-playful and, in the context of the book as a whole, does not justify attributing to Marx
the synoptic fallacy that the world economy could be run by an omniscient planner. The
Comtean 'socialism' which did lead to such a view had no attractions for Marx. It was
precisely *Capital* that persuaded Louis Althusser to reject the notion that social relations
could be an 'expressive totality', possessed of the coherence and simplicity of an idea, and
to prefer what he saw as Marx's concept of the mode of production as an 'already-given
complex totality', which could never be commanded by a *prise de conscience*. See Louis
Althusser and Etienne Balibar, *Reading Capital*, London 1970, pp. 97, 180, 194.

7. Friedrich Engels, *Anti-Dühring*, Moscow 1978. Though overshadowed by the
disquisitions on dialectic, this work does contain, *faut de mieux*, the most extensive discussion to be found in the works of Marx and Engels of the socio-economic order they
believed might supersede capitalism (see, in particular, pp. 343–79). Whatever the failings
in Engels's work, he was always insistent as to both the limits placed by objective economic
conditions and the importance of democratic development. Engels was, of course, responsible for one of the most memorable and prophetic utterances on the former topic to be
issued by the founders of historical materialism. Referring to the situation of Münzer, the
leader of the Peasant War of the early sixteenth century, he wrote: 'Not only the movement
of his time, but the whole century, was not ripe for the realization of the ideas for which he
had himself only just begun to grope. The class which he represented not only was not
developed enough and incapable of subduing and transforming the whole of society, but it
was just beginning to come into existence. The social transformation that he pictured in his
fantasy was so little grounded in the then existing economic conditions that the latter were
a preparation for a social system diametrically opposed to that of which he dreamt.'
Friedrich Engels, 'The Peasant War in Germany', in *The German Revolutions*, edited by
Leonard Krieger, Chicago 1967, p. 105. The Bolsheviks would have known this passage
well, with its conclusion that nevertheless Münzer was right to act as he did. From the

Menshevik position the important point would be that, whatever his dreams, Münzer was right to engage in a struggle that could not go beyond the horizon of some early bourgeois republic. In endorsing Münzer's struggle, Engels was certainly not recommending an attempted direct leap to communism regardless of conditions. He would have agreed with his friend Plekhanov that such an attempt in an isolated and backward country could only result in the sort of 'patriarchal despotism' practised by the Incas. (Quoted by Michael Ellman, *Socialist Planning*, 2nd edn, Cambridge 1990, p. 350.)

8. August Bebel, *Woman in the Past, Present and Future*, London 1988, pp. 178–228.

9. 'Marx, the Bismarck of Socialism', in Leonard Krimmerman and Louis Perry, eds, *Patterns of Anarchy*, New York 1966, p. 86.

10. Daniel Guèrin, 'Marxism and Anarchism', in David Goodway, ed., *For Anarchism: History, Theory, and Practice*, London 1989, pp. 109–26.

11. Robert Graham, Introduction to Pierre-Joseph Proudhon, *General Idea of the Revolution in the Nineteenth Century*, London 1989.

12. The *Critique of the Gotha Programme* had already denounced the idea that the non-proletarian classes were simply 'one reactionary mass'. For Marx's thinking on the peasantry see, in particular, Teodor Shanin, *The Late Marx and the Russian Road*, London 1983; and Robert Bideleux, *Communism and Development*, New York 1985.

13. Hal Draper, *Karl Marx's Theory of Revolution*, Vol. IV, *Critique of Other Socialisms*, New York 1990, pp. 126–9. Anyone tempted to make a plaster saint out of either Proudhon or Bakunin would be disabused by this author's informative, if overly partisan, account. At the same time Marx and Engels were themselves fallible and, as Draper shows, their ideas developed through encounters with such chosen antagonists and collaborators as Proudhon and Bakunin.

14. John Stuart Mill, *On Socialism*, Buffalo, New York 1976, pp. 134–5.

15. See Wolfgang Mommsen, 'Max Weber and Social Democracy', in Carl Levy, ed., *Sociliasm and the Intelligentsia*, London 1987, pp. 90–105. Mommsen summarizes Weber's view at this time in the following formula: 'While there might be many varieties of socialism, the only viable one, compatible with modern civilization, was bound to be some type of centrally directed "planned economy"' (p. 92). For Durkheim see Stephen Yeo, 'Notes on Three Socialisms', in Levy, *Socialism and the Intelligentsia* pp. 219–70, p. 221. For the idea that social antagonisms and economic fluctuations should be curbed from above by national assembly or professional corporations, see Emile Durkheim, *Socialism*, New York 1962, pp. 245–7. Pareto's famous calculus of social equity was also prompted by engagement with socialism; note that he saw the latter as a vigorous but threatening and fundamentally sentimental and irrational force which needed to be harshly disciplined, by Fascist means if really necessary. However, his views on socialism oscillated widely, see Richard Bellamy, 'From Ethical to Economic Liberalism', *Economy and Society*, vol. 19, no. 4, November 1990.

16. It was, of course, possible to support a labour theory of value while not questioning capitalism, as did Ricardo, just as it was possible to be a socialist while rejecting the labour theory, as did Alfred Marshall. Böhm-Bawerk specifically separated his critique of Marx from his estimation of socialism; see Eugene Böhm-Bawerk, *Karl Marx and the Close of His System*, edited by P.M. Sweezy, New York 1948, pp. 117–18.

17. Karl Kautsky, 'The Day After the Revolution', *The Social Revolution*, Chicago 1907, pp. 103–89, the quoted passages being at pp. 150–1, 152–3. See also the entry for Kautsky by T. Kowalik in John Eatwell, ed., *The New Palgrave Dictionary of Marxian Economics*, London 1990, pp. 218–21.

18. For English versions of the articles by Pierson and Barone see F.A. Hayek, ed., *Collectivist Economic Planning*, London 1935.

19. Friedrich von Wieser, *Social Economics*, London 1927 (1914), pp. 396–7.

20. Quoted in Edward Thompson, *William Morris*, London 1977, p. 575. See also pp. 542, 693. Morris's lectures and essays on socialism combined a most eloquent indictment of the degradation of the human and natural environment by commercial war with occasional recourse to the 'simplifying' thesis. But the latter is balanced and qualified by tributes to Marx's doctrine of necessary social 'evolution', by his rejection of 'asceticism',

and by his ready acknowledgment that his own vision was partial. In 'How we live and How We Might Live' he writes of the need for 'regulation of the markets' while he opens 'The Society of the Future' with the assertion that 'monopoly must come to an end', See *Political Writings of William Morris*, edited by A.L. Morton, London 1979, pp. 145, 188.

21. A. Chilosi elaborates the sophisticated implications of the specific form of the 'right to work' outlined in Hertzka's *Freeland* in 'The Right to Employment Principle and Self-Managed Market Socialism', EUP Working Paper, European University Institute, Florence 1986. In Hertzka's novel the settler colony becomes a major industrial power set in the heart of Africa; it defeats the warlike African Kingdom of Ethiopia and helps to inspire a bloody revolution against the Tsar. Theodore Hertzka, *Freeland, a Social Anticipation*, London 1891, especially pp. 96–7 for the 'model statute' and p. 131 for the problems with the natives: 'Their military organization had to be broken up, their morality suppressed, their prejudice against labour overcome.' Hertzka was himself an Austrian economist of some prominence, having helped to found the Association of National Economists.

22. Quoted in Salvadori, *Karl Kautsky*, p. 232.

23. Rosa Luxemburg, *Organizational Questions of Russian Social Democracy* (1904), New York 1934; Leon Trotsky, *Our Political Tasks*, Geneva 1904. (*Nos taches politiques*, Paris 1970.)

24. For this context see Arno Mayer, *The Politics and Diplomacy of Peace-Making*, Princeton 1970, and *Why Did the Heavens Not Darken?*, London 1990, pp. 4–8.

25. The key text on the introduction of 'War Communism' is probably 'Report on Combating the Famine', *Lenin's Economic Writings*, edited by Meghnad Desai, London 1989, pp. 268–86. For the influence of the German war economy model on Lenin's thinking see the editor's introduction (p. 27) and also Meghnad Desai et al., (The Transition from Actually Existing Capitalism' in NLR 170, July–August 1988.

26. Moshe Lewin, *Lenin's Last Struggle*, London 1970; Isaac Deutscher, *Stalin*, Harmondsworth 1966, pp. 238–70.

27. V.I. Lenin, 'How to Organize Competition', *Selected Works* Volume 2.

28. Samuel Farber, *Before Stalinism*, New York and Cambridge 1990. Farber discusses War Communism, pp. 43–50, and throughout notes the many dissentient voices who resisted Bolshevik policy or practice from within the revolutionary camp. For further evidence see also Vladimir Brovkin, *The Mensheviks after October*, Ithaca and London 1990. Farber considers that the dispersal of the Constituent Assembly can be justified but not the subsequent suppression of Soviet democracy, commencing in the spring and summer of 1918—thus the Central Executive Committee of the Soviets, supposedly the permanent expression of the sovereign institution of the country, only met rarely in 1918 and not at all in 1919 (p. 29). Farber's type of criticism is, of course, not new, though it is comprehensive and systematic. See, for example, the last chapter, 'Defeat in Victory', in Isaac Deutscher, *The Prophet Armed*, Oxford 1954. But Deutscher, like Victor Serge in his *Memoirs* (Oxford 1962), makes greater allowance for the pressures of war.

29. Bertrand Russell, *The Practice and Theory of Bolshevism* (1920), London 1948; see, in particular, pp. 47–55, 114–23.

30. Kautsky's views on socialization in 1918 are discussed in Salvadori, *Karl Kautsky*, pp. 233–4. For Martov, see Jane Burbank, *Intelligentsia and Revolution: The Russian View of Bolshevism 1917–1922*, Oxford 1986, pp. 16–35, especially pp. 19 and 32–4; also Julius Martov, *The State and the Socialist Revolution*, New York 1938, and *Le bolshevisme mondial*, Paris 1934. Note that as a Marxist Martov championed *both* a strengthening of the democratic institutions of civil society *and* the construction of an authoritative, democratic state. Rather than counter-posing the state to civil society he argued that the former, if democratic, would be the guarantee of the latter. Indeed he attacked the Bolsheviks for a sort of lumpen anarchism which failed to see the importance of establishing a lawful and democratic polity based on an authoritative state. Martov died in 1923.

31. *Lenin's Economic Writings*, pp. 301–44.

32. Such features of the Soviet impact on mid-twentieth century history are explored by Eric Hobsbawm in 'Goodbye to All That', Chapter 10 above.

33. Martin Malia observes: 'the term *totalitarian*, coined by Mussolini with a positive connotation to designate his new order and first applied in a negative sense to Stalin's Russia by Trotsky, was taken up by Hannah Arendt to produce a general theory of perverse modernity.' Z, 'The Stalin Mausoleum', *Daedalus*. Winter 1990, p. 300. Of course Trotsky would not have endorsed the use of this concept made by his former follower. For him totalitarianism was a delusive as well as dangerous project. In 1940 he wrote: 'A totalitarian regime, whether of the Stalinist or fascist type, by its very essence, can only be a temporary transitional regime. Naked dictatorship in history has generally been the product and the symptom of an especially severe social crisis, and not at all of a stable regime. Severe crisis cannot be a permanent condition of society. A totalitarian state is capable of suppressing social contradictions during a certain period, but it is incapable of perpetuating itself.' *In Defence of Marxism*, New York 1940, p. 13.

34. Rosa Luxemburg, *The Russian Revolution*, Michigan 1961, pp. 71–2. While Luxemburg argued for democratic structures on grounds of principle, she also argued that they were essential because of the unpreparedness of Marxists for tackling the problems of a transition beyond capitalism: 'The tacit assumption underlying the Lenin–Trotsky theory of the dictatorship is this: that the socialist transformation is something for which a ready-made formula lies completed in the pocket of the revolutionary party, which needs only to be carried out energetically in practice. This is, unfortunately—or perhaps fortunately—not the case. Far from being a sum of ready-made prescriptions which have only to be applied, the practical realization of socialism as an economic, social and juridical system is something which lies completely hidden in the mists of the future. What we possess in our programme is nothing but a few main signposts' (pp. 69–70). The sketchy, tentative and experimental nature of socialist proposals thus required the fullest democracy or they could not be refined and developed.

35. Marcel Liebman, *Leninism under Lenin*, London 1970.

36. Quoted in P. Sedgewick, Introduction to Victor Serge, *Memoirs of a Revolutionary, 1901–41*, Oxford 1962, pp. xv–xvi.

37. Luxemburg, *The Russian Revolution*, pp. 41–56.

38. C.L.R. James, *Mariners, Renegades and Castaways*, New York 1953, p. 12.

39. Kautsky, *Bolshevism at a Deadlock*, p. 81. Kautsky wrote: 'The Soviet leaders would think themselves very clever and economical if they found means of trebling the number of available machines by the adoption of methods which reduced the productive capacity, intelligence and independence of the existing industrial workers to a minimum. They have failed to realize that the vital problem is to raise the efficiency of labour, and that the products of labour would then yield a surplus automatically, while such a policy would at the same time increase the capacity for turning out new and improved means of production. The Bolsheviks would not profit by recognising this, for this method of increasing the productive capacity of the workers pre-supposes a high degree of freedom, and this requires a far-reaching democracy.' Ibid., pp. 14–15. See also Salvadori, *Karl Kautsky*, especially pp. 301–12. Kautsky knew both of Soviet Taylorism and of the role of leading Mensheviks is resisting it.

40. A.C. Sutton, *Western Technology and Soviet Development* Volume II, Stamford 1971.

41. For an account of widespread unrest in the camps, see Alexander Solzhenitsyn, *The Gulag Archipelago* Volume 3, London 1978, pp. 229–86.

42. The articles outlining this proposal will be found in Leon Trotsky, *Writings 1930*, New York 1975, edited by G. Breitman and S. Lovell, pp. 123–9, 147.

43. 'The Five Year Plan in Crisis', *Bulletin of the Opposition*, no. 25/26, 1931. This article was published in an English translation in *Critique*, no. 13, 1981.

44. Leon Trotsky, 'The Soviet Economy in Danger', *Bulletin of the Opposition*, no. 31, November 1932, available in English in *Writings 1932*, edited by G. Breitman and S. Lovell, New York 1973, pp. 258–84, the quoted passage being at pp. 273–4. For an interesting discussion of this text see Alec Nove, *Socialism, Economics and Development*, London 1987, pp. 97–8.

45. Trotsky, *Writings 1932*, pp. 273, 276.

46. Deutscher, *The Prophet Armed*, pp. 496–7. Deutscher has a vivid account of a

vital incident prompting Trotsky's rethinking. While drafting an eloquent new decree mobilizing labour, aboard his military train, there is a sudden jolt as the train is thrown into a snow drift. Despite the controls supposedly monitoring rail traffic and the presence of a nearby village, the chief of the Soviet Military Committee and his party were left for two days to ponder the deficiency of planning and popular motivations.

47. Quoted in Nove, *Socialism, Economics and Development*, p. 89, where a helpful discussion will be found of Trotsky's views on these questions.

48. Quoted in ibid, p. 98.

49. Andrei Sakharov, *Memoirs*, London 1990. p. 164.

50. Stalin's last writings on the continued operation of the law of value in a socialist economy should be read as his own back-handed and partial recognition that planning could not sort out Soviet economic problems. With his love of a phoney argument, he declared that one reason for this was that the cooperative farms, unlike the *sovkoz*, were an independent property form. J.V. Stalin, *Economic Problems of Socialism in the USSR*, Moscow 1952.

51. Mises's 1920 essay can be found in Hayek, *Collectivist Economic Planning* pp. 87–130; most of it was reprinted in Alec Nove and Mario Nuti, eds., *Socialist Economics*, Harmondsworth 1972. Neurath's writings prompted Max Weber to a similar critique around the same time, see Max Weber, *The Theory of Social and Economic Organization* (1921), New York 1966, pp. 202–18. Weber, and possibly Mises as well, were influenced by the failings of the war economy (see p. 209).

52. See L. von Mises, *Socialism*, London 1936, especially pp. 113–50 and pp. 516–21 for his critique of Karl Polanyi and Eduard Heimann. The quoted passages are from L. von Mises, *Human Action*, Chicago 1947, pp. 60–71, 698, based on a work first published in Switzerland in 1943.

53. See Carl Landauer, *European Socialism* Volume II, Berkeley 1959, pp. 1641–50. See also the articles by Rosner and Mendell in K. Polanyi-Levitt, ed., *The Life and Work of Karl Polanyi*, Montreal 1991.

54. H.D. Dickinson published an essay outlining his model in the *Economic Journal*, June 1933. The Lange/Breit model was published in 1935 in the *Zeitschrift für National-ökonomie* and is discussed in A. Chilosi, 'The Right to Employment Principle and Self-Managed Market Socialism', EUI, Florence 1986. Lange's more formalized essay, 'On the Economic Theory of Socialism', appeared in two parts in the *Review of Economic Studies*, vol. IV, nos. 1 and 2, 1936–37. It was later reprinted in book form and a shortened version appears in Nove and Nuti, *Socialist Economics*. In an appendix to the second part of his essay, Lange reviewed Marxist writing on the economics of socialism, favourably citing Kautsky's work and quoting extensively from Trotsky's essay of 1932, 'The Soviet Economy in Danger'; this latter reference he undoubtedly took over from an earlier essay by Lerner, 'Economic Theory and Socialist Economy', *Review of Economic Studies*, vol. II, no. 1, 1934, which had criticized Dobb's ideas. The best recent discussion of the 'calculation debate', with many helpful references, is Don Lavoie, *Rivalry and Central Planning*, Cambridge 1985. However, he does not fully acknowledge the extent to which Lerner anticipated key points to be made by the Austrians. Lerner was later to develop his position further in *The Economics of Control*, London 1944.

55. A.P. Lerner, 'A Note on Socialist Economy', *Review of Economic Studies*, vol. IV, no. 2, 1936–37, pp. 72–6. Lerner was himself one of three editors of this journal, together with Paul Sweezy and Ursula Hicks.

56. Hayek's first essay took the form of a review of the book version of Lange's essay and of Dickinson's book, *The Economics of Socialism*: F.A. von Hayek, 'Socialist Calculation: the Competitive Solution', *Economica*, 1940, p. 145. Mises had argued like this in the 1920s, responding to the 'market socialist' theories of Karl Polanyi and Eduard Heimann; see Don Lavoie, *Rivalry and Central Planning*, Cambridge 1985, pp. 174–6.

57. At this point, Hayek may have been influenced by the work of his teacher, Böhm-Bawerk, who had written, in the context of discussing which types of knowledge were operative in capitalism, 'in the region of economics where we have to deal so largely with conscious and calculating human action, the first of the two sources of knowledge, the objective source, can at best be considered a very poor and, especially when standing alone,

an altogether inadequate part of the total attainable knowledge.' *Karl Marx and the Close of His System*, p. 115. But Böhm-Bawerk immediately goes on to concede that the knowledge and motives of economic actors do play a part in Marx's system (p. 116). Indeed among several affinities between the Marxist and Austrian schools is a tendency to distrust over-generalized or reified aggregates, where socio-economic relations are represented by strings of mathematical equations. While Marx did write an algebra of exploitation, he also argued that capitalism and the market brought about a reduction of quality to quantity, an idea which can illuminate the double-sided character of the processes of entrepreneurial appropriation. With regard to Hayek's argument from knowledge, note also that Abba Lerner had produced a more weakly formulated version of this point in 1935: 'Where there are thousands of factors, being combined in thousands of different ways in millions of different productive units, and where a re-shuffling of factors may have to be of the most complicated kind, it seems to be that it would not be easy to find a technical expert who knows all that is going on everywhere.' A.P. Lerner, 'A Rejoinder to Mr Dobb', *Review of Economic Studies*, 1935, p. 153.

58. F.A. von Hayek, 'The Uses of Knowledge in Society', *American Economic Review*, September 1945, p. 530. Hayek's various contributions to the 'calculation debate' between 1935 and 1945 were republished in *Individualism and Economic Order*, London 1948.

59. Ibid., p. 529. Hayek will have read of this article in Lange's appendix, which cited both the passage referred to here and the lengthy quotation I have myself given above (p. 201).

Trotsky's stature as one of the key leaders of the Russian Revolution undoubtedly lent piquancy to his qualified espousal of market mechanisms. But his way of conceptualizing the problem of the command economy made its own intellectual contribution and might have been cited even if he had not been the founder of the Red Army. This raises the question of how and why he arrived at his ideas on this issue. It is not impossible that he had read Friedrich von Wieser, whose work prepares the ground for the single-mind argument. His prominence in the Soviet government in the War Communism period will, as Deutscher emphasizes, have given him first-hand experience. To this we may add that Soviet intellectual life in the twenties also witnessed a fascinating concern with complex structure and the 'dialogic'—as in Voloshinov/Bakhtin. Finally Trotsky's own revulsion from totalitarian projects and his (somewhat belated) vindication of political pluralism will also have assisted his capacity to pierce to the roots of the economic problem.

60. That Hayek developed new ideas in the debate with the socialists is argued by Israel Kirzner in Ellen F. Paul et al., eds, *Capitalism*, New York 1990. Dobb reviewed Hayek's *Collectivist Economic Planning* in *The Economic Journal* in 1935, but did not respond directly to his later essays.

61. For a critique of Austrian assumptions see Geoffrey M. Hodgson, *Economics and Institutions*, Cambridge 1988.

62. See the interesting discussion of Neurath by Juan Martinez-Alier in *Capitalism, Nature and Society*, no. 2, Summer 1989. Neurath had been economic adviser to the Munich Soviet, and later a prominent member of the Vienna circle of Logic Positivists, and later, analytical philosophers. See also the discussion of Neurath in Martinez Alier's *Ecological Economics*, Oxford 1989 and in Carl Landauer, *European Socialism* Volume II, pp. 1636-9. The ideas of Polanyi and Neurath, with their refusal of the reductionism of the market and concern with natural limits, may have had some influence on the Frankfurt School via the writings of Weil and Pollock. Karl Polanyi was to furnish a memorable indictment of Mises and laissez-faire economics in general in his book *The Great Transformation*, London 1944, see especially pp. 68-76, 163-200. Another left response to Mises—combined on this occasion with a critique of Lange—can be found in *Living Marxism* (Chicago), September 1939, pp. 235-44, where it is argued, from a 'Council Communist' standpoint that 'the Russian development destroyed a number of illusions in ... the desirability of a state controlled economic system' (ibid p. 241).

63. For Hayek's discomfort with ecological arguments and attempt to argue away 'neighbourhood effects', see *The Constitution of Liberty*, Chicago 1960, pp. 367-75. The very term 'neighbourhood effects' has an unduly localized and cosy ring to it. Hayek's later

writings, such as those in the series *Law, Legislation and Liberty*, propose stringent limitations on who should be allowed to vote and how often, as well as narrowly circumscribed
powers for the government of the day—all this in the interest of protecting the
'spontaneous order' of the catallaxy from the short-sighted passions of the citizenry. For a
discussion of this, see Nick Bosanquet, *After the New Right*, London 1983, pp. 26–42.
We socialists should, however, be gentle in our critiques of the Austrian notion of a catallaxy since it is so obviously first cousin to the notion of 'freely associated producers' in a
world where the state has withered away.

64. See F.A. von Hayek, *Prices and Production*, 2nd edn, London 1931, with its
attack on 'the well-meaning but dangerous proposals to fight depression with "a little
inflation"', p. 125; though note that one of the most prominent left thinkers of the time,
John Strachey, shared Hayek's view that Keynesianism would generate uncontrollable
inflation; see John Strachey, *The Coming Struggle for Power*, London 1934, where
Hayek's critique of Keynes is at least partially endorsed.

65. See Hayek's speech to the Montpelerin society reprinted in *Individualism and
Economic Order* and his later *Knowledge, Evolution and Society*, London 1985.

66. H.D. Dickinson, *The Economics of Socialism*, London 1939, p. 32. As well as
devoting critical attention to consumption, this book argues that socialism should advance
equality for women. The respectful tone of Hayek's critique was a tribute both to its quality
and to the influence of Wieser on Dickinson's thought; for the latter see H.D. Dickinson's
review of Ernest Mandel's *Treatise on Marxist Economics* in NLR 21, September–October
1963. At this time Dickinson formed part of an academic support group for Tony Benn.

67. For the involvement of Dickinson, Lerner and other 'market socialists' on Labour
thinking see Elizabeth Durbin, *New Jerusalems: The Labour Party and the Economics of
Democratic Socialism*, London 1985, pp. 169–71, 232–41. It is worth noting that the
reformism of this epoch at least produced real reforms, such as the National Health
Service. Another peripheral contributor to the 'calculation debate', A.C. Pigou, came
closest to anticipating the 1945 Labour government's approach to nationalization in his
Socialism versus Capitalism, London 1947.

68. Maurice Dobb, *Soviet Economic Planning since 1917*, London 1966, p. 373. On
the basis of simple correlation it could be argued that as the ability of Gosplan increased,
with the elaboration of more sophisticated control techniques and the application of
computers, so Soviet economic growth rates dropped. By the seventies, data on millions of
products were being fed into the central computers and thousands of millions of bits of
paper were being shuffled between the ministries and the enterprises. Yet all along, Soviet
successes, such as they were, may have owed more to the motivation of the cadres in the
factories. This was the characteristic emphasis of the Polish Marxist economists. Thus W.
Brus courageously reminded his readers of Rosa Luxemburg's verdict on the Russian
Revolution in his book, *The Market in a Socialist Economy*, London 1972, pp. 97, 100.
Dobb wrote an introduction to this English edition where he drew attention to this latter
point and expressed support for a variety of market socialism. M. Kalecki wrote in 1942 as
follows: 'No socialist government can hope to succeed unless its efforts are seconded by a
feeling of heightened tempo of development permeating the whole of society and, above
all, of *self-confidence* amongst the workers and lower strata of society. Such a mood cannot
be artificially created—it can be stimulated by propaganda but only if a real basis for it
exists.' Quoted in J. Osiatynkski, *Michal Kalecki on a Socialist Economy*, London 1988,
p. 184. Of course a mixture of illusion, terror and propaganda, combined with fear of
German invasion, could for a time effectively mobilize the cadres and 'little cogs', but
Kalecki was right to suppose that mobilization of this type could not be sustained for more
than a decade or two. Kalecki himself proposed not only greater worker participation but
also perspective plans that would give priority to investment in consumer goods
industries.

69. Hayek, *The Constitution of Liberty*, p. 392.

70. For an assessment of these debates pinpointing the failure to establish a rational
pricing system, see Charles Bettelheim, *The Transition to Socialist Economy*, Brighton
1975, pp. 184–243.

71. Nove was, of course, far from alone in advocating market socialism and freely

drew on the important work of East European economists such as Sik, Kornai and Brus. However, for the reasons given above, Nove's work has had a critical role in discussion of socialist economics in the English-speaking world. See *The Soviet Economic System*, London 1977; 'Market Socialism and its Critics', *Soviet Studies*, vol. XXIV, no. 1, 1972: 'Problems and Prospects of the Soviet Economy', NLR 119, January–February 1980; *The Economics of Feasible Socialism*, London 1983, rev. ed., London 1991. For the reappearance of some themes from the 'calculation debate', see Milton Friedman, *Plan and Market*, with a reply by Alec Nove, Committee for the Study of Communist Economies, London 1984. For one strand of the debate on Nove see W. Brus, 'Viable Socialism?' NLR 153, September–October 1985; Ernest Mandel, 'The Case for Socialist Planning', NLR 159, September–October 1986; Alec Nove, 'Reply to Mandel', NLR 161, January–February 1987; Ernest Mandel, 'The Perils of Marketization', NLR 169, May–June 1988; Meghnad Desai et al., 'The Transition from Actually Existing Capitalism', NLR 170, July–August, 1988; Diane Elson, 'Socialization of the Market', NLR 172, November–December 1988.

72. See Anders Aslund, *Gorbachev's Struggle for Economic Reform*, London 1989, pp. 76–87.

73. In the sixties I worked for the Cuban Ministry of Soviet Trade. The section chief told us of a story about an economic conference convened by the then President, Oswaldo Dorticos, who had general oversight in the economic field at the time. One of the economic advisers argued that in drawing up such and such a plan for a given sector the aim must be to produce the maximum output for the minimum effort and expense. Dorticos emphatically disagreed: 'This is not the revolutionary way', he insisted, 'instead we aim to achieve the maximum of output with the maximum forces (*fuerzas*).' Unfortunately the attitude expressed by Dorticos, the cavalry charge method of economic mobilization, was to become all too typical of Cuban economic management, as in the attempted Ten Million Ton Harvest of 1970.

74. For the failure of Soviet management to make effective use of computers see Mark R. Beissinger, *Scientific Management, Socialist Discipline, and Soviet Power*, London 1988, pp. 246–60.

75. For an exhaustive account of the irrationalities of the 'traditional' Soviet model, see Michael Ellman, *The Socialist Economies*, 2nd edn, Cambridge 1989, pp. 17–52.

76. 'Planning and Consciousness in the Transition to Socialism (On the Budgetary Finance System)', *Che Guevara and the Cuban Revolution: Writings and Speeches of Che Guevara*, edited by David Deutschmann, Sydney 1987, pp. 203–30, 220–1. Guevara, of course, remained an advocate of planning, but he did clearly face up to the consequent problems. The argument quoted shows that the absolute levels of world market prices can only be ignored at peril. But because of the segmentation of markets, and because it is comparative prices not absolute prices which are the operative factor, a development strategy could work by deliberately 'getting prices wrong'. See, for example, Alice Amsden's account of South Korean practice, 'Third World Industrialization: "Global Fordism" or a New Model?', NLR 182, July–August 1990, pp. 5–31.

77. This point is made by Jaques Bidet, *Théorie de la modernité, suivi de, Marx et le marché*, Paris 1990, pp. 161–7. For the logic of competition in capitalist conditions, see Robert Brenner, 'The Origins of Capitalist Development: a Critique of Neo-Smithian Marxism', NLR 104, July–August 1977; and the same author's contribution to J. Elster, ed., *Analytic Marxism*, Cambridge 1987; also Israel Kirzner, *Competition and Entrepreneurship*, New York 1973; and the same author's contribution to Ellen F. Paul et al., *Capitalism*, pp. 165–82.

78. See NLR 172, November–December 1988.

79. Elson's approach has some affinity with that of Pat Devine in his *Democracy and Economic Planning*, Oxford 1988, with his outline of a scheme of 'negotiated coordination' of production. Devine is willing to accept that a market will be needed in a socialist economy but not 'market forces'. However, there are several crucial problems which Devine's approach does not address. While the multi-million complexity of a modern economy can be monitored, requiring it to be positively 'negotiated' is asking a very great deal. Devine contemplates inter-industry negotiating boards; but who determines which are the most appropriate links and who ensures that outcomes are compatible with one another

if they have been freely and separately negotiated? How do negotiations establish commonly accepted prices where there are difference of views and, perhaps, interest? In a democratic political structure one person has one vote. In a market structure the distribution of economic resources distributes power, whether evenly or otherwise, but at least a decision can be reached. But in a process of negotiated coordination, how are differences decided? Clearly, it would not do for larger enterprises to prevail over smaller ones, or for those in a strategic position always to have their way. While market forces might remain fallible even where large concentrations of wealth are absent, at least a 'socialized market' could seek, by trial and error, to promote generally egalitarian and responsible, as well as reasonably efficient, outcomes. (The efficiency I refer to here is not, of course, to be identified with capitalist efficiency, since both costs and benefits would be established in different ways.) Notwithstanding these comments, Devine's book does helpfully address questions of democracy in a socialist economy; his suggestions in this area would probably work all the better if 'negotiated coordination' were not overloaded with tasks that would be beyond it.

80. For the 'can ban' system see Masahiko Aoki, *Information, Incentives and Bargaining in the Japanese Economy*, Cambridge 1988, pp. 20–26.

81. Thus life expectancy in China is 64 years compared with 52 years in India. For a most illuminating discussion, see Jean Dreze and Amartya Sen, *Hunger and Public Action*, Oxford 1989, pp. 204–25.

82. For a comparative view of Japanese banks and *kieretsu*, see Aoki, *Information, Incentives and Bargaining*, pp. 119–22, 148–9, 232–3.

83. Julian Le Grand and Saul Estrin, eds., *Market Socialism*, Oxford 1989, developing an earlier Fabian pamphlet of 1986; Wlodzimierz Brus and Kazimierz Laski, *From Marx to the Market*, Cambridge 1989, especially pp. 103–53; Anthony de Jasay, *Market Socialism: A Scrutiny*, Institute of Economic Affairs 1990.

84. Engels would have smiled at such a concession. He mocked Dühring's pompous suggestion that 'society honours itself in conferring distinction on the higher types of professional ability by a moderate additional allocation for consumption', riposting that 'Herr Dühring, too, honours himself, when, combining the innocence of the dove with the subtleness of a serpent, he displays such touching concern for the moderate additional consumption of the Dührings of the future.' *Anti-Dühring*, p. 365. In general Engels's critical comments in this text on Dühring's proposals have a certain bearing on market socialist projects and should not be dismissed out of hand, even if his own brief sketch of a fully planned alternative is unconvincing. On the question of pay differentials, a problem that would present itself to any socialist economy that was not entirely global would be the need to discourage specialists from emigrating; this practical consideration says nothing about social justice, which would have to take account of the fact that specialists have usually benefited from support during training.

85. Ignacio Ortuño Ortin, J.E. Roemer and J. Silvestre, 'Market Socialism', Working Paper no. 355, Department of Economics, University of California at Davis. Clearly it is beyond the scope of this article to further explicate this impressive model here.

86. See, for example, André Gorz, Chapter 17 below. For the 'basic income' proposal see Philippe van Parijs' *Arguing for Basic Income*, London 1992.

87. For these and many further examples, see Robin Murray, 'Ownership, Control and the Market', NLR 164, July–August 1987, pp. 87–112.

88. See André Gorz, *The Critique of Economic Reason*, London 1989, pp. 127–33 for Gorz's discussion of this point. I have myself sought to show the crucial and progressive role of the anti-mercantile impulse in the construction of anti-slavery in *The Overthrow of Colonial Slavery*, London 1988, especially pp. 27–8, 59, 89, 93–5, 118–19, 223, 446, 499, 533–6. I was drawn to focus on this question because of a recent attempt to endow the market with moral qualities unsuspected even by Mises and Hayek. See Thomas Haskell, 'Capitalism and the Origins of the Humanitarian Sensibility, Part I', *American Historical Review*, vol. 90, no. 2, April 1985; 'Part 2', *American Historical Review*, vol. 90, no. 3, June 1985; and the same author's reply to critics in the *American Historical Review*, vol. 92, no. 4, 1987.

89. Polanyi, who eloquently denounces the destructive impact of the market on

natural and human resources, nevertheless writes: 'the end of market society means in no way the absence of markets'. *The Great Transformation*, p. 252.

90. *The Economist*, 14 July 1990.

91. See, in particular, Alice Amsden, 'Third World Industrialization'; see also Robert Wade, *Governing the Market: Economic Theory and the Role of Government in East Asian Industrialization*, Princeton 1990.

92. See Karel van Wolferen, *The Enigma of Japanese Power*, New York 1989, pp. 375–408. The general point I am trying to make here is similar to Hodgson's discussion of the 'impurity principle'—see *Economics and Institutions*, pp. 167–71, 254–62.

93. Jasay, *Market Socialism*, p. 15.

94. *The Economist*, 'Capitalism Survey', 5–11 May 1990, p. 10.

95. Ibid. provides evidence for the claims in this paragraph.

96. F.A. Hayek, *The Road to Serfdom*, London 1944, pp. 140–1.

97. In international bodies there would be a strong case for representation to be allotted according to population. Ensuring representativity is a difficulty in international bodies where it is governments that do the representing. The following proposal would meet this problem, though its purpose might be frustrated by intimidation; juries chosen at random, on the classical Athenian model, could be asked either to reduce or increase their own country's share of votes according to their evaluation of their government's success in representing them. While this might prove quite unworkable, the principle that only governments should be represented in international bodies should not just be accepted and assumed.

98. Submission on the Future of the Multifibre Arrangement, Women Working Worldwide, Textile and Garment Project, University of Manchester 1990.

99. As it happens, one of the best recent summary statements of the case for state intervention and social planning comes from Nove, doubtless drawing upon his experience of Margaret Thatcher's Britain on this occasion. See Alec Nove, 'The Role of Central Planning under Capitalism and Market Socialism', in Jon Elster and Karl Ove Moene, eds, *Alternatives to Capitalism*, Cambridge 1989, pp. 98–109.

100. The statement issued by the December meeting in Leningrad of the Soviet Socialist Party declared: 'Market relations are necessary but should not become the chief regulator of economic and social life. The market should play the role of a regulating mechanism, facilitating the responsiveness of the economy, but its action should not extend to the extra-economic sphere and should not determine the priorities of development.' Peter Uhl, interviewed in NLR 179, January–February 1990, took a similar stance, as does the veteran Vietnamese revolutionary N.K. Vien whose oppositional letter is published in *International Viewpoint*, no. 204, 15 April 1991.

101. That the crisis of Marxism is located in the weakness of potential agencies of socialism is argued by Joe McCarney, *Social Theory and the Crisis of Marxism*, London 1990.

102. See Lewis Seigelbaum and Theodore Friedgut, 'The Soviet Miners' Strike and its Aftermath', NLR 181, May–June 1990, pp. 5–32. See also the remarks of the Soviet miners' leader, quoted in *International Viewpoint* no. 207, 27 May 1991.

103. Kautsky, *Dictatorship of the Proletariat*, p. 3. Kautsky was here echoing a phrase from the Erfurt programme.

104. Raymond Williams, *Politics and Letters: Interviews with New Left Review*, London 1979, p. 437.

13

'A Child Lost in the Storm'

Eduardo Galeano

Lenin's statue removed by a crane in Bucharest. An eager multitude lined up outside McDonald's in Moscow. The odious Berlin Wall for sale in souvenir-size chunks. In Warsaw and Budapest, the ministers of economy talking exactly like Margaret Thatcher—and in Beijing, too, as tanks crush students. The Italian Communist Party, largest in the West, announcing its forthcoming suicide. Soviet aid to Ethiopia cut back and Colonel Mengistu suddenly discovering that capitalism is good. The Sandinistas, mainstay of the finest revolution in the world, lose the elections, the headlines proclaiming: 'The revolution in Nicaragua falls.'

It seems that there is no place for revolutions anymore other than in archaeological museum display cases, nor room for the Left, except the repentant Left willing to sit to the right of the bankers. We are all invited to the world burial of socialism. All of humanity is in the funeral procession, they claim.

I must confess, I don't believe it. This funeral is for the wrong corpse.

Perestroika and the passion for freedom which it unleashed have everywhere burst the seams of an unbearable straitjacket. Everything is exploding. Changes proliferate at a dizzying pace founded on the certainty that there is no reason why social justice should be the enemy of freedom or efficiency. There was an urgency, a collective necessity: the people were at the end of their tether; fed up to the teeth with a bureaucracy as powerful as it was futile, that forbade them in the name of Marx to say what they thought, to live what they felt. Spontaneity of any kind could be considered treason or insanity.

Socialism, Communism? Was it all nothing but a historical fraud? I write from the Latin American viewpoint and say to myself: If that was the case, or might have been, why should we be the ones to pay for the fraud? Our face was never in that mirror.

National dignity lost the battle in the recent Nicaraguan elections. It was vanquished by hunger and war; but it was vanquished as well by the international winds that are buffeting the Left with greater fury than ever. Unjustly, the just paid for the sinners. The Sandinistas are not to blame either for the war or the hunger. Nor do they bear the slightest responsibility for what happened in Eastern Europe.

Paradox of paradoxes: a democratic, pluralistic, independent revolution that borrowed nothing from the Soviets, the Chinese, the Cubans, or anybody else, has paid for the crockery broken by others, while the local Communist Party voted for Violeta Chamorro.

Those responsible for the war and the hunger are now celebrating the outcome of an election that punishes the victims. The day after it, the US government announced the end of the economic embargo against Nicaragua. That was just what happened years ago at the time of the military coup in Chile. The day after President Allende's death, the price of copper miraculously rose on the world market.

Actually, the revolution that overthrew the Somoza family dictatorship did not have a moment's respite over these last ten long years. It was invaded on a daily basis by a foreign power and its hired criminals and underwent at the same time the unrelenting pressure of a state of siege on the part of the bankers and commercial masters of the world.

In spite of all this, it managed to be a more civilized revolution than the French Revolution, not having guillotined or stood anybody against the wall, and a more tolerant one than that of the United States, having granted freedom of expression, with some restrictions, to the local spokespeople of the colonial overlord.

The Sandinistas brought literacy to Nicaragua, reduced infant mortality significantly and distributed land to the peasantry. But the country was bled white by war. War damage amounted to one-and-a-half times the gross domestic product, which means that Nicaragua was destroyed one-and-a-half times. The magistrates of the International Court of Justice in The Hague found against the United States but their decision had no effect. Nor were the congratulations of the United Nations specialized organizations for education, food and health of any avail. Praise is inedible.

The invaders rarely attacked military objectives. Farm cooperatives were their favourite targets. How many thousands of Nicaraguans were killed or wounded on orders of the US government over the past decade? Proportionately, the number would come to three million North Americans. Yet, many thousands of North Americans visited Nicaragua, were always welcomed and nothing ever happened to any of them. Only one died. He was killed by the Contras. (His name was Ben

Linder. He was very young, an engineer and a clown. He was followed about by a swarm of children. He organized the first Clown School in Nicaragua. The Contras killed him as he measured the water in a lake for a reservoir that was being built.)

But what about Cuba? Didn't the same thing happen there as in Eastern Europe, a divorce between the power and the people? Aren't the people fed up there, too, with one party, one press, one truth?

Fidel Castro has said: 'If I am Stalin, my dead are enjoying good health.' And that, to be sure, is not the only difference. Cuba did not import a prefabricated model of vertical power from Moscow, but was obliged to transform itself into a fortress to keep from ending up on its all-powerful enemy's dinner plate. And it was under those conditions that this tiny developing country made astonishing strides. There is less illiteracy and less infant mortality today in Cuba than in the United States. Furthermore, in contrast to a number of East European countries, Cuban socialism was not orthopaedically imposed from above and outside but was born deep inside and grew from way below. The many Cubans who died for Angola, or gave the best of themselves for Nicaragua expecting no recompense, did not do so against the dictates of their hearts, submissively obeying the orders of a police state. Had that been the case, it would be inexplicable that there were never desertions but always fervour.

Now Cuba is living in a time of tragic isolation, a time of danger: the invasion of Panama and the disintegration of the so-called socialist camp are, I am afraid, influencing its internal process in the worst way, abetting bureaucratic obduracy, ideological rigidity and the militarization of society.

The US government invokes democracy with respect to Panama, Nicaragua or Cuba in the way the East European governments invoked socialism—as an alibi. Latin America has been invaded by the United States more than a hundred times in this century—always in the name of democracy and always to impose military dictatorships or puppet governments which safeguarded the money that was in danger. The imperial power system does not want democracies; it wants humbled countries.

The invasion of Panama was scandalous, with its 7,000 victims among the ruins of the poor barrios levelled by the bombings. But more scandalous than the invasion was the impunity with which it was effected. Impunity, which encourages repetition of a misdeed, stimulates the malefactor. President Mitterrand greeted this crime of sovereignty with discreet applause, and the whole world—after the tithe of a statement had been paid here and there—sat back.

In this context, silence and even thinly disguised complaisance on the part of some of the East European countries speaks eloquently. Does the liberation there give the green light to oppression of the West? I never went along with the attitude of those who condemned imperialism in the Caribbean but applauded or kept their mouths shut when national sovereignty was trampled in Hungary, Poland, Czechoslovakia or Afghanistan.

I can say this because I have never operated under a double standard: the right of self-determination of nations is sacred in all places at all times. It is well said by those who point out that Gorbachev's democratic reforms were possible because the Soviet Union ran no risk of being invaded by the Soviet Union; and likewise by those who point out that the United States is safe from coups and military dictatorships because there is no US Embassy in the United States.

Without the shadow of a doubt, freedom is always good news, for the East European countries now enjoying it and for the entire world. But, at the same time, are the paeans to money and the virtues of the market-place good news? The idolatry of the American way of life? The naive illusions of an invitation to membership in the International Club for the Rich? The bureaucracy, nimble only for stepping into better positions, is rapidly adapting to the new situation and the old bureaucrats are beginning to transform themselves into a new bourgeoisie.

It must be understood that from the standpoint of Latin America and the so-called Third World, the defunct Soviet bloc at least had one fundamental virtue: it did not get fat by feeding off the poor, did not take part in the raping by the international capitalist market. On the contrary, it helped to fund justice in Cuba, Nicaragua and many other countries. I suspect that in the not very distant future this will be recalled with nostalgia.

For us, capitalism is not a dream to be made reality, but a nightmare come true. Our challenge lies not in privatizing the state but in de-privatizing it. Our states have been bought at bargain prices by the owners of the land, the banks and everything else. And for us, the market—the local market and the world market—is nothing more than a pirate ship—the greater its freedom, the worse its behaviour. The world market robs us with both arms. The commercial arm keeps charging us more and more for what it sells us and paying less and less for what it buys from us. The financial arm that lends us our own money keeps paying us less and charging us more.

We live in a region where European prices and African wages prevail, where capitalism acts like the kind man who said, 'I'm so fond of poor people that it seems to me there are never enough of them.' In Brazil alone, for example, the system kills 1,000 children a day by disease or starvation.

With or without elections, capitalism in Latin America is antidemocratic—most of the people are the prisoners of need, doomed to isolation and violence. Hunger lies, violence lies: they claim that they are part of nature, they feign belonging to the natural order of things. When that 'natural order' grows disorderly, the military comes on the scene, hooded or barefaced. As they say in Colombia, 'The more the cost of living goes up, the less life is worth.'

The elections in Nicaragua were a very cruel blow, a blow like hatred from God, as the poet said. When I heard the result, I was, and still am, a lost child in the storm. A lost child, yes, but not alone. We are many. Throughout the world, we are many.

I sometimes feel as though they have stolen even our words. The term 'socialism' is applied in the West as make-up for injustice; in Eastern Europe, it evokes purgatory or maybe hell. The word 'imperialism' is out of style and no longer to be found in the dominant political lexicon, even though imperialism is present and does pillage and kill.

And the term 'militancy'? And the very fact of militant fervour? For the theoreticians of disenchantment it is a ridiculous old relic; for the repentant, a memory disturbance.

In a few months we have witnessed the turbulent shipwreck of a system that usurped socialism, that treated the people like a kid that never grew up and dragged it by the ear. Three or four centuries ago, the Inquisitors slandered God in saying that they were carrying out his orders; but I believe that Christianity is not the Holy Inquisition. In our time, the bureaucrats have stigmatized hope and besmirched the most beautiful of human adventures; but I also believe that socialism is not Stalinism.

Now, we must begin all over again; step by step, with no shields but those born of our own bodies. It is necessary to discover, create, imagine. In a speech shortly after his defeat, Jesse Jackson championed the right to dream: 'Let us defend that right', he said. 'Let us not permit anybody to take that right from us.' And today more than ever it is necessary to dream. To dream together dreams that undream themselves and become incarnate in mortal matter, as was said, wished, by another poet. My best friends live fighting for that right; and some of them have given their lives for it.

This is my testimony. A dinosaur's confession? Perhaps. In any case, it is the affirmation of one who believes that the human condition is not doomed to selfishness and the obscene pursuit of money, and that socialism did not die, because it had not yet been—that today is the first day of the long life before it.

May 1990
Translated by Asa Katz

14

Conversations on the New World Order

Fredric Jameson

World history is a house that has more staircases than rooms.

Börne

The collapse of the party–state in Eastern Europe (although not in China) has consequences significantly different from those implicit in yesterday's three great news items—the failure of socialism, the collapse of Communism, and the bankruptcy of Marxism. Journalists might better, as it turns out, have evoked the return with a vengeance of classical imperialism; those of us who used to insist on the existence of 'three' worlds rather than the North–South dualism pushed by liberals and convergence theorists now ruefully contemplate the emergence of this dualism, in the vocation of the North American superstate to try out its postmodern technology by enforcing its 'new world order' on the former Third World.

That is news, I suppose; but it does not seem to make much sense to talk about the bankruptcy of Marxism, when Marxism is very precisely the science and the study of just that capitalism whose global triumph is affirmed in talk of Marxism's demise. Marxism was capable of predicting the race to spend the 'peace dividend' in the skies over Baghdad, and the transubstantiation of the abortive 'star wars' research into actually existing weapons budgets for the unforeseeable future. For, according to Marx, the nature of the beast is expansion, and that means new imperial tasks abroad and an indefinite postponement of social investments:

> Das wahre Tier, das wilde schöne Tier,
> Das—meine Damen!—sehen Sie nur bei mir!

As for the failure of socialism, you may well wonder where it was ever given a chance to fail. But here too the interest of the proposition is displaced, for what has in reality been revealed is the profound ambivalence of the Soviet Union as an object (now, as the Lacanians might put it, a lost object, an *objet petit a*). Few could be found to admire the Soviet system in these last years, but (with the exception of Eastern Europe and, perhaps, Afghanistan) their foreign policy was different and they generally supported the right causes: who will support them now? (Or, in true poststructuralist fashion, were the 'causes' themselves caused by the support, rather than the other way round?) Meanwhile, even non- or anti-communist socialists and social democrats seem stunned, and in mourning. Having tirelessly denounced Soviet totalitarianism as 'having nothing to do with genuine socialism', they have evidently discovered within themselves, the unsuspected existence of a deeper unconscious belief: that the Soviet system could somehow be transformed into genuine socialism after all, in the course of just such a liberalization as we have witnessed. But these leftists were in reality liberals (in the American sense) after all; they still believed in some kind of progress—whereas on a more dialectical view of history, there is progress, but it proceeds by catastrophe and defeat. The events in Eastern Europe, indeed, seem richly to justify the view tirelessly propounded by Immanuel Wallerstein that the Soviet system is not to be considered a 'system' at all; that today—as yesterday—there is still only one system, and even the seventy years of Soviet power are only to be considered the provisional occupation of an 'anti-systemic' enclave. That enclave has now been colonized (or recolonized) in its turn. In its loss of autonomy and in the collapse of its independent structures it resembles nothing quite so much as those mining towns in the far west of the USA: disfigured by strip mining and, more ominously, hollowed out everywhere underground, with tunnels under a surface that here and there (virtually soundlessly) gives way, sucking the collapsing woodwork of the houses down with it into the earth like the vortex of an antlion— Well grubbed, old mole! But this particular mole is an absence; and the dusty, abandoned, yet mortal void marks the non-appearance of the collective project; the waning and then the eclipse of mass commitment and resolve; the naive belief of the party–state in the capability of 'socialist institutions' (including the police and the army) to substitute for 'moral incentives'. But socialism was supposed to involve the primacy of the political and constitute the true 'moral equivalent of war'; to eschew the mechanical and non-political, economic and institutional, modes of social reproduction available to other social formations and other modes of production.

And if socialism cannot be said to have failed, so also capitalism cannot be said to have succeeded, on any meaningful reading of the market system as such. All true reactionary ideologues affirm this, who complain that there is not yet a genuinely free market under the interventionist state of late capitalism; and Galbraith observed long ago that there is a way in which, for us, oligopoly has been a substitute for planning (in the 'socialist' sense). Surely it remains fair to suppose that whatever the fortunes of the three great emergent centres of late capitalism—Japan, post-1922 Europe and the North American superstate—capitalism still has no future in the Third World (or in the Second World either, if one believes those few economists willing to speak their mind against the grain). The Rostowian 'takeoff stage' remains as chimerical for most underdeveloped countries of the periphery and semi-periphery—the countries of the Debt—as it did before the equally legendary 'collapse of socialism': the only difference now is that such countries can more plausibly be offered a future as client and dependent states, sources of cheap labour and raw materials. It is a future calculated to warm the hearts of only a prospective comprador bourgeoisie; the overpopulated and unemployed masses will still wait impatiently for the reinvention of some alternative system (for which you had better now find another name, if you don't want to call it socialism any longer).

As for Communism itself, what needs to be affirmed is that the most recent developments are due not to its failure but to its success. It was not left-wing economists who sung the praises of Marxism-Leninism and the one-party state as a vehicle for the rapid industrialization of underdeveloped societies (whether in the Second or the Third Worlds). It is strange to hear right-wing historians now assure us that Russia would have reached greater heights of productivity today had the liberals been left undisturbed. The fact is that Stalinism was a success, fulfilling its modernizing mission, developing political and social subjects of a new type. I am not the only one to point out that (leaving aside the industrial transformation of an overwhelmingly peasant Poland in the first place), Solidarity would not have been possible without the concentration of the workforce against a single employer in the form of the Communist state. But in a more general way, and with more specific emphasis on the Soviet Union, the denial that industrial Communism has collapsed will be paradoxical only for those who, as Marx put it, 'believe that there once was history, but there isn't any any more'. From a dialectical standpoint, to affirm that something is a success is also to posit the emergence of new contradictions, inherent in that very success. This is surely different from the disorder that would have attended some early failure. It is just such an emergence that has to be posited on the occasion of the recent events—about which I certainly agree that something happened, but not exactly what we have been told.

What happened is that suddenly a whole new world-system of late capitalism—a sudden breakthrough and expansion of the former system on an unparalleled global scale—came into being (or better still, was revealed to have come into being), in terms of which all the constituent parts and elements become radically revalued and structurally modified. Let me touch on three economic phenomena or categories in this respect: the national debt, efficiency, and productivity. One of the most mysterious developments in my own lifetime is the inexplicable passage from wealth to poverty of great nations which essentially remain unchanged as far as one can see: in the sixties everything was possible, from new schools and new welfare programmes to new wars and weapons; in the eighties, the same countries can no longer afford those things and everybody begins to mouth pious noises about the necessity of balancing the budget (a media unanimity which preceded and formulated the bleating unanimity on our present topics). But as Heilbroner and others have shown, not only would it be disastrous to pay off the national debt, it is essentially other countries who force us to balance our budget in the first place, by beginning to doubt our essential worth and soundness. A strong regime that enjoys the collective confidence of its people can perfectly well issue bonds and indulge in deficit spending, provided it is not obliged to worry about its standing in the eyes of its neighbours; but that worry is very precisely what is at issue when a formerly autonomous nation-state finds itself part of a world-system of the present kind. The same can be said for efficiency (and has been, by Paul Sweezy and Harry Magdoff long ago, on the occasion of the Chinese Revolution): even in modernizing situations efficiency in production is by no means an absolute and indispensable value—one can equally well imagine other priorities; for example, the industrial education or reeducation of peasants, or even the political education of industrial workers themselves and their training in self-management. But in a world-system, non-competitive industrial practices (and physical plants) clearly become a disaster, and drag a revolutionary collectivity down to sordid Third- or even Fourth-World status. Productivity is equally the result of a unified market, as Marx taught us long ago in *Capital*; it is not some timeless absolute either: what is perfectly productive in an isolated village or province suddenly drops to a very low level of productivity when its goods are juxtaposed with those of the metropolis in a more unified system. This is precisely what happened to the Soviet Union and its client states when they formed the project of plunging into the capitalist world-market; of linking their star—or, rather, chariot—to the newly emergent world-system of late capitalism that has come into being in the last twenty years.

Such were some of the thoughts that crossed my mind when I had occasion to have some discussions with intellectuals from a range of 'Eastern' countries, in a relatively more neutral one of those. On the very day of what used to be called 'reunification', but which is now oddly merely called the 'unification' of Germany, I stopped on my way in the formerly divided Berlin. I was struck by people's anxiety, their lack of anything but the most formal and official joyous enthusiasm (the all night long citywide party closely resembled the *Oktoberfest* or some prolonged and drunken American New Year's Eve). I was also struck by the dismay of the intellectuals on both sides: the chagrin of the West Berliners about to become something they always thought themselves to be different and distinct from, namely mere Germans—it is as though New Yorkers suddenly found themselves part of Ohio; the panic of East Berliners, most of whom were now out of a job, whatever their former employment. In the former East, all the scientific institutes have been shut down; the publishing houses have disappeared; expensive new cafés have suddenly appeared out of nowhere, in the wake of currency reunification; people with houses are preparing to be thrown out by Westerners with property claims dating back forty-five years; people in flats are preparing to see their rents triple or quadruple. Those in the West are also confronting a prodigious increase in rents and other expenses now that federal subsidies are about to disappear. It is promised that Berlin will be the new capital but it will also be a city full of unemployment, far to the Eastern border of the new Europe; once again a city of economic refugees from further East, as in the days of Weimar—Poles, Russians, Russian Jews—but without Weimar Berlin's wonderfully tawdry and suspect glitter and fascination. Nobody seems to want to think much about Weimar these days; the most prestigious exhibition in the city at the time of unificiation was an enormous life and times of Bismarck.

It does not meanwhile seem irrelevant to pause on the uniqueness of this changeover in systems, which the East Germans think of as a kind of colonization, and which surely has few historical precedents (if only for the obvious fact that social or socialist property relations have not existed before this century). More is at stake, clearly, than mere power; the displacement by the personnel of the victorious party of personnel of the vanquished one. I can myself only think of one distant analogy: namely, reconstruction in the American south after the Civil War, in which what was in that case a revolutionary change in political and property relations was implemented by a triumphant occupying military regime.

What happens to culture and politics after this particular Thermidor is discontinuous. It has for example been said[1] of recent West German 'neo-expressionistic' painters that they were lucky to have had Hitler as an inexhaustible source of raw material. If the War is now definitively over, then that material is clearly used up, along with the much-publicized Wall. The former West German intellectuals are people without a vocation, stumbling about in a witless search for this or that even minor cause; the former East German intellectuals meanwhile are dazed (they now have to catch up on their West German reading), while a few brave souls like Heiner Müller or Christa Wolf continue to defend the plausibility of the already unsuccessful idea of a possible East German cultural and political autonomy. Business as usual means land speculation and unemployment; while for the intellectuals it means the search for new topics and inspiration, and also for new forms of the perennial third party.

Of the lands further east I will only now be talking about Yugoslavia, Bulgaria and the Soviet Union; three very different places with relatively different preoccupations from each other, as well as from what I will—abusively and for the sake of convenience—call 'us', namely North Americans. That all three are unevenly obsessed with Stalin, his system or *nomenklatura*, is not so natural or self-evident as it might seem. That they are all profoundly convinced that 'we' (in the West) can understand nothing of this, that we cannot in the deeper senses even begin to imagine it, is probably less incomprehensible, since it is always the opening gambit in any serious international exchange to assert the originality of one's cards; it would be self-defeating to acknowledge that the other side already knows all about you in advance. Unfortunately Cold War anticommunism has lavishly supplied all possible and imaginable stereotypes along these lines in the course of the last forty-five years, most particularly in the 1940s and 50s; so that even experiential truth from the East now looks indistinguishable, not merely from media commonplaces and simulacra but from its most ancient Cold War forms. Here too then language and representation intervene to complicate the simplest forms of communication: the more their truths are couched in Orwellian language, the more tedious they become for us; the more our truths demand expression in even the weakest forms of Marxian language—that of simple social democracy say, or even the welfare state or social justice, or equality—the more immediately do the Eastern hearing aids get switched off.

For it is language itself, not only its individual words or message, that is situation-specific. In the West, Marxism as a code still gives a certain number of specific oppositional signals: disbelief in whatever liberal apologias for universal prosperity, social equality and political democracy are still current; scepticism about the ongoing collective benefits of production for profit, and specifically about the takeoff possibilities of 'minorities' either internal or external; a loathing for the new corporate style (if not for corporate culture, which often seems ambivalently to fascinate); or—to put all this positively—a profound conviction that the system itself as a structural unity cannot be reformed in either the pious traditional liberal sense or its cynically optimistic postmodern variant. In the West, then, the Marxian code is still the ultimate signal for a stubborn and lucid pessimism about 'the system' itself; a system which produces social misery as its necessary by-product and goes to war driven by an irresistible compulsion of which it is not even aware.

But in the East this same code means authority, the state and the police; attempting to change it means ending up in a discussion of why we need to use it in the first place, until the Westerners finally begin to grasp the fact that, virtually as a matter of toilet training, people in the East already think in Marxist ways without needing to say so. They are more interested in devising a wealth of new fables and figures (such as the image of mummification under socialism, by now virtually a stereotype of the newer literature), most of them turning on Stalin himself. It seems crucial for people to affirm that he was at one with a whole system: that is to say, first of all, that historical explanations of Stalinism by way of contingency and the dialectic are absolutely undesirable (the fully formed embryo being already present in Lenin himself, if not in Marx); and, conversely, that what exists in capitalism—famously baptized 'civil society'—is not a system at all but simply life itself, natural life, in its two major sub-varieties: private and public. The recent Western conception that civil society in this sense may itself be coming to an end in the corporate West, and that we no longer really have a public sphere in the classical sense, or a private one either—this could not be conveyed, even with the fanciest theoretical brand-names and wrapping.

But what Stalin means now is more interesting; no longer the terror or violence particularly, but three other things, each of which may strike us as peculiar: collectivity, utopia and modernism. One of the marks of the omnipotence of the media, even in its more rudimentary forms, is the way in which, for Eastern intellectuals, the word 'utopia' has become as automatically stigmatized as the words 'totality' and 'totalization' are for us—although in more limited circles no doubt, and for different reasons. The grotesque idea that Stalin represented the most illustrious embodiment of the utopian impulse; that his deepest drives, motives and projects were utopian in the purest sense (despite being occasionally and aberrantly compared to Hitler, whom surely no idea of utopianism could encompass) is now an unquestioned principle of doxa. It does no good to point out that utopia, or Lafargue's 'right to laziness', is hard to reconcile with the forced labour and primitive accumulation of value in early modernization and industrialization; the point here has nothing to do with facts, but rather with the intellectual's and the ideologue's will to model a seamless web of ideal values and positions, in which one automatically leads to the rest—in classical idealist or even religious fashion. History and events must, once again, be excluded from such moral ideal types, such ethical 'total systems', which, from the ethical religions onwards, remain the intellectual's preferred way of thinking about events; that is to say, from systems of idealism that turn events first into ideas before producing what look like iron-clad explanations but what are in fact rewarmed rehashings of our old friends Good and Evil. Old-fashioned materialism still has a mission here, it would seem, to break up—with its contingencies, its discontinuities, its accidents and its dialectical leaps—such moralizing views of history's 'total systems' that can be seen at work in our own seemingly post-idealistic postmodern philosophizing and theorizing, fully as much as in these now canonical anti-utopianisms from the East.

At a time when in the West a hegemonic philosophy has proclaimed the end, if not the death, of the subject, or the centred subject; the old inner-directed individual, the unique personality, if not the individual genius—at a time when other marginal or subaltern groups in the West are on the contrary speaking out for a conquest of local collective identities, which seem to offer the multiple shimmering of that same 'subject' that was supposed to have disappeared on the individual level—what is interesting is the sense in the former Soviet East, of the failure of the individual subject to constitute itself in the first place (I'm reminded of a Japanese colleague who observed that 'we' (Japanese) never needed deconstruction because we never had centred subjects to begin with). The absence of the moment of individualism in the Soviet East, staged with all the loss and pathos of a classic Habermasian unfinished project, is strengthened by the nightmarish vision of the Stalinian collective body—under the hegemony of which, as one theorist put it, 'bodies cannot exist separately'; or, as this is expressed by the great Soviet utopian writer Andrei Platonov, where the miseries of famine and civil war drive individual bodies to huddle together for warmth. Stalinism is thereby the deliberate plot or strategy whereby such a collective body was lashed together by force and terror—for what reason, of course, it is difficult to say without a certain dose of paranoia, even if one does not subscribe to the silliness of Orwell's 'lust for power'.

Much in current Soviet anti-utopianism seems to me, as I've said, derivative of the most banal Western anticommunism, largely consolidated as a rhetoric in the golden years of the 1950s; however, this part about the collective body seems to me relatively original, or at least never stressed or foregrounded in the same way by the ideologues of the Cold War. If they failed to do so, it was probably because, in the West, precisely such a vision of the collective body has tended to have utopian rather than dystopian overtones—but utopian now in the good, rather than Eastern and Stalinist bad, sense. Let's leave social psychology or human nature out of it, and lower the tone to a more banal form of psychological common sense: it does make sense to me that people suffering from an excess of individualism and anomie will be stirred by just such compensatory visions of collective life; while others, who have been huddled together for warmth for a long time, without a room of their own, as someone once put it in an analogous situation, would naturally enough develop a horror of togetherness in everyday situations, and would long for a little privacy as for the private property of the individual or individualist psyche. Indeed, the Russian participants in our conversations were very open about this experiential motivation behind the ostensible concept or value named anti-utopianism. These resonances, and the deeper unconscious family and childhood representations that accompany them in the form of affect, are not yet, in my opinion, political or social positions, but rather the libidinal machinery mobilized in political or class struggle (on either side, I may add).

But for us in the West, it is perhaps more interesting to tell this story another way, one which anticipates more fundamental East–West opposition which I will speak about in a moment. For the US version of huddling together—the great collective crisis in the American thirties that offers an equivalent to the famine, civil war and forced collectivization in the Soviet Union—was of course the Great Depression. Symbolically, the Depression meant for us not only collective huddling together, but also impoverishment and the stripping away of objects. It thus becomes 'natural' and a matter of 'common sense' that after the thirties have finally come to an end, after the great experience of World War II (the only true utopian moment in American history) and after the boom period of 1947–48, when shortages are finally overcome and all the new postwar products have begun to be marketed, what happens is a violent revulsion against the trauma of the previous decade. Now the horror of collective life is psychically compensated for by an individualism of consumption, by a security blanket of commodities and new objects of all kinds. Consumption in that sense is thus not in human nature as such: the passion for consumption is a historical, North American experience which has been reified and then projected out onto the rest of the world as a value, shorn of its symbolic meaning and transformed into something that looks like an attribute of some eternal human nature. It thereupon becomes equally 'natural' when the post-Eisenhower generation of the sixties, in its turn, reacts against this reaction against the collective by dreaming and acting out new forms of solidarity—against which the present generation of yuppies seems itself to be in full historical reaction. And this historically symbolic mode or generational alternation is of course also the way in which an Eastern anti-utopianism and horror of collectivity is to be understood.

The other feature of current Eastern or Soviet anti-utopianism which strikes me as truly original has to do with the aesthetic and with modernism; it is a position that has been worked out most program-matically by Boris Groys in his remarkable book, *Gesamtkunstwerk Stalin.*[2] The idea—and it is a striking and perverse, provocative historical revision, a scandalously fresh historical narrative, to replace some of the older more tired ones according to which the rise of aesthetic modernism has so often been told—consists in identifying two things and periods long held to be antithetical to one another, the great avant garde modernisms of the Soviet cultural revolution of the 1920s, and the dismal hegemony of a standard and stereotypical socialist realism that followed in the Stalin period. These two periods might for us in the West correspond to the supersession of the great aesthetic vanguards of the visual arts by the primacy of Hollywood and mass culture; and indeed, a previous and very exciting revision of Soviet art history had already been offered by Katarina Clark in her thesis that, in the USSR, socialist realism *is* mass culture as such. But for Groys and his generation (and I don't mean to attribute to him personally a position which now seems standard among the Soviet intelligentsia as a whole today), these two periods are not to be seen as a break but rather a continuity. For them, socialist realism, Stalinism and Stalin himself as a Wagnerian total work of art, are the continuation of the high modernist avant garde project by other means. Stalin is the true successor of Malevich; what the latter was unable to bring into being by fiat and dictatorship in the mystical realm of the spirit, the former brought into being in the realm of bodies in the real world. It had already been said of Hitler (by Syberberg) that he was the greatest twentieth-century film-maker; now however the Stalinist system as a whole is seen as the enactment of everything dictatorial and utopian in the high modernist project as a whole. The Gulag becomes the true Mallarméan *Livre*, or Book of the World, and daily life suffers under the burden of an ultimate fusion of aesthetics and politics that the futurists and surrealists could only live out in warfare or dreams. Whether or not this position is postmodern, it certainly implies the most thoroughgoing repudiation of the values of aesthetic high modernism that has ever been articulated in the postmodern era as a whole. Once again, it is Edmund Burke's old idea of the evils of intentionality—the damage done by planning and planification, the submission of all of the existent and the contingent to the single all-encompassing Will of the individual genius—which is the original sin, of both Joyce and Zhdanov; of Mallarmé, Picasso or Schoenberg; of Yezov and Vishynsky; of Ulbricht and of Gottwald; indeed, of Lenin himself.

This would then certainly seem to be the one propitious topic, in full Western postmodernism, for an East–West dialogue; it being understood that the Western argument about such matters would have to begin with Galbraith's fundamental observation that the Western or capitalist equivalent for planning in the East is called oligopoly, and that the capitalist West is no less an art work, no less subject to corporate decision and flat, arbitrary and isolated undemocratic will, than the Stalinist East—save that for us what is active is not the Politburo but the will of the corporations and the high modernist or postmodernist business community. If you feel, for example, that freedom has something to do with immunity from the arbitrary decisions of other, mostly unseen and unknown, people, what do you make of that corporate junk-language, American English, which incorporates boardroom decisions in shorthand and advertisting-type political and daily life slogans—such as 'lifestyle' itself, or 'smoke-free', or 'sexual preference' or indeed more philosophically laden verbal concepts such as 'anti-essentialist' or 'totalization'. That such linguistic decisions are taken by an essentially liberal-oriented hegemonic corporate culture does not particularly redeem them in the absolute, any more than the Marxian flavour of Stalin's culture redeemed it. (The explanation, however, would probably have something to do with the availability, to conservatives and reactionaries, of an older, already existing language or code for such matters; but in postmodernity, they are driven, in spite of themselves, into an apprenticeship to the corporate neologism.)

But even arguments of this kind, let alone dialogues, are difficult to sustain with our opposite numbers from the East; and the difficulty is not even related to basic informational doubts on either side—such as when our Eastern friends refuse to believe that the Americans engineered Allende's overthrow, or doubt (perhaps rightly) that we can ever be trusted fully to grasp what it was like to live under Stalin or Brezhnev. The principal difficulty, rather, lies in the utter disparity or incommensurability of the explanatory terms in which each side seeks to stage its discourse. To put it briefly, the East wishes to talk in terms of power and oppression; the West in terms of culture and commodification. There are really no common denominators in this initial struggle for discursive rules, and what we end up with is the inevitable comedy of each side muttering irrelevant replies in its own favourite language.

But this would be distressing only if you thought some noise-free communication between the various national and collective situations were possible in the first place. But with what is euphemistically called the 'new world order', we witness the return of all the national stereo-types (the nationalisms and neo-ethnicities are included within this process), and also a wellnigh Lacanian investment of fantasy in such images of the collective Other, about which it is essential to understand: that we can never do without them; and that they can never be 'accurate' or even corrected (whatever that might mean)—like readings and misreadings, they are necessarily and structurally distorted. The global dialogue is in that sense always a fascination on each side with what the other does not want to be.

At any rate, our own (Western) denial would probably sound something like this: The superstate—this enormously powerful and unconscious force, innocent of tragedy or history, deeply hypocritical in its moralizing Protestant heritage, and as dangerous for others as a football team or a rogue investment combined—these United States are now, after the sudden disappearance of the Soviet counterweight, as threatening for the outside world as a loose cannon. Although the differences in the very principle of the Soviet system offered a reassurance which the systemic kinship of the other powers scarcely affords, one might none the less have felt that the imminent emergence of the two other new superpowers—post-1992 Europe and Japan—would create some new balance of power in which North American irresponsibility could be safely contained. The recent conflict in the Gulf, however, does not speak well for this optimistic idea; less favourable still is the cultural conjunction itself.

We used to speak—now so long ago that it seems another epoch—about something called 'cultural imperialism'; it was seemingly concomitant with real imperialism, like a shipment of Hollywood film cans and boxes of hit cassettes loaded onto the gunboats. But it is a peculiar feature of such language—one that in many ways confirms the dialectic itself—that as its content fulfils itself and grows ever truer, more completely realized, its form falls away as though the words in which it was originally formulated had been a lie all the time without our realizing it. So it was with that form of modernization called, years ago, 'Americanization': as the process realized itself ever more faithfully, the term seemed ever more inept and unsatisfactory, being at length replaced by the word 'postmodernism', which still says it all, but also seems to deny the original attempt at naming the system.

Something like this also seems to me to have happened to the idea of cultural imperialism. Not untrue, indeed truer than ever, it has burst open the dead cocoon of its older name and spread its glamorous wings against a new sky, which it darkens with all the feeding frenzy of a plague of locusts. For in the era of postmodern global marketing strategies and of so-called 'post-Fordism',[3] the tyranny of the older product, the violent standardization and imposition of the American-style commodity (whether powdered milk, shampoo, fifties TV programming or armaments systems), seems to be at an end, and a new flexibility, difficult to reconcile with domination or hegemony, is the order of the day. Indeed, 'pluralism' itself, whether as a social and political slogan or a fact of theoretical and philosophical life, would seem to be a faithful superstructural reflection of post-Fordism: however, it links the phenomena of imperialism and domination much more intricately to the structures of commodification, making what was once a fairly open and evident kind of violence into subtle and metaphysical intricacies. The old Marcusean–Platonic question about false happiness then begins to return, as though it had, in its sixties form, been a mere anticipation of our own seemingly new and original cultural and political problems.

The guiding thread has to be the role of US corporate power (sometimes loosely and inaccurately called multinational)—something brought home vividly to me in an earlier trip to a new waterfront project in Rotterdam of which the city planners are most proud, which will replace the now-decaying docks and port facilities (modern, those, rather than postmodern) with a whole new complex of housing, entertainment and office buildings. Money will be made on this new urban 'inner colonization', to be sure, but the centrally controlled plan is in fact intended to avoid the disaster of the London docklands—a truly horrible example of 'deregulation' and of the desecration of city space by the speculators—and is indeed offered by and to students of architecture as another illustration of the way in which the older, modern, building of 'genius' has been in our time replaced by a new collective ensemble aesthetic of a type not witnessed since the age of Haussmann. It is thus with the grimmest surprise that the North American observer discovers the role of the Rouse corporation in all of this, American corporate advisers now playing the same role in postmodern global cultural development that their expert counterparts have played in counterinsurgency techniques and the training of local police forces. That this outfit, whose credentials are exhibited in Baltimore's harbourfront, and which is alleged to have deeper relations with the Disney empire, is the mover behind an old-world project on the eve of a united Europe will surely be a shock for anyone still clinging to some vestigial notion of cultural autonomy. Never mind the fact that the Russians and their friends, incapable of designing a proper hotel room, were obliged to call in the Hiltons for elementary pointers—that merely proved the bankruptcy of socialism! But here the oldest bourgeois culture in Europe—presumably still a fitting prototype for everything supposed to be distinctively European in style and *Weltanschauung*, in daily life and in social attitudes and priorities—turns out to have declared itself so culturally bankrupt in the postmodern age as to be obliged to call in the businessmen and commodity designers of a new world now older than they are; to supplement Rembrandt with Walt Disney, and the great social housing projects of the twenties and thirties with Epcot and Horton Plaza.

Can the prospect of political and economic autonomy be held out for the new Europe when—despite the proud nationalistic travelling mega-art shows of the various European nation-states—cultural autonomy proves there also to be so dismal a failure? That last hope, which in architecture was called 'critical regionalism', and which promised at least an attempt at the resistance of national and local styles to the new global Americanization—is that really still on the agenda in an age where any self-respecting American post-Fordist transnational understands the importance of packaging the product in the appropriate local colour and national style? Today cultural imperialism lies in the export of the experts: not even the national tradition is safe from them if they win; but can we still imagine their losing?

For those who may think all this pessimistic, may I now mildly suggest that we need not leave Nietzsche to the enemy, but rather find our own consolation in his deeply held conviction that only the deepest pessimism is the source of genuine strength. We must be deeply, unremittingly pessimistic about this system, just as my Eastern friends were about the other one; only for those who have nothing against being used and manipulated is optimism, of even the weakest variety, recommended.

March 1991

Notes

1. By Christo; what he thinks of the indebtedness to Stalin of recent Soviet painting is not recorded, but a similar position becomes a virtual manifesto in Boris Groys's book *Gesamtkunstwerk Stalin.*

2. Munich: Hanserverlag, 1988 (an English version is forthcoming from Princeton University Press in 1991).

3. Expertly characterized by Robin Murray as follows:

In contrast to the discount stores which are confined to a few, fast-selling items, Sainsbury's, like the new wave of high street shops, can handle ranges of products geared to segments of the market. Market niching has become the slogan of the high street. Market researchers break down market by age (youth, young adults, 'grey power'), by household types (dinkies, single-gender couples, one-parent families), by income, occupation, housing and, increasingly, by locality. They analyse 'lifestyles,' correlating consumption patterns across commodities, from food to clothing, and health to holidays.... The most successful manufacturing regions have been ones which have linked flexible manufacturing systems, with innovative organisation and an emphasis on 'customisation' design and quality. Part of the flexibility has been achieved through new technology, and the introduction of programmable machines which can switch from product to product with little manual resetting and downtime. Benetton's automatic dyeing plant, for example, allows it to change its colours in time with demand.

'Fordism and Post-Fordism', *New Times*, ed. Stuart Hall and Martin Jacques, London: Lawerence & Wishart 1989, pp. 43–4.

15

The Intellectuals in Power?

Iván Szelényi

The Intellectuals on the Road to Class Power, which I co-wrote with George Konrad in 1974,[1] ended with these sentences:

> Paradoxically, no transcendent intellectual activity is thinkable in Eastern Europe so long as intellectuals do not formulate the immanence of the intelligentsia's evolution into a class. That however must wait for the abolition of the ruling elite's hegemony and the consolidation of the power of the intellectual class as a whole. As to when that hypothetical third period of socialism will arrive, we can only say that when some East European publisher accepts this essay for publication it will be here, and not before.

(We had distinguished two earlier periods of socialism: Stalinism, in which the bureaucracy monopolizes power, and Brezhnevism, in which the bureaucracy begins to open up to the intelligentsia but retains a hegemonic position.)

In November 1989, amidst crumbling walls and Communist regimes, our book finally was published in Budapest by Gondolat, a government-owned publishing company. We owe answers to a few questions our readers may pose:

1. Is this an indication that intellectuals form a dominant class; does this support the claim that with the rise of Gorbachev to power one could detect a revitalization of the 'New Class project'?
2. If the answer to this question is yes, is the newly won power of the intellectuals a lasting phenomenon or just a brief era of transition? If it is likely to constitute a whole *epoch*, can it be called 'socialist' in any meaningful way?

A proper answer to these questions would require more time and distance from current events. During the summer of 1989, after discussing these issues with Konrad in Budapest, we thought that we might eventually write a 'second volume' on intellectuals and power. All we can do at this moment is offer a few working hypotheses.

My answer to the first question is a qualified *yes*. The bureaucratic rank collapsed all over in Eastern Europe and is in a shambles even in the USSR. This is consistent with the New Class theory we offered in *The Intellectuals on the Road to Class Power* in two ways.

First: intellectuals—or, to be more specific, what could be called the intellectualization of the bureaucracy—undoubtedly played a significant role in the rather unexpected collapse of Communism, in the bloodless 'velvet revolutions' against the bureaucracy, and in the astonishing readiness of the elite to dissolve itself and its organizations, such as the Communist Party.

One of the reasons why the bureaucracy demonstrated so little resistance can be attributed to the changing pattern of recruitment into the party and state bureaucracy over the last two decades. In Hungary, at least during the Kádárist consolidation, the Party consciously tried to appeal to the highly educated and went out of its way to bring good young professionals into *nomenklatura* positions, in particular into the Party apparatus.

As these 'Communist yuppies' replaced the old-line bureaucrats, the ethos of the Party apparatus changed. These young professional cadres, unlike those recruited from the working class and peasantry, did not depend exclusively on political bosses. Their personal fate is not tied to the future of the Party. If their Party job goes, they believe that with their marketable skills they can return to their professions and earn better salaries by working for multinational corporations than by working for the Party.

This has turned out to be a highly bourgeoisified Party elite, whose loyalties do not lie with Communism. While some critics of *The Intellectuals on the Road to Class Power* ridiculed us for thinking that a Party cadre member can be an intellectual, our prediction about the intellectualization of the bureaucracy—with its consequently devastating impact on the bureaucratic rank's order—proved to be a surprisingly accurate one.

Second: there is a power vacuum today in Eastern Europe. The old elite has collapsed; in the absence of a domestic bourgeoisie, the only serious contender to replace them is the intelligentsia.

A new political class is in formation, and this emergent new elite is exclusively recruited from the intelligentsia. Its members are historians, economists, sociologists, jurists, media-professionals. They all claim power—they all aspire to positions such as members of parliament, government ministers, presidents and mayors—on the grounds of their expertise as professionals.

If one wants to describe the power structure of Eastern Europe today (the last days of January 1990), it can fairly confidently be characterized by the power struggles between different fractions of the intelligentsia. In Hungary, society, silently and quite apathetically, watches this struggle. The new elite freezes wages and boosts prices, tries to control strikes and offers Lenin shipyard in Gdansk, the birthplace of *Solidarność* in 1980, to Mrs Barbara Piasecka-Johnson, a US millionaire, while promising her industrial peace.

Undoubtedly intellectuals today in Eastern Europe have more power than they have ever had in their history. And what used to be a conflict between 'society and powers' is rapidly becoming a conflict between intellectual elites and the rest of the society.

My answer to the second question is: I do not know. Intellectuals usually play a prominent, vanguard role in revolutionary social change, when one social formation collapses and a new one is emerging. But these vanguard intellectuals usually are unable to keep the power that they grab during revolutions.

As the new social order consolidates itself, they lose their power and surrender some of their political privileges to other classes or social categories, such as the propertied bourgeoisie or the bureaucracy—the former happened after the French Revolution, the latter after the Russian.

Will the intelligentsia be able to set a new historic precedent this time? Will it keep its power, constituting itself as a genuine new class which can reproduce itself in the position of power? Or will it simply surrender its power to a new bourgeoisie? In other words, is the current revolution other than a probably historically brief transition from socialism or Communism to capitalism?

I think that at the current historic conjuncture it is impossible to answer this question. The social formation that exists at present in Eastern Europe is unquestionably *not a capitalist* formation. *Eastern Europe today is a socialist mixed economy* with a dominant statist sector, or state mode of production—which still employs full time probably up to 85–90 per cent of the labour force—combined with a rapidly growing private sector. In terms of its economic institutions and social structure, then, contemporary Eastern Europe is almost exactly what George Konrad and myself predicted the third epoch of socialism would be.

At the same time, there are indications of the total collapse of the statist sector. A significant fraction of the intelligentsia by now wants to 'go all the way'. Liberalism is the major political ideology, which, coupled with neo-classical economics and with deep sympathies toward the economic policies of Margaret Thatcher and Ronald Reagan, calls for 'shock therapy' for an unrestrained re-privatization, for the whole-sale, unrestricted transformation of public property into private property.

This re-privatization may mean just transforming the public firms into the private property of managers—according to Elemer Hankiss and Jadwiga Staniszkis a great deal of this is happening both in Hungary and in Poland—or it may mean transferring Hungarian and Polish firms into the hands of foreigners, sometimes for real but more frequently for symbolic amounts of money.

This process of re-privatization to foreign capital took place in Hungary under the tutelage of Mr Palmer, US ambassador to Budapest. In an interview granted to the *New York Times* in January 1990, he talked about a 'gold fever' in Hungary, comparing Budapest to a 'boom town'. A week later he resigned his ambassadorial position, announcing his acceptance of a job as the chief executive of the investment firm that funds Hungarian re-privatization. What a smart man. He knows what he is talking about.

This sudden and somewhat unexpected opening to capitalism created new perspectives for East European intellectuals. I would not be surprised if the young Hungarian prime minister, a Harvard-trained economist known to be Mr Palmer's tennis partner, emerges eventually as a board member of one of the new 'joint ventures', and I would not be worried about his future, either professionally or financially, after the electoral defeat of his party (the successor of the Communist Party) in March 1990. There is a New Class project unfolding in Eastern Europe, but it may not last long. Just by the time the intelligentsia gets hold of power, it may let it slip away.

Intellectuals may decide they are more interested either in well-paid jobs at multinational corporations, or in becoming private proprietors—a new bourgeoisie themselves—either by receiving rewards from the foreign investors for whom they facilitate good deals or by figuring out ways to transform their positions as managers into proprietors of the formerly public firms.

Anyway, I just do not know at present which way Eastern Europe may go. Does it have a chance to consolidate itself in a mixed economy? This would mean preservation of a significant portion of its state sector, with the unleashing of some private business. In this dual economy a dual structure may emerge: A social balance may be created between bureaucracy and a new bourgeoisie under supervision of a 'super-master', the political class of the intelligentsia.

But it is equally possible that Eastern Europe will go all the way to market capitalism. My liberal friends in Hungary enthusiastically believe this will mean 'joining Europe'. I hope they are right, but I fear they are wrong. 'Europe' is a long way from Eastern Europe, which never belonged to the West and moved rapidly East over the last forty years. A big jump from where these countries are now right into Western Europe impresses me as a courageous if somewhat adventurous move.

If this jump is not forceful enough, the region may land not in Stockholm or Amsterdam—where it is aspiring to be—but rather in Istanbul, Seoul or Honduras, where Hungarians, Poles and Romanians may not feel that comfortable.

The punch-line: yes, intellectuals gained a lot of power, more than critics of the New Class theories or of *The Intellectuals on the Road to Power* usually liked to admit would ever be possible. But who knows if they can hold on to this power? They probably will not, and, like vanguard intellectuals after the 'big bang', they will pass their power on to some other historical agent.

In this case that new agent will most probably be international capital.

Note

1. Translated by Andrew Arato and R.E. Allen and published in English translation in 1979.

16

Whose Left?
Socialism, Feminism and the Future*

Lynne Segal

Political generations appear and disappear with astonishing speed. Thirty years ago, as a budding anarchist and sixties student radical, I shared with certain others of my generation and class a politics of generalized anti-authoritarianism and free love. In Australia at the time, coming out of the rigid conformity of the Cold War, such a politics was not as vapid as it sounds today. The Communist Party was banned outright, along with James Joyce, James Baldwin, and any sex at all that dared to speak its name. Non-white people were denied entry into Australia, black Australians were denied legal rights, even the right to vote, and devotion to monarchy, marriage and hyper-hypocrisy remained our sacred birthright. We read Reich, Nomad and Bakunin, remaining oddly innocent of any more solid socialist tradition.

Ten years later, student anarchism quickly transformed itself into the more class-oriented, anti-imperialist libertarian socialism of the seventies. In Britain now, I joined those attempting to win 'Power for the People' on the streets of London, in the local struggles of the day. And, just in time—as a single parent and comical colonial relic—I discovered women's liberation, then closely linked in with alternative or libertarian socialism.

Two decades on again, and it is hard indeed for socialist and movement activists of the sixties and seventies to contemplate the passing of our own one and only (and the Left's hopefully more cyclical) heyday. Today, depression, cynicism or political turnabouts are hard to avoid, even knowing we are not the first—and will not be the last—to face the defeat and disorderly retreat of the ideals, activities and lifestyles that transformed and gave meaning to our lives. Depression hits hardest when the withering of former struggles and aspirations begins to feel like personal defeat; often ending the friendships, the shared activities and the opening up of public spaces, so necessary for the survival of any sense of optimism in the future. The excitement of believing in the possibility of collective action for change has been replaced by the gloom of witnessing the erasure of the history of such struggles: an erasure which stems not only from the mainstream media, but from sections of the Left as well, busy exchanging new ideas for old, or else recoiling memoryless from the corpse of Soviet socialism.

Libertarian Socialism

Yet for over three and a half decades most Western socialists had battled not only against the destructive consequences of capitalist development, but also against Stalinism and the stifling, authoritarian regimes of Soviet-style state or bureaucratic socialism. And now, just when in Britain more people seem a little more aware again of some of the problems accompanying the inequalities tolerated, indeed promoted, by the unregulated free market of Thatcherism—if only to welcome the minor shift to Major—and just when, in the East, Stalinism is finally in irreversible retreat, those who worked hardest and longest for a more democratic socialism seem most silenced. Ten years of defeat for almost all egalitarian and collectivist endeavours has caused many of us on the Left to fall into chronic mutual abuse, to fall upon our own swords, or to fall—some never to rise again— on to the analytic couch.

The resounding victory for the conservative alliance in Eastern Germany, the one country of the Soviet bloc which appeared to have a democratic Left opposition in New Forum, has been registered by many across the political spectrum as the proof that socialism of any kind will never have popular appeal. In fact, New Forum, a heterogeneous alliance of peace, environmental and human-rights activists under the umbrella of the Church, was never itself organized as a *political*, let alone a *socialist*, opposition. Its recent dramatic rise and fall tells us much about the extreme isolation of dissident intellectuals in East Germany, as well as the effectiveness of four decades of Stalinist rule in massively discrediting and impoverishing both socialist *and* democratic ideals and values.

What inspired the upsurge of Western radicalism in the sixties, which in turn spawned the feminist and other movements of the seventies, was never, in any case, 'actually existing socialism'. Every type of anarchist, dreamer, utopian, syndicalist, Trotskyist, pacifist, revolutionary, reformist and third roader appeared in the radical metropolitan scene at that time, but one rarely encountered a Stalinist, a command-economy 'socialist', the creature whose aspirations and beliefs today apparently typify 'socialism' itself, although we were all aware of their existence. Anti-Stalinism was our common home, the place from which we all began, the air we breathed. The 'Party' member was, and remains to me, something of a puzzle: critical of Soviet societies, committed to democratic transition, but until recently (before some, like Gorbachev, swung over to become apparently uncritical allies of the market) still prepared to defend the obviously bleak and authoritarian, undemocratic Soviet regimes. The Leninist and social-democratic Left *shared* the belief that their own parties (despite mirroring existing race, gender and, in the main, class hierarchies) could be trusted to administer a centralized state in the interests of all working people and their dependents: the former after the revolution, and the latter on election.

It was precisely these vanguardist and bureaucratic beliefs, precisely these hierarchical and centralized structures, that were *rejected* by New Left writers like E.P. Thompson, Raymond Williams and Stuart Hall from the late fifties, as well as by the emerging social movements from the late sixties—the largest and most influential, of course, being the women's liberation movement. They sought instead more devolved and participatory structures of organization and practice, which could empower people in their communities and workplaces. In one sizable segment of the independent or non-aligned Left that flourished in Britain in the 1970s, influenced by and often overlapping with the women's movement and other liberation struggles, 'democracy'—today's 'new' buzz-word—was fetishized: steering committees had to rotate regularly, skills had to be shared to prevent the growth of bureaucracy, committees sought equal representation of women and men, and discussion endlessly picked over the problem of the under-representation of Black, working-class and other subordinated groups. Indeed, if anything, the lack of commitment to working out types of viable and responsive centralized economic planning—today's new bogey word—or to building national structures capable of providing long-term support for grass-roots initiatives, was the problem for this part of the Left. The socialist case for some form of public ownership remains as strong as ever, if only because, despite the failures of the past, it alone provides the greatest possibilities for using resources and labour in ways which are more egalitarian, innovative and supportive.

The participatory democratic ideals of the libertarian Left never had a mass appeal, but they did play a critical role in grass-roots agitation over the most diverse array of popular needs and interests throughout the 1970s. Whether campaigning around single issues, foregoing careers to establish local information and resource centres, creating housing or workplace cooperatives, attempting to change local or national state policies, or supporting international struggles, the problems of that Left were many. But they were not those of adopting coercive, bureaucratic or economistic ideas and practices. Even though goals often bore slight relation to achievements, they were not those of ignorance of or un-concern about male-domination, class privilege, racism, homophobia or other forms of invalidation and exclusion long associated with more traditional labour movement and Left party politics.

By the close of the seventies, this Left, which had widened its own socialist agendas to include personal relations and social identities, was facing increasing problems building support and maintaining optimism against the combined obstacles fast overwhelming it: economic recession and the Right in power. It was the growing difficulties of finding strategies to overcome fragmentation and of forming new alliances that were to lead many into closer engagement with the machinery of local government and other mainstream institutions in the 1980s, moving outside the demoralization of dwindling autonomous bases for jobs or other forms of contact inside the state or perhaps trade-union structures. These internal weaknesses in libertarian socialism, which contributed to its inability to withstand Thatcher, need to be studied. But what we have seen instead—for example in the 'new' politics of *Marxism Today*—is merely the removal of its innovations and influences (full recognition of autonomous groups, multiple sites of oppression, rejection of vanguardism and authoritarianism) from the messy terrain of political engagement into the calmer waters and cosier spaces of cultural studies.

A Wilful, Deliberate Forgetting

'With the onset of economic recession the libertarian Left died out in the early 1980s', Jonathan Rutherford declares in his introduction to the latest Lawrence and Wishart collection of essays, *Identity*.[1] But Rutherford's burial of this particular socialist tradition is premature, indeed illustrative of the very problem it faced. The early to mid eighties actually saw a resurgence of alternative Left ideas, still committed to creating structures and resources for grass-roots democracy and the recognition of the diversity of subordinated groups, finally beginning to influence the mainstream Left of the Labour Party and labour move-ment. It would be foolish to ignore the problems or exaggerate the significance of the burst of creativity and democratic and egalitarian hopes raised when, for example, the Labour Left took control of the Greater London Council in 1981 and opened its doors for direct dis-cussion with Black and women's groups, trade unionists or housing coop-eratives, seeking to channel institutional power and resources into marginalized and disadvantaged sectors organizing on their own behalf. But it is even more foolish to 'forget', within a few short years, that such attempts were made. A wilful, deliberate forgetting.

The GLC's economic-policy unit under Robin Murray was, ironically, the first to theorize post-Fordism in Britain, as it ambitiously set out to find ways of encouraging viable alternative forms of industrial production which might, though adopting more human, creative and egalitarian employment practices, nevertheless survive the rigours of multinational competition. We cannot assess the ultimate fate of these initiatives, as within a few short years the GLC and its policy units were closed down. By the mid 1980s Thatcher's generals, having provoked and defeated every trade-union struggle since their election, knew just where next to direct their fire. Ignoring overwhelming opposition and the widespread personal popularity of Ken Livingstone, Thatcher first abolished the GLC and other metropolitan councils outright, and then launched one attack after another on the capacity of local government to provide any focus or hope for popular resistance.

Yet throughout most of the 1980s, right up until the third Thatcher victory in 1987 (and in pockets still today), more libertarian, less bureaucratic ideas kept emerging in the new terrain of local government and in women's and other sections of the trade unions, which, *significantly*, effected official recognition of issues of racism, sexism, harassment, abuse and other forms of specific discrimination, while for a time at least providing some focus for creative if conflict-ridden interaction with political activists—whether Black, feminist, or collective consumer campaigners. But these developments were also to highlight some of the weaknesses which can follow from commitment to notions of the absolute autonomy of each oppressed group to organize itself and assert its own needs and identity. Splits and hostilities rapidly appear, often demoralizing if not immobilizing the pursuit of political ends, as one group competes against another, claiming the mantle of the most oppressed.

Incessant problems spring to life when attempting to rethink our concepts of democracy in practice, attempting to move beyond the limitations of either representative democracy or purely individual understandings of rights, towards the dismantling of inequalities. But rather than assessing such problems in practice, this politics of autonomy has been adapted for the 'New Times' outlined in *Marxism Today* and re-theorized, as though quite new, to become the politics of 'identity' or (confusingly displaying its deep ambivalence) of 'difference'. But old songs resung by different bards, now more removed from sites of political engagement, will not overcome the rifts arising when autonomy becomes fragmentation, and the mere affirmation of difference replaces strategic thought—whatever the hopeful appeal to the thinking of Laclau and Mouffe, who suggest we may call upon some conceptual 'chain of equivalence' between different identities.[2]

Identity Politics, Feminism and 'Difference' Theory

The problem is that social identities are not necessarily or even desirably political identities.[3] Nothing illustrates this better than the pains and perils of contemporary feminism. We may wish to celebrate our lives as women, but be desperately seeking to cast aside the bewitching female romance of virtue and maternal connectedness: the identity of woman as we have known it, and attempted, so hazardously, to live it. No clear political strategies follow from our either embracing or rejecting a gendered identity as such. In the name of women's specific needs and interests, women have fought progressively for peace and public welfare. But they have also at times made 'cowards' of reluctant warriors, and opposed women's professional, creative and employment prospects. In the name of shared human rights, women have fought tenaciously against exclusion from the economic, political and cultural citadels men dominate. But this may also invalidate the significance of inter-dependence and community, a reality that can weigh so heavily upon the backs of women.

Pointing out the inevitability of women's oscillation around their gendered identities, and the need to embrace rather than reject or attempt to transcend its multiple contradictions, US feminist Ann Snitow points out: 'The urgent contradiction women constantly experience between the pressure to be a woman and the pressure not to be one will change only through a historical process; it cannot be dissolved through thought alone.'[4] Yet feminism has torn itself apart over the recurring divisions between those who stress the similarities and those, increasing in number and influence since the late 1970s, who stress the differences between women and men.[5] As constructed within contemporary feminism, the former have tended to pursue strategies for equality and power sharing, the latter to assert the significance of 'maternal' ways to celebrate 'female' pleasures and to denounce and seek protection from 'male' violence and abuse. But outside feminist thought, women have stressed either similarity or difference with quite other objectives in mind: perhaps to assert similarity in constructing a shared superiority over 'inferior breeds', perhaps to stress gender difference in deference to the word of God the Father, or in the service of more mortal *Führers*.

The point is that identities do not spring directly from gender, class,

race or ethnic position, or from sexual, religious or any other particular
orientation, so much as from a sense of belonging to specific social and
historical milieux. The strength and confirmation that context can offer,
and the currently unfashionable consideration of its political orientation
on the Left/Right divide, will determine whether the contemporary
Western proliferation of identities offers new forms of resistance, or
conservative retrenchments in the face of change.

Within feminism, these conflicts and the extent to which gender
similarities or differences have been the focus of debate, are not unconnected to feminism's declining relationship to socialism from the
close of the seventies, which in turn is not unconnected to the declining
fate of socialism itself. Little more than a decade ago many feminists
who were also socialists still believed (despite the difficulties of working
with the traditional Left and the labour movement) that what was
important and distinctive about our politics was its capacity to change
and enrich male-centred socialist agendas and theories to include
women's experience, personal life and cultural politics, alongside the
interests of all oppressed groups. Today, with the Left itself battling to
survive a cold destructive climate, more would agree with the North
American feminist Zillah Eisenstein, a leading theoretician of socialist
feminism in the USA in the 1970s, who recently declared—adapting to
what she sees as new realities, rather than expressing anger or sectarian
sentiment—that 'the specification of feminism *as* socialist has little
political context today'.[6] Socialism, she feels, seems to hold out little
promise for women, and the radical edge of feminism is now to be maintained through a focus on 'the particularities of women's lives'. In agreement with those known as 'difference theorists', Eisenstein now argues
that it is in their specific identity as women that feminists should seek a
politics which unites all women through the assertion and revaluing of
our experience of 'difference'.

Illustrating her argument, Eisenstein cites the feminist struggle over
reproductive rights: 'the starting point for theory and politics here is
both the individual (her specificity) and her right to reproductive
freedom (which is universal)'.[7] But, despite the importance of the issue
of abortion, this is a less than convincing strategy for a common political
struggle to unite all women. Nothing, in fact, so *polarizes* women,
including a small number of women who call themselves feminists, as the
issue of abortion: the main and ferocious opponents of women's
abortion rights in the West are other women. They fight their battle—
blowing up clinics and terrorizing pregnant women—expressly in
defence of women's specificity, women's difference (backed, of course,
by the Catholic Church, and other forces of the Moral Right).

It is precisely the issues arising from what is most distinctively female that today most dramatically *divide* rather than unite feminists fighting for women's interests. Feminists stressing 'difference' unsurprisingly emphasize the female body, sexuality and human reproduction (or, in the more sophisticated versions of 'French feminism', the unconscious and psychic meanings attaching themselves to the female body and maternal experience). Yet it is easier for women to unite over demands on the economic front than it is for women to unite around sexuality and the meanings of the female body. While many feminists now give most of their time and energy to combatting 'pornographic' representations of sexuality and the female body as the root of women's oppression, others battle against what they see as sex-negative positions on pornography (or erotica) which threaten to enclose women anew in repressive, patriarchal fictions of female virtue.[8]

That there is such fierce disagreement over what many see as the bedrock of feminism is not so surprising. At least it is not so surprising once we recognize the complexities at the heart of all talk about 'identities'. We can never stress enough, it seems to me, that both 'femininity' and 'masculinity' are always more complex and nuanced than any cultural symbolism can register.[9] That which at one minute we may wish to embrace, in defiance of shared oppression, we may, at the next, wish to discard as trapping us within traditional cultural discourses, institutions and practices. The celebration of female specificity makes use of the existing structures of meaning that establish sexual difference, which as feminists we also need to contest, even when we try to invert the existing androcentric system of values that accompany such difference. Women as women, however oppressed, do not necessarily adopt oppositional identities. Indeed, the reverse is more likely. This paradox of difference theory for feminists is shared, I believe, by any politics of identity, as divisions inevitably proliferate both inside and around the assertion of any specific identity.

Does Feminism Need Socialism?

It is certainly true that twenty years of feminism have *failed* to improve the economic and social position of all women, although they have brought many gains for some. This is as true in Britain as in most other Western countries. But nowhere is it quite so clear, nowhere are the contrasts between the lives of women after twenty years of feminism quite so stark, or the conflicts within feminism and their declining relationship to socialism quite so dramatic, as in the United States. The USA best illustrate the problems around feminism, identity politics and the Left.

Despite the existence of the largest, most influential and vociferous feminist movement in the world, it is US women who have seen least *overall* change in the relative disadvantages of their sex, compared to other Western democracies. As Barbara Ehrenreich illustrates, within the professional middle class, women have made huge gains, increasing their representation among the most prestigious and lucrative professions by 300 to 400 per cent within a decade.[10] They have also cracked open the corporate business world, in which 30 per cent of managerial employees are now women, while Masters' graduates from business school jumped from 4.9 per cent in 1973 to 40 per cent by 1986.[11] But outside the professional middle class, the situation for many women has been one of frustration, defeat and, for a significant number, increasing misery.

The first big defeat for the women's movement in the USA came in 1977 when the initial Hyde amendment was passed and Medicaid abortion was withdrawn, just four years after the right to abortion, affordable for women of all classes, had been won. The next, deeply symbolic defeat, ensuring frustration and retrenchment for feminist organizers and activists throughout the USA, came with the dismantling of the ERA (Equal Rights Amendment), exactly ten years after its resounding success when passed in 1972. Meanwhile, and connected with the defeat of ERA (as women of the New Right like Phyllis Schlafly mobilized around the slogan 'STOP ERA'), the Reagan decade of the 1980s had ushered in massive welfare cuts and steep increases in poverty—especially among Black and ethnic-minority women and men. More women, particularly women raising children on their own, were not only poorer than women of their class and race had been twenty years earlier, but their poverty, with new spending cuts, became the more disabling. (They now battle to survive and raise children in an environment where, it is said, more people have been murdered in the streets of New York in the last fifteen years than Americans died in the Vietnam war.[12])

In this time of triumphal victory for the Right, some formerly self-declared feminists, like Sylvia Ann Hewlett, have drawn massive media attention by blaming feminism for the current plight of so many women in the USA. Feminism failed to protect women who are mothers, she accuses; claiming, falsely, that it never made demands of the state around child care and welfare.[13] Hewlett now opposes all equal-rights legislation in favour of an exclusive focus on child-care support for women. But her argument that it is women, and women alone, who in the end perform all the labour of caring is itself a capitulation to the very cornerstone of conservative thinking: the thinking that has overseen the deterioration in the lives of the poor, rewarded the rich, and—with its traditional family rhetoric and judicial removal of relevant funding—

fought till it has all but smashed the seventies' feminist vision of moving beyond existing gendered conceptions of 'public' and 'private' to a world where nurturing and instrumental tasks could be mutually shared by women and men.

The growing immiseration of the US poor was not a product of the failure of feminist equal-rights and affirmative-action programmes for women; indeed many succeeded. It resulted from the now historic weakness of the US labour movement in protecting either male or female workers' rights, or winning any comprehensive welfare system.[14] From its already battered and shrunken state in the early 1950s (around 30 per cent), after direct attacks from both corporate capital and the state, trade-union membership declined calamitously in the USA, down to its current 17 per cent. And, as research like that of Pippa Norris and others indicates, political parties and the level of trade unionism do seem to matter in assessing women's relative disadvantages compared to men. In countries where there have been longer periods of social-democratic government and stronger trade unions, there is far less pay-differential and occupational segregation (both vertical and horizontal) between women and men, and far greater expansion of welfare services. In Sweden, that familiar example in many ways similar to other Scandinavian countries, where the Social Democratic Party has been in government since the 1920s and trade unionism in both the public and private sector is around 90 per cent, we find the highest levels of welfare spending and the lowest discrepancy between women and men's wages (women's wages are around 87 per cent of men's).[15]

Given that the USA is the *only* major Western democracy where women have failed to improve their wages at all relative to men's over the last two decades (remaining at 59 per cent of men's hourly wage, compared to Britain's 69 per cent), and given the favourable contrasts between the Scandinavian countries and the USA regarding child-care facilities and other welfare benefits (again, Britain comes somewhere in between), as well as women's proportionately far higher representation in parliament, it seems strange for feminists to ignore the traditional objectives of socialist or social-democratic parties and organized labour in their search for feminist goals and strategies, whatever their limitations and weaknesses, and however much their successes have depended on the hard and difficult slog of women within them. At a time when the advances made by some women are so clearly overshadowed by the increasing poverty experienced so acutely by others (alongside the unemployment of the men of their class and group), it seems perverse to pose women's specific interests *against* rather than *alongside* more traditional socialist goals.[16]

The question is whether, as so many now feel and Eisenstein

expresses, 'socialism seems to hold out little new theoretical or political promise for feminism'.[17] The answer, I suggest, depends upon where you look, and whether you allow what has been the most creative and dynamic rethinking on the Left to be forgotten, or perhaps resuscitated as flimsier new fashions eager to flaunt their distance from what remains of the theoretical and organizational strengths of the 'old' (New) Left and labour movement. Today's critics who would say goodbye to socialism for a politics which recognizes 'the centrality of difference' usually reject as inevitably oppressive the 'totalizations' of *any* socialist project in the name of the 'irreducible plurality and indeterminacy' of the social. Yet the force of their argument (esoteric philosophical con-fusions aside) comes from what should by now be *familiar* criticisms of Leninist and Labourist forms of socialist politics. That Marxism, let alone the Left, rarely did and does not now reduce to either Leninism or Labourism is ignored, along with the writings of Marx and Engels them-selves, not to mention the libertarian critics of Lenin.

There are many weaknesses in the Marxism that has inspired most of the Left for over a hundred years—its economism, homogenizing of class interests, and inability adequately to theorize the position of women and other non-class oppressions. But that tradition was never *synonymous* with the elitism and authoritarianism that has characterized Leninist notions of the vanguard party substituting itself for mass support, any more than it was synonymous with the paternalism that has character-ized Fabian notions of the democratic state reforming from above and hostile to extra-parliamentary culture, movements and struggles.

Today we face a cultural climate where much of the Left, like those associated with 'Charter 88', has moved so far to the right that nineteenth-century liberalism has become its centre. Few people across the political spectrum could object to a project that seeks 'a constitution which protects *individual* rights and the institutions of a *modern* and *pluralistic* democracy'. The USA has precisely such a Constitution, as does Colombia. At a time when Thatcher was so aggressively attacking existing democratic rights, 'Charter 88' provided a rallying point for a broad oppositional democratic alliance. It also highlighted the many anachronistic structures of the existing British state—from the House of Lords to the nature of the judiciary. However, it left open for debate the crucial issue of whether social needs for health, housing, education and adequate welfare, which must be met *before* people can put to any good use their rights as citizens, should be guaranteed as well. In the face of the real economic and cultural factors which limit the participation of many in active citizenship (not least the many women whose primary relationship to the state is one of dependence rather than autonomy), the Charter once again exposes the very real limits of liberalism, however progressive, articulated over a hundred years ago in the contradictions of John Stuart Mill.[18]

Desperate to adapt in this new cultural climate, there was little discernible trace of socialist strategies in the most recent Labour Party Policy Review. Much of the Trotskyist Left, on the other hand, which has now taken up some of the rhetoric of the new social movements around women, Blacks, gays and lesbians, has done so only, or primarily, as part of a politics of confrontation with what remains of the reformist structures of social democracy in local government and the trade unions.

But, before we say goodbye to socialism, should we not take the time to learn from the mistakes of the past, and reject, as did the social movements of the seventies, the centralized, authoritarian, top-down practices of *both* social democracy and Leninism? Should we not also pause a moment to recognize the weaknesses of the new social movements themselves? Without access to the resources of strengthened social-democratic reformist structures, as decentralized and accountable as possible, and without strong trade unions, the social movements (particularly as conceived by the theorists of difference) can offer little more than the enjoyment of an endless game of self-exploration played out on the great board of Identity.

January 1991

Notes

*This article is an expanded version of a talk delivered to the Radical Philosophy Conference, 'Values, Resistance and Social Change', at the Polytechnic of Central London, in November 1990.

1. Jonathan Rutherford, 'A Place Called Home', in J. Rutherford, ed., *Identity: Community, Culture, Difference*, London 1990, p. 14.

2. See, for example, Chantal Mouffe, 'Radical Democracy or Liberal Democracy?', *Socialist Review*, vol. 90, no. 2, 1990, p. 63.

3. For a useful exposition and critique of the thinking of Laclau and Mouffe along these lines, see Peter Osborne, 'Radicalism Without Limit?: Discourse, Democracy and the Politics of Identity', in P. Osborne, ed., *Socialism and the Limits of Liberalism*, Verso, London 1991.

4. Ann Snitow, 'A Gender Diary', in M. Hirsch and E. Fox Keller, eds., *Conflicts in Feminism*, New York 1990, p. 19.

5. For a fuller exploration of the development of these conflicts in British and North American feminism over the last two decades, see Lynne Segal, *Is the Future Female?: Troubled Thoughts on Contemporary Feminism*, London 1987.

6. Zillah Eisenstein, 'Specifying US Feminism in the 1990s: The Problem of Naming', *Socialist Review*, vol. 90, no. 2, 1990, p. 48 (emphasis in original).

7. Ibid., p. 53.

8. See Ann Ferguson, 'Sex War: The Debate between Radical and Libertarian Feminists', *Signs* 10, 1984; Estelle Freedman and Barrie Thorne, 'Introduction to the Feminist

Sexuality Debates', *Signs* 10, 1984; Carol Vance, ed., *Pleasure and Danger: Exploring Female Sexuality*, London 1984; Catherine MacKinnon, *Feminism Unmodified: Discourses on Life and Law*, Cambridge, Mass. 1987; J. Dickey, ed., *Feminism and Censorship*, Bridport 1988.

   9. This is the theme of my latest book, *Slow Motion: Changing Masculinities, Changing Men*, London 1990. Snitow has asked, pertinently, referring to some feminists' fear that seeking gender equality will lead only to women becoming more like men, 'are we perhaps quite close to men already at the moment when we fear absorption into the other?' Snitow, 'A Gender Diary', p. 27.

   10. Barbara Ehrenreich, *Fear of Falling: The Inner Life of the Middle Class*, New York 1989, p. 217.

   11. Idem, *The Worst Years of Our Lives*, New York 1990, p. 164.

   12. See Kate Soper, *Troubled Pleasures: Writings on Politics, Gender and Hedonism*, London 1990, p. 61.

   13. Sylvia Ann Hewlett, *A Lesser Life: The Myth of Women's Liberation in America*, New York 1986.

   14. See, for example, David Plotke, 'What's So New About New Social Movements?', *Socialist Review*, vol. 90, no. 1, 1990.

   15. Pippa Norris, *Politics and Sexual Equality: The Comparative Position of Women in Western Democracies*, Brighton 1987.

   16. Here, like Kate Soper in her excellent collection of essays *Troubled Pleasures* (see note 12), I refer to 'socialist' goals as those which 'conflict with the logic of the untrammelled market' involving forms of planning and redistribution of wealth at odds with the logic of capital accumulation.

   17. Eisenstein, 'Specifying US Feminism', p. 50.

   18. The first of still very few left critiques of 'Charter 88', pointing out the complicated and confusing politics behind it, and the crucial omissions for socialists within it, is Peter Osborne's brief but lucid 'Extensions of Liberty: What *Charter 88* Leaves Out', *Interlink*, February/March 1989, pp. 22–3.

17

The New Agenda

André Gorz

In the developed late-capitalist societies the reality of class as organized power is destroyed on the terrain of class society.

Detlev Claussen[1]

Everyday solidarity is based on the search for open communication free of domination. It is, therefore, from the first, more comprehensive than workers' solidarity; it does not have the latter's constantly re-emerging limitations, indeed it even has universalist tendencies.

Rainer Zoll[2]

The socialist movements, and later the socialist parties, developed out of the struggle against the exploitation and oppression of the wage-earning masses, but also against the social goals and conceptions of the bourgeois leading strata. The socialist project of a new society at first contained two elements. On the one hand, there was the claim to leadership by a class of skilled workers, which tested its ability to direct the production process itself in daily practice; it was simultaneously determined to seize power from the class of owners, whom it regarded as parasites and exploiters, in order to place the development of the productive forces at the service of emancipation and human needs. And on the other hand, there was the resistance of a disenfranchised and oppressed proletariat of women, children and men who toiled in workshops and factories at starvation wages, and had to fight for their political and economic rights. These unskilled labouring masses could only achieve the cultural and social perspectives with which to overcome oppression through an alliance with the skilled workers. Equally, the potential leading class of skilled workers drew, in part, legitimation for

its claim to leadership from the unbearable immiseration of the proletarian masses, for whom the elimination of capitalist domination was a
question of life and death; however, legitimation was also provided by
man's domination of the forces of nature, embodied in the worker—
above all in the versatile craft worker. The real subject of this domination was the worker himself, not only as 'global worker', but also as
individualized bearer of irreplaceable human capacities and human
skills.

Beyond the historicity of the central conflict between labour and
capital, however, socialism signified more than its manifest political and
social contents: more than emancipation of the disenfranchised,
oppressed and exploited; more than just the claim to power of the
immediate masters of nature. Resistance and the claim to power of the
working class contained a fundamental critique, not only of the capitalist
relations of production, but also of capitalist rationality itself, as
expressed in commodity, market and competitive relationships.

Actions are economically rational in so far as they aim at the maximization of productivity. But this only becomes possible under two
conditions: (1) productivity has to be separated from the individual
singularity of the labourer, and it must be expressed as a calculable and
measurable quantity; and (2) the economic goal of the maximization of
productivity cannot be subordinated to any non-economic social,
cultural or religious goals; it must be possible to pursue it ruthlessly.
Only unlimited competition in a free market makes such ruthlessness
possible, indeed compels it. Only the 'free-market economy' permits
economic rationality to make itself independent of the demands of
sociality, in which it is embedded in all non-capitalist societies, and to
withdraw from society's control—in fact, even to put society at its service.

The socialist workers' movement came into being as the positive
negation of capitalist development. Against the principle of the maximization of output, it set the necessary self-limitation of the amount of
labour performed by the workers; against the principle of competitive
struggle between isolated individuals, it set the principle of solidarity and
mutual support, without which self-limitation would be practically
impossible. The socialist workers' movement aimed, therefore, to place
limits on economic rationality, and ultimately to place them at the
service of a humane society.

The Central Conflict

The central conflict out of which the socialist movement has developed,
revolves, then, around the expansion or limitation of the areas in which

economic rationality is allowed to evolve unhindered in market and commodity relationships. It is characteristic of capitalist society that relationships conducive to the realization of capital predominate in conceptions of value, in everyday life and in politics. The socialist movement opposes this with the striving after a society in which the rationality of the maximization of productivity and profit is locked into a total social framework in such a way that it is subordinated to non-quantifiable values and goals, and that economically rational labour no longer plays the principal role in the life of society or of the individual. Socialism, understood as the abolition of economic rationality, assumes, consequently, that this has already fully evolved. Where, in the absence of market and commodity relations, it has not yet established itself, 'socialism' cannot put economic rationality at the service of a social project intended to dissolve it. Where 'socialism' understands itself as the planned development of not-yet-existing economic structures, it necessarily turns into its opposite: it reconstructs a society so that it is devoted to the economic development of capital accumulation. Such a society cannot assert its independence of economic rationality. It is 'economized' through and through.

The central conflict over the extent and limits of economic rationality has lost nothing of its sharpness and historical significance. If one understands socialism as a form of society in which the demands deriving from this rationality are subordinated to social and cultural goals, then socialism remains more relevant than ever. Nevertheless, the concrete historical contents as well as the actors of the central conflict have changed. This used to be conducted, culturally and politically, at the level of workplace struggles; it has gradually spread to other areas of social life. Other kinds of antagonism have been superimposed on the contradiction between living labour and capital, and have relativized it. The striving after emancipation, after free self-development, and to shape one's own life cannot assert itself without trade-union struggles for a reshaping of work and conditions of work, but it also demands actions on other levels and on other fronts, which may be equally important and at times even more so. The question as to the 'subject' that will decide the central conflict, and in practice carry out the socialist transformation, can consequently not be answered by means of traditional class analysis.

In Marxian analysis, the class of skilled workers was destined to rule over a totality of productive forces, so that a totality of human capacities would develop in each worker. The all-round developed individual would consequently be able to make himself the subject of that which he already was; that is, he would resist every external determination, take command of the production process, and set himself the goal of the 'free development of individuality' within and outside productive cooperation. Now unfortunately actual developments have not confirmed these predictions. Although in parts of industry an 'integral adaptation of tasks' (Kern/Schumann) becomes possible or even necessary, there can be no question—even in the case of the new, versatile, skilled production workers—of a totality of skills commanding a totality of productive forces. The integrally adapted task always affects only the manufacture of parts of an end product (for example, of crank shafts, cylinder heads, gear boxes) or of their assembly and control. As a consequence of its ever greater complexity the total social production process demands a functional specialization of tasks in all areas. Max Weber spoke in this context of *Fachmenschentum* (specialized mankind). But specialization always stands in contradiction to the free all-round unfolding of individual capacities, even if it demands initiative, responsibility and personal commitment to the job. A computer specialist, a maintenance worker, a chemicals worker or a postman cannot experience and develop themselves in their work as creative human beings, materially shaping with hand and mind the world experienced through their senses. They can only succeed in doing so outside their professional employment. Specialization— that is, the total social division of labour beyond the level of the individual plant—renders the production process opaque. In the course of their work the operatives can hardly influence at all the decisions which relate to the character, determination, use-value and social utility of the end products. A process worker is in no way different, according to Oskar Negt, from the civil servant in a public body, who is also responsible only for sections of work cycles and for the precise execution of tasks that are placed before him. He makes a contribution to the functioning of areas which as a rule he knows nothing about.[3]

The concept, which appears in Hegel and is then taken over by Marx, according to which labour is the material shaping of the world experienced by the senses, through which man becomes the producer of himself, was still valid seventy years ago for the overwhelming majority of the working class: it was employed in non-formalized activities in which individual know-how, physical strength, planning and self-organization of the sequence of tasks played a decisive role. Today the majority of wage-earners work in administration, banks, shops, transport, postal, caring and education services, where individual performance is usually not measurable, and labour has lost its materiality.

The 'modern male and female workers', who now take the place of the former versatile skilled worker, are not in a position, on the basis of their own direct experience of work, to question the meaning and social purpose of production simply by identifying themselves with their work.

With 'modern male and female workers', the 'transformation of labour-process power' into a political claim to power can no longer develop, if at all, through an identification with their position in the production process. Rather, starting from the total social relationships of society, it demands a distancing from the experienced work task. Such a capacity is founded on the socialization of male and female workers, because this socialization does not in the first instance pass by way of learning a social role. In addition, professional training develops capacities which are never utilized to the full within labour. This may require a sense of responsibility and independence, but always only to fulfil predetermined functions: it demands 'autonomy within heteronomy'.

However, the capacity to put capitalist relations of production fundamentally in question does not, at the same time, automatically incorporate practical possibilities that could lead in this direction. Such possibilities cannot be grasped by the male and female workers as such at the workplace (one thinks of the maintenance specialists in automated plants, of employees in nuclear power stations or in the chemical industry), but only in their capacity as citizen, as consumer, as tenant, or as the user of private and public facilities; here they participate in social relationships outside the workplace and experience themselves as belonging to a much larger community.

New Cultures of Resistance

It can or should be the task of trade-union work to animate this feeling of an expanded belonging, responsibility and solidarity, and the related distancing from a predetermined professional role. However, the trade-union movement's understanding of itself would have to change. Its task would then no longer consist solely of representing and defending the interests of modern workers as such, but also of giving them the possibility of seeing their professional activity in relationship to an economic and political development determined by the logic of capital realization. This can happen in many forms: through working groups; through public discussions and critical investigations, whose content is the social and political implications of technological innovations and their effect on the environment. What may be advantageous to the employees of one company, writes Hinrich Ötjen, may under certain circumstances involve disadvantages or reduced future opportunities for others; and he continues: 'If the trade unions want to remain relevant, then at the very least a public debate on such conflicts of interest should be organized on the spot, because otherwise new movements, in which the workers can draw on their various interests, will be more relevant to them than the trade unions. Up to now, trade-union immobility has frequently given workers cause to set up citizens' initiatives; they capitulate in the face of the trade unions' difficulties in organizing such a dialogue internally.'[4]

At this point it becomes clear: for modern workers, socialist consciousness and the critique of capitalism do not usually have any direct connection with, or derive from, the lived experience of work. The 'subject' of a socialist project of society therefore no longer develops in the capitalist relation of production as class consciousness of the worker as such, but rather in a worker who as a citizen, for example, in his neighbourhood, is deprived of his social and natural lifeworld by the consequences of capitalist development, just as are most of the rest of his fellow human beings. It's very much in this sense that Horst Kern writes that there is no such thing as 'the natural recalcitrance of experience in the face of hegemonic limitations'. It is rather the case that modern workers' critical reflections are set free by the fact that they 'are confronted by the imperfection of the capitalist version of modern life not within, but largely outside, their actual professional roles'.[5] Alain Touraine's thesis may also be valid here.

According to him, the central conflict is no longer the antagonism between living labour and capital, but that between the large scientific-technical-bureaucratic apparatuses,[6] which I—following Max Weber and Lewis Mumford—have called the 'bureaucratic–industrial megamachine', and a population which feels itself robbed of the possibility of shaping its own life by a culture of experts, by external determination of its interests, by professional know-alls, and by technological appropriation of the environment. However, nothing should prevent one recognizing the bureaucratic–industrial megamachine and its leading stratum as also the expression of an economic rationality characteristic of capitalism, which takes the shape of industrial growth, the realization of ever larger quantities of capital, the monetarization and professionalization of social and interpersonal relationships.

The inadequacy of an analysis that relies principally on the cultural resistance to the 'colonization of the lifeworld' contained in the 'new social movements' is that these movements do not consciously and concretely attack the domination of the economic rationality embodied in capitalism. These movements are certainly anti-technocratic, that is, directed against the cultural hegemony of the leading stratum of the ruling class, but they only strike at the cultural assumptions and social consequences of the relation of domination, not, however, at their economic-material core. The new social movements will become the bearers of socialist transformation when they ally themselves not only with the 'modern worker' but also with the contemporary equivalent of the disenfranchised, oppressed and immiserated proletariat—that is, with the post-industrial proletariat of the unemployed, occasionally employed, working short-term or part-time, who neither can nor want to identify themselves with their employment or their place in the production process. Estimates, according to which this group is likely to make up 50 per cent of the wage-earning population in the 1990s, are proving by now to be realistic: in West Germany, as well as in France, more than half of the workers newly started in recent years are employed in precarious or part-time jobs. Workers who are employed in this way already constitute in total more than a third of the wage-earning population. Together with the unemployed, that makes a 'post-industrial proletariat' of 40–45 per cent in Great Britain, and in the United States as much as 45–50 per cent. The two-thirds society has already been left behind.[7]

Now it would be a mistake to see in the 40 per cent excluded from normal full-time working relationships only people who long for a full-time job. In its most recent research into the subject of the 35-hour week,[8] the Italian metalworkers' union, FIOM-CGIL, comes to the same conclusion as similar studies in France and West Germany. According to this, we are dealing with a social transformation that is leading to a situation in which work occupies only a modest place in people's lives. Work as wage-labour is losing its centrality, though it is more a question of a decline of the socialization function of work than of a refusal to work. Work is only desired if it possesses the character of autonomous and creative activity. Otherwise it is viewed solely with respect to the income deriving from it, and for women also as a way of achieving independence from the family.

Rainer Zoll also came to similar conclusions as a result of exhaustive research with reference above all to young people. He concludes that 'the breaking up of the old identity structures' throws young people back on themselves 'in their search for an identity of their own'. They could never achieve the total, fixed identity that results from traditional family and corporate professional roles, but at best an open one, based on 'self-realization', legitimated by communicative intercourse, but never definitive. The choice of professions potentially available to a young person was greater than ever, but the chances of actually finding what s/he was looking for—namely a job with creative and socially useful aspects in which s/he could realize him/herself—were extremely limited. The number of such workplaces is estimated at 5 per cent. It was therefore understandable that many had already given up the race before it had even begun. The evident consequence of this situation was that individuals transferred the search for self-realization to other terrains.[9] It should therefore be no surprise that, according to an Italian survey already a few years old, young people frequently prefer to take part-time work, to enter precarious or short-term work situations, and to pursue if possible, by turns, a variety of activities; even among university students with limited means, the professional activity most frequently preferred was that which left most time for one's own cultural activities.[10] The impossibility of creating stable, socially useful, and economically rational full-time jobs for almost half of the wage-earning population corresponds, therefore, to the desire of a significant proportion of younger wage-earners not to be tied, either full-time or for life, to a career or professional employment which only very rarely makes use of all personal capacities and cannot be regarded as self-realization.

Limiting the Sphere of Economic Rationality

Now what connects this post-industrial proletariat of wage-earners, who cannot identify themselves with their position in the productive process, with the 'modern worker'? Both strata experience the fragility of a wage relation based on measurable work performance. It is the case, both for those not working full-time or all the year round, or precariously employed, as it is for the core workforces of 'modern workers', that their effective labour is not constantly required. The first group is needed for limited, usually short-term, foreseeable units of time; the second is needed for situations that are frequently quite unpredictable, which can occur several times a day or only relatively seldom. 'Process workers', maintenance specialists, also firemen or caring professionals, must be constantly available, and in an emergency also work twenty hours without a break. They are paid for their availability and not only for their qualifications. They are on duty even when they are not active. In the case of the precariously employed, by contrast, only that time is paid during which they are performing effective work, even though it is of the utmost importance to industry and services that flexible, willing and capable labour is available at short notice. It is for exactly this reason that the demand of the precariously employed—usually less than six months a year—that they also be paid for their availability during interruptions of the wage relation, which are no fault of theirs but advantageous to business, is quite legitimate.

It is therefore a question of uncoupling income and work time, and not income and work itself. This demand is altogether rational, since as a consequence of increases in productivity through technical innovation the total economic production process requires less and less labour. Under these circumstances it is absurd to continue to make the wages paid out by the economy as a whole dependent on the volume of labour performed, and the individual income dependent on individually performed work time. Work time as the basis for the distribution of socially produced wealth is clung to solely for reasons of ideology and political domination. For the post-industrial proletariat that is not employed full-time or all the year round, the wage relation becomes the manifest expression of a relation of dominance whose previous legitimacy derived from the now untenable rationality of the production ethic. The common goal of the 'modern workers' and the post-industrial proletariat is to free themselves from this relation of dominance. However, this goal is pursued by them in very different ways. For the post-industrial proletariat of marginal men and women workers, it is principally a matter of being able to transform the frequent interruptions to their wage-labour relationship into new areas of freedom; that is, to be entitled to periodic unemployment, instead of being condemned to it. For this purpose they need the right to a sufficient basic income which permits new lifestyles and forms of self-activity. For the core workforces of 'modern male and female workers', as for others with full-time jobs, forms of control over working time, such as self-determined flexibility of working hours or even linear reductions in the length of the working week, may seem more attractive.

This may appear to be a new form of the earlier social stratification, with its distinction between skilled workers on the one side and proletariat on the other. As in earlier times, the contemporary proletariat is rebelling principally against the arbitrariness of relations of dominance that express themselves in the absurd compulsion to live from wage labour of which not enough is available; while autonomy within and outside professional life becomes the main desire of 'modern male and female workers'. The divisions between the two strata are consequently much more fluid than they may first appear to be, and could to a great extent be removed. Progressive general reductions in working hours must logically lead to a redistribution of work, whereby the skilled jobs would be made available to a much larger number of wage-earners; and at the same time the right and the possibility of interruptions of the wage-labour relation could apply to everyone. An alliance of both strata does indeed seem feasible, especially on the question of the demand for reduced working hours, provided that such a demand does not become a straitjacket but enhances autonomy within and outside labour.

Reduction in the average annual working time, or even in the quantity of labour performed in the course of four or six years, entitling the wage-earner to an uncut income, offers in this respect the greatest scope and possibilities of choice. The 30-hour week, for example, whose achievement the trade unions and left-wing parties of most European countries have set themselves as a goal, corresponds to an annual working time of approximately 1,380 hours, and combined with the right to a sabbatical year, an average of approximately 1,150 hours annually. A society that no longer needs all its labour-power full time and all the year round can also easily provide for reductions in working hours, without loss of income, in the form of the right to longer breaks from work. Until the beginning of the twentieth century, journeymen and skilled workers always took this right. Variety, tramping, collecting experiences, were for them part of human dignity. Consequently a reduction in working time must be regarded 'not only as a technocratic means to a more just distribution of work', which allows everyone to acquire an indisputable right to their share of social wealth, 'but as the society-transforming goal of procuring more "disposable time" for human beings'.[11] This time may be used however one likes, depending on one's situation in life, to experiment with other lifestyles or a second life outside work. In any case it limits the sphere of economic rationality. It has a socialist significance in so far as it is combined with a social project that puts economic goals at the service of individual and social autonomy.

Jacques Delors has pointed out that forty years ago a twenty-year-old worker had to be prepared to spend a third of his waking life at work. Today his working time only amounts to a fifth of his waking time, and it will shrink further. From the age of fifteen, one spends more time in front of the television today than at work.[12] If a socialist movement does not focus on cultural, interpersonal, community life as intensively as it does on working life, it will not be able to succeed against the capital-realizing leisure and culture industry. It only has a chance if it consciously insists on the creation of expanding free spaces for the development of a many-sided, communicative, everyday culture and everyday solidarity liberated from commodified relations of buying and selling.

The expansion of areas freed from economic calculation and immanent economic necessities cannot mean that a socialist economy or alternative economy is taking the place of the capitalist one. There exists, up till now, no other science of management except the capitalist one. The question is solely to what extent the criteria of economic rationality should be subordinated to other types of rationality within and between companies. Capitalist economic rationality aims at the greatest possible efficiency, which is measured by the 'surplus' obtained per unit of circulating and fixed capital. Socialism must be conceived as the binding of capitalist rationality within a democratically planned framework, which should serve the achievement of democratically determined goals, and also, of course, be reflected in the limitation of economic rationality within companies.

Consequently, there can be no question of dictating to public or private companies conditions which make the calculation of real costs and performance impossible, or which are incompatible with initiatives aiming at economic efficiency, and consequently prevent economically rational company management. Reduction in working time cannot, if it is to have general validity—which on the grounds of justice it must have—take place purely at the individual company level and be dependent on a particular company's increases in productivity. The equalization of incomes, together with a general reduction in working hours guaranteed to all, can also not be financed by a general taxation on increases in company productivity (machine tax), but must be guaranteed by indirect taxes, applicable to every European Community country, which are cost-neutral for the businesses. But that is already another chapter.

January 1990
Translated by Martin Chalmers

Notes

1. Detlev Claussen, 'Postmoderne Zeiten', in H.L. Krämer and C. Leggewie, eds., *Wege ins Reich der Freiheit*, Berlin 1989, p. 51.

2. Rainer Zoll, 'Neuer Individualismus und Alltagssolidarität' in ibid., p. 185.

3. Oskar Negt, *Lebendige Arbeit, enteignete Zeit*, Frankfurt 1984, p. 188.

4. Hinrich Ötjen, *Krise der Gewekschaften*, MS, Hattingen 1989.

5. Horst Kern, 'Zur Aktualität des Kampfs um die Arbeit', in Krämer and Leggewie, p. 217.

6. Alain Touraine, *Le Retour de l'acteur*, Paris 1984.

7. W. Lecher, 'Zum zukünftigen Verhältnis von Erwerbsarbeit und Eigenarbeit aus gewerkschaftlicher Sicht', *WSI Mitteilungen* 3, 1986, p. 256.

8. According to the report by Bruno Vecchi in *Il Manifesto*, 1 July 1989.

9. Rainer Zoll, *Nicht so wie unsere Eltern?—Ein neues kulturelles Modell?*, Opladen and Wiesbaden 1988.

10. S. Benvenuto and R. Scartenazzi, *Verso la fine del Giovanilism Inchiesta*, Bari 1981, p. 72.

11. Peter Glotz, 'Die Malaise der Linken', in *Der Spiegel*, no. 51, 1987.

12. Jacques Delors, *La France par l'Europe*, Paris 1988, p. 107.

18

Vorsprung durch Rethink

Göran Therborn

Three concepts are sufficient to sum up a long-term socialist or, if you prefer, radical-humanist project: human life-realization, universality and history. Universal human life-realization is, in a nutshell, what socialism is about, with the addition that it has a location and a range in historical time. It is not a moment, or even a lifetime, of bliss only, but a period rooted in the past and connecting itself with the future.

A *vision* of it may be seen as the outside of a sphere, with open horizons in every direction, some spaces in varying shades of daylight with people peacefully and autonomously going about myriad activities, difficult to distinguish between work or play, not to speak of between rewarding and bare subsistence-yielding activities. Some people are acting alone, others in smaller or larger groups, leaders and led may exist, but are impossible to distinguish from afar. Locales vary seemingly infinitely, but slums, rural holes of misery or concentration camps are nowhere to be seen. A certain clean freshness is hanging in the air and sparkles in the water. Other spaces are in the dark but penetrable to the visionary, who sees well-fed people in safe, well-sheltered sleep, people in the passion of love-making, individuals awake with sleepless eyes wrestling with the demons of creation, or others being born, lying sick or dying, with caring fellow-humans at their bedside. The visionary is looking at Earth from inner space and sees a multi-faceted human life without systematic violence, coercion, misery and degradation, without sorting mechanisms condemning categories of human beings to having a large portion of their children die as babies, falling prey to famines, preventable diseases, poverty, humiliation, exploitation, lack of care and to a cruel or unnecessary death.

As this vision is meant to be part of a rational political discourse, it is open to a number of objections. In other words, in forwarding a planetary vision of humanity in daylight and at night, I accept the obligation of a rational reasoner to provide reasons for sceptics to see it as a possible future, and as a future worth striving for. Indeed, I am trying to develop an argument in dialogue with critics.

A Debate with a Liberal Sceptic and a Modern Socialist

Round One: About Evil and Emancipation

Liberal Sceptic: Your so-called socialist vision is little more than a dream of a world without evil. That may be a noble dream, but it provides no indications of how to get there. And, after all, is it worthy of a rational social scientist (politician, writer, activist, citizen—delete what is not appropriate) to promise a world without evil?

Modern Socialist: On this point, if only on this, I agree completely with my liberal enemy, but I would add ...

Answer: Wait a minute, let us stop here for a moment. My vision is something significantly different from, or less than, a wish for a world without evil. The world I am talking of is a world without systems of evil, without systematic mechanisms allocating fortune or misery, without, to echo an already half-forgotten Hollywood actor, 'empires of evil'. I am assuming no change in the everyday mixture of good and evil in Mr Smith and Ms Jones. And I think I am rare among utopians having envisaged, in one paragraph summary of paradise, people bed-ridden with sickness, and people dying.

Modern Socialist: All right, but it is still very abstract and vapoury. More than that, even at the level of supreme principles you seem to be fucking things up. The Communist and socialist project has always had a clear goal, universal human emancipation. Why are you leaving out the goal of emancipation? Has it become too revolutionary, 'fundamentalist' even, perhaps?

Answer: This is a crucial difference between modernism and postmodernity, which has dawned upon me only lately. I honestly do not think that a socialist or radical project can be summed up in terms of 'emancipation' any more. Emancipation is a key to the politics of modernity, a politics of liberation from the shackles of the *ancien régime*, or of traditional society, monarchical rule supposedly by the grace of God, class exploitation, bigotry, prejudice, patriarchy, racism. Emancipation remains on the agenda in most parts of the world, above all, in the form of women's emancipation, but also of ethnicity/ nationality and class. However, the concept of emancipation presupposes that of oppression/exploitation as a clear baseline from which to move. In advanced capitalist democracies it is difficult, and unconvincing, to conceive of women or workers as generally and unqualifiedly oppressed and as exploited (other than in the accountant's sense of an academic class analysis). Such societies do contain features of oppression and exploitation, and thereby tasks of emancipation, but the former do not hold as general characteristics of life in those societies. *Human life-realization* has the advantage of not being tied to one linear movement, from oppression to freedom, but of connoting, at the same time, an infinite plurality of life— projects and a universal yardstick, the human life-span universally possible at a given level of world resources and medical knowledge.

Round Two: About Life and the Economy

Liberal Sceptic: Your vision seems to entail a biologization of politics and of social life. Does that mean that you accept the current capitalist economy as the most efficient one?

Answer: No one but a fool would say that the present is the best of all possible worlds. Only hopeless utopians may dream of capitalism lasting for ever. But it is true that I have reformulated the socialist project, from being couched in terms of property, markets and the state, into basic concerns of human life.

Liberal Sceptic: But that implies a recognition of markets and of capitalism, doesn't it?

Answer: Of markets yes, of capitalism no. The Marxist conception of socialism was based on an analysis of capitalism asserting its intrinsic contradictoriness. The development of capitalism would bring about an increasing dysfunctionality between the private relations of production and the increasingly public(ly dependent) forces of production. That did happen, up to about 1950, expressed in the socialization of mass communications and mass transport, even of natural resources held to constitute the 'commanding heights' of the economy. For another fifteen years there was the establishment of a public management of the economy, of its growth rate and its business cycle. The process of international cartelization, which culminated in the 1930s, was part of the same tendency. Since then, however, the world market and the multinational corporation have reasserted themselves against both cartels and states, although the publicly managed economy remains—and will remain.

Liberal Sceptic: But why don't you then accept the superiority of the capitalist market? Isn't that what is implied both in the reforms of Deng Xiaoping and the perestroika of Gorbachev?

Answer: The functioning of the market is dependent on the initial distribution of endowments, and the current distribution of resources in the world denies the possibility of a decent human life to hundreds of millions of people. That distribution has to be changed. There seems to be no empirical evidence that speculative financial markets have any positive function in what serious liberal economists sometimes call 'the real economy', and often the former have clearly negative effects on production and work. The increasing power of financial capital has to be reversed. The market is furthermore a poor mechanism for dealing with fundamental human questions—for which there are no clear compensatory trade-offs—with choices of rare frequency and/or of special information requirement. The market can function rather well with regard to your choice of consumer goods, but rather badly, for instance, with respect to what old-age care you, as a resourceful prime-age adult, may need in the far-off future as an elderly person.

Intellectually, it is interesting that probably the most popular metaphor of contemporary rational action theory is 'the prisoner's dilemma', which is a sad story or two or more people who cannot communicate and cooperate with each other, and who therefore, as rational egoists, end up much worse than they would have scored if they had been able to cooperate. This example teaches us a lesson exactly opposite to that of the 'invisible hand' of the market.

Round Three: About Socialism and Liberalism

Modern Socialist: But if you hold those views, why don't you present a clear picture of a socialist economy? Instead you are presenting a vision devoid of any concrete institutions. Wouldn't it be more honest to say, in your case, that you are abandoning the idea of socialism for another vision or utopia of a more general humanistic kind?

Answer: The vision I am seeing presupposes a complete overhaul of the distribution of endowments, of property and propertylessness, and a complete change of the relationships between financial and productive institutions. Those changes would entail a universal equalization of life-chances and a decisive role allotted to productive, in contrast to merely appropriating, creativity. Therefore, my vision implies a number of crucial institutional changes, which are all contained within the traditions of socialism. However, in contrast to classical socialists, I am not sure what the new institutions needed would look like exactly.

Liberal Sceptic: Fine, but isn't that tantamount to civilized liberalism?

Answer: In case you should recognize your liberalism in my vision, or somebody else social democracy, christian democracy, ecologism, or x-, y- or z-ism, I would be happy, because that would mean a broadened support for it. The sectarian preoccupation with drawing demarcation lines is alien to me.

Liberal Sceptic: Thank you, but doesn't that amount to an abandonment of socialism as a specific political tendency?

Answer: There is a basic continuity with modern socialism, in universalism, in historicity, and in concentrating on scrutinizing and changing the content of social and political forms, the social human contents of political constitutions and sets of juridical rights, and the structuring of situations of choice with systematic outcomes of affluence on the one side and misery on the other.

Round Four: On History and Historical Tendencies

Modern Socialist: Why do you put such an emphasis on history in your three concepts summary? Isn't that more than anything else a cover-up for the fact that you have substituted a utopian vision for the Marxist theory of history?

Answer: No, the reason is an aim at retaining a link with 'scientific socialism', that is, with the location of socialism in actually existing history. But I had also something else in mind, more directly related to my conception of life politics. A vision of a better world must contain a sense of link with, and thereby responsibility for, the future, for coming generations. No generation has the right to destroy life-chances for the next one(s). That is a constraint on universal life-realization.

Modern Socialist: Talk about 'history' is not enough! The scientificity of historical materialism's conception of socialism was that it analysed how the latter developed out of the contradictions and the social conflicts of capitalism. But your so-called vision is not derived from any analysis of historical tendencies of contradiction and conflict. You are only holding up a picture, hoping that some people will find it attractive. Do you see any social forces with an interest or tendency to bring them about?

Answer: The most concrete answer to your first question is that my vision involves a universalization and a deepening of the institutions of the most advanced welfare states. Secondly, it follows up the vital issues brought on to the historical agenda by the progressive women's movement, namely gender relations, modes of human reproduction, and the quality of personal relations in the systems of institutional forms. Thirdly, my vision expresses the actualization of basic questions of the human environment put forward by the ecological movement. What I see are all tendencies of the new times.

Modern Socialist: Is it deliberate that you refrain from referring to any economic tendencies of contemporary capitalism?

Answer: The welfare state, the women's uprising, environmental concerns, have all grown out of affluent developed capitalism, out of forces and issues generated within it, although the processes have been very complex and are irreducible to a purely economic dialectic. Between these tendencies and capitalism, there are fundamental conflicts, which does not mean incompatibility or impossibility of co-existence, however. After all, life is not incompatible with violence, cruelty and fraud, for instance. But wouldn't you admit that life would be more pleasant without them?

Liberal Sceptic: Why don't you relate to the rise of the post-industrial knowledge economy with its substitution of information for toil and capital, of networks for hierarchy, of flexibility for rigid rules, of de-centralization for centralization?

Answer: The tendencies of contemporary capitalism are ambiguous in their social implications. While Taylorist, army-type bureaucracies are clearly on their way out, industrial production is of declining economic weight, and the computerization of information and of the use of infor-mation are clearly of rapidly growing economic importance, no clear pattern is emerging, bestseller ideologies notwithstanding. The global centralization of corporate power is growing simultaneously with de-centralization within corporate organizations. Union busting and idiosyncratic personal management are increasing alongside more and more autonomous personnel involvement. Rent for attractive, increas-ingly scare natural estate and for urban real estate is rapidly growing in importance in contemporary capitalism. The manipulation of, or privi-leged exclusive access to, information is becoming an increasingly important means of capital accumulation. And so forth. Very significant in these ambiguously contradictory economic tendencies is, I think, the growing role of a large category of qualified employees, overcoming manual/non-manual divisions, the commitment and the sophisticated life-demands of whom productive capital is getting crucially dependent upon. People of this kind are already providing much of the support for new humanistic movements, and given an institutional chance they could also give a new impetus to the labour movement. The counter-strategy of capital and conservatism, however, is to try to segment these employees in corporate and local loyalties and to isolate them from the rest of the population, from the bulk of the service workers, traditional production workers, the unemployed and the retired.

The two basic institutions of welfare states are (membership) rights and care. As a member of a relevant category, as a citizen, or as a member of some other group, you as a person have a right to certain services and forms of support, regardless of your property status and of your ability to pay the going market price. Secondly, most of what existing welfare states do is to provide care for people, care for the sick, the infirm, and the elderly, care for children to grow up and learn. The rights of persons and taking care of people have a tense, conflictual relation to the principle of exclusion inherent in the notions of property and purchase, and to the production and circulation of commodities.

The women's movement challenged the male particularisms in the prevailing conceptions of freedom and equality, solidarity and socialism. In that respect the movement has been a tendency of universalism. Pertinent in this context is also another feature of the feminist insurrection: its concern with the quality of personal human relations—between men and women above all, but also among women, among men, and between adults and children. Autonomy, dignity, authenticity, concern in human relations, are standards or demands raised in defiance of instrumentalism and commodification. A third aspect of the women's movement, one that I find particularly appealing, is its combination of a radical individualism with collective action and solidarity. Feminism challenged the unproblematized collectivity of the family—the hidden cupboard of most bourgeois individualism, a cupboard full of victims of patriarchal power and despotism. It did that by pointing towards a more authentic individualism, which at the same time entailed a universalistic concern with and care for other human beings.

The ecological movement has put life environment at the centre of attention. Like all radical movements, including the classical socialist one, it also contains dubious elements, fragile prophecies of imminent doom, puritanical moralisms and upper middle-class neglect of the work and housing environment of ordinary people. However, ecologists have made invaluable contributions to a new life politics, demonstrating the lethal or seriously damaging, unnecessary threats of pullution, poisoning and the destruction of nature.

Round Five: The Welfare State and Statism

Liberal Sceptic: But isn't the welfare state a bureaucratic dinosaur which is now being challenged both from the Left and the Right as something which has to be replaced, or at least cut down, by a 'welfare society', of one form or another?

Answer: You are mistaking the current institutional forms for the basic principles of the welfare state, and the current ideological steam around those forms. The core of the welfare state is that the reproduction of the population of a given political entity is a public, political responsibility. Neither Thatcher nor Reagan and their acolytes have been able to challenge the right of people in need to support and to service. Neither has been able to do away with institutions of human care and concern. The development of the productive forces, of science and technology, will require more education, rather than less. The growth of medical knowledge and technology will raise the demand and the supply of care in the future. Ageing populations will need much more care.

It is certainly not inconceivable that the current right-wing tendencies of restricting to the shoddiest possible minimum the services and the care given to the ordinary human being without property or a properly conducted insurance policy will continue, and even be aggravated. But the life politics issues of human reproduction, of the education, the curing, the caring, and the maintenance of the population's health will not go away. Nor will they be buried in families and networks outside common political responsibility and organization. The traditional socialist Left has lost sight of the meaning of the welfare state through a myopia of economic functionalism and a macho preoccupation with 'high politics'.

Liberal Sceptic: But surely, any serious attempt at new thinking would have to break with the statism of the traditional Left?

Answer: It is true that the public corporation and the planning commissariat, even some of the large public health care authorities, no longer inspire the confidence and enthusiasm they once did. But statism or anti-statism is not the real issue. To put the choices in those terms is a diversionary manoeuvre. What is needed is to put the most important social problems into focus, and then to discuss the proper institutional forms. For everybody on this earth to have a chance to realize a decent life, in view of the resources and the knowledge available to humankind today, a great deal of public political intervention and regulation will be absolutely necessary. But new forms of public intervention and organization will certainly be called for. I am no reliable defender of actually existing welfare state forms, but you will never lure me into any statism/anti-statism debate.

Round Six: Social Forces

Modern Socialist: You never answered directly my question about the possible social forces that might be mobilized for your utopia. I also wonder, from what you did say, if you mean that there is a growing contradiction between capitalism and what you call universal life-realization?

Answer: There has been so much growth in the contradictions of capitalism in past socialist rhetoric that considerable caution seems proper for a while. I am not saying that the internal contradictions of contemporary capitalism are growing or are likely to grow in the fore-seeable future. What I am saying is that the conflicts between capitalism, even advanced affluent capitalism, and the universal possibility of realizing a meaningful, dignified and reasonably decent and healthy life do not show the slightest tendency of disappearing. And at least in some areas the gap between the potential and the actuality of human life is definitely increasing. We see this in the expansion of poverty in the United States, in the enduring, American-type ghetto-producing mass unemployment in most parts of Western Europe, in the increased pollu-tion of many cities and waters, in the growing destruction of children and youth (visible in addiction, violence, crime and prostitution), in the glaringly inadequate care for the elderly also in the richest countries, in the increase of misery in large parts of the Third World, and in the persisting threats of ecological disaster.

Life politics has no single or even central subject. That is a handicap in short-term power politics. On the other hand, it can, or might, draw upon a broad spectrum of social and cultural forces, which in terms of long- and medium-term societal transformations is a source of strength.

The labour movement, in so far as it is a class movement rather than an aggregate of interest groups pursuing sectional interests, and the movements of the popular classes or the poor people of the Third World, in so far as they are movements of popular needs rather than merely waves of frustration or objects of demagogy, are certainly neces-sary forces. Without them, life politics would tend to become concern for the quality of life among the affluent and prosperous only.

Women, not just the women's movement, are and will probably become another major force. Whatever the reasons, women are, and seem likely to remain (as far as we can see), over-represented in repro-ductive work (paid as well as unpaid) and tend to be more concerned with the quality of the human condition. In the past, family seclusion and confinement to a narrowly religious interpretation of existential issues tended to make women more politically conservative than men. That is now changing, and turning the other way around. Of course, women constitute no one tendency, and they will continue to spread over the political spectrum. But it seems likely that they will have a strong—stronger than men—tendency to support radical politics for universal human life-realization.

Various aspects of what I have here called life politics is also what various groups of concerned middle-class people, mostly professionals of one kind or another, have already committed themselves to. Environmentalist groups, human-rights groups, people concerned with helping victims of famines, disasters and of persecution. While here there has been an erosion and a demoralization of the traditional Left, the right-wing politics currently in vogue in several countries does not seem to have extinguished, or even lowered, commitments to specific issues of humanistic concern, and does not seem to have lowered the vistas of the whole middle classes to political concerns with taxation rates, mortgage interests and portfolio trajectories only.

Liberal Sceptic: But if there are so many people and movements of goodwill, why does the world then look the way you say it does? Or do you mean that paradise is imminent?

Answer: My answer to your second question is no, and to your first would be too long to print here. But, as a general point, the people of this world are caught up in a welter of conflicting situations, structured by a starkly unequal distribution of resources, constrained by economic competition and power rivalry, and affected by unintended and unforeseen, as well as by conflicting, consequences of action. The progressive forces I referred to above are also entangled in this web. What is needed is to cut a path on which a life politics can stand tall, can see its own vista, and can walk forward. That task of clearance is first a task of re-orienting the political debate, such as we are doing here. How such a re-orientation should take shape in line-ups for power for a change is a later question. And changing the terms of prevailing discussion will already in itself bring about some changes in existing institutions and configurations of power.

Round Seven: A Summing-up of Issues

Modern Socialist: Please, could you formulate the re-orientation you are talking about into an understandable everyday political language? What do you want us to do?

Answer: I am not going to present a party platform or a blueprint for the next socialist revolution. But I will sum up my argument in a few points. What I am suggesting is, first of all, to take a step behind economic and political institutions and to begin to formulate the tasks of radical (socialist, progressive, humanist, democratic) politics in terms of people's life environment and their life chances, of everybody's possibility of realizing the full potentiality of human life, with the constraint that this possibility should be preserved for future members of humankind.

This perspective puts certain issues and political tasks in the foreground.

1. Disarmament (not necessarily unilateral), arms control, attempts at preventing or defusing armed conflicts.
2. Universalistic human solidarity, fighting racism, sexism and ethnic oppression, overcoming exclusivist nationalisms.
3. Health and adequate healthcare for everybody, which means a frontal assault on national, ethnic and class differences in mortality, morbidity and well-being; provision of decent care for the infirm and for the elderly.
4. Education to enable a full participation in a continuously developing society with a secure milieu of growth for all children and youth, and possibilities for further education for adults.
5. A distribution of material resources and rewards egalitarian enough to make a decent human life a possibility for everybody, which means massive efforts at restructuring the material life chances of people within most countries (not least Britain), and the construction of new forms of cross-national support and development co-operation.
6. A restructuring of personal and social relations so as to render individual antonomy possible for all women as well as for all men.
7. Work, with basic health safety, and potential for human growth for everybody who wants to take part in the economy. An organization of social time which makes it possible and easy for people to arrange their life-time according to their choice of remunerated work, care for children, kin and friends, education and re-training, and of leisure and recreation.
8. De-pollution of air and water, economic growth and life-realization only under the constraint of nature conservation. Nature has to be recognized politically and economically for what most of us know privately already, that nature should not just be an object of human conquest, since it is a basic aspect of the quality of human life. Large efforts have to be made at finding out and doing something about the life-damaging consequences of produced substances and waste products, and of various human practices.
9. A reorganization of urban life and of the different opportunities in

cities and in the countryside with a view to the abolition of slums and metropolitan congestion and to steering the trade-off between anonymous freedom and, on the other hand, vandalism, violence, criminality and abandoned despair into more positive directions.

Liberal Sceptic: Beautiful! And who is to foot the bill?

Answer: All of us. This cannot be paid for by the rich only. But almost all of us will also benefit from it, to a larger or smaller extent.

Modern Socialist: You didn't say a word about capitalism, or, for that matter, socialism!

Answer: The gist of my argument is that the issues of life environment and life chances should be put first, and that the economic institutions most adequate to the former will have to be found out later. The issues I give priority to are certainly different from maximizing capital accumulation. Nay, they require a drastic restriction of the sway of capitalist property and capital accumulation. In that sense they follow a classical socialist line. On the other hand, I am quite aware of the dynamism of a market economy and of the requirement of economic and administrative managerial competence. In order to give everybody on this earth a decent life environment and decent life chances we need a very efficient economy and very efficient forms of organization in all walks of life. Markets and professional management will without doubt be necessary. But for the rest, what organizational forms and systems we should head for, I am not sure. The crucial thing is, in my opinion, that the latter will be geared to the goal of giving everybody the possibility of realizing the full potential of a human life in a fresh environment.

Round Eight...

The Editor: You haven't allowed your opponents to concede defeat or to be knocked out, so this could go on for ever. But, in case you should want to publish these scribbles you had better stop now!

Answer: Yes sir.

19

The Economics of a Socialized Market

Diane Elson

The socialist tradition has always stressed the conscious social direction of the economy to meet needs rather than make profits. It is important to hang on to that objective at a time when the failure of central planning in Eastern Europe and the Soviet Union has led to its wholesale repudiation. We need to rethink what this objective means and the methods by which to achieve it. Some suggestions to stimulate discussion are offered here.[1]

We need to think of conscious social direction in terms of enabling rather than of control. The economy is not a machine; it is the aggregation of millions of individual and collective actions and decisions. It is not possible to control all of these to achieve a predetermined result. Attempts to do so lead to undemocratic and overcentralized political and economic institutions side by side with corruption, black markets, inefficiency and queues. We need to create institutions that enable people to produce to meet needs; that direct people in terms of showing them the way, creating routes, creating channels of communication between different producers and between producers and users. This requires some preventative measures, just as a road system requires measures to stop people travelling against the flow of the traffic. But it does not require a central authority telling people what they should all be producing and how.

These measures are required to prevent people using resources without being socially accountable for them; and to prevent people from treating others as simply resources to meet their needs rather than as fellow citizens. The mistake in the past has been to see this mainly in terms of state control and ownership overriding and displacing private property rights. Certainly strong limits on the individual exercise of property rights are necessary, but this must be coupled with the creation of new citizenship rights: rights to basic goods and services and rights of participation and accountability in decisions about what and how to produce. These individual rights need collective institutions for their effective exercise, but these institutions must operate in a way that preserves some link to individuals. Workers' cooperatives are one important means of achieving this. However, cooperatives are probably better suited to some kinds of production than to others—municipal ownership and ownership by regional and national bodies will also be required. We also need to pay much more attention to the way in which such production units link to the wider community. Internal democracy is certainly necessary, but this is not enough. Rights of participation and accountability have to extend beyond those who work in these units to provide a broader social accountability. How can this be achieved?

The answer given by some socialists is that markets are the best way to do this, providing that the distribution of income and wealth is relatively egalitarian. My view is that while there is certainly an important and indispensible role for buying and selling in the organization of a socialist economy, the cash nexus by itself does not adequately convey information about needs. Moreover, it tends to take on a life of its own and to encourage a narrow pursuit of individual and group interests rather than an appreciation of the interests of others and an attempt to arrive at decisions which are truly social. In fact, the pursuit of individual and group self-interests irrespective of what others are doing is ultimately self-defeating—as the growing environmental crisis is now revealing. (This is also the root cause of unemployment, inflation and other manifestations of economic dislocation.) A socialist economy has to be organized in a way that encourages and enables people to appreciate their interdependence with others and to be more public-spirited in their decisions. This is not the utopian goal of selflessness; rather it is the practical goal of enabling people to see and take account of interconnections that may not be immediately apparent but which are none the less real. New social movements—the green movement, the women's movement, the peace movement—have been far in advance of traditional socialist movements in working on this.

A variety of ways can be envisaged of enabling people to be more social and less narrowly selfish in their decision-making. One way is by means of negotiations (as suggested by Pat Devine): all substantial investment decisions would be subject to negotiations between the investing enterprise and those likely to be affected by the investment—community groups, consumer groups, etc.[2] This seems likely to work most efficiently where the effects are relatively localized, or in the case of really large projects, such as power stations. Another way is by means of leasing (as suggestd by Robin Murray): enterprises would be leased to groups of operators for a fixed period and leases would only be renewed to groups which satisfied certain social performance criteria (including efficiency).[3] The ultimate owners, issuing the leases, would be some kind of social investment trust. But this in turn would need to be accountable to the community for its stewardship—elected representatives on the board might be an answer here. In many cases direct representation of the interests of users would be a good idea—perhaps in the former users' committees or a consumers' director on the board. A further way would be by means of requiring all enterprises above a certain size to have community directors on their boards—a democratic extension of the current role of the non-executive director.

Clearly, social accountability for the use of resources is going to require individuals to serve as community directors, members of users' committees, members of negotiating groups, etc. (The role of school governors is a good example of what will be required.) This kind of responsibility needs to be evenly spread and might be seen as an obligation of citizenship, rather like jury service, which is undertaken in return for the benefits of citizenships, such as a basic guaranteed income.[4] There is also going to be a need for a considerable amount of campaigning and for activist groups to supply information and keep up the pressure for people to take all-encompassing rather than narrow views. Social accountability cannot be effective if it is left to state institutions; these are necessary, but need to be complemented by a wide range of independent initiatives. Campaigning and activist groups need subscriptions, donations and grants. A socialist state must facilitate their access to these resources while allowing them to remain independent.

The key to democratic social direction of economic activity is an ongoing interaction between state institutions (regulated by elections); production units (internally democratized); individual citizens exercising social supervision through users' committees, community directorships, etc.; and a wide range of campaigning and activist groups expressing a variety of community needs and interests.

This interaction will involve planning processes, in which particular goals for the future are spelled out and the means to achieve them are specified. It will also involve decisions about buying and selling and setting prices, and using financial criteria. But the organization of both planning and market processes will be structured by networks of mutuality of the types described above, which will serve to bring them under social direction. For this to work successfully there will need to be easy and open access to a wide variety of information. A key role for the state will be to use its unique power of taxation to provide as public goods the necessary communications infrastructure and the training necessary for citizens to make sense of the information. As much transparency as possible in all forms of decision-making is absolutely essential to a democratically directed socialist economy. Such an economy will not avoid mistakes and problems—but it was always an illusion to think of 'planning' as a magic wand that could achieve a perfect allocation of resources always in line with everyone's needs. What will be avoided, however, is the entrenchment of processes that perpetuate and intensify the domination of purchasing power over need satisfaction.

So where do we begin? Demands for the state to do this or that in isolation from the self-activity of the citizens themselves is *not* the appropriate starting point. We have to start from existing demands for greater social accountability and from existing attempts to develop a wider vision among people as they decide what to buy or how to bargain in the workplace.

That consumers are willing to look beyond the immediate characteristics, in terms of price and quality, of what they buy is shown by successful anti-apartheid campagins to boycott South African goods; and by Green consumer campaigns to create pressure for the availability of household cleaning materials that do not pollute. Less well known are Dutch and British campaigns for Clean Clothing—that is, clothing produced under decent working conditions—which aim to mobilize consumers to put pressure on big retail chains not to source from sweatshops, whether in Europe or the South. Such campaigns have attracted trade-union support and participation on a number of occasions. There have also been examples of joint campaigns by consumer groups, local communities and trade unions in defence of jobs. For instance when General Motors threatened to close its last remaining plant in California a union–community coalition was formed which began to organize a boycott of GM cars in the Los Angeles area. This succeeded in securing a commitment to keep the plant open.

Going beyond purely defensive actions, workers have shown themselves willing to take account of the needs of consumers in the organization of work. This includes others besides the well-known example of the Lucas Aerospace shop stewards; for instance, unions in British local government preparing tenders for groups of workers to supply local services such as rubbish removal and street cleaning.

We might think of building on these kinds of actions to institutionalize regular networks that link workers and consumers and other activist organizations; sharing information; providing education to a wider public; developing techniques of social audit which could eventually supersede purely financial audit, formulating strategies for technological innovation and economic restructuring. We could then demand of the state resources to facilitate such networks; and the integration of such networks into the regulatory process through which laws are formulated and enforced. The regulatory process could then be expanded to require more social accountability from property owners. To the extent that the regulatory process is democratized, with people gaining experience of exercising regulatory functions and seeing the restriction of private property rights as something they take part in rather than as imposed by an alien state, support can be built up for a decisive moment, in which social accountability takes precedence over private profitability. The establishment and maintenance of democratic social accountability for resource use is at the core of what socialism will be about.

Note

1. I explain this approach further in 'Socializing the Market', *New Left Review*, 172, 1988.
2. Pat Devine, *Democracy and Economic Planning*, Oxford 1988.
3. Robin Murray, 'Ownership, Control and the Market', *New Left Review* 164, 1984.
4, See Philippe Van Parijs, ed., *Arguing for Basic Income*, London 1992.

20

Out of the Ashes

Eric Hobsbawm

What is the future of socialism? As a historian my first instinct, you
might say my professional deformation, is to ask: what is its past and
how does it affect the present situation and future possibilities? And this
is a plausible approach, because the word, the concept, the programme,
the realizations of socialism and socialist policies are not simple objective data like, say, the situation of London on the Thames opposite the
Low Countries, but mental constructs. They are names, patterns, labels
which we use to make sense of the situation in which humanity has
found itself since the age of revolution of the late eighteenth and early
nineteenth centuries, and which we give to certain human attempts to
improve and/or transform society.

   Initially the word 'socialism' was neither political nor did it imply any
specific way of organizing society; unlike the older word 'communism',
which from the start clearly meant a society based on common rather
than private property, and managed as such—and pretty soon from
Babeuf on, a political movement to bring it about. 'Socialism' and 'socialist' were simply derived from the word 'social', and meant little more than
that the human is by nature a social and sociable being. It only began to
have something like our sense in the 1830s when it became part of the
social and political vocabulary, spreading outwards from Britain and
France. Of course the thing had already existed under other names
before, though not for very long: it was called 'cooperation' and 'cooperative' in Britain, or 'collective' or 'collectism' in France—later it
became 'collectivism', and known by such names as 'mutualism'. We
have to note two things about it.

   First, the opposite of 'socialism' was not yet 'capitalism' but 'individualism'. What made 'socialism' anti-capitalist was simply that it seemed

logical enough, in the early nineteenth century, to say that the core of an individualist society was *competition*, that is, the market, and consequently the base of a social(ist) society had to be *cooperation* or *solidarity*. Now that left a very wide range of possibilities. Anything ranging from a slight modification of laissez-faire in the interests of social security, to communist colonies entirely without private property or money could count as 'socialism'. In Britain this original sense of socialism remained central until the end of the nineteenth century, and the rise of socialist labour movements. That is why the Fabians thought they could convert the Liberal Party to socialism without anyone noticing.

Second, socialism originally had no political implications (here again it differed from communism). It could be instituted by the state or by any other kind of effective authority, but mostly it could be established by voluntary communities; by what Bernard Shaw called 'socialism by private enterprise'. That, by the way, is probably why there was more socialism—that is, more socialist colonies—in the USA in the 1840s than anywhere else in the world. In fact, until the 1880s when people thought of working-class socialism they thought of socialism through voluntary associations, cooperatives and other forms of voluntary mutual and collective action. It was only when the labour movements, following both the Jacobin tradition of democracy and the Marxists, took the road of collective political action that socialism became tied to the conquest of state power. Naturally the state then became the central element in the construction of socialism.

But remember one thing. The object of this exercise was not primarily a particular way of organizing production, distribution and exchange. It was, to quote an intelligent anti-socialist of the 1880s, John Rae, 'at bottom a demand for social justice'. That is why, unlike the constructors of utopias for voluntary colonies, the new socialist working-class parties and their thinkers and writers paid surprisingly little attention to what they were going to do when they got into office and power—before they actually did so at the end of the First World War. The Marxists actually made a virtue out of refusing to think about the future. 'The Socialist Party,' said Kautsky, speaking for the largest of them, 'can make positive propositions only for the existing social order. Suggestions that go beyond that cannot deal with facts, but most proceed from suppositions; they are accordingly phantasies and dreams.'[1] The real content of socialism until 1917–18 was capitalism turned upside down: what was bad now would be good then. The details didn't matter. Even the people who bothered about details, like the British Fabians, did not seriously consider how a socialized economy would work. It stood to reason that it *had* to work better than capitalism.

As it happened, for most of the first half of the twentieth century capitalism itself seemed to prove the socialists right. Between 1914 and 1950 or so, everything that could conceivably go wrong with it did so. It went through two world wars, and two bouts of national and social revolution which killed off, or at any rate passed the death sentence on, the great colonial empires and transferred one third of humanity out of the capitalist system. The typical political regimes of bourgeois society, liberal democracies, were overthrown all over the world. By 1940–41 they barely survived outside the USA, a fringe of Europe and the Americas and in Australasia. Above all, the capitalist economy itself was sick, and almost collapsed in the worst slump it had ever suffered, the only one in which it actually looked as though it might break down entirely. Any kind of socialism had to do better than this. Nothing is more obvious to us today than the economic inefficiency of the primitive centrally planned state-run command economy which claimed to be socialism in the Soviet Union. Yet sixty years ago non-Communist politicians and intellectuals were queuing up for tickets to Moscow to get the secrets of the 'planning' which apparently made the Soviets immune to the slump that was devastating their own countries.

The socialists, of course, had been forced to give some thought to what socialism meant concretely, rather than just as a slogan; for in 1917 the Bolsheviks took power and from 1918 on the important social-democratic parties became or joined governments, and therefore had to have real policies. But, not having given any systematic thought to what they wanted, let alone to what a socialist society should be like, they had to think out their policies at short notice, or work them out under the pressures of the most immediate problems. In a word, they reacted to particular situations. And most of the current troubles of socialism today arise from the fact that socialist policies which were devised to fit the situation of capitalist crisis and breakdown—roughly 1914 to 1950—are no longer suited to the situations of the late twentieth century. Or rather, that we have never decided what is time-bound and obsolete in them, and what isn't.

I said 'socialism' in the singular. But after 1917 we must speak of at least two different branches of socialism, of which one is at present collapsing or has collapsed, namely social democracy and the Soviet or Soviet-inspired Communist systems. The Soviet systems are the only ones which actually claimed to have established fully socialist economies and societies. To the best of my knowledge no social-democratic government or party, however radical or long-lived, has ever made such a claim, and it is worth recalling that even the USSR didn't actually claim that it had achieved socialism until 1936. Maybe they should have waited a bit longer ...

Soviet-type socialism was essentially dominated by the conditions under which the Soviets found themselves after the October Revolution: in a very poor and spectacularly backward country, whose only political tradition was autocracy, lacking all known conditions for socialism, totally isolated, and under constant threat. Rapid economic and techno- logical development, that is, breakneck industrialization, was the obvi- ous top priority. Bolshevism turned itself into an ideology for rapid economic development for countries in which the conditions of capitalist development don't exist, and for a while it was so successful that it provided an economic model for a lot of Third World countries like India, even those who had no sympathy for its ruthless dictatorship. It operated essentially like a war economy, in which certain priorities are accepted as given—like the need to win the war—and costs are not counted, or rather all other objectives are subordinated to the main one. Even though the centralized command economy at its best was a pretty rough-and-ready instrument, and enormously wasteful, it chalked up some very impressive achievements. While capitalism was flat on its back, these achievements looked even more impressive than they were. What the Soviet economy could not do, as it turned out, was to keep pace with capitalism once, after the 1950s, that system got into top gear again. In terms of ordinary people's lives, it could provide the basic needs of life—food, housing and clothes and leisure at a very low level, but nothing beyond. On the other hand it was better than capitalism at providing mass education and (until the economy started to seize up in the 1970s and 1980s) it was much better than other Third World coun- tries at providing health and welfare.

The comparison with a war economy is not casual. For the only real model of public policy which socialists had, who had never previously thought about what to do in power or office, was a war economy, start- ing with those of the First World War. This applies not only to the Bolsheviks, but also to Western social democrats, at all events in the belligerent countries. For a war economy required planning, the public management or operation of large parts of the economy—and, not least, the mobilization of labour, preferably with the help of labour organiz- ations and some element of systematic public welfare. One by-product of this influence of the war model—and Lenin's idea of planning was specifically inspired by the German war economy—was to intensify the socialist bias in favour of centralized state action. When both Bolsheviks and social democrats thought of socialism they thought almost exclus- ively of the conflict between state planning and market priorities.

If the communist idea of socialism was determined by the imperative of backward countries to get economic growth as quickly as possible, whatever the cost, the social-democratic policies were to be dominated by another special historical situation, namely the great interwar slump, the crisis of capitalism; to be more precise, by mass unemployment. They were, of course, influenced by other considerations. In addition to the experience of war economies, they took the politics of electoral democracy for granted, because they were the ones which had enabled them to become mass movements; and what is more, they had sometimes been the chief architects of democracy which they had won through long agitations and general strikes in Sweden, Belgium and Austria. Curiously enough, while social democracy took enthusiastically to what came to be called the 'welfare state' after 1945, it didn't originate it, and the welfare state hadn't played much part in their thinking. In Britain it was elaborated mainly by Liberals, in France by social Catholics, in Germany by socially conscious bureaucrats. The socialist (or, for that matter, the Western Communist) input into its development came primarily via local government, which left-wing authorities often controlled even under anti-Left national governments. Hence the importance of public housing which socialist councils pioneered: as in Vienna and in London. And we must also say that non-socialist experience provided them with models of socialist economic organization (as was also the case with the Bolsheviks).

The very word 'trusts' was used in Soviet Russia for the bodies which coordinated all factories producing similar commodities. This indicates the inspiration: monopoly-capitalist enterprise. And there is no doubt that in Britain the model for Labour's nationalizations after 1945 was not the government ministry, which Victorian capitalism had simply used for whatever bits of the economy needed to be publicly run— notably the postal services—but a public and in some sense autonomous corporation. Nevertheless, mass unemployment was the key to postwar social-democratic policy, as to the policy of Keynesian and New Deal capitalism which merged with it: its key policy imperative was 'full employment'.

As a matter of fact this policy was brilliantly successful, if not from a socialist point of view, then from the point of view of restoring the dynamics of a reformed social security capitalism based on mass consumption—so successful that full employment ran into its own difficulties in the 1970s and 1980s, for reasons which need not concern us here. And when it did, the consensus of reform capitalism and social democracy broke down. Free market neo-liberalism and the critique of the welfare state gained ground, although only in one or two unhappy countries did they triumph—notably in Reagan's USA and Thatcher's Britain. Well, not quite triumph. It proved politically impossible even under the extremists to liquidate, or even significantly to reduce, the social security expenditure. On the other hand social democrats found themselves saddled with a set of policies which undoubtedly did not

work as well as they had in the golden years from 1945 to 1973. And
they had nothing else except Keynes and nationalization to fall back on.
Mitterrand's experience in the early 1980s was bitter but conclusive.

So both Communists and social democrats found in the 1970s and
1980s that they simply could no longer coast along with the policies
which they'd more or less improvised or adapted after the First World
War, never having given any real thought to them before. History had
given them an impressive spell of success, or at least of relative or apparent success for a while. That success had now run out. For the first time
socialists had to think out socialism.

What has the second half of the twentieth century taught us, this most
revolutionary period in human history? In 1950 people who lived by
farming were a majority of the population even in some of the most
industrial countries of today: Japan, Italy, Spain. Today they are a
minority, sometimes a very small minority, almost everywhere in
Europe, the western Islamic world and the western hemisphere. An era
of such dramatic and unprecedented changes in society must inevitably
lead socialists to have another look at their assumptions and expectations. And it is clear that a number of them can no longer be maintained.

First, it has become clear that capitalism has produced an abundance
of goods and services beyond the expectations of our fathers; and that
most ordinary people in the West enjoy a standard of living far beyond
anything conceivable fifty years ago. And thanks to the welfare state,
poor people have more shelter against the winds of misfortune. The
argument that socialism is needed to abolish hunger and poverty is no
longer convincing. Even the argument, which sounded so convincing in
my young days, that only socialism could end mass unemployment is no
longer persuasive. The West has lived through a generation of full
employment under capitalism, and although we are once again in an era
of mass unemployment in Europe, in fact it is neither felt to be as intol-
erable as it was in the 1930s, nor do many people believe that it can only
be eliminated by a totally different economic system. In short, the *material* argument for socialism has been weakened.

Second, much that was once regarded as typical of a socialist economy
has, since the 1930s, been co-opted and assimilated by non-socialist
systems, notably a planned economy, and state or public ownership
of industries and services. This may surprise you, since the talk of the
last ten years or so has been all about the triumph of the free market and
the dismantling of the state, and the ideological victory of economic
neo-liberalism, but the fact that Thatcher's ideologists and their
colleagues were so convinced that the clock needed turning back, actually demonstrates how far it had been put forward in most capitalist

states after the war. And, in structural terms, it has not been possible to move it back all that far. The World Bank calculated that from 1980 to 1987, in *all* the world, there were just over 400 privatizations, and half of these in five countries: Brazil, Thatcher's Britain, Chile, Italy and Spain. If you add up all the privatizations in the three greatest economies, the USA, Japan and Germany, they amount to the grand total of fourteen cases. In short, the capitalist economies which emerged from the Second World War and presided over the greatest economic burst of growth in history were not pure market economies but mixed economies with very substantial public sectors and very considerable public planning. That didn't make them *socialist* economies, but it made it considerably harder to say exactly what socialist economies were and how they differed structurally from non-socialist ones.

Suppose, for instance, that you looked at two neighbouring countries, one of which claimed to be socialist and the other not, namely Hungary and Austria in the 1970s (that is, before the Eastern crisis). Both, incidentally, were extremely successful by the standards of their systems. In capitalist Austria, for historical reasons, all the big banks were nationalized, together with virtually all heavy industry and energy production as well as a large part of engineering, electrical and electronic and armaments: in short, what used to be called the 'commanding heights' of the economy. In socialist Hungary, as we know, the economy had been substantially liberalized with considerable scope for (minor) non-state enterprise. Just where, in these two cases, should the line between capitalist and socialist systems be drawn? In a word, the *structural* criterion of socialism had been weakened.

Except—and this is my third point—in the Soviet-type 100 per cent state-run centrally planned economies. But from the 1960s on it became increasingly clear, not least to their governments, that this type of socialist economy worked badly and was running into increasing trouble: and this because it lacked any criterion of economic rationality, that is, of comparative costs; not to mention any way in which consumers could indicate what they wanted. In short, it lacked the market element. All attempts to reform these systems aimed at introducing this element. So while capitalist economies since the war introduced elements that had been regarded as characteristically socialist before the war, socialist ones tried to introduce elements regarded as characteristically capitalist. The West was more successful in this than the East, but the simple either/or distinctions between the systems were getting fuzzier.

However, one thing has not changed. It is indeed more obvious than ever. This is my fourth point. The market as a guide to economic efficiency and effectiveness is one thing. The market as the *only* mechanism for the allocation of resources in an economy, in the way the

fanatics of Reaganism and Thatcherism or the Institute of Economic
Affairs and other ultra-capitalist think-tanks see it, is quite another. It
produces inequality as naturally as fossil fuels produce air pollution.
And, as Adam Smith long ago pointed out, there are some things—
essentially public goods—that it doesn't produce at all, because nobody
can make any money out of them; or not as much money as could be
made in other ways. No modern national or big city transport system
can be adequately financed by profit-seeking enterprise even if it ends
by not actually losing money. In the 'social market economies' (to use
the German phrase) or the Keynesian and social-democrat-influenced
economies of the West, these tendencies are to some extent kept in
check by public policy and management. But we can see what happens
when, in Reagan's America or Thatcher's Britain, house-building is
supposed to be left entirely to the market. Houses are only built for
those who can afford them, and today the number of people who have
no roof over their head at all in New York is 70,000. Moreover, under
such conditions the rich get very much richer, and the gap between them
and the poor grows steadily wider. This has also visibly happened both
in Britain and the USA. In the rich and developed countries people
console themselves with the reflection that the ones who are dropped
down the plug-hole of society are, after all, only a minority of at most a
third of the population. And even they have TV and don't actually
starve. Two-thirds are doing all right. The terrible word 'underclass' has
surfaced in the 1980s to describe the victims of the market. They live
under the floorboards of respectable society, and we have to look underneath the floorboards to see them—unless they come out into the open
as in New York, where there is no way of not seeing the armies of homeless grubbing through the dustbins, or of not smelling the characteristic
odour of the greatest and most splendid city of the globe, the smell of
stale urine of those who have nowhere to live except the street.

You may say that all this is an argument not for socialism but for a
humanized mixed economy, ranging from the social market (which is
capitalism with a bit of social christian input) to social-democratic states
like the Scandinavian ones and Austria, which is capitalism with rather
more of a socialist input. I won't say no. I agree with John Kenneth
Galbraith that 'in a very real sense in both East and West our task is the
same: it is to seek and find the system that combines the best in market-
motivated and socially-motivated action'. And I also agree with him that
whether a particular industry or service is provided by public or private
enterprise is not necessarily a matter of basic principle. At present, for
instance, there is a serious demand among large American corporations
for something like the British National Health Service, simply because
the system of private medical insurance there has turned out to be

incredibly bureaucratized and crazily expensive. But in some other European countries, for instance France, government-sponsored health insurance seems to work quite well. The crucial question isn't about technicalities, but about whether a country accepts the obligation to provide adequate health and medical care for all its citizens and sees to it that they have access to it.

But let us never forget that, while the bad results of the market can be and have been to some extent controlled—more and more successfully in countries like Austria and the Scandinavian ones, where labour and social-democratic parties have been in government—nevertheless there are at least three consequences of world capitalist development which have escaped from control. These help us to define the socialist agenda of the twenty-first century.

The first is ecology. Humanity has now got to the point where it can actually destroy the biosphere—the plant, animal and human habitation of the globe—or at any rate change it for the worse in unpredictable and dramatic ways. The 'greenhouse effect' is something we all have got to learn to live with. Now this is the result of unrestricted economic growth at an accelerating speed. True, socialist theory also used to favour this, and socialist practice, especially in Eastern Europe, created massive pollution. But capitalism is committed *by its nature* to unlimited growth, whereas socialism isn't. And growth must henceforth be controlled in some way. 'Sustainable development' cannot work through the market, but must work *against* it. It cannot work by free consumer choice but by planning, and, where necessary, going against free choice. At this very moment the EC has decided to stop all fishermen going into the North Sea for a week every month, otherwise it will run out of fish.

The second is the appalling way in which the gap between the inhabitants of the rich and developed countries and those of the poor ones is widening, in spite of one or two of the 'newly industrializing countries' and a handful of Opec billionaire states. The 'developed world' which represented one third of humanity in 1900 today represents between 15 and 20 per cent—about the same as in 1750. And whereas in 1900 the developed world had roughly three times the GNP per head of the population as the rest of humanity, in 1950 it had five times as much, in 1970 seven times and—according to Unctad—in the middle 1980s $12\frac{1}{2}$ times as much. As for the richest tenth of the world's countries, their GNP per head is 58 times that of the poorest tenth. There is no 'trickle-down effect' as the world gets richer. On the contrary, without systematic action this explosive situation will get more explosive.

The third is that by subordinating humanity to economics, capitalism undermines and rots away the relations between human beings which constitute societies, and creates a moral vacuum, in which nothing counts except what the individual wants, here and now. At the top, men sacrifice entire cities to profitability, as in the film *Roger and Me*, which shows what happened to the town of Flint when General Motors shut down its works. At the bottom, teenage boys kill others for their sheepskin jackets or fashionable trainers, as happens every day in New York. Because, you see, human beings don't fit into capitalism. Capitalism needs an endless rise in productivity. Unlike machines and their products, which become ever more efficient and cheap, human beings stay obstinately human. They are best dispensed with and replaced by robots as in the car industry. Where they can't be replaced by machines, like in hospitals or in the social services in general, they still have to be sacked, because, unlike machines, their wages go up like other people's and we all know from the business economists that wages mustn't go up faster than productivity. It would be simpler all round if we could do without them. Well, the economy can do without them to an extraordinary extent, but they don't disappear. They are still there. But what happens to them?

Let me give you one example of what happens to them: the American motor industry. Once upon a time it provided jobs. Working on the assembly line in Henry Ford's Willow Run or River Rouge plant was not much fun, but it was well paid, and it provided endless jobs for blacks and poor whites from the American South. They were not skilled, not educated, often perhaps not too brainy, but they were ready to work, and assembly-line labour gave them the chance to bring up a family decently, with some self-respect and a little bit of dignity, as citizens and members of the United Autoworkers Union. Today the auto industry doesn't need them anymore. The only body that offers a poor American black a self-respecting job of this kind today is the army, which is why one-third of troops in the Gulf were black. And what happened to the communities left high and dry by the decision that their labour was no longer needed? They have become the embittered, anarchic ghettos stalked by fear, drugs and guns, where men and women live either on welfare or crime.

Socialists are there to remind the world that people and not production come first. That people must not be sacrificed. Not any special kinds of people—the clever, the strong, the ambitious, the beautiful, the ones that one day may do great things, or even the ones that feel that their personal interests are not being taken into account in this society—but all of them. Especially the ones who are just plain people, not very interesting, 'just there to make up the numbers', as the mother of one of my friends used to say. As a character says in the most moving line of Arthur Miller's *Death Of A Salesman*, which is about just such a nondescript and rather useless person: 'Attention must be paid. Attention must be paid to such a man.' They are what socialism is for and about.

The future of socialism rests on the fact that the need for it remains as great as ever, though the case for it is not the same as it was in some respects. It rests on the fact that capitalism still generates contradictions and problems it cannot solve, and that it generates both inequality (which can be mitigated by moderate reforms) and inhumanity, which can't. If the miserable and deserved collapse of the Soviet-type socialist systems had not filled the headlines in 1989 and 1990, there would be fewer commercials about how marvellously capitalism is doing these days. It isn't. It is back in a world of hunger and war. And even where it is not creating visible ruin as in parts of Latin America and Africa, it is not all that it is cracked up to be. As J.K. Galbraith said while Eastern Europe was still nominally socialist: 'It is a grim but wholly unshakeable fact that no one in search of a better life would move from East Berlin to the South Bronx.'

The problems of the world cannot be solved either by social democracy—or at least by the sort of social democracy existing in Sweden and perhaps Austria, which still lives up to its name—or by the 'social market economy'—the sort of moralized and socially conscious enterprise which, if I may hazard a guess, the Catholic Church will favour in the next papal encyclical this year. For if you have forgotten, the Holy Father has not forgotten that 1991 is the centenary of the Church's first social encyclical, *Rerum Novarum*. These things are better than Reaganism and Thatcherism, and in the case of social democracy far better, and probably they are in practice the best horses to back for the socialist punter at the moment. That is to say that they are the best sort of governments at present available. But the problems of a globe which can today be made uninhabitable by sheer exponential growth in production and pollution, not to mention the technological capacity to destroy which the Gulf War demonstrated; the problems of a world divided into a vast majority of extraordinarily rich states, cannot be solved in this way. Sooner or later they will require systematic and planned action by states and internationally, and an attack on the central strongholds of the consumer market economy. They will require not just a better society than in the past, but, as socialists always held, a different kind of society. A society which is not only able to save humanity from a productive system that has got out of its control, but in which people can live lives worthy of human beings: not just in comfort, but together, and in dignity.

That is why socialism still has an agenda 150 years after Marx and Engels's manifesto. That is why it is still on the agenda.

Notes

1. *The Class Struggle (Erfurt Program)*, Chicago 1910, p. 125.

Contributors

Giovanni Arrighi is Professor of Sociology at SUNY, Binghamton, New York, and the author of *The Geometry of Imperialism*.

Robin Blackburn is Editor of *New Left Review* and the author of *The Overthrow of Colonial Slavery*.

Norberto Bobbio is the author of many works of political science, including most recently in English *Liberalism and Democracy*. He is a member of the Italian Senate.

Alexander Cockburn is author of *Corruptions of Empire*, co-author (with Susanna Hecht) of *The Fate of the Forest*, and an editor of *New Left Review*.

Diane Elson is a Lecturer in the Economics Department, University of Manchester, and an editor of *New Left Review*.

Hans Magnus Enzensberger is a poet, novelist and essayist. His most recent books in English include *Europe, Europe!* and *Political Crumbs*.

Eduardo Galeano is a Uruguayan writer whose recent published work in English includes *Memories of Fire*.

André Gorz is the author of many works on economics and philosophy including most recently in English *Critique of Economic Reason*.

Jürgen Habermas is the author of many works of social theory and is Professor at the Goethe University, Frankfurt.

Fred Halliday is Professor of International Relations at the London School of Economics. He is the author of *The Making of the Second Cold War*.

Eric Hobsbawm is Emeritus Professor of History at London University, and the author of *The Age of Empire* and *Politics for A Rational Left.*

Fredric Jameson is Professor of Literature at Duke University, North Carolina, and the author, most recently, of *Postmodernism* and *Late Marxism.*

Ralph Miliband is an editor of *The Socialist Register* and author of *Divided Societies* and *Marxism and Politics.*

Maxine Molyneux is a Lecturer in Sociology at the University of Essex and and a member of the *Feminist Review* collective.

Lynne Segal is Lecturer in Psychology at Middlesex Polytechnic and the author of *Is the Future Female?* and is in the collective of *Feminist Review.*

Iván Szelényi is Professor of Sociology at the University of California at Los Angeles and the author, with George Konrad, of *The Intellectuals on the Road to Class Power*, as well as many more recent studies.

Göran Therborn is Professor of Sociology at the University of Gothenburg and the author of *Why Some People Are More Unemployed Than Others, The Ideology of Power*, and *Science, Class and Society.*

Edward Thompson is the author of *The Making of the English Working Class* and was a founder of European Nuclear Disarmament.